Magistra Doctissima

Medieval Institute Publications is a program of
The Medieval Institute, College of Arts and Sciences

WESTERN MICHIGAN UNIVERSITY

Magistra Doctissima

Essays in Honor of Bonnie Wheeler

Edited by
Dorsey Armstrong, Ann W. Astell,
and Howell Chickering

MEDIEVAL INSTITUTE PUBLICATIONS
Western Michigan University
Kalamazoo

Publication of this work has been supported in part by grants
from the University of Notre Dame and an anonymous donor.

Copyright © 2013 by the Board of Trustees of Western Michigan University
Copyright to "The Testamentary Strategies of Jeanne d'Évreux: The
Endowment of Saint-Denis in 1343" is retained by Elizabeth A. R. Brown

Manufactured in the United States of America
This book is printed on acid-free paper.

Library of Congress Cataloging-in-Publication Data

Magistra Doctissima : Essays in Honor of Bonnie Wheeler / Edited by Dorsey Armstrong, Ann W. Astell, and Howell Chickering.
   pages cm
  Includes bibliographical references and index.
  ISBN 978-1-58044-177-3 (clothbound : acid-free paper)
 1. Literature, Medieval--History and criticism. 2. Arthurian romances--History and criticism. I. Armstrong, Dorsey, 1970- editor of compilation. II. Astell, Ann W, editor of compilation. III. Chickering, Howell D, editor of compilation. IV. Wheeler, Bonnie, 1944- honouree.
  PN671.M28 2013
  809'.02--dc23
                                                2012040810

C 5 4 3 2 1

Contents

Acknowledgments — vii

Introduction — 1
    Ann W. Astell and Howell Chickering

Part 1. Old and Middle English Literature

Kiyoko Nagase and Her "Grendel's Mother" — 17
    Toshiyuki Takamiya

British Chaucer — 25
    Jeffrey Jerome Cohen

Just How Loathly Is the "Wyf"?: Deconstructing Chaucer's "Hag" in *The Wife of Bath's Tale* — 34
    Lorraine Kochanske Stock

Lectio difficilior and All That: Another Look at Arcite's Injury — 43
    †Stephen Stallcup

Part 2. Arthuriana Then and Now

Arthurian Bones and English Kings, ca. 1180–ca. 1550 — 61
    †Maurice Keen

The *Prophecies of Merlin*: Their Originality and Importance — 71
    Geoffrey Ashe, MBE

Notes toward a Reappraisal of Malory's Prose Style — 80
    D. Thomas Hanks, Jr.

The Scottish *Lancelot of the Laik* and Malory's *Morte Darthur*:
Contrasting Approaches to the Same Story   89
    Edward Donald Kennedy
"The Strength of Ten": The Cultural Resonance of Tennyson's "Sir Galahad" 97
    Alan Lupack
Googling the Grail   111
    Donald L. Hoffman and Elizabeth S. Sklar

Part 3. Joan of Arc Then and Now

"Because It Was Paris": Joan of Arc's Attack on Paris Reconsidered   123
    Kelly R. DeVries
Warrior not Warmonger: Screen Joans during World War I   132
    Kevin Harty
The Drama of Left-Wing Joan: From "Merlin's Prophecy" to Hellman's *Lark* 142
    Nadia Margolis

Part 4. Nuns and Spirituality

A Letter to the Abbess of Fontevrault from the Abbot of Clairvaux   155
    Giles Constable
The Nuns of Bival in the Thirteenth Century   159
    William Chester Jordan
The Sonic Presence of Mary Magdalene at the Last Supper: The
Maundy of the Poor at Barking Abbey   169
    Anne Bagnall Yardley
The Royal Purple Mantle of El Greco's *Espolio*   183
    Annemarie Weyl Carr

Part 5. Royal Women

Signed, Sealed and Delivered: The Patronage of Constance de France   201
    William W. Clark
The Testamentary Strategies of Jeanne d'Évreux: The
Endowment of Saint-Denis in 1343   217
    Elizabeth A. R. Brown

Contributors   249

Index   255

Acknowledgments

The editors gratefully thank Jo Goyne of Southern Methodist University for her crucial role in helping develop this volume and then assisting in the editing in its early stages. Susan Raymond-Fic and Julie R. Howland of the Amherst College English Department provided much-appreciated secretarial help, assistance in copy-editing, and computer support. Brigitte Buettner (Art History, Smith College) helped us locate the image of Christine de Pizan that is the basis for the jacket cover, which was designed by Ben Chickering and Tom Krol. We extend special thanks to our expert indexer, Margie Towery. We are grateful to have had the chance to work with Patricia Hollahan, our editor at Medieval Institute Publications, who has been a model of efficiency, grace, and good humor. We thank the University of Notre Dame and an anonymous donor for generous subventions that supported the publication of the volume.

Introduction

Ann W. Astell and Howell Chickering

Answering Boccaccio's *De mulieribus claris* in her *Book of the City of Ladies* (*Le Livre de la Cité des Dames,* 1405), Christine de Pizan celebrates queens, female warriors, prophetesses, foundresses, inventors of arts and science, instructors, and saints, drawing not only upon classical legends but also from her own experience of educated women, talented artisans, virtuous and valiant women from all the social classes—magisterial women, in short, who have instructed others by word and example. Against those who would oppose the education of women, Christine bears witness to "the benefits accrued and still accruing because of good women—particularly the wise and literary ones and those educated in the natural sciences" (2.36.1).[1]

Medieval writers and artists certainly knew how to depict the words and deeds of vitally alive, authoritative women, each of whom merits the title of *magistra* in one or more of its various senses: Boethius's Lady Philosophy with her blazing eyes, Dante's radiant Beatrice, Alan de Lille's and Geoffrey Chaucer's Dame Natura, Hildegard of Bingen's towering and bejewelled Ecclesia, Christine de Pizan's city-building ladies, the potent Virgin Mary of the miracle-tales, Queen Guenevere on her dais, the Wife of Bath pontificating from her ambling horse, the *Pearl*-poet's consoling and correcting maiden. Inspiring these images and, in part, inspired by them, stood, in turn, the historical women of the Middle Ages—among them, famous figures such as Eleanor of Aquitaine, the abbess Heloise of the Paraclete, and Joan of Arc. Christine de Pizan likened her pen to Joan of Arc's banner and sword, rejoicing in the Maid's victories, her womanly accomplishments, and drawing hope from them.

Magistra doctissima. Each one's true name remains hidden in heaven, according to the Scriptures (Rev. 2:17), but here on earth a word, an expression, can

1

still capture a defining quality. The editors of this volume use its title to name and to honor Bonnie Wheeler. The idea for this book originated several years ago when the editors realized that the time had come—was in fact overdue— to honor her many scholarly achievements and to celebrate her wide-ranging contributions to medieval studies in the United States. The volume was quickly and confidently conceived; the call for papers went out, and the contributors to this volume responded with equal alacrity. It is no exaggeration to say that Bonnie has effectively shaped medieval studies over the course of the last three decades. Not only is Bonnie most expert (*doctissima*) in her chosen scholarly fields as well as a master teacher in the classroom and lecture hall, she has also guided innumerable national committees, often as their chief, and, above all, has been a beloved mentor to generations of students and colleagues. During her career she has played the role of *magistra* in so many different contexts that the title seemed inevitable.

While to many medievalists Latin *magister/magistra* primarily means "teacher" in the sense of a schoolmaster or classroom teacher, to classicists it has a broader range of meaning: not only "teacher" but also "guide, tutor, expert, mentor, guardian, shepherd, master, chief, instigator, author, and judge," depending on the context and date of use. Medieval Latin preserves this same rich array of meanings.[2] Middle English similarly reflects the plural senses of *magister/magistra* in its related Latin-derived words: *maieste* (majesty), *maistres* (masters), *magistrat* (censor, judge, magistrate), *mages/magis* (magicians), *magi* (philosophers), and *magisteri* (the academic degree of Master).[3]

One could easily use the full semantic range to gloss the career of Bonnie Wheeler. Among her many contributions to medieval studies in North America, the one for which she is perhaps best known, and which definitely has had a profound and long-lasting effect upon the field, has been her role, beginning in 1980, as the founding chair of the Committee on Teaching Medieval Studies of the Medieval Academy of America. Subsequently this standing committee metamorphosed into TEAMS, an independent nonprofit organization dedicated to improving the teaching of the Middle Ages in North America. For more than two decades Bonnie served on its board of directors. Its acronymic name (*TEAching Medieval Studies*) emphasizes the necessity for interdisciplinary cooperation that characterizes the medieval field. Since 1984 Bonnie has been a member of the advisory board for the Middle English Texts Series published for TEAMS by Medieval Institute Publications, which makes available inexpensive student-friendly editions of high scholarly quality. These two themes of teamwork and outreach appear again and again in the record of her achievements.

Bonnie is widely known as an editor. She was the founder and longtime editor of *Arthuriana*, the quarterly journal of the International Arthurian Society–

North American Branch. She has edited or co-edited twelve books, among them *Mindful Spirit in Late Medieval Literature: Essays in Honor of Elizabeth D. Kirk* (2006), *Arthurian Studies in Honour of P. J. C. Field* (2004), *Joan of Arc and Spirituality* (2003), *Eleanor of Aquitaine: Lord and Lady* (2003), *On Arthurian Women* (2001), *The Malory Debate: Essays on the Texts of Le Morte Darthur* (2000), *Listening to Heloise: The Voice of A Twelfth-Century Woman* (2000), *Becoming Male in the Middle Ages* (1997), *Fresh Verdicts on Joan of Arc* (1996), and *Medieval Mothering* (1996).

Equally valuable to the profession has been her long service as general editor of the peer-reviewed book series The New Middle Ages, which to date has published close to 150 titles on a wide variety of subjects in literary history, art, music, philosophy, and theology. By founding this series, Bonnie single-handedly created a whole new venue for contemporary book-length research in medieval studies. As series editor, she carefully mentored many young medievalists whose first books appeared in print partially through her efforts. Contributing to the series herself as the editor or co-editor of several collections of essays, Bonnie has led by example, providing collaborative forums for scholarly work on neglected topics, as well as for work on daring new approaches to familiar subjects.

Among her several nationally elected positions, she has been vice president of the Council of Editors of Learned Journals; a councillor of the Medieval Academy of America; and a member of the national nominating committee of the Phi Beta Kappa Society. She has given nearly one hundred invited scholarly lectures and conference presentations. At the same time, she has sought to bring the Middle Ages to the general public, appearing frequently as historical and literary consultant for the Arts and Entertainment Network, the History Channel, and the BBC. She also has given two courses for The Teaching Company on educational television, of thirty-six half-hour lectures each: "Medieval Heroines in History and Legend" and "King Arthur and Chivalry."

The red thread connecting all of her many activities has been Bonnie's role as an enabler and encourager of other scholars. It is no accident that back in 1982 she and Jeremy Adams, in a joint article in *Medieval Studies in North America: Past, Present, and Future*, turned to Socrates's metaphor of a midwife to describe the ideal teacher and mentor in medieval studies.[4] To paraphrase their description: in the *Theaetetus*, Plato has Socrates propose that the teacher should behave like a *maias*, an honored officer in Athenian society who actually does much more than physical midwifery. First, she acts as a marriage broker: Thus Socrates's teacher-*maias* introduces students and ideas to each other, hoping for legitimate noble unions. Then comes the gestation of new ideas, and their care, nurture, and clarification. Finally, she presides over the birth of a work, thereafter judging its soundness. Mentor, editor, and scholar-critic all rolled into one.

Bonnie has acted in many areas as a model scholarly and caring *maias*. Endlessly energetic and creative herself, she stimulates creativity in others, be they students, colleagues, national committee members, or contributors to *Arthuriana* or to her book series. Her mentoring and intellectual midwifery are cause for praise—indeed, are major reasons for our wishing to honor her with this book. She is a personal force for good in our profession, as was made movingly clear by the spoken and written testimonies of the hundreds who gathered in May 2009, in Kalamazoo, Michigan, to toast her sixty-fifth birthday and her many achievements.

Given Bonnie's status in the profession, one might well expect that this book would focus on the teaching of the Middle Ages. However, that is not what this collection is about, nor the side of Bonnie's achievements that it celebrates. While these contributions may prove useful to teachers as well as scholars, their principal raison d'être is that they extend or complement the scholarly work that Bonnie has done in these several fields.

Unusually for such a volume, none of the contributors (with one exception) are former students of Bonnie's but instead are her peers and colleagues. Many are preeminent in their respective fields. We have organized their contributions into five sections focused on Bonnie's major scholarly interests: medieval English literature, especially Chaucer; Arthuriana past and present; Joan of Arc, then and now; nuns and spirituality; and royal women. The book also reflects a more general and enduring concern of Bonnie's: nearly half the essays (nine of twenty) deal with the roles and activities of medieval women. In addition, her long-standing interest in using primary sources in scholarship and teaching is represented by five contributions presenting previously unpublished or untranslated documents.

The volume is necessarily multidisciplinary in character. The editors solicited new work in the several fields of Bonnie's scholarly expertise and believe that the excellence and originality of the contributions make them valuable in themselves. Beyond that, however, they link up to Bonnie's own prior work in each field, as we point out below. Also, within each of the five sections, different essays resonate with each other, and we think that readers may also see interrelationships between the topics in each section. Taken *in toto*, the collection confirms Bonnie's commitment to the multidisciplinary study of the Middle Ages. Moreover, the inclusion of essays on modern treatments of medieval subjects, such as Arthur, Joan of Arc, and Grendel's Mother, derives from the conviction held by Bonnie and many others that the medieval and the modern are best viewed not as "the past" and "the present" but as interpenetrative categories.

Old and Middle English Literature

Bonnie's initial graduate training as a medievalist, under Elizabeth Kirk and George Anderson at Brown, was in Old and Middle English literature,[5] and thus the first section of this volume is on that topic. Taken as a group, its essays recall the tensions that Bonnie and many of her generation felt between canonical views and subsequent challenges to them. Toshiyuki Takamiya's lead essay on the Japanese feminist Kiyoko Nagase's poem "Grendel's Mother," composed in 1929, gives us the historical context and first English translation of this interesting document. The poem emphasizes the maternal aspect of Grendel's Mother, and juxtaposes a medieval and a modern scene. In doing so, it claims a sympathy for the medieval character that has resurfaced among postmodern Beowulfians.[6] There is an obvious link to the 1996 collection *Medieval Mothering*, co-edited by Bonnie and John Carmi Parsons, as well as to Bonnie's earlier edited volume, *Representations of the Feminine in the Middle Ages* (Academia Press, 1993). Less obviously but aptly, Bonnie accomplished the medieval Japanese/Chaucer comparison in her 1995 *Poetica* article "Grammar, Genre, and Gender in Chaucer and Murasaki Shikibu" (Lady Murasaki wrote *The Tale of Genji*).

The next three articles are about Chaucer, an author Bonnie engaged with deeply in 1982 in a major article in *Philological Quarterly*, "Dante, Chaucer and the Ending of *Troilus and Criseyde*," and later returned to from a different angle in "Trouthe without Consequences: Rhetoric and Gender in Chaucer's *Franklin's Tale*," in *Feminea Medievalia I: Representations of the Feminine in the Middle Ages* (1993).

Jeffrey Jerome Cohen's present essay, "British Chaucer," offers yet another approach to "the father of English poetry," challenging not his alleged paternity so much as his persistent marginalization of the non-Anglophone peoples of the British Isles. Cohen sees Chaucer as "a writer within a polyglot, culturally restless archipelago" who, like others before him, promulgated "London's dialect and metropolitan culture over regional differences." The Britain presented in his poetry, particularly in the romance genre, exists as the realm of the dead past, to be encountered only in the land of "Faerye." Cohen's postcolonial approach leads him to explore why, and how, the vigorous contemporary cultures of Ireland, Wales, and Scotland are so diminished in Chaucer's version of "Britain." He freshly contexualizes *The Wife of Bath's Tale*, *Sir Thopas*, and *The Man of Law's Tale*, suggesting that Chaucer's version of a past Britain existing in the land of Faerye can be seen as "inventive and demeaning."

Lorraine Kochanske Stock's essay, "Just How Loathly Is the 'Wyf'?: Deconstructing Chaucer's 'Hag' in *The Wife of Bath's Tale*," continues the theme of questioning canonical views, in this case challenging critics' use of the term "hag" (never used by Chaucer) in preference to the "olde wyf" found in the text. With impressive philological arguments, Stock shows that the automatic presumption of physical monstrousness relies on slender textual evidence. She notes that critics (male critics particularly) have moved the grotesque descriptions of the "wyf" found in the analogues over into their readings of Chaucer's text, which omits any physical details. The article energetically deconstructs such overdetermined, male-gendered readings.

In "*Lectio difficilior* and All That: Another Look at Arcite's Injury," the late Stephen Stallcup (1970–2009) reexamines lines 2684–91 of Chaucer's *Knight's Tale*, which he shows to be ambiguous and probably misread by medieval and modern readers alike. In the standard editions an "infernale furie" (line 2684) is the cause of Arcite's horse rising up and his fatal fall, but only sixteen of fifty-six manuscripts contain the "fury" reading; the forty other manuscripts give us some version of "fire." The *Teseida*, telling the same story, names the Fury as Erinys but the dominant reading of the manuscripts makes equally good sense (the horse rears up at an infernal fire sent by Saturn). Thus the manuscript evidence is at odds with the editorial assumption that Chaucer followed his source without alteration. How exactly Arcite falls to his death in line 2689 ("He pighte hym on the pomel of his heed") is equally ambiguous, with "pighte" and "pomel" having ranges of meanings that lead to a welter of possible readings. Stallcup carefully sorts through the lexicographical and semantic data to arrive at the likeliest possibilities. After discussing readers' assumptions as they have tried to determine the sense of the line, he offers a tentative new emendation. His article represents an advance on the critical analysis by E. Talbot Donaldson in his 1983 essay "Arcite's Injury." Donaldson was Bonnie's mentor through her early career and Stallcup was her student, so this article, published posthumously—itself a model of the critical reexamination of evidence—stands as homage not only to Bonnie but also to her revered mentor.[7]

Arthuriana Then and Now

The six essays in the next section of the collection focus on Arthurian topics. In a recent programmatic essay, "The Project of Arthurian Studies: Quondam et Futurus" (2002), Bonnie traced the colorful history of the academic study of Arthuriana from the foundation of the Arthurian Society at Oxford University in 1927. Assessing its current state and its possibilities for the future, Bonnie declared, "In my view, Arthurian studies have never been healthier or more vibrant than they are at present."[8] If that is the case, Bonnie herself deserves much of the credit for this flourishing. The editor (1993–2009) of the journal *Arthuriana* and of the scholarly book series Studies in Arthurian and Courtly Cultures (Palgrave Macmillan, St. Martin's Press), Bonnie has also edited or co-edited three Arthurian collections. *The Malory Debate: The Texts of "Le Morte Darthur"* (co-edited with Robert L. Kindrick and Michael N. Salda, 2000) provides a critical assessment of the arguments concerning the authorship and the structure of the great fifteenth-century Arthuriad, especially in the wake of Eugène Vinaver's edition of the Winchester Manuscript. The collected essays in *Arthurian Studies in Honour of P. J. C. Field* (2004), edited by Bonnie, and *On Arthurian Women: Essays in Memory of Maureen Fries* (2001), co-edited with Fiona Tolhurst, pay tribute, in varying ways, to great Arthurian scholars and highlight, especially, women scholars' important contributions to the field. An "Arthurian woman" herself, Bonnie has penned many articles on Arthurian topics, exploring such themes as masculinity, reputation, slander, humiliation, and the psychology of grief.

The Arthurian essays in this volume reflect many of the directions for research that Bonnie predicted in her 2002 programmatic essay cited above. In "Arthurian Bones and English Kings, c. 1180–c. 1550," the late Maurice Keen narrates the history of the supposed discoveries at Glastonbury: first, in 1191, of the tombs of Arthur and Guenevere, and second, in 1421, of a group of ancient coffins, which the abbot and his monks clearly hoped could be identified as those of Joseph of Arimithea and the companions who had come to Britain with him. Drawing from a rich variety of sources, he documents the interest of English kings, from Henry II to Henry VIII, in the quest for physical Arthurian remains, and he analyzes that interest from the perspective of a developing English national patriotism.

In "The *Prophecies of Merlin*: Their Originality and Importance" (a topic to which Nadia Margolis returns in her essay on Joan of Arc), Geoffrey Ashe studies the contribution made by Geoffrey of Monmouth (c. 1100–1155) to the Arthurian legend, focusing, in particular, on the medieval Welsh historian's depiction of Merlin in the *Historia Regum Britanniae* (1138), which also records the Arthurian wizard's historically influential, cryptic prophecies, including his prophecy of Arthur. Ashe emphasizes the originality of these prophecies, the hope they gave to Welsh political aspirations, and the theological audacity shown in Geoffrey's authorship of (most of) them. He argues that they contributed indirectly to the later Joachite prophecies of the Angelic Pope and the Second Charlemagne and to the historical repercussions of these predictions.

Turning from Arthurian history to literature, D. Thomas Hanks, Jr., praises Bonnie's 1993 study of Malorian parataxis in his essay, "Notes toward a Reappraisal of Malory's Prose Style." Taking into account the oral-aural culture in which Malory composed his *Le Morte Darthur*—a context largely neglected by previous scholars of Malory's prose—Hanks emphasizes that Malory's verbal cues, especially his coordinating conjunctions, serve syntactic functions similar to those served by punctuation within a print culture. Modern editions duplicate these functions by adding commas where Malory's manuscript had none. As a result, Hanks argues, Malory's masterful style, repetitive in its sounds and balanced structures as is appropriate for a listening audience, has not been appreciated properly and needs to be reevaluated on its own terms.

Edward Donald Kennedy's essay, "The Scottish *Lancelot of the Laik* and Malory's *Morte Darthur*: Contrasting Approaches to the Same Story," focuses not on Malory's style but on his plotline. That plotline, Kennedy argues, reflects upon national and political boundaries, similar to those cited in Jeffrey J. Cohen's essay. Kennedy shows that Malory must have known the noncyclic *Lancelot en prose*, the source upon which the Scottish writer based his Arthurian romance, but chose not to use many of its episodes, judging them inappropriate to his preferred, loftier view of King Arthur's character. Malory, moreover, wove together material from different sources, drawing especially upon the Vulgate (Lancelot-Grail) Cycle, to construct a tragic tale of Camelot's rise and fall, redeemed at the end by the penitence of Lancelot and Guenevere. Kennedy speculates that the Scottish romancer may have written in response to Malory, calling attention to his omissions from the *Lancelot* and imagining an alternative, comic ending, which leaves Arthur a better king and Lancelot happily rewarded with Guenevere's love. Such an optimistic ending, Kennedy observes, falls far short of Malory's truer sense of the costs of a queen's adultery.

Noting the endurance and mythic power of the Arthurian legends, Bonnie has insisted that "Arthurian Studies . . . lives at the core of what is now termed 'cultural studies.'"[9] The last two essays in the Arthurian section of this volume prove the truth of this judgment. In his essay "'The Strength of Ten': The Cultural Resonance of Tennyson's 'Sir Galahad,'" Alan Lupack traces the occurrences in popular culture of quotations of, and allusions to, the opening lines of Alfred Lord Tennyson's poem "Sir Galahad": "My strength is as the strength of ten, / Because my heart is pure." As Lupack shows, the lines quickly came to be associated with the painting *Sir Galahad* (1862) by George Frederic Watts, and the combined text and image were frequently used to inspire young soldiers during the era of World War I and, afterwards, to memorialize the dead. According to Lupack, the painted image of Sir Galahad and the Tennysonian phrase were taken up with enthusiasm in the United States by Arthurian youth groups as an emblem of manly moral purity. Works of fiction, from Annie Fellows Johnston's *Two Little Knights of Kentucky* (1899) to John Steinbeck's *Winter of Our Discontent*, echo the line from Tennyson, and it is heard, too, from the lips of politicians and basketball coaches. Tennyson's idea of Sir Galahad provided a paradigm, Lupack argues, for a new democratic chivalry, accessible to all.

The essay co-authored by Donald L. Hoffman and Elizabeth S. Sklar, "Googling the Grail," takes its readers on a merry chase through cyberspace, looking for websites that somehow allude to the Grail, the sacred object of the greatest and most demanding Arthurian quest. In most cases, they discover, the word "grail" simply designates an obscure object of desire, without any deeper signification. The term has undergone a drastic "semantic deterioration." Noticing that "the differences between the Googled grails and the canonical Holy Grail impressively outnumber the similarities," Hoffman and Sklar enumerate, define, and illustrate those differences. They conclude on a wistful note: perhaps the web search has, at least, "remind[ed] us of what has been lost."

Joan of Arc Then and Now

Bonnie's essay, "Joan of Arc's Sword in the Stone," compares the saint's discovery of a lost sword in the shrine of St. Catherine in Fierbois to King Arthur's legendary discovery of the sword in the stone.[10] The section of the present collection entitled "Joan of Arc Then and Now" includes three essays that honor Bonnie as the founding president of the International Joan of Arc Society (Société Internationale de l'étude de Jeanne d'Arc) (1999) and the editor of three books on the young French visionary, battle leader, and martyr (d. 1431). According to Bonnie's candid admission, she "had no interest in Joan of Arc as a girl," considered her "either crazed or fictional or both," and was repulsed by Joan's monarchist militarism, which put her "on the wrong side of all [Bonnie's] secular, democratic, antiwar sentiments."[11] The writings of Jean Gerson and Christine de Pizan concerning Joan moved Bonnie, however, to reconsider the challenging figure of the Maid and to read for the first time the historical records of Joan's trial. Finding those documents "staggering," Bonnie "was entirely swept away by them," hearing in them the "piercingly clear voice of a young woman"[12] who was braving her male judges and their condemnation. Bonnie went on to edit (with historian Charles T. Wood) the 1996 collection *Fresh Verdicts on Joan of Arc* and the 2003 collection *Joan of Arc and Spirituality* (with Ann W. Astell), as well as Jeremy DuQuesnay Adam's English-language translation and revision of Régine Pernoud and Marie Véronique Clin's classic text *Joan of Arc: Her Story*. That volume appeared in 1998, shortly after Pernoud's death. A "voracious" reader of writings about Joan, Bonnie confesses, "I can't get her out of my head."[13]

The three essays about Joan included here attest to the historical and political questions she continues to raise, as well as to her cultural significance. In his study, "'Because It Was Paris': Joan of Arc's Attack on Paris Reconsidered," Kelly DeVries reevaluates the conditions in which Joan launched her attack on Paris in September 1429. A Burgundian stronghold, the city was heavily fortified by walls, gatehouses, and a wide moat. The French assault lasted for only one day, at the end of which Joan was wounded in the thigh, and her wearied soldiers withdrew. Most historians blame the Maid's humiliating defeat after so many victories on Charles VII, who initially delayed and then, over Joan's protests, precipitously ended the siege. DeVries complicates this judgment against the king by comparing Joan's fruitless attempt to the successful attack of Paris by John the Fearless in 1418. In his case, the Parisians themselves were initially divided in their choice of allegiance between the Burgundians and the Armagnacs and eventually rose up for him. Joan did not benefit from a similar internal division among the citizens.

Lacking sufficient support from within Paris, DeVries concludes, Joan could not achieve the victory she so ardently desired.

Kevin Harty's essay, "Warrior not Warmonger: Screen Joans during World War I," also examines the figure of the embattled Maid. Observing that Joan of Arc is often invoked in pro-war films, Harty traces this trend back to its cinematic origins. Harty shows that filmmakers during World War I readily used Joan of Arc to rally support for the Allied cause. They likened historical women like Edith Cavell and Émilienne Moreau explicitly to Joan and presented them as models for those at home and on the front. Filmmakers also created fictional characters, such as the Joan in *Joan of Plattsburg*, to typify a properly patriotic response to the war effort. Geraldine Ferrar stars in the most famous of these pro-war films, Cecil B. DeMille's *Joan the Woman* (1916). Through the self-sacrificing heroines of such films, Harty argues, filmmakers sought to overcome opposition in the United States and elsewhere to further involvement in the Great War.

Nadia Margolis explores the political implications of Jehannine theater in her essay, "The Drama of Left-Wing Joan: From 'Merlin's Prophecy' to Hellman's *Lark*." Although more often associated with right-wing authors such as Robert Brasillach and Jean Anouilh, both of whom wrote for the Vichy press, Joan of Arc, as a populist heroine, has also demonstrably attracted left-wing writers, including the notable Marxist playwrights Bertolt Brecht and Lillian Hellman. Margolis first provides a critical commentary on Brecht's three (co-written) plays about Joan, especially *Heilige Johanna der Schlachthöfe* (1928–29), in which the gradual unblinding of the idealistic champion of the workers, Joan Dark, is designed to enable the audience's own ideological enlightenment. Contrasting Brecht's Marxism with Hellman's, on the one hand, and Brasillach's patriotism with Anouilh's right-leaning humanism, on the other, Margolis studies the encounter of right and left in Hellman's adaptation of Anouilh's famous play about Joan of Arc. As Margolis demonstrates, in Hellman's Broadway success, *The Lark*, Anouilh's right-wing-based ideals finally differ little fundamentally from Hellman's. In the courage of her convictions, Joan speaks for them all.

Nuns and Spirituality

This section follows the section on Joan of Arc, complementing its primarily historical and political treatments of a saintly medieval lay woman with historical, spiritual, and liturgical considerations relevant to her religious women contemporaries. Bonnie Wheeler's own scholarship concerning nuns of the Middle Ages has mainly focused on a single, highly celebrated nun of the twelfth century, the abbess Heloise of the monastery of the Paraclete. Heloise's correspondence with her former teacher, lover, separated husband, and spiritual director Peter Abelard about the monastery's Rule offers proof, Bonnie has argued, that "their intellectual union continued until death," and that "their collaboration . . . in the creation of the convent of the Paraclete" was "equal in every sense."[14] The fifteen essays edited by Bonnie in *Listening to Heloise: The Voice of a Twelfth-Century Woman* (2000) combine to produce "a richer sense of the several strands of Heloise's life" than is usually available in scholarly sources.[15] Answering to the deathbed request of Mary Martin McLaughlin (d. 2006), Bonnie has subsequently carried through to its completion McLaughlin's lifelong work, publishing in 2009 *The Letters of Heloise and Abelard: A Translation of Their Collected Correspondence and Related Writings* and, soon thereafter, *Heloise and the Paraclete: A Twelfth-Century Quest*.[16]

In "A Letter to the Abbess of Fontevrault from the Abbot of Clairvaux," Giles Constable pays tribute to Bonnie's interest in the correspondence between Heloise and Abelard by offering an edition and translation of a hitherto unpublished letter, incompletely copied by two scribes, probably at Admont. Constable presumes the letter to be genuine, and not a rhetorical exercise, but admits that it may be fictive. Published and translated here for the first time, the letter from "P" (the abbot) addresses "M" (the abbess) with affection and respect and praises Christ, the bridegroom of souls, whose grace has united them in love. Its diction, tone, and spiritual content shed some interesting light, he argues, on the historical relations between the heads of two of the most important of the new religious orders, one male and the other female, in the twelfth century.

Like Constable, historian William Chester Jordan draws upon manuscript sources in his study, "The Nuns of Bival in the Thirteenth Century." Building upon work begun by the late Joseph Strayer, Jordan utilizes the unpublished late twelfth- and thirteenth-century charters of Bival, a Cistercian nunnery in Normandy. Combining their data with information from the famous *Register* of Archbishop Eudes Rigaud of Rouen, who visited the house at least fourteen times from 1248 to 1269, Jordan charts the precarious conditions of life at the house, which was almost always close to bankruptcy, and its communal struggles. The picture Jordan paints of the specific points of contention between the nuns and the archbishop offers a fascinating view into monastic discipline, governance, and economy.

Anne Bagnall Yardley's essay, "The Sonic Presence of Mary Magdalene at the Last Supper: The Maundy of the Poor at Barking Abbey," provides yet another avenue for insight into medieval women's monastic life. Yardley shows that the music chanted by Benedictine nuns during the *mandatum pauperum* (ritual footwashing of the poor on Maundy Thursday) at Barking Abbey in the later Middle Ages is almost entirely derived from the liturgy for Saint Mary Magdalene, whose cult had grown in popularity. The sung antiphons thus suggest a different set of biblical precedents for this liturgical action than the usual one of Jesus washing the disciples' feet. The effect, Yardley proposes, is almost as if one looked at a picture of the Last Supper and saw Mary Magdalene washing the disciples' feet, even as the sinful woman of Luke 7:37–38 had washed the feet of Jesus with her tears of penitence and love. Yardley examines the precedents for these liturgical chants and the aural significance of their incorporation into this central monastic ritual of a large English convent.

Drawing upon mnemonic rather than stylistic or iconographic sources for Christian piety, Annemarie Weyl Carr studies the contrasting Greek and Italian iconography of Christ's Passion in her essay, "The Royal Purple Mantle of El Greco's *Espolio*." She seeks to discover Theotokopoulos's bond to his Greek background not, as art historians usually do, through compositional parallels between his paintings and Cretan icons or through his style but rather in his use of visual images that were steeped in meaning by Greek liturgical painting, poetry, and performance. In particular, Carr relates the blood-red robe of Christ in El Greco's *Espolio* (1577), commissioned for the cathedral of Toledo, to the red robe of Christ in Cretan icons of Christ at the cross. This red robe, Carr explains, which is about to be stripped from Christ, symbolizes in Byzantine tradition Christ's very body, the mantle of his flesh. The robe is thus linked with the theme of flaying, current in European awareness in the 1570s through the historic flaying of a Venetian general in Cyprus. El Greco's *Espolio* of Christ is, Carr argues, a transcendent allegory of the flaying that is, for Michelangelo and Titian, a potent image of artistic ambition.

Royal Women

As the essays in the concluding section, "Royal Women," demonstrate, the queens of the Middle Ages controlled their possessions and directed their households in ways expressive both of their personal piety and of their desire for independence. Bonnie Wheeler's edition (with John Carmi Parsons) of the essays collected in *Eleanor of Aquitaine: Lord and Lady* (2003) shows her own abiding fascination with a powerful queen. Of Eleanor, Bonnie observes, "As the wife and mother of kings, her wealth and influence afforded her fields of action by no means insignificant to her husbands' governments."[17]

The same may be said, *mutatis mutandi*, of the royal women studied here by historians William W. Clark and Elizabeth A. R. Brown. In his essay, "Signed, Sealed, and Delivered: The Patronage of Constance de France," Clark offers an arresting portrait of King Louis VII's sister Constance (1124–ca. 1190), the only daughter of Adelaide de Maurienne and Louis VI. Although twice married, Constance de France spent the last period of her life, beginning in 1165, living independently in Paris and traveling as a pilgrim to the Holy Land. Clark examines the royal and aristocratic iconography of Constance's unusual round and double-sided personal seal, which he redates to ca. 1165. As Clark shows, Constance used this seal to manage her properties shrewdly and to make timely donations to religious institutions associated with the royal family, particularly the financially hard pressed nunnery on Montmartre, which had been founded by her mother. To Constance, who countered her royal brother's decisions regarding the nunnery, Clark credits "the first significant matrilineal patronage in the Capetian dynasty."

In her essay, "The Testamentary Strategies of Jeanne d'Évreux: The Endowment of Saint-Denis in 1343," Elizabeth A. R. Brown similarly examines the bequests to a religious institution by a royal woman. Queen Jeanne d'Évreux, widow of King Charles IV of France (1294–1328), lived forty-three years beyond the death of her husband. During those years, she "made a cult of widowhood and philanthropy," according to Brown, offering charitable donations in Charles's memory and in pious anticipation of her own death and afterlife. Brown pays particular attention to the novel strategy Queen Jeanne d'Évreux devised to ensure the fulfillment of her last will and testament. With the reigning king's permission, she took the unusual step on August 1, 1343, of giving the abbey of Saint-Denis, where she hoped to be buried next to her husband, a lavish anticipatory endowment. In two acts, she gave the abbey three precious objects: a gold statue of St. John the Evangelist, a silver-gilt statue of the Virgin and Child, and a crown, as well as a substantial annuity to support the monks in their work of intercessory prayer. Brown has edited the complete text of these two previously unpublished acts, which appear in an appendix to her essay.

The testamentary, memorial themes of the last two essays in this collection make them a fitting conclusion to a volume in honor of Bonnie Wheeler, who has been so exemplary in honoring the lives and the work of those from whom she and many others have learned. The titles of many of her publications indicate the bonds of filial piety and faithful friendship. It was Bonnie who edited Festschriften in honor of E. Talbot Donaldson, P. J. C. Field, Maureen Fries, Elizabeth D. Kirk, and Charles T. Wood, and Bonnie, too, who helped to carry forward the lifework of the great, recently deceased medievalists Régine Pernoud, Mary Martin McLaughlin, and George Bond. Once again, Bonnie, you have proven yourself a *magistra doctissima*, leading us—contributors to this volume and editors alike—by your example in the art of grateful remembrance and faithful *traditio*.

NOTES

1. Christine de Pizan, *The Book of the City of Ladies*, trans. Earl Jeffrey Richards (New York: Persea Books, 1982), p. 153.

2. See Charlton T. Lewis and Charles Short, *A Latin Dictionary* (Oxford: Clarendon Press, 1879, repr. 1955), p. 1097.

3. See *The Middle English Dictionary*, ed. Sherman M. Kuhn and John Reidy, vol. 10 (Ann Arbor: University of Michigan Press, 1975), pp. 9–11.

4. Jeremy DuQ. Adams and Bonnie Wheeler, "Medievalists as Teachers: North American Models," in *Medieval Studies in North America: Past, Present, and Future*, ed. Francis G.

Gentry and Christopher Kleinhenz (Kalamazoo, MI: Medieval Institute Publications, 1982), pp. 201–21 (at pp. 219–20).

5. As well as Old Norse and, simultaneously, medieval history under the direction of Bryce Lyon, since at the time Brown University did not have an interdisciplinary graduate medieval studies program.

6. See for example Gillian R. Overing, *Language, Sign, and Gender in "Beowulf"* (Carbondale: Southern Illinois University Press, 1990), and *The Postmodern "Beowulf,"* ed. Eileen A. Joy and Mary K. Ramsey (Morgantown: West Virginia University Press, 2006).

7. Bonnie wrote about Donaldson's influence in "The Legacy of 'New Criticism' in the Study of Chaucer: Revisiting E. Talbot Donaldson," *Chaucer Review* 41:3 (2007), 216–24. Stephen Stallcup graduated magna cum laude in 1992 from Southern Methodist University, where he studied with Bonnie. He completed his PhD in English literature at Princeton University in 2000 and taught at the University of North Carolina-Greensboro from 2001 to 2008. A sudden illness caused his death on January 8, 2009, while this volume was in preparation.

8. Bonnie Wheeler, "The Project of Arthurian Studies: Quondam et Futurus," in *New Directions in Arthurian Studies*, ed. Alan Lupack (Woodbridge: Boydell and Brewer, 2002), pp. 123–34, at p. 124.

9. Ibid., p. 125.

10. Bonnie Wheeler, "Joan of Arc's Sword in the Stone," in *Fresh Verdicts on Joan of Arc*, ed. Bonnie Wheeler and Charles T. Wood (New York: Garland, 1996), pp. xi–xvi.

11. Bonnie Wheeler, "Introduction," in *Joan of Arc and Spirituality*, ed. Ann W. Astell and Bonnie Wheeler (New York: Palgrave, 2003), p. 2.

12. Ibid., p. 3.

13. Ibid.

14. Mary Martin McLaughlin with Bonnie Wheeler, "Introduction," in *The Letters of Heloise and Abelard: A Translation of Their Collected Correspondence and Related Writings*, trans. and ed. Mary Martin McLaughlin with Bonnie Wheeler (New York: Palgrave Macmillan, 2009), p. 2.

15. Ibid., p. 8.

16. The latter title has not yet appeared in print but has been announced as forthcoming.

17. John Carmi Parsons and Bonnie Wheeler, "Prologue: Lady and Lord: Eleanor of Aquitaine," in *Eleanor of Aquitaine: Lord and Lady* (New York: Palgrave Macmillan, 2003), p. xiv.

Part 1
Old and Middle English Literature

Kiyoko Nagase and Her "Grendel's Mother"

Toshiyuki Takamiya

In February 1996 Professor Fred C. Robinson was generous enough to send me a copy of a portfolio file entitled "*Beowulf* in the Floating World: The Poem Illustrated with Japanese Block Prints from Several Centuries," edited and compiled by his former student, Professor Marijane Osborn. His cover note indicated that as his birthday gift she presented him with two copies of this privately made file, suggesting that one of these should be delivered to anyone who could appreciate her cross-cultural efforts to juxtapose some scenes from *Beowulf* and their matching pictures selected from among Japanese *Ukiyoe* prints by such artists as Hokusai, Kuniyoshi, and Yoshitoshi.[1] The *e* of *Ukiyoe* signifies "picture(s)" and *Ukiyo* serves as a pun in Japanese meaning "the Floating or Gloomy World": the latter would surely suit the grim world of *Beowulf*.

In her afterword, she maintains as follows:

> It comes as a surprise that the Japanese, who have produced more work on *Beowulf* than any other single nation outside the English-speaking world and Germany, have not, to my knowledge, produced a single picture of the hero or his exploits. The omission is all the more surprising in view of the fact that models for suitable pictures exist ready at hand in Japan's world-famous art of block prints, which includes imaginings of ancient stories. When I began to put some of these pictures with the poem, the project practically took off by itself because of the art waiting for it.[2]

Certainly Professor Osborn is right in assuming that there has been no modern Japanese artist who has attempted to illustrate *Beowulf,* mainly because its reputation has remained within the confines of academia. There is a case, however, of an extraordinary reception of the epic, reflected in a Japanese poem written by Kiyoko Nagase as early as April 1929. I find it more than gratifying, therefore, to celebrate Professor Bonnie Wheeler's sixty-fifth birthday by contributing a short essay on the poet and her poem on mothering, because we know that one of Bonnie's books is on medieval mothering.[3]

❖

The eldest daughter of an intellectual middle-class family, Kiyoko Nagase was born in a small town in Okayama Prefecture, situated between Kobe and Hiroshima, on February 17, 1906; she died on the same day in 1995.[4] Her parents owned a small piece of farmland, but it had to be abandoned due to the Land Reform, which was put into effect immediately after the Second World War. Nevertheless, as their eldest daughter, she somehow managed to hold a few acres for her own cultivation. This was partly why she used to be referred to as an "agricultural poet," but it was only in 1946, when she was forty years old, that she started agriculture.

Her father, a graduate of the Imperial University of Kyoto, worked as a chief engineer for an electric company based in Kanazawa, an ancient and cultural city located on the Japan Sea. So from the age of two to sixteen she was brought up in Kanazawa, where she was deeply attached to Japanese gothic novels in her formative years. Then her family moved to Nagoya, and when she was seventeen she encountered a best-selling selection of English romantic and French symbolist poems, translated by Bin Ueda and first published in 1905, which made her determined to be a poet—apparently rather an unusual decision, one might say, because poetry is something that will naturally come out of the poet's mind rather than something deliberately chosen as a profession. Since childhood, she had not been good at expressing herself with spoken words, which she felt was rather disadvantageous, and so she wanted to make use of poetry writing as her means of communication. She assiduously and repeatedly read these poems at the bedside of her younger sister, who was then confined to a hospital bed.

Kiyoko was impressed by the greater intricacy and expansiveness she found in them compared to earlier Japanese poetry. In this period there was virtually no woman poet active in Japan, and even male poets were often ill spoken of by lay people as "bohemian outsiders." Arising in Europe and the United States during the First World War, Dadaism found its way into Japan, if belatedly, orchestrating the rebellious and destructive movement against established art and tradition.[5] There is no doubt that the popularity and rapid dissemination of the movement in Japan had something to do with the aftermath of the Great Earthquake, which totally devastated Tokyo and its neighboring areas in 1923.

At the age of eighteen, in 1924, Kiyoko was admitted as a mature pupil to the English Department of the Advanced Courses, attached to the Aichi Prefectural First Women's High School. In the department, all subjects were taught using English textbooks, and one of the classes she attended was the history of English literature. There she was immediately touched by the description of Grendel's mother, whose exploit was mentioned in a summary of *Beowulf*.

In this period there were two epoch-making incidents which took place in her life: her poetic training under the guidance of Sonosuke Sato, a poet who had a life-enduring influence on her; and her marriage in 1927 to a law graduate of the Imperial University of Tokyo, which led to the birth of their eldest daughter in the following year. Hers was what is called an arranged marriage, as was the ordinary case with many prewar generations of Japanese, but she successfully persuaded her husband to let her continue writing poetry. In 1930 *Grendel's Mother* was published as her first collection of thirty-nine poems, some experimental and some fairy tale-ish, which included a short poem of the same title.[6]

From 1912 to 1926, during Emperor Taisho's reign, and even some time after, there was a short-lived liberalistic and democratic movement in politics, society, culture, and art, later called the Taisho Democracy Movement, prevailing all over Japan. It certainly included the movement for women's liberation and emancipation and for universal suffrage.[7] Perhaps it will be no exaggeration to argue that Kiyoko Nagase was one of the daughters of the movement, although she did not firmly maintain her antiestablishment stance at the time of the Second World War, which she later regretted.

Beowulf was virtually unknown to the general public in Japan, of course, and interest in the Anglo-Saxon epic was limited to university students of English literature, such as Soseki Natsume,[8] who attended the lectures given by Professor Lafcadio Hearn at the University of Tokyo. In one of these lectures, Professor Hearn referred to the affinity between Beowulf's fight with Grendel and his mother and Watanabe-no-Tsuna's seizure of an ogre's arm,[9] a similarity that was first pointed out by F. York Powell as early as 1901.[10]

On his return to Keio University after four years of study in Oxford, Professor Junzaburo Nishiwaki started teaching Old and Middle English and English philology to Keio undergraduates in 1926, and soon found the very best student in Fumio Kuriyagawa, who was to become the doyen of medieval English studies in Japan. At the age of only twenty-two, Kuriyagawa translated *Beowulf* into antiquated Japanese based on the medieval Japanese war epic entitled *The Tale of Heike*. This pioneering translation was first published with a full critical apparatus in 1932 in a Keio journal,[11] while its popular edition appeared in 1941.[12]

It is evident from the above account that when Kiyoko composed her short poem "Grendel's Mother" there was no Japanese translation of the Old English available, but her poem appeared at a propitious moment, when *Beowulf* studies in Japan were about to emerge: now we have as many as ten complete translations in Japanese.[13] To the best of my knowledge, the hitherto unprecedented reception of *Beowulf* by Kiyoko, a Japanese feminist poet, has not been known to *Beowulf* scholars until quite recently,[14] but the poem, originally written in Japanese free verse of twenty-seven lines without rhyme and spiced with some archaic vocabulary, is remarkably impressive even in the following English translation:

> Grendel's mother is
> In the recesses of an ancient cave
> On the far side of a blue swamp
> (Or at the bottom of a dark metropolis
> Where streetlights cast shadows)
> With her bronze-colored hair
> Hugging her children tightly.
>
> With those old monstrous eyes
> She stares at the entrance, arachnid-like.
> With her stalwart maternal instinct
> Shield-like she protects
>
> Her children who will eventually
> Become colossal monsters of the north
> (Or will become those who drink firmly and silently
> The tears of multitudes of people).
>
> Even among the horrifically sacrificed
> Each will walk alone toward the sublime,
> They will remain unsmelted by evil and rage.
> And other than in their mother's arms
> They will let out neither shrieks nor roars!
>
> The light shed from the moon rising
> From the depths of the night like fresh metal
> In that ancient swamp
> (Or on the roof-tiles of the city)
> Is burning blue.
> Grendel's mother is
> Even now lurking in the recesses of her cave.[15]

In a preface to the poem, Kiyoko gives an introductory remark as follows:

> I must admit that I do not have enough knowledge of Grendel. All I know is that he is a northern monster mentioned in an Old English poem; although he has assailed the royal palace every night for twelve years, putting all the courtiers into terror, he is attacked by Beowulf the hero, who came to rescue the king; Grendel's mother, who attempted to take a revenge, is also killed by Beowulf in a cave deep in the bottom

> of the mere. I do not think that my poem will need any background information. My Grendel is not necessarily based on an accurate legend, but rather my own idealized figure. He may well be identified not as a Grendel observed by a biographer who stands for his hero, but as a Grendel from the mother's point of view.[16]

But Kiyoko was always willing to elucidate the motivation and background of her poetry: in 1984, almost fifty years after the composition of the piece, she makes a summary of *Beowulf*, and then gives the following comment:

> In all the heroic tales, however, the opponents are always wicked ogres or filthy monsters, and the hero who conquers them is in victorious glory praised for his generous conduct of giving away captured goods or hailed with laudatory words.
>
> But can it be right? I doubt whether it is a poet's role to praise the victorious hero. It may not be right if one inadvertently praises the winner alone. The thing is that the Danish King [Hrothgar] had a splendid palace built and held endlessly extravagant feasts with his subjects, enjoying mead and everything, and this orgy angered the monster Grendel who had lived there, and triggered the conflict. We can never regard his anger as groundless. However troublesome he may have been to the king or hero, Grendel was a child whom his mother loved and cherished since his birth, wishing him to grow strong and happy as a family column or supporter. I believe that she had an honorable right to fight against the intruder and her fight was remarkably heroic.
>
> People tend to make their opponents either ogres or monsters without any knowledge of their real heart or living. As a youth, I wanted to be a human who could appreciate the real heart of these oppressed victims.[17]

The final passage should be taken as Kiyoko's manifesto as a mother-poet. In her poem one will be struck by the determination of Grendel's mother to protect her children in a medieval cave, which is interestingly juxtaposed with a modern setting in which Kiyoko seems to place herself. Kiyoko had four children in her life, which naturally led her to write more poems resulting from her domestic experiences and feelings of mothering, but we have found no more intense sentiments as a mother determined to guard and foster her children than in "Grendel's Mother."

Perhaps Setsuko Haruta was one of the first medievalists to draw comprehensive attention to the role of the women in the epic including Grendel's mother.[18] Haruta argues that the poet betrays too much sympathy for Grendel's mother to allow us to brush her aside as the mother-villain and emphasizes her femininity in mentality and in appearance (*Beowulf* 1351a): "The motive of

Grendel's mother's attack is understood as revenge by both the poet (1276b–78 and 1546b–47a) and by Hrothgar (1333b). Among all the characters bereft of their children, she is the only parent who dares to act as an avenger, and, even to a modern audience, her act is 'understandable,' 'acceptable,' and even 'laudable.'"[19]

I wonder if Kiyoko would agree to the final quotation in Haruta's account, because one day in 1976, Kiyoko watched a Kabuki play "Ibaraki" (sometimes pronounced "Ibaragi") on television. This is reminiscent of the story of Grendel's arm, first linked by York Powell to that of Watanabe-no-Tsuna. A legend has it that in the late tenth century Ibaraki, an outrageous female ogre or demon residing at Rashomon or Rajohmon Gate in Kyoto, harassed the people who tried to pass it. Watanabe-no-Tsuna, one of the renowned retainers of Minamoto-no-Raiko, goes to get rid of her, but the battle rages on until Tsuna draws his sword and severs her arm, which he sweeps up as a trophy. Returning to his mansion, he locks it in a chest for safekeeping. He is advised to keep it hidden for seven days without allowing anyone to enter the mansion. On the seventh day, however, the female demon comes to visit him, disguised as his aunt Mashiba, who happens to be his foster mother. He reluctantly lets her in, and then she successfully persuades him to show her the ogre's arm. She abruptly grabs at it and reveals herself as Ibaraki, escaping triumphantly from Tsuna's mansion.

The medieval story of Watanabe-no-tsuna and his fight with Ibaraki had been very popular in prewar Japan, but alas, virtually no undergraduates are now familiar with it. A poet of the prewar generation, Kiyoko must have been well versed in Japanese literature and popular tradition on the subject of the medieval woman ogre, who is related topically to motherhood.[20]

Immensely touched and satisfied by the dramatic ending of the Kabuki drama, which gives final victory to the female ogre, Kiyoko almost identified herself with her: "The blue river, which has continuously run in my heart since my youth, is now suddenly visible. I have now realized that the armless ogre is nothing but the source of my poetry writing."[21] It is possible to argue that the blue river bears the symbolism of the real heart of these oppressed victims mentioned above, which Kiyoko connected with the light burning blue in the last stanza of the poem. Thus she was able to confirm that "Grendel's Mother" had become a work that forecast her life.

NOTES

N.B. [J] indicates publications in Japanese. I am very grateful to Professor Howell Chickering for valuable suggestions he has given during the course of the preparation of the present article and to Professor John Scahill for improving my English.

1. Osborn selected forty-three scenes from *Beowulf*, often adding a Japanese text translated by Professor Tsunenori Karibe. This well-selected and carefully prepared portfolio contains a preface, afterword, list of plates, and bibliography. The woodblock prints used

here are diverse and varied in genre as well as artists. In her email message dated May 20, 2007, Osborn admits that her work proved to be too esoteric to be published by a university press in the United States, but I believe it is high time that it receives critical attention in published form. For the last twelve years I have shown the portfolio around among undergraduate students attending my lectures on the history of English literature conducted at Keio University: thus more than one thousand young Japanese have enjoyed with admiration and amazement this extraordinary cross-cultural undertaking.

2. Afterword, p. 2. I am very grateful to both Professor Marijane Osborn and Professor Fred C. Robinson for their kindness in allowing me to have access to her work and to quote from it.

3. *Medieval Mothering*, ed. John Carmi Parsons and Bonnie Wheeler (New York: Garland, 1996).

4. For a biographical account of the poet's early life, see Yoko Isaka, *Kiyoko Nagase* [J] (Tokyo: Goryu Shoin, 2000), pp. 7–25; and Itoko Ikubo, *Kiyoko Nagase in Women's History: Before and during the War* [J] (Tokyo: Domesu Shuppan, 2007), pp. 9–160.

5. A general discussion of the literary movement in modern Japan will be found in Donald Keene, *Dawn to the West: Japanese Literature of the Modern Era, Poetry, Drama and Criticism* (New York: Holt, Rinehart and Winston, 1984), pp. 255–91.

6. Kiyoko Nagase, *Gurenderu no Hahaoya (Grendel's Mother)* (Osaka: Kajinbo, 1930).

7. See Yoshio Iwamoto, "Aspects of the Proletarian Literary Movement in Japan," in *Japan in Crisis: Essays on Taisho Democracy*, ed. Bernard S. Silberman and H. D. Harootunian (Princeton: Princeton University Press, 1974), pp. 156–82.

8. Soseki Natsume seems to have been the first novelist to refer to *Beowulf* in Japanese. For Soseki as the first Japanese writer to encounter the western concept of ego, see Hisaaki Yamanouchi, "The Agonies of Individualism: Natsume Soseki," in *The Search for Authenticity in Modern Japanese Literature* (Cambridge: Cambridge University Press, 1978), pp. 40–81, and Toshiyuki Takamiya and Andrew Armour, "*Kairo-ko*: A Dirge," in *Arthurian Literature* 2 (1981): 92–126.

9. Lafcadio Hearn, *A History of English Literature* (Tokyo: Hokuseido, 1927), 1:15–16.

10. F. York Powell, "Beowulf and Watanabe-no-Tsuna," in *An English Miscellany Presented to Dr Furnivall in Honour of His Seventy-Fifth Birthday*, ed. William P. Ker, Arthur S. Napier, and Walter W. Skeat (Oxford: Clarendon Press, 1901), pp. 395–96. For more recent and detailed studies of the affinity see the following: Kinshiro Oshitari, "A Japanese Analogue of *Beowulf*," in *Philologica Anglica: Essays Presented to Professor Yoshio Terasawa on the Occasion of His Sixtieth Birthday*, ed. Kinshiro Oshitari et al. (Tokyo: Kenkyusha, 1988), pp. 259–69; Michiko Ogura, "An Ogre's Arm: Japanese Analogues of *Beowulf*," in *Words and Works: Studies in Medieval English Language and Literature in Honour of Fred C. Robinson*, ed. Nicholas Howe and Peter S. Baker (Toronto: University of Toronto Press, 1998), pp. 59–66; and Yuko Tagaya, *Sword of the King and the Hero: King Arthur, Beowulf and Yamato Takeru* [J] (Tokyo: Hokuseido, 2008), pp. 167–227.

11. Fumio Kuriyagawa, "*Beowulf* and *The Fight at Finnsburg*" [J], *English Literature and Philology* 3 (1931–32): 1–284.

12. Fumio Kuriyagawa, trans., "*Beowulf*" and "*The Fight at Finnsburg*" [J] (Tokyo: Iwanami, 1941).

13. Hideki Watanabe, "Beowulfiana in Japan: A Brief Survey of the Past 75 Years, with Special Focus on the Japanese Translations and Interpretative Studies," *Studies in Medieval English Language and Literature* 21 (2006): 45–54; Kazutomo Karasawa, "An Aspect of *Beowulf* Scholarship in Japan" [J], *Universals and Variation in Language* 2 (Tokyo: Senshu

University, 2007), pp. 75–97. The latest translation is found in *The Old English Epic Beowulf: A Bilingual Edition* [J], ed. Tsunenori Karibe and Ryoichi Koyama, with translation, glossary, and commentary (Tokyo: Kenkyusha, 2007).

14. I touched on the subject in a lecture entitled "Beyond the Middle Ages and Medievalism," delivered at the 79th Annual General Meeting of the English Literary Society of Japan held at Keio University on May 20, 2007, and subsequently published under the same title [J] in *Rising Generation* 153:6 (2007): 358–63.

15. The text is based on Ikubo, *Kiyoko Nagase in Women's History*, pp. 131–33, and translated by Professor Yuko Matsukawa, to whom I am deeply indebted.

16. Quoted in Isaka, *Kiyoko Nagase*, p. 23, my translation.

17. Quoted in Isaka, *Kiyoko Nagase*, p. 24, my translation.

18. Setsuko Haruta, "The Women in *Beowulf*," *Poetica* (Tokyo) 23 (1986): 1–15, esp. p. 11.

19. Ibid., p. 12.

20. Ogura, "Ogre's Arm: Japanese Analogues of *Beowulf*," in Howe and Baker, *Words and Works*, pp. 62–64. Making a succinct summary of the woman ogre in the Japanese tradition, Ogura indicates that many ogres turn into women in old age (sometimes eating their children) and that the woman ogre is related to motherhood.

21. Ikubo, *Kiyoko Nagase in Women's History*, p. 142.

British Chaucer

Jeffrey Jerome Cohen

The ambit of Chaucer's works ranges from England to Africa, from the "errtik sterres" wandering the firmament to the literal bowels of hell. Yet the island from which he writes is a strangely diminished geography. This essay examines Chaucer not as an English poet, not as an international man of letters, but as a writer within a polyglot, culturally restless archipelago. Chaucer's attenuated Britain reveals an essential component of his Englishness: participation in a long tradition of passing over in silence the vitality and contemporary diversity of the isles, imagining that the only modernity Britain can possess is singular and English.[1]

Dipesh Chakrabarty has written of the need to *provincialize* Europe, to break it into "different Europes," allowing history to admit "contradictory, plural, and heterogeneous struggles whose outcomes are never predictable, even retrospectively."[2] Medievalists have in fact long been laboring at such epistemological dismantling. Robert Bartlett details how peoples undertook to Europeanize themselves, a fraught process of internal harmonization essential to imagining transnational community.[3] Post-Conquest England was long absorbed in a similarly difficult process of self-colonization, Anglicizing its inhabitants to effect an insular unity.[4] R. R. Davies has emphasized the high price paid for this emergent Englishness by the "Celtic Fringe" that such circumscription produced. The Scots, Irish, and Welsh found themselves denigrated as barbarians so that England as a single kingdom could pass itself off as an entity coterminous with the whole of Britain.

The transformation of a boisterously multicultural archipelago into an "exclusive orbit of power" dominated by one of its four constituent countries was well advanced long before Chaucer's birth.[5] Yet the marginalization of Britain's nonanglophone peoples and the promulgation of London's dialect and metropolitan culture over regional differences were ongoing throughout the fourteenth century. Though the Canterbury pilgrims arrive in Southwark from various provinces, they speak the vernacular of the nearby city.[6] Characters who in life would have been bilingual utter no French. London saturates *The Canterbury Tales*, serving as the work's unacknowledged structuring principle.[7] Chaucer spent many of his adult years living in an apartment built into one of the city's medieval gates. Beneath his dwelling at Aldgate passed diverse peoples. With a population approaching 50,000, fourteenth-century London was a multilingual and culturally intermixed space. Chaucer's family home in the Vintry Ward was close enough to the Thames to behold ships sailing between London and Scandinavia, Iberia, the Mediterranean. His London was a place of great intellectual and artistic achievement, of violence, intolerance, and sheer possibility.

Early in his life Chaucer was attached to the household of Lionel, second in line for the English crown. While the prince was young, a marriage had been arranged with the lone heiress of William, Earl of Ulster, ensuring that at his majority half of Ireland would come under Lionel's dominion. In 1366 he presided over a parliament at Kilkenny that attempted to establish an Anglo-Irish apartheid system in England's western colonial frontier. Statutes forbade the English from absorbing indigenous language, customs, and dress, upon penalty of immediate dispossession.[8] Davies aptly writes of these decrees and of similar laws addressed to Wales: "When national customs become the subject of legislative enactments, we begin to realize what an important place they occupied in the framework of race relations in the past as well as the present. In the eyes of medieval Englishmen the customs and habits of the Welshmen . . . marked them as a different race."[9] Yet no matter their aspirations, such "legislative enactments" never obtained much success. The Statutes of Kilkenny failed to enact the keen separations they envisioned. A dispirited Lionel abandoned Ireland for other campaigns.

Even if he never crossed the Severn, Chaucer moved within courtly circles where the Irish and the Welsh were denigrated peoples, sometimes even a different species. He knew of England's Hibernian entanglements from London events as well. A formal submission of Irish chiefs to Richard II was staged just as the poet was most intensely engaged in his *Canterbury Tales* project in the mid-1390s, a submission that did little to ameliorate the violence in that country. Chaucer would also have been well aware of the military history of England in Wales, where native resistance flared regularly long after the country's conquest came to its official close. He would have been frequently reminded of the fluctuating alliances that English nobles forged with Scotland, especially because John of Gaunt (for whom he composed *The Book of the Duchess*) enmeshed himself with such gusto in Scottish politics. Ireland, Wales, and Scotland were not absent from Chaucer's life. How strange, then, that these places should be so difficult to glimpse in his work.

Vanishing Britain

Romance, the most popular vernacular genre of the Middle Ages, is replete with mysterious geographies. Accessed by boats that move of their own volition, steeds that tread the clouds, ancient caves, or numinous mounds, these fantastic realms have been christened by scholarly convention "Other Worlds." They appear at once impossibly distant and unbearably close, intrusions of alternate realities into the quotidian. Through their portals beckon spaces where the rules structuring mundane existence are exchanged for eruptions of magic, unforeseen transformations, fabulous wealth, landscapes fashioned of desire and dread. Jeff Rider describes these oneiric expanses as "dream worlds, wish worlds."[10] They seem to be intimately related to the Other Worlds of medieval Welsh and Irish narratives, spaces that combine the familiar with the disconcerting, the present with the fading past.[11]

The action of the Middle English poem *Sir Orfeo* is set into motion by the impingement of such a world, a geographically unlocatable space that intrudes with fearsome allure into the Winchester court.[12] In this self-described Breton lay, Queen Heurodis of England slumbers beneath a grafted tree and is abducted by a radiant host. The "king o fairy" (283) shows her a land and a people of exorbitant beauty, then announces that Heurodis must join him forever. Should she refuse, her body will be torn to fragments. The fey realm to which the queen is conveyed is accessed by passing through a rock ("In at a roche the levidis rideth" [347]), making it similar to the subterranean worlds described by William of Newburgh, William Map, Gerald of Wales, and Marie de France. As in these realms, there seems something quite British about the Other World of *Sir Orfeo*, existing in queer contiguity to ordinary England. From at least the twelfth century onward, English writers imagined Wales as frozen in time. Modernity belonged to England, while across the Severn awaited a living museum of the primitive. The fairy realm in *Sir Orfeo* takes temporal stasis to an extreme: bodies injured in war continue to bleed; the moribund are locked perpetually in the agony of perishing; everyday life yields neither goal nor progress (when the Fairy King and his retinue go to hunt, they do not seem to pursue any animal but simply make their mysterious way through the woods).

Though a mere 605 lines of brisk verse, *Sir Orfeo* is one of the most ambitious colonial projects ever launched in English literature, transforming the realm of classical myth into an English kingdom (an Orpheus pilfered from Greek mythology is thus "king / In Inglond" [39–40]; his father and mother are Pluto and Juno; Winchester is declared the English name for Thrace). While the Greek and Roman past is engulfed and anglicized, contemporary Britain is made to vanish entirely. Like all examples from this very English genre of writing, this "Breton lay" claims origin not on the island of Britain but from its near homonym, Brittany (*Breteyne*). This small feat of geographical acrobatics, familiar as well from Marie de France, makes it seem as if the story arrives from a direct line of communication between England and a magical place across the channel, dooming nearby Wales and a potentially multicultural Britain to an oblivion of silence.

Chaucer performs a similar displacement, though with more subtlety than the author of *Sir Orfeo*. *The Wife of Bath's Tale*, his single Arthurian narrative, implies that this hero intimately tied to Welsh nationalism is outdated. The regal warrior who in Geoffrey of Monmouth's seminal narration conquered most of the known world becomes in Chaucer's story as insubstantial as the elves and fairies who once populated Britain but have since dwindled to their vanishing point:

> In th'olde dayes of the Kyng Arthour,
> Of which that Britons speken greet honour,
> Al was this land fulfild of fayerye.
> The elf-queene, with hir joly compaignye,
> Daunced ful ofte in many a grene mede. (857–61)[13]

The Britons (that is, the Welsh) are aligned with the "olde dayes" of the island (857), with the stillness of ancient history.[14] The "grene mede" where the elf queen dances seems to be Chaucer's flattened version of the fairy mound of Irish and Welsh narratives of the Other World. "I speke of manye hundred yeres ago," the Wife of Bath declares as she gives her Arthurian romance its temporal setting. "But now kan no man se none elves mo" (3.863–64): Nowadays no one sees elves any more. Fairies and elves, like the Welsh for whom they seem doppelgängers, are the island's lost past. Its present, she states, belongs to lusty "lymytours," friars who divide the land among themselves to farm its revenue. Such men might from time to time spice their conversation with some urbane French ("Je vous dy sanz doute" declares the unctuous Friar of *The Summoner's Tale* [3.1838]), but such men, like the land itself, are wholly English. The Wife of Bath populates modernity with English content, just as Chaucer populates the same space with English characters like the Wife of Bath: neither the artist nor his creation leave any space open for lingering Britishness, except in the dwindled state that Fairy represents.

"Fairy" can indicate either a people or their land. The noun is common in the Breton lays, and nearly always participates in the process of divorcing the non-English from a vitality in the insular present. "Fairy" marks the lostness of a Britain long ago swallowed by England. This Britain survives only as nostalgic remnant, as a magical intrusion into English stories. Contemporary people are thereby robbed of their coevalness. Of Breton lays the author of *Sir Orfeo* declares "mani ther beth of fairy" (10). The land so designated in that poem is a shadowy space in which a British past is collapsed with classical and English histories, creating a lost time with little connection to the contemporary nation, similar to a modern Hall of Man where dioramas of Neanderthals mingle with Maori warriors and Roman foot soldiers. Such amalgamating dismissal of history renders the fourteenth-century domination of England over the rest of the island as natural as it is unquestioned.

The Wife of Bath's Tale allows, however, a certain danger behind the fairy allure: she implies (3.880) that incubi, a kind of demon with some similarities to fairies, are rapists, and even King Arthur's court is a place where that same crime unfolds. A rapist fairy knight features in *Sir Orfeo* and *Sir Degaré* as well. Chaucer uses the word *fairy* in attenuating ways that nonetheless suggest lurking ambivalence. *The Squire's Tale* banishes the Arthurian court to an impossibly distant time and place with the lines "Gawayn, with his olde curteisye / Though he were comen ayeyn out of Fairye" (5.95–96). Lancelot fares worse (declared dead, 287). *The Nun's Priest's Tale* at least allows Lancelot a dwindled existence in the mendacities that present-day women read to amuse themselves (7.3212). *Fairye* is ultimately reduced in *The Squire's Tale* to a deracinated synonym for a mechanical marvel or *gyn* (5.322), applied to a robotic steed presented to the Mongol court: "It was a fairye, as the peple semed" (5.201). "Fairye" cannot here easily be glossed as *illusion*, since the materiality of the artifact is made to matter so much in the narrative: the brass horse is a wondrous transport device, but the long explication of exactly how it works (not contained in Chaucer's sources) disenchants the object, stripping the noun of both danger and magic.[15] "Fairy" is suddenly as ordinary as any artifact on display, not even associated with the Welsh or the Irish or any aboriginal island dweller—and therefore intimately related to the process of disenchanting Gawain and Lancelot, of leaving that non-English past well behind.

Thus when Sir Thopas arrives in the "contree of Fairye / So wilde" (7.802–3), rather than promise the danger and desire evident in the fairy realms of the Breton lays, this childlike geography offers a three-headed giant who hurls stones from a slingshot. Its perturbations are easily calmed by munching "gyngebreed" and "lycorys" (854–55). *The Merchant's Tale*, meanwhile, follows *Sir Orfeo* in combining the Fairy realm with classical mythology, envisioning Proserpina as a Fairy Queen who resembles no one so much as the sharp-tongued Wife of Bath. Pluto, "that is kyng of Fayerye" (4.2227), finds himself silenced by the "suffisant answere" (4.2266) of his wife, rendering him just another version of January or Jankyn. May herself is described as "fayerye" in her husband's eager eyes, ensuring that the word is thoroughly euhemerized (4.1743). The ability of Fairy to contain Arthurian content is Chaucer's acknowledgment of its British potential, but his diminution of Fairy into a space for burlesque, an arena for domestic comedy, and a mere marvel ultimately relegates Britain to ancient history and present silence.

Chaucer's only avowedly "Celtic" narrative, the Breton lay told by the Franklin, ignores the non-English inhabitants with whom the writer shares his island by placing its action in Brittany rather than proximate Wales. The setting seems especially perverse given that the names of the protagonists (Aurelius, Arveragus, and perhaps Dorigen) are taken from Geoffrey of Monmouth's *History of the Kings of Britain*, a profoundly influential text that provided the island a rich, pre-English history.[16] With its resplendent envisioning of Arthur, Geoffrey's *History* was also central to contemporary Welsh nationalism. Like all the Canterbury tales set abroad, however, the "speech and customs" of the characters in *The Franklin's Tale* are "thoroughly anglicized," as if the Bretons were Londoners and all the world England.[17] When the knight Arveragus travels abroad to hone his chivalry, he goes to "Engelond, that cleped was eek Briteyne" (810), silently granting as primordial fact an equivalence of island and nation for which only England would argue.

The Man of Law's Tale is the single Chaucerian narrative in which we behold living Britons. Wandering Custance arrives in Northumbria, a realm that remains pagan but carries already the seeds of its Christian, English future. "To Walys fledde the Cristyanytee / Of olde Britons dwellynge in this ile" states the narrator (2.545–46), at once acknowledging the aboriginal status of the Britons but making it clear that their time has passed. The few "olde Britons" who have not withdrawn to Wales lead furtive, invisible lives. Having "bigiled" (549) the heathens they dwell among, they practice their faith only "in hir privitee" (548). The communal conversion that will signal the arrival of English modernity will be precipitated by Roman Custance, not by these secretive future Welshmen. Even if they provide the "Britoun book, written with Evaungiles" (666) that will enable Custance's missionary work, that book becomes a palimpsest in which their history is overwritten by a narrative focused upon Rome, Northumbria, and an expanse that can be designated "oure occian" (505) no matter at what historical moment its waters appear.[18] Thus when King Alla goes to war, he fights anachronistically against his "foomen" of Scotland (580, 718), a country and a people that did not exist at the time.[19]

Chaucer's England, Chaucer's Britain

Chaucer knew well that "in forme of speche is chaunge / Withinne a thousand yeer," that words once familiar could become "straunge" (*Troilus and Criseyde* 2.22–24). Yet to his mind he wrote *englissh*, not "Middle English." That periodizing distinction was not made until Henry Sweet divided the language into Old, Middle, and Modern English in 1874, an act of separation that underscored the discontinuities between an undeveloped past and a confidently complete present.[20] John Ganim has demonstrated how the medieval period was imagined at the time of Sweet's linguistic partitioning as an analogue to England's new possessions overseas. In order to justify the absorption of India into the empire, its people were represented as medieval. Acculturating the subcontinent to English modernity meant the eradication of indigenous languages, customs, religions. These could be taken from the colonized under the banner of progress, as a healthful movement from Old and Middle into Modern: "Where the English were in the Middle Ages, so was India in the nineteenth century."[21] This otherness of the Middle Ages—and the medievalness of places like India—was emphasized not only in scholarly and popular writings of the time but through pedagogical public exhibits like the World's Fair, where "authentic" medieval villages could be re-created next to "authentic" villages from the colonies as if the two were versions of the same universal human journey. In reaction to this transformation of the Middle Ages into an underdeveloped country, medievalists eventually claimed a modernity for their era of study, describing an early Europe full of familiar, contemporary ideas. As a result, an exploration of the relations between courtly Arthurian romance and the supposedly unrefined Celtic world by R. S. Loomis (a postcolonial theorist *avant la lettre*) scandalized traditionalists, while the possibility of a deep connection between courtly love and Arabic literature likewise provoked outrage when first proposed.

Chaucer escaped some of the debate over the possible primitiveness of the Middle Ages because he was considered not a great poet of the fourteenth century but "a great English poet who happened to live in the Middle Ages," and his timelessness enabled a convenient escape from history.[22] The fact that he monsterized Jews and Muslims, that his vision of Britain (or perhaps more accurately, his programmatic diminution of Britain to the point at which it could be neither coeval nor coequal) emptied the island of Welsh, Scottish, and Irish content, did not disturb scholars for whom poetic universality was a synonym for an exclusive kind of contemporary Englishness. Chaucer's fifteenth-century followers discovered in him a founding father whose sophisticated, musical language they could harness to their own nationalistic literary aspirations. Eventually Chaucer became not simply the father of English poetry but the consummate poet of Englishness. G. K. Chesterton declared "Chaucer is the father of his country, rather in the style of George Washington"—a hyperbolic claim that Derek Pearsall has with typical understatement labeled "dizzying." Pearsall observes that in *The Canterbury Tales*, "England is being fully *recognised*, so to speak, perhaps for the first time, as a real place."[23]

Dryden famously praised Chaucer for his depictions of "oure Fore-fathers and Great Grand-dames," as if human nature were immutable over time, invariable over cultures.[24] Chaucer was a medieval English poet, limited and fallible. His works call into being an intoxicatingly imperfect series of worlds, wide expanses that nonetheless omit more than they include. It is difficult to reduce these realms to jingoistic paean or to harness them to some xenophobic nationalism. Yet Chaucer's emptying his isle of British content is hardly innocuous. A postcolonial, British Chaucer is a complicated character, inventive and demeaning, haunted by that which he absents. Chaucer's "Fairye" seems at first glance the realm of the dead past, but on closer examination a life can be glimpsed still animating the word, even as it becomes a supposedly inanimate object shelved in the museum of English literature. The contemporary study of Chaucer, as of the Middle Ages more generally, must never stop asking how we have come to know the past and must attempt not to repeat history's violence and exclusions as we study the medieval anew.

NOTES

Early versions of some sections of this essay appear in "Postcolonialism," in *Chaucer: An Oxford Guide*, ed. Steven Ellis (Oxford: Oxford University Press, 2004), pp. 448–62. I thank James P. Wade for sharing his research and conversation.

1. R. R. Davies traces this disappearance in twelfth-century English historiography in *The Matter of Britain and the Matter of England* (Oxford: Clarendon Press, 1996).

2. Dipesh Chakrabarty, *Provincializing Europe: Postcolonial Thought and Historical Difference* (Princeton: Princeton University Press, 2000), p. 42.

3. Robert Bartlett, *The Making of Europe: Conquest, Colonization and Cultural Change, 950–1350* (Princeton: Princeton University Press, 1993).

4. John Gillingham, *The English in the Twelfth-Century: Imperialism, National Identity and Political Values* (Woodbridge: D. S. Brewer, 2000); Jeffrey Jerome Cohen, *Hybridity, Identity and Monstrosity in Medieval Britain: On Difficult Middles* (New York: Palgrave, 2006).

5. R. R. Davies, *The First English Empire: Power and Identities in the British Isles, 1093–1343* (Oxford: Oxford University Press, 2000), p. 83.

6. John Bowers details London's ascendancy: "Chaucer after Smithfield," in *The Postcolonial Middle Ages*, ed. Jeffrey Jerome Cohen (New York: Palgrave, 2000), pp. 53–66.

7. David Wallace writes that this permeation foregrounds London as a space of "fragments, discontinuities, and contradictions" (*Chaucerian Polity: Absolutist Lineages and Associational Forms in England and Italy* [Stanford: Stanford University Press, 1997], p. 177).

8. *Statutes, Ordinances and Acts of the Parliament of Ireland, King John to King Henry V*, ed. Henry F. Berry (Dublin: Her Majesty's Stationery Office, 1907), pp. 430–69. Kathleen Biddick discusses the statutes as colonial violence in *The Shock of Medievalism* (Durham, NC: Duke University Press, 1998), p. 54.

9. R. R. Davies, "Race Relations in Post-Conquest Wales: Confrontation and Compromise," *Transactions of the Honourable Society of Cymmrodorion* (1974–75): 36.

10. Jeff Ryder, "The Other Worlds of Romance," in *Cambridge Companion to Medieval Romance*, ed. Roberta L. Krueger (Cambridge: Cambridge University Press, 2000), p. 122.

11. The materials gathered by Howard Rollin Patch, in *The Other World according to Descriptions in Medieval Literature* (New York: Octagon Books, 1970), are useful, especially pp. 27–59. I have written about these mounds in my introduction to *Cultural Diversity in the British Middle Ages* (New York: Palgrave, 2008), pp. 1–16.

12. I quote from the edition of Anne Laskaya and Eve Salisbury in *The Middle English Breton Lays* (Kalamazoo, MI: Medieval Institute Publications, 1995), pp. 15–59. The following have been essential to my thinking about this complicated text: Corinne J. Saunders, *The Forest of Medieval Romance: Avernus, Broceliande, Arden* (Woodbridge: D. S. Brewer, 1993), pp. 133–42; Neil Cartlidge, "Sir Orfeo in the Otherworld: Courting Chaos?" *Studies in the Age of Chaucer* 26 (2004): 195–226; L. O. Aranye Fradenburg, "Simply Marvelous," *Studies in the Age of Chaucer* 26 (2004):1–27.

13. *The Riverside Chaucer*, ed. Larry D. Benson, 3rd ed. (Boston: Houghton Mifflin, 1987), p. 860.

14. On Arthur, Welsh nationalism, and the complexities of postcolonial identities, see Patricia Clare Ingham, *Sovereign Fantasies: Arthurian Romance and the Making of Britain* (Philadelphia: University of Pennsylvania Press, 2001), and Michelle R. Warren, *History on the Edge: Excalibur and the Borders of Britain, 1100–1300* (Minneapolis: University of Minnesota Press, 2000). Ingham powerfully reads *The Wife of Bath's Tale* as creating a pastoral space in which the present struggles of the Welsh are made invisible by an idealized, lost history: see her "Pastoral Histories: Utopia, Conquest, and the Wife of Bath's Tale," *Texas Studies in Literature and Language* 44 (2002): 35–46.

15. The *Middle English Dictionary* offers as a secondary definition of *fairie* "supernatural contrivance, enchantment, magic, illusion . . . something incredible or fictitious" (accessed at ets.umdl.umich.edu). That the detailed instructions are Chaucer's introduction to the source material is well argued by Kathryn L. Lynch in "East Meets West in Chaucer's Squire's and Franklin's Tale," in *Chaucer's Cultural Geography*, ed. Kathryn L. Lynch (New York: Routledge, 2002), p. 85. The inexplicability of *fairie* is emphasized by James Wade in "Abduction, Surgery, Madness: An Account of a Little Red Man in Thomas Walsingham's *Chronica Maiora*," *Medium Aevum* 77 (2008): 10–29.

16. Lynch, "East Meets West," p. 89.

17. Bowers, "Chaucer after Smithfield," p. 56.

18. In this way Chaucer is merely repeating the geographic structuration of Bede: see Nicholas Howe, "Rome: Capital of Anglo-Saxon England," *Journal of Medieval and Early Modern Studies* 34 (2004): 147–72.

19. Chaucer's vanquishing the present Welsh, Irish, and Scots to silence does not necessarily mean that they cannot be glimpsed or heard in his texts. As Patricia Ingham argues "taking the utopian dreams of the medieval colonized as a serious strategy of resistance will change how we understand, and indeed define, history. It affects, for one thing, where we might look for traces of those texts and traditions judged not worthy of preservation, and not recovered for the archives. It suggests, more precisely, that the genres of folklore and romance might offer a different kind of evidence within which we might read a fantasmatic colonial archive" ("Pastoral Histories." p. 37).

20. David Matthews, *The Making of Middle English: 1765–1910* (Minneapolis: University of Minnesota Press, 1999), p. xxxi.

21. John Ganim, "Native Studies: Orientalism and the Origins of the Middle Ages," in *The Postcolonial Middle Ages*, ed. Jeffrey Jerome Cohen (New York: St Martin's Press, 2000), pp. 123–34; quotation p. 127.

22. G. K. Chesterton, "The Greatness of Chaucer," in *G. K. Chesterton: Collected Works* (San Francisco: Ignatius Press, 1991), p. 155.

23. Derek Pearsall, "Chaucer and Englishness," in Lynch, *Chaucer's Cultural Geography*, pp. 296, 291. Pearsall adds "But it is not a place for which we are encouraged to feel a particular affection, as a beloved land or heritage-site, and the pilgrims and the people who inhabit those of the Canterbury Tales that are set in England are on the whole a pretty unsavoury lot" (p. 291).

24. John Dryden, "Preface to Fables Ancient and Modern," in *Of Dramatic Poesy and Other Critical Essays*, ed. George Watson (London: J. M. Dent, 1962), 2:285.

Just How Loathly Is the "Wyf"?: Deconstructing Chaucer's "Hag" in *The Wife of Bath's Tale*

Lorraine Kochanske Stock

Throughout his *oeuvre*, Chaucer betrays extreme authorial anxiety about being misinterpreted by readers, about his texts being erroneously transmitted, and about misrepresenting other "auctours" himself.[1] He curses future readers/critics who for various reasons "mysdeme" his dream report about visiting Fame's House (*House of Fame* [*HF*] 94–100). He curses his scribe, Adam Scriveyn, in the poem of the same name, with a case of scalp disease to ensure that he "wryte . . . true" rather than "wryte newe." His *Troilus*-narrator apologizes for "in eche-ing" details beyond his "auctour's" intent while narrating his text and invites more experienced lovers to "encresse" or "maken dymynucioun" of "myne wordes" (*Troilus and Criseyde* [*TC*] 3.1324–37). Notoriously, Chaucer's relation to his sources and literary analogues involves considerable "encresse" and "dymynucioun" of what he found in his ur-texts. This is especially true in *The Wife of Bath's Tale* (*WBT*), his rendering of the "Loathly Lady" or "Irish Sovereignty" tale type which enjoyed a flowering in other late Middle English texts such as John Gower's *Tale of Florent* (*Florent*), *The Wedding of Sir Gawain and Dame Ragnell* (*Ragnell*), and *The Marriage of Sir Gawain* (*Marriage*). Compared with these versions, Chaucer makes significant "encresse," notably precipitating the plot with an Arthurian knight's rape of a maiden, expiation of which requires his learning what women really want. As in the analogues, the Knight makes a rash promise to an old woman, the Loathly Lady character. In return for the answer that will save him from decapitation, he must marry her. Chaucer practices "dymynucioun" by eliminating the detailed blazon of the grotesque physical appearance of a female figure who in *Florent*, *Marriage*, and especially *Ragnell* can justifiably be termed a "hag."

Judging by the considerable body of interpretive commentary about *WBT*, Chaucer had good reason to worry about being "mysdemed" or "wryten newe" by critics who have taken his narrator's offer in *Troilus* as an open invitation not only to "eche in" their own interpretations of what Chaucer does say in *WBT* but also, as if seeing a textual mirage, to completely fabricate details and language that Chaucer never wrote. Although this tendency holds true about other aspects of *WBT*, I now focus on what commentators have "eched in" about Chaucer's Loathly Lady, especially their relentless designation of the figure as a "hag," a label that I argue carried pejorative resonance that Chaucer chose not to burden *his* female character with.

"Hag" as a Category of Medieval Female Otherness

"Hag" is a verbal signifier that attaches to aging females a vast spectrum of benevolent and malevolent presumptions and projections, as exemplified in the scholarly treatment of the female protagonist in *WBT*, an unnamed old woman whose nominal signifier is the "olde wyf."[2] Importantly, as is duly acknowledged by critics, the usually garrulous Wife's uncharacteristically, and therefore significantly, reticent presentation of her female subject never physically describes the "wyf." Nevertheless, from early modern "translators" through contemporary scholars, Chaucerians almost universally represent this woman by the culturally loaded designator "the hag." In over one hundred journal articles and book chapters devoted to *WBT* published in the past century,[3] at least seventy-five of the critics refer to the "wyf" as some variant of "loathly," "old," or "ugly" "hag." Only about twenty critics label her "old wife," "wife,"[4] or "old woman,"[5] echoing Chaucer's own term, the "olde wyf." Taking a neutral position, some call her "loathly lady."[6] The "image" of the "wyf" as a hag in *WBT* originates in the eye of her first beholder, the rapist/Knight to whom she gives the life-saving answer to the riddle that will determine the outcome of his rape trial. Similarly, the alleged transformation of the "wyf" to a young, beautiful bride at the tale's conclusion is also a product of the Knight's gaze. I intend to challenge the accumulated scholarly misreadings of the "wyf" as "hag" and to recuperate Chaucer's wise old "wyf" in *WBT*.

Before we proceed, some operating definitions are in order. Middle English "wyf" denotes: a human biological female or generic woman (of any marital status); the mistress of a household; a married woman; a sexually experienced woman; or a non-virgin (MED, s.v. "wif" 1.a, b; 2. a, b). Modified by "olde," "wyf" may denote a disparaging term for an elderly woman (MED "wif" 1.b). Middle English "hagge" (derived from Old English "haegtesse" meaning "fury, witch, hag") denotes an *ugly* old woman, a witch, or "*hag*," defined in the OED as "evil spirit, daemon, infernal being in female form"; "malicious female sprites or fairies"; "a woman supposed to have dealings with the infernal world, a witch"; and "an ugly, repulsive old woman, often with the implication of viciousness or maliciousness" (OED, s.v. "hag"). This three-letter word encompasses a broad continuum of meaning, including negatively evaluated physical appearance, fairy mischief, moral perversity, and utterly malign supernatural power. How could critics transform Chaucer's explicitly designated "wyf," a neutral, even benign designation of "female," to "hag," a term invested with so much medieval and modern misogyny?

The Critics' "queynte fantasye"—The Wife's "Hag"

The hallowed tradition of constructing the "wyf" as a loathsome, grotesquely ugly female begins early. In 1615, Richard Brathwaite published his observations about *WBT*, in which he identifies with the rapist/Knight's discomfiture at having to marry "this unwieldy Beldame, who was a very Fardel of Diseases":

> For to describe her, . . . what was she, but a sapless seer stock without verdure; a crawling creeping cricket without vigour; a proportionless feature without favour? One, whose mouth like a common sewer, was ever driveling; whose Nose, like a perpetual Limbeck, was ever dropping. The *Sciatica* had taken possession of her Hip; the Megrim of her head; An aged film had quite covered her eyes; And an incessant Cough taken seizure of her Lungs. Her mouth was discharged of the Grinders; from which issued such a Steam, as it would have put a Serjeant in mind of his Mortality. Yet must this proper Puss be this Knight's dainty Bride.[7]

Brathwaite's meticulous *effictio* of the visual appearance and physical disabilities of the "wyf" rewrites the description of "our ancient, renovvned, and ever living poet Sr. Jeffray Chaucer," who chose to offer not one detail of the "olde wyf's" appearance in *WBT*.

Besides the epithet "hag," other descriptive terms used by later critics include: "an amazingly ugly woman";[8] "an ancient female . . . uglier than any man could imagine,""ancient beldame,""antique monster uglier than any could ever devise";[9] "a shrewd and tricky, decidedly equivocating beldame";[10] "grizzled bride";[11] "ugly and somewhat run-down old woman";[12] "beastly bride" evincing her "fleshly incongruity in the nuptial bed";[13] "old and battered crone";[14] "loathsome old hag";[15] and "more than hag."[16] How could a mere "wyf" be "more than hag"? This automatic assumption of the physical monstrousness of the "wyf" relies on slender, if not totally invented, textual evidence and betrays preconceived constructions of the character.

What the Knight "saugh" on the green replacing the vanished dancers was a projection of patriarchal construction—not just an old "wyf" or woman but a "creature" or "wight"[17] whose foulness could be amplified by "no man's" devising. The passage is narrated from the Knight's point of view, with his thoughts and feelings mediating the events.[18] From this patriarchal, aristocratic perspective, what the Knight "sees"—or perhaps what any *man* would devise (the line's inflection should fall on "man")—is a "hag."[19] Unduly influenced by the tale's analogues—which present the encounter between a hero and a loathly lady who aids him in return for the promise of a kiss or sex and then is magically transformed from grotesqueness to beauty—critics project on to Chaucer's "creature" the attributes of the other physically loathsome hags of this tale type, which Chaucer deliberately resists in creating his "olde wyf." Never mind the softer sounding "loathly damsel or lady" of the analogues; Chaucer's character is nearly universally labeled the "hag," connoting not only the malevolent witch associations but also the extreme physical deformity associated with the loathly ladies of the analogues. If he wanted, Chaucer could have used the explicit label "hagge," as Langland did in *Piers Plowman B.* 5.191, referring to an old woman with bleary eyes "as a blynde *hagge.*" Chaucer, selecting the more gender-generic "wyf," denoting "woman," neutralizes the potentially pejorative valence that "hagge" would connote, especially as a signifier of witchcraft.[20] Nonetheless, Hollis views the "wyf" as "a succubus" or "an otherworldly being"; the Knight's consummation with her is "tantamount to engaging in intercourse with evil spirits."[21]

As most critics acknowledge, Chaucer alters his Loathly Lady story most significantly by omitting a graphic "portrait" of the physical ugliness of his loathly damsel. Silverstein asks, "How ugly is ugly? How loathsome the loathly lady? The Wife of Bath never tells us the details."[22] The Knight claims she is "so *loothly*, and so oold" (1100), a token nod to the Loathly Lady analogues, usually featuring detailed portraits of hideous hags. And the analogues of *WBT* are unequivocal in depicting their hags' physical deformities, especially *Ragnell*'s monstrous female. The absence of a graphic description of the supposedly "loothly" "wyf" in *WBT* is all the more striking, considering the use of such negative feminine types by his fourteenth-century literary contemporaries: Gower in *Florent*, the *Gawain*-poet in the long description of another loathly damsel, the "auncian" in *Sir Gawain and the Green Knight*,[23] and Langland in the previously cited reference to *Piers Plowman*. Yet, when he chooses to, Chaucer is capable of creating graphic descriptions of physical ugliness or deformity; witness the General Prologue's depiction of the Miller's cavernous mouth and hairy wart and the Summoner's terrifying-looking facial protuberances. In the analogue temporally and stylistically closest to Chaucer's version, Gower's *Florent*, the "hag-ness" of what Gower terms a "creature," "a lothly wommannysch figure" (1529–30),[24] and the "olde wyht" (1548) is unequivocal.

Despite such incontrovertible textual evidence, it is still possible to be blind to the legitimate "hag-ness" of Gower's character in order to project that physical grotesqueness on to Chaucer's "olde wyf." For instance, comparing Gower's and Chaucer's handling of what he calls "the forest hag," Beidler reverses the two terms. He notes, "Florent sees an ugly old woman sitting under a tree. When she calls to him he turns his horse aside and goes to her." Chaucer's Knight finds in place of the dancing ladies "*a foul old hag*. We should note, of course, that he approaches her out of lust for the dancing ladies, not—like Florent—out of kindness *to help an old lady*."[25] Here the critic not only "transforms" Gower's hag into a benign "old woman" or "old lady" and Chaucer's into a "foul old hag" but also projects "kindness" upon Florent's motives, when in fact the text states that Florent "wolde have passed by" this ugly creature had she not "cleped him and bade abide" (1534–35).[26] In contrast, Chaucer's Knight eagerly approaches the fairy dancers, motivated by the "hope that som wysdom sholde he lerne."

Chaucer's version omits another feature of the analogues: the public acknowledgment of their hags' loathliness, the verification, even documentation, of the unquestionable physical ugliness of the analogues' genuine hags by members of Arthur's court. In *Marriage*, when Gawain meets his new bride, Lancelot, Tristram, and Kay accompany him and swear that they would not kiss this hag, much less marry her. When she is released from her literal bewitchment at the end of the story, the court duly notes her transformation. Similarly, in *Ragnell*, during both her arrival with Arthur to his court and her wedding reception, Ragnell's ugliness is confirmed universally by "kyng and knyghte," "bothe knyghte and squyre," "*alle* the contraye," Queen Guenevere and "*alle* the ladyes in her bower," and "*alle* men" (545, 618, 521, 542–43, 603, 612, 616; emphasis added). At the wedding, a second hideous portrait is offered (545–56), her uncouth table manners are noted (601–18), and despite being dressed more richly for the wedding than even Guenevere, "Ffor alle her rayment she bare the belle / Of fowlnesse" (595–96).

However, in *WBT*, there is no such documentation of the foul appearance of the "wyf"; only the Knight seems to "see" her as loathly. When she accompanies him to court for the queen's judgment, none of the assembled women remarks upon the purported physical ugliness of the "wyf," and thus it remains unverified, and perhaps is "real" to the Knight only. Moreover, his revulsion at her supposed grotesque physiognomy masks his deeper objection, his class-based embarrassment at marrying someone "comen of so lough a kynde" (1101). Besides class, the Knight seems to object most to the advanced age of his potential spouse, the attribute of the "wyf" that is most often acknowledged *textually* in the tale, unlike the other Loathly Lady stories where not so much the age but the abhorrent physical appearance of those hags is emphasized. In *WBT*, "wyf" is modified with the adjective "olde" three times (1000, 1046, 1072). The "wyf" claims to be one of "thise *olde* folk" (1004) and admits publicly before the court to being "foul, and *oold*, and poore" (1063). Although most critics take "foul" to mean its second MED denotation, "unattractive, ugly," when describing "persons," the adjective also means "abject, low, miserable, wretched," all signifying low social or economic station.[27] The "wyf's" defense of economic poverty and redefinition of God-given "gentillesse" in the pillow lecture suggest that Chaucer was more concerned with the economic meaning of "foul" than with the cosmetic one.

Notwithstanding the etymology of the term "hag" from the Anglo-Saxon word for witch or hag, other more positively valenced origins of the word are the Greek *hagia*, or "holy one," and Old High German *Hagazussa*, priestess of the underground, mother Hel. Walker argues that "hag" derives from and refers to traditional wise women figures, crones associated with Mother Goddess worship.[28] Significantly, the educative role of the "wyf" and her signification as a source of wisdom are stressed repeatedly throughout Chaucer's version. The Knight's first sight of her occurs when she replaces the vanished ladies, to whom he raced "In hope that *som wysdom* sholde he lerne" (994). Her pillow lecture on the true source of "gentillesse" amply extends that dispensation of wisdom. If bestowing wisdom is what being a "hag" is about, then I agree with those many critics who have constructed the "wyf" as a "hag." However, most scholarly labels of "hag" are about her imagined grotesque physical appearance and advanced age, not wisdom. Her equivocal transformation at the end of the tale, from being old and ugly to being young and fair, is another point of critical contention that space limitations preclude developing here. Based on the evidence of the text, however, I would argue that the most demonstrable transformation of Chaucer's character has not been from "hag" to beautiful bride but rather from "wyf" to "hag," especially in the sense of "wise woman." Taking their cue from the male protagonist, critics have seen what they wanted to see in the "wyf": a "hag" in the pejorative sense. They have "eched" their own antifeminist and misogynist projections upon Chaucer's creation and "wryte newe" his text.[29] Chaucer had good reason to be anxious about being "mysdemed"! Medieval paradigms of female otherness subsume not only the Loathly Lady but also the benevolent wise crone who, in the absence of a hideous physical description, informs Chaucer's creation of the "wyf" in *WBT* much more than the Loathly Lady does. It's time for the deconstruction of the critics' "hag" and the reconstitution of *Chaucer's* wise "wyf."

NOTES

An earlier version of this essay was delivered at the 1994 Southeastern Medieval Association with Bonnie Wheeler, always an important presence at SEMA, attending. In 2001, I contributed an essay, cited in note 23 below, connecting the Celtic Sheela-na-gigs and an authentic literary "hag," the *auncian* in *Sir Gawain and the Green Knight*, to a collection honoring Maureen Fries that Bonnie edited. For this volume honoring Bonnie, I extend my study of the "loathly lady" to Chaucer's "olde wyf." To Bonnie go my warmest thanks for her longtime support and friendship.

1. Chaucer quotations are taken from *The Riverside Chaucer*, ed. Larry D. Benson, 3rd ed. (Boston: Houghton Mifflin, 1987).

2. To differentiate between the Wife of Bath and her created character, the pilgrim is designated "Wife"; the character, "wyf."

3. Space limitations preclude listing all examples; I selectively discuss the most inventive constructions of the "wyf" as "hag" and other critical labels.

4. See W. W. Allman and D. Thomas Hanks, Jr., "Rough Love: Notes toward an Erotics of the *Canterbury Tales*," *Chaucer Review* 38.1 (2003): 36–65; Meredith Cary, "Sovereignty and Old Wife," *Papers in Language and Literature* 5 (1969): 375–88; Sarah Disbrow, "The Wife of Bath's Old Wives' Tale," *Studies in the Age of Chaucer* 8 (1986): 59–71; S. Elizabeth Passmore, "Through the Counsel of a Lady: The Irish and English Loathly Lady Tales and the 'Mirror for Princes' Genre," in *The English "Loathly Lady" Tales: Boundaries, Traditions, Motifs*, ed. S. Elizabeth Passmore and Susan Carter (Kalamazoo, MI: Medieval Institute Publications, 2008), pp. 3–41; Lee Patterson, "'Experience woot well it is noght so': Marriage and the Pursuit of Happiness in the Wife of Bath's Prologue and Tale," in *Geoffrey Chaucer: The Wife of Bath*, ed. Peter G. Beidler (Boston: Bedford, 1996), pp. 133–54; Nancy Rosenfeld, "'Who Peyntede the Leon?' The Olde Wyf Confronts the Wife of Bath and Criseyde," *Atenea* 23.1 (2003): 69–82; Barrie Ruth Straus, "The Subversive Discourse of the Wife of Bath: Phallocentric Discourse and the Imprisonment of Criticism," *English Literary History* 55 (1988): 527–54.

5. See Muriel Brown, "'Gentilesse' in Chaucer's *Wife of Bath's Tale*," in *Proceedings of the 11th Annual Northern Plains Conference on Early British Literature*, ed. Michelle Sauer (Minot, ND: Minot State University, 2003), pp. 82–89; Laurie Finke, "All is for to sele': Breeding Capital in the Wife of Bath's Prologue and Tale," in Beidler, *Geoffrey Chaucer*, pp. 171–88; Olga C. M. Fischer, "Gower's *Tale of Florent* and Chaucer's *Wife of Bath's Tale*: A Stylistic Comparison," *English Studies* 3 (1985): 205–25; Louise O. Fradenburg, "'Fulfild of fairye': The Social Meaning of Fantasy in the Wife of Bath's Prologue and Tale," in Beidler, *Geoffrey Chaucer*, pp. 205–20; Susan Hagen, "The Wife of Bath: Chaucer's Inchoate Experiment in Feminist Hermeneutics," in *Rebels and Rivals: The Contestive Spirit in The Canterbury Tales*, ed. Susanna Greer Fein, David Raybin, and Peter C. Braeger (Kalamazoo, MI: Medieval Institute Publications, 1991), pp. 105–24; Elaine Tuttle Hansen, "'Of his love daungerous to me': Liberation, Subversion, and Domestic Violence in the Wife of Bath's Prologue and Tale," in Beidler, *Geoffrey Chaucer*, pp. 273–89; H. Marshall Leicester, Jr., "'My bed was ful of verray blood': Subject, Dream, and Rape in the Wife of Bath's Prologue and Tale," in Beidler, *Geoffrey Chaucer*, pp. 234–54; Susan Signe Morrison, "Don't Ask, Don't Tell: The Wife of Bath and Vernacular Translations," *Exemplaria* 8.1 (1996): 97–123; Katherine M. Morsberger, "Voices of Translation: Poet's Voice and Woman's Voice," *Pacific Coast Philology* 28.1 (1993): 3–19; Esther Quinn, "Chaucer's Arthurian Romance," *Chaucer Review* 18.3 (1984): 211–20; John Stephens and Marcella Ryan, "Metafictional Strategies and the Theme of Sexual Power in the Wife of Bath's and Franklin's Tales," *Nottingham Medieval Studies* 33 (1989): 56–75; Robert S. Sturges, "*The Canterbury Tales*' Women Narrators: Three Traditions of Female Authority," *Modern Language Studies* 13 (1983): 41–51.

6. See W. P. Albrecht, "The Sermon on Gentilesse," *College English* 12.8 (1951): 459; Elizabeth M. Biebel-Stanley, "Sovereignty through the Lady: 'The Wife of Bath's Tale' and the Queenship of Anne of Bohemia," in Passmore and Carter, *English "Loathly Lady" Tales*, pp. 73–82; Merrill Black, "Three Readings of the Wife of Bath," in *Autobiographical Writing across the Disciplines: A Reader*, ed. Diane P. Freedman and Olivia Frey (Durham, NC: Duke University Press, 2003), pp. 85–95; Muriel Brown, "'Gentilesse' in Chaucer's *Wife of Bath's Tale*," in Sauer, *Proceedings*, pp. 82–89; Rafal Boryslawski, "Sirith-na-Gig? Dame

Sirith and the Fabliau Hags as Textual Analogues to the Sheela-figures," in *To Make His Englissh Sweete upon His Tonge*, ed. Marcin Krygier and Liliana Sikorska (Frankfurt: Peter Lang, 2007), pp. 121–33; Paul Gaffney, "Controlling the Loathly Lady, Or What Really Frees Dame Ragnelle," in Passmore and Carter, *English "Loathly Lady" Tales*, pp. 146–62; Stephanie Hollis, "'The Marriage of Sir Gawain': Piecing the Fragments Together," in Passmore and Carter, *English "Loathly Lady" Tales*, pp. 163–85; Bernard F. Huppé, "Rape and Woman's Sovereignty in the *Wife of Bath's Tale*," *Modern Language Notes* 63 (1948): 378–81; Martin Puhvel, "*The Wife of Bath's Tale*: Mirror of Her Mind," *Neuphilologische Mitteilungen* 100.3 (1999): 291–300; A. C. Spearing, "Rewriting Romance: Chaucer's and Dryden's *Wife of Bath's Tale*," in *Chaucer Traditions: Studies in Honour of Derek Brewer*, ed. Ruth Morse and Barry Windeatt (Cambridge: Cambridge University Press, 1990), pp. 234–48; Francis G. Townsend, "Chaucer's Nameless Knight," *Modern Language Review* 49 (1954): 1-4; Edward Vasta, "Chaucer, Gower, and the Unknown Minstrel: The Literary Liberation of the Loathly Lady," *Exemplaria* 7.2 (1995): 395–418; Michael E. Williams, "Three Metaphors of Criticism and the *Wife of Bath's Tale*," *Chaucer Review* 20.2 (1985): 144–57. 7. Richard Brathwaite, *A comment upon the two tales of our ancient, renovvned, and ever living poet Sr. Jeffray Chaucer, Knight . . . The miller's tale, and the wife of Bath* (1665), Early English Books Online: Wing/ 16:01, pp. 174–75. I thank Mikee Deloney for drawing my attention to this text.

   8. Joseph P. Roppolo, "The Converted Knight in Chaucer's *Wife of Bath's Tale*," *College English* 12 (1951): 263–69.

   9. Theodore Silverstein, "The Wife of Bath and the Rhetoric of Enchantment: Or, How to Make a Hero See in the Dark," *Modern Philology* 58 (1961): 153–73.

   10. Douglas J. Wurtele, "Chaucer's Wife of Bath and Her Distorted Arthurian Motifs," *Arthurian Interpretations* 2.1 (1987): 47–61.

   11. Norman N. Holland, "Meaning as Transformation: The Wife of Bath's Tale," *College English* 28.4 (1967): 279–90.

   12. Penn R. Szittya, "The Green Yeoman as Loathly Lady: The Friar's Parody of the Wife of Bath's Tale," *Publications of the Modern Language Association* 90.3 (1975): 386–94.

   13. Susan Carter, "Coupling the Beastly Bride and the Hunter Hunted: What Lies Behind Chaucer's *Wife of Bath's Tale*," *Chaucer Review* 37.4 (2003): 329–45.

   14. Marc Glasser, "'He Nedes Moste Hire Wedde': The Forced Marriage in the 'Wife of Bath's Tale' and Its Middle English Analogues," *Neuphilologische Mitteilungen* 85 (1984): 239–41.

   15. Dorothy Colmer, "Character and Class in *The Wife of Bath's Tale*," *Journal of English and Germanic Philology* 72 (1973): 329–39.

   16. Russell A. Peck, "Folklore and Powerful Women in Gower's 'Tale of Florent,'" in Passmore and Carter, *English "Loathly Lady" Tales*, pp. 100–145.

   17. Through increased application to bad or good spirits, "wight," a Germanic word meaning "being" or "creature," acquired a supernatural connotation. See Katherine Briggs, *An Encyclopedia of Fairies* (New York: Pantheon, 1976), p. 434. Chaucer's Miller equates "wightes" with "elves" (*MT* 3479).

   18. Helen Cooper, *Oxford Guides to Chaucer: The Canterbury Tales* (Oxford: Oxford University Press, 1989), p. 165.

   19. H. Marshall Leicester, Jr., chooses to inflect "man" in *The Disenchanted Self: Representing the Subject in the Canterbury Tales* (Berkeley: University of California Press, 1990), p. 147.

20. For "hagge," the MED also cites the ca. 1475 *Idly Instr.* 2.A.448, "The[r] was an olde wycche, a foul hagge, That of hir believe was full unstable," associating hags and witches explicitly. Critics who designate the "wyf" as a "witch" include Gloria K. Shapiro, "Dame Alice as Deceptive Narrator," *Chaucer Review* 6 (1971): 130–41; Julia Fernández Cuesta, "A Pragmatic Approach to The Wife of Bath's Tale," *Selim* 3 (1993): 103–16; Nanda Hopenwasser, "The Wife of Bath as Storyteller: 'Alle is for to selle' or Is It? Idealism and Spiritual Growth as Evidenced in the Wife of Bath's Tale," *Medieval Perspectives* 10 (1995): 101–15.

21. Stephanie Hollis, "'The Marriage of Sir Gawain': Piecing the Fragments Together," in Passmore and Carter, *English "Loathly Lady" Tales*, p. 177.

22. Silverstein, "Wife of Bath and the Rhetoric of Enchantment," p. 166.

23. Comparing Chaucer's "wyf" with *SGGK's* graphically described "auncian," Meyer implicitly projects a similar grotesque ugliness on Chaucer's "strange old hag." See Robert J. Meyer, "Chaucer's Tandem Romances: A Generic Approach to the *Wife of Bath's Tale* as Palinode," *Chaucer Review* 18 (1984): 221–38, at p. 228. For another study of the "auncian," see Lorraine Kochanske Stock, "The Hag of Castle Hautdesert: The Celtic Sheela-na-gig and the *Auncian* in *Sir Gawain and the Green Knight*," in *On Arthurian Women: Essays in Memory of Maureen Fries*, ed. Bonnie Wheeler and Fiona Tolhurst (Dallas: Scriptorium, 2001), pp. 121–48.

24. Quotations from *Florent* and other analogues come from Bartlett J. Whiting, "The Wife of Bath's Tale," in *Sources and Analogues of Chaucer's Canterbury Tales*, ed. W. F. Bryan and Germaine Dempster (Chicago: University of Chicago Press, 1941), pp. 224–35.

25. Peter G. Beidler, "Transformations in Gower's *Tale of Florent* and Chaucer's *Wife of Bath's Tale*," in *Chaucer and Gower: Difference, Mutuality, Exchange*, ed. R. F. Yeager (Victoria: University of Victoria Press, 1991), p. 104. The emphasis is mine. Lucas also reverses the terms: Chaucer's heroine is an "old hag"; Gower's is an "old woman." See Angela M. Lucas, "The Knight in Chaucer's *Wife of Bath's Tale*," *Poetica* 35 (1992): 29–40.

26. Peter Beidler attended my 1994 SEMA presentation. In a personal email (June 30, 2008), he admitted that, when editing his excellent edition/essay collection *The Wife of Bath* in 1996, "I set it as a ground rule for my essayists not to use that term ('hag'). And, yes, my decision to make that a 'given' was for sure the result of my having heard your fine SEMA paper, Lorraine." A case of conference paper as "pillow lecture"?

27. MED, s.v. "foul," 4.

28. Barbara Walker, *The Crone: Woman of Age, Wisdom, and Power* (San Francisco: Harper & Row, 1985), p. 53.

29. Preferring "old woman" or "wise woman," Thomas argues polemically that "hag" should be discouraged because it is not in the tale and is "painfully sexist." See Susanne Sara Thomas, "The Problem of Defining *Sovereyntee* in the *Wife of Bath's Tale*," *Chaucer Review* 41.1 (2006): 87–97, at p. 88.

Lectio difficilior and All That: Another Look at Arcite's Injury

†Stephen Stallcup

As anyone who has tried to parse Theseus's "first moevere" speech (perhaps *ex tempore* before a classroom of undergraduates) will agree, the language of Chaucer's *Knight's Tale* is anything but straightforward and precise. Yet much Chaucer criticism has followed Theseus's injunction to "make a virtue of necessite" and has systematically disregarded or glossed over many of the knotty verbal problems that litter the poem.

The description of the fatal accident that befalls Arcite following the conclusion of the tournament appears, upon close inspection, much less clear than at first glance. Indeed, were it not for the fact that we have Boccaccio's *Teseida* as a guide, one would be hard pressed to explain two crucial features of this episode: what exactly is it that spooks Arcite's horse and how exactly is Arcite injured? E. Talbot Donaldson made a stab at the second question in a brief, speculative piece a quarter-century ago, but he himself was not entirely satisfied with his conclusions, hopefully suggesting that the great philologist Norman Davis might be able to solve this textual problem.[1]

The former question has not, I believe, received any critical attention. Although my own answers to these questions must remain speculative, too, I hope to show that the meaning of this passage is much less secure than our modern editions would have us believe.

The scene of Arcite's mortal injury is as dramatic as it is unexpected. Having just won the tournament against his cousin and rival Palamon and thus won the hand of Emily, Arcite removes his helmet and takes a victory lap around the arena. Emily, having accepted her fate that she must marry instead of remaining in Diana's service, casts a "freendlich ye" upon the victor. Yet there remain Olympian scores to settle. Mars's promise to Arcite ("Victorie!") has been fulfilled, yet Venus's promise to Palamon (love) remains and, seeing her tears, Saturn declares, "Mars hath his wille, his knyght hath al his boone, / And, by myn heed, thow shalt been esed soone" (2669–70).[2] Within moments, the goddess's will is put in motion: Palamon will get the girl by default, owing to the untimely death of his rival. At the moment of Arcite's greatest joy—Emily "was al his chiere, as in his herte" (2683)—disaster strikes, from an unexpected quarter:

> Out of the ground a furie infernal sterte,
> From Pluto sent at requeste of Saturne,
> For which his hors for fere gan to turne,
> And leep aside, and foundred as he leep;
> And er that Arcite may taken keep,
> He pighte hym on the pomel of his heed,
> That in the place he lay as he were deed,
> His brest tobrosten with his sadel-bowe. (2684–91)

Within the space of eight lines, Arcite goes from victory to near death.
But what exactly has happened here?

The Fury

The *Riverside Chaucer* says that a "furie" spooked Arcite's horse, and commentors on the scene (Donaldson included) talk about this Fury as if everyone knew what it was. But this is not the case. A survey of the fifty-six manuscripts containing *The Knight's Tale* reveals a surprising (though ultimately explicable) lack of uniformity here. The reading of "furie"—adopted by all the modern editors of the poem—is present in only sixteen of the manuscripts. The remaining forty—which include the prominent manuscripts Cambridge, Cambridge University Library MS Gg.4.27 and London, British Library, MS Harley 7334—contain some variant of the word "fire." Thus for many readers, not only of the tale in manuscript but also in the early printed editions, the horse is frightened not by a monster but by a flame.

Two reasons account for this misreading (for indeed it is an error in light of the unambiguous evidence of Chaucer's source): a textual one and an authorial one. Nine of the extant manuscripts have "fuyre" for "furye," and it is easy to see how the transposition of *r* and *y* might lead a subsequent reader or scribe to interpret "fuyre" as "fyre" rather than "furye," especially since the narrative gives the reader no clue as to what a "furye" actually is. A confused scribe might see a hellish fire as a logical device for Pluto to use to scare Arcite's horse, given horses' well-known fear of fire.

Yet the fact that such a large majority of the manuscripts effectively *change the plot* at this moment in the story highlights—if not exactly a weakness in the narrative—an unintended consequence of Chaucer's method of translation. Boccaccio's *Teseida* is unambiguous about the Fury's role in effecting Arcite's death.

Not only does it name the specific Fury responsible for the event, it describes her in gruesome detail and almost revels in depicting her terrible power:

> Venne costei di ceraste crinita,
> e di verdi idre li suoi ornamenti
> erano a cui in Elisso la vita
> riconfortata avea, le quai lambenti
> le sulfuree fiamme, che uscita
> di bocca le facevan puzzolenti,
> piú fiera la faceano; e questa Dea
> di serpi scurïata in man tenea.
> ....
> Costei, nel chiaro dí rassicurata,
> non mutò forma né cangiò sembiante;
> ma giú nel campo tosto se n'è andata,
> lá dove Arcita correva festante,
> e orribil come era, fu parata
> al corrente destrier tosto davante,
> il qual per ispavento in piè levossi
> e indietro cader tutto lasciossi.   (book 9, stanzas 5 and 7)[3]

[Erinys came forth with her long serpent-tresses, and her ornaments were green hydras whose lives she had restored in the Elisos, and the sulphurous flames that they flashed forth from their mouths made them more foul-smelling as they made her more fearsome. And this Goddess carried a whip of snakes in her hand.... More clearly defined in the bright light of day, she did not change her shape nor alter her appearance. She immediately went down the field where Arcite rode about jubilantly, and, dreadful as she was, she stood right in the path of the running horse, which reared on its hind legs in fright and let itself fall over backwards.]

If Boccaccio (who in the *Teseida* is always fascinated by the mythological) leaves nothing to the imagination in his narrative here, Chaucer, by contrast, leaves everything to the reader's mind, collapsing three stanzas of the *Teseida* into a single line.

As a reader of Dante, Statius, and Virgil, Chaucer would have been well versed in the literary tradition of the Furies that Boccaccio makes use of in his poem. Just as Dante's Virgil "ben conobbe" (well knew) the Furies when he met them in the *Inferno*,[4] so Chaucer perhaps assumed that the brief tag "furie infernal" would be enough to evoke the required image in the minds of his more literate readers.[5] Indeed, this was an assumption he would make throughout his literary career, culminating in his invocation of the fury Tisiphone at the very beginning of *Troilus and Criseyde* (1.6).[6]

But it is one thing to make decorative mythological allusions for the benefit of an imagined or actual coterie of *literati*; it is quite another to hang an important plot point on a brief, oblique reference as Chaucer does here. A scribe's misreading can have serious and lasting consequences: in most of the manuscripts and in all of the printed editions through the nineteenth century, Arcite's horse is frightened by a fire, not a Fury. Even a classically trained poet such as John Dryden notices nothing amiss in Speght's edition of *The Canterbury Tales*, and so in his translation of *The Knight's Tale* in 1700, he, too, unknowingly accepts the corrupt reading: "Just then from earth sprung out a flashing fire, / By Pluto sent, at Saturn's bad desire."[7]

Yet if scribes of *The Knight's Tale* did not know what a fury was, they are in good company. Although (as quoted above) Boccaccio is specific in his description of the Fury, the miniature depicting this scene in the single medieval illuminated copy of the *Teseida* (Vienna, Österreichisches Nationalbibliothek, Cod. 2617, fol. 138v) shows no awareness at all of what a fury was supposed to look like.[8] In this image, the fury looks like something out of *Beowulf*, a winged, fire-breathing dragon that appears in a cloud of smoke just above the tournament lists. The effect, however, is the same. The center of the image shows Arcite's horse on its back, legs flailing, and the unfortunate rider trapped beneath it.

Although so many English scribes misinterpreted the fury in *The Knight's Tale*, their misreading has no real effect on the poem. As Kolve notes, "Though Saturn's procedures may lack elegance, no one could fault their economy: he resolves the claims of two petitioners by killing one."[9] Be it by fury, fire, or fire-breathing dragon, Arcite still meets his untimely but fated end.

If, from the point of view of editors and readers, Chaucer's handling of Boccaccio's fury is clumsy, there remains a certain art to it. On the one hand, Chaucer's elimination of Boccaccio's description of the fury is consonant with *The Knight's Tale*'s consistent reduction of the *Teseida*'s epic machinery and its attempts at philosophical closure. Giving too much narrative space to the supernatural elements in the story might problematize Theseus's subsequent explanation of divine justice. On the other hand, by making the fury barely visible or, indeed, invisible (depending on the manuscript), the text replicates the ambiguous sighting of the fury in the *Teseida* as the spectators see or seem to see *something* that is fearsome but inexpressible:

> La cui venuta diè tanto d'orrore
> a chi nel teatro stava a vedere,
> ch'ognuno stava con tremante core,
> né il perché nessun potea sapere.
> Li venti dièr non usato romore,
> e 'l ciel piú ner cominciò a parere;
> il teatro tremò, e ogni porta
> cigolò forte ne' cardini storta.   (book 9, stanza 6)[10]

[Her arrival into the theater caused such horror in everyone who saw her, that each man trembled in his heart, *and yet no one was able to explain why.* The winds made a strange noise and the sky began to seem blacker. The theater shook and every gate writhed and rattled on its hinges.] (my emphasis)

In his *chiose* (or glosses) that accompany most of the *Teseida* manuscripts in one form or another, Boccaccio emphasizes the obscure quality of the episode:

> Certissima cosa è le bestie adombrare per alcuna spaventevole cosa la quale loro pare vedere; ma quello che egli si veggano, overo vedere si credono, niuno il sa. Finge adunque l'autore essere stata Erinis, l'una delle infernali furie, quella che spaventò il cavallo, e disegnala forte spaventevole a vedere, acciò che piú renda scusata l'animositá del cavallo.[11]

> [It is a very certain thing that animals shy at some frightening object that they see, but what they see, or what they think they see, no one knows. So the author imagines that it was Erinys, one of the infernal furies, who terrified the horse, and he describes her as frightful to behold so that the revulsion of the horse might be understood.]

Here, the supposedly authoritative gloss casts doubt on the narrative. Arcite's horse either saw something or might have seen something—but no one knows for sure (*niuno il sa*). Despite the fact that the *Teseida* explicitly narrates Venus's summoning of the Fury, the gloss curiously places the omniscient author as one of the spectators at the tournament who "imagines" (*finge*, literally "pretends") that the cause of the horse's behavior was a frightful Fury.[12]

Did the horse see something or not? Did the spectators see something or not? The way the *Teseida* consistently undermines its own authority here gives Chaucer the license to be as ambiguous as he wishes. And editors have given Chaucer wide latitude. The note in the *Riverside Chaucer* unhelpfully refers students to an analogous passage in Statius that describes "a monstrous figure with snakes for hair" ("anguicomam monstri effigiem") sent by Apollo but it is clearly *not* one of the Furies itself.[13] If, as Kolve suggests, Chaucer "sought imaginative vividness . . . as a special goal" of his narrative art, this moment of curious opacity, of a kind of "anti-visuality" in an otherwise thickly descriptive poem, should give us pause.[14]

The Fall

The potential ambiguities surrounding the "furie" that spooks Arcite's horse pale in comparison to those around the actual injury that Arcite suffers when the horse falls on him. As with the Fury, the description of the fall in the *Teseida* leaves no doubt as to what exactly happens:

> [il] corrente destrier . . .
> il qual per ispavento in piè levossi
> e indietro cader tutto lasciossi.   (9.7.7–8)

48   Stephen Stallcup

> Sotto il qual cadde il giá contento Arcita,
> e 'l forte arcione li premette 'l petto
> e sí il ruppe, che una fedita
> tutto pareva il corpo al giovinetto   (9.8.1–4)[15]

> [the galloping steed, which reared up in fear, lost all control and fell backwards. Happy Arcita fell under it, and the hard saddlebow crushed his chest and pierced it. It seemed as if the whole body of the young man was a single wound]

Yet the version in *The Knight's Tale* is not nearly so clear cut. The first two lines of the description render Boccaccio's Italian faithfully: "his hors for fere gan to turne, / And leep aside, and foundered as he leep" (2686–87). But the Middle English of the ensuing lines is muddy and difficult:

> And er that Arcite may taken keep,
> He pighte hym on the pomel of his heed,
> That in the place he lay as he were deed,
> His brest tobrosten with his sadel-bowe. (2688–91)

The crux lies in line 2689, a difficulty noticed and briefly explored by Donaldson but glossed over or explained away by all the modern editors. The line does not stand up to much critical pressure; upon close inspection, the exact meaning of practically every word in the line is in doubt. What does the verb "pighte" mean? What is a "pomel"? How is it related to a "heed"? To whom (or what) do the pronouns "he," "hym," and "his" refer—Arcite or Arcite's horse—and how do we know?

With two notable exceptions, the line has been (and continues to be) interpreted as "Arcite's horse pitched Arcite on the crown of Arcite's head." But this interpretation assumes stable meanings for "pighte" and "pomel," which, as Donaldson demonstrated, is not the case. The definitions of "pighte," "pomel," and all the pronouns are mutually dependent; to define one is to define the others.

Writing in 1983 before the publication of the "P" volume of the *Middle English Dictionary* (*MED*) and with only the first edition of the *OED* available, Donaldson categorically denied that *pighte* in this line could mean "pitched" in the sense of thrown or cast.[16] Scholarship in the intervening quarter century, which has seen the completion of the *MED* and a second (now continuously emended) edition of the *OED*, has done nothing to question this assertion. In fact, the entries in these two venerable lexicons reinforce each other with respect to the notion that the early uses of *picchen* (the infinitive form of *pighte*) revolve around the act of piercing, either literally or figuratively.

The earliest recorded uses of the Middle English *picchen* date to around 1275 and establish the word's primary meaning throughout the medieval and early modern periods: to thrust, pierce, implant, make fast by means of driving.[17]

This meaning slides into the secondary use of *picchen*, to set up, build, or erect a structure such as a tower, pillar, pavilion, or tent, a usage that continues to the present day.[18] These definitions are closely related since erecting a structure (such as a tent) very often involved penetrating the ground on which it stood. Because "pitching" in these senses almost always leads to some kind of more or less permanent embedding (e.g., a sword in a body or a stake in the earth), one finds that the tertiary use of *picchen* is also closely connected to the other two: to array or adorn someone or something, to stud with gems.[19] This last usage also involves the idea of "fixing," though in a less permanent or less severe way.

Whereas the uses of *picchen* involving thrusting or fixing cluster in the thirteenth and fourteenth centuries, the unambiguous association of the word with the act of throwing or falling dates from the sixteenth century. (Its use in connection with such sports as cricket, baseball, and golf does not come until the eighteenth and nineteenth centuries.) Though both the dictionaries cite a handful of pre-1500 examples of *picchen* in the context of throwing or falling, most of these instances do not, under close scrutiny, appear to support this definition. Rather, they recall the word's primary meaning and imply, as Donaldson (working from considerably less data than is now available) asserts, "if not penetration of an object, sufficient force to cause penetration if the object is penetrable."[20]

When we examine the few examples of this ambiguous usage that antedate *The Knight's Tale* (now generally dated ca. 1385), it becomes clear that they are either insufficiently early or insufficiently unambiguous to establish the meaning of *picchen* as "to throw" in Chaucer's day. The earliest example is an intransitive use and comes from the *Metrical Chronicle* of Robert of Gloucester (ca. 1300), where the poet describes the Icarus-like fall of an unbeliever, one King Bathulf, magician and legendary founder of the city of Bath:

> And vor þe King Baþulf þat it made gret enchanteor was
> And þat him miʒte suþþe rewe—Ich wolle telle þat cas—
> Vor þat men ssolde is enchantement se
> He let him makie wengen an hei vor to fle.
> And þo he was iflowe an hei and ne couþe noʒt aliʒte
> Adoun mid so gret eir to þen erþe he vel and *piʒte*
> Þat al to peces he to rod þat betere him adde ibe
> Abbe bileued þer doune þan ilerned vor to fle. (668–75)[21]

[And because King Bathulf who founded it (i.e., Bath) was a great sorcerer and would come to regret that afterwards, I will tell that story. So that men might see his magical ability, he made wings so as to fly on high. And when he had flown and could not land, he fell to the ground and plummeted with such great speed that he was torn all to pieces. It would have been better for him to have believed down below (i.e., on earth) than to have learned to fly.]

Robert's verse, never particularly graceful, is especially dense here, and it is hard to tell just what *piȝte* is supposed to denote. Its meaning can only be inferred, and the *OED* glosses it as "to fall headlong, esp. landing heavily," to which Donaldson adds, "it is likely that the faller made something of a dent in the earth."[22] As such, *piȝte* seems simply to be a synonym for *vel* (= fell), employed, we may guess, primarily as a rhyme for *aliȝte* in the previous line.[23]

The next attested example comes nearly a century after the previous one and is found in a manuscript of the Middle English romance *Sir Ferumbras* (ca. 1380):

> Wanne þe kyng hym vnderstod,
> His herte wax angry and ful of mod,
>   And was ful heghe y-pyȝt.
> His armes he asked anon with cry,
> And hy were broȝt wel hastely,
>   And sone þan was he dyȝt.   (3636–38)[24]

[When the king (i.e., Claryoun) understood him (i.e., King Bruyllant), his heart grew angry and full of wrath and was set very high. He straightway called for his arms and they were quickly brought, and soon he was armed.]

As the *OED* entry notes, the figurative usage here means something like "uplifted." But although "uplifted" certainly makes sense in this context, it seems unnecessary to create a meaning for *y-pyȝt* when an established one would work just as well. Since one of the primary meanings of *picchen* is "to fix, or place," one could just as well apply this meaning in a figurative sense here, as in an earlier line in *Sir Ferumbras*:

> Þan hur spak þe damesel,
>   "Myn herte now waxeþ liȝt.
> Þat þyng now hope y gete wel
>   On wham myn herte ys piȝt."   (2068–69)

[Then said the maiden (i.e., Floripas), "Now my heart grows happy. Now I hope I get that thing on which my heart is set (i.e., Sir Guy of Burgundy)."]

Though the difference between "uplifting" one's heart and "setting it high" is one of degree rather than kind, it remains the case that this pre–*Knight's Tale* usage does not necessarily have anything to do with throwing as the dictionaries suggest.

Likewise, the example drawn from the Middle English translation of the Bible (attributed to John Wycliffe or his followers) does not support a reading of *pighte* as "thrown" and again employs the word in a highly figurative sense. Lamentations 2 contains a dramatic image of divine punishment of Jerusalem:

[8] *Heth*. Thoȝte the Lord to scateren the wal of the doȝter of Sion; he straȝte out his litil corde, and turnede not awei his hond fro perdicioun; and he weilede biforn the walling, and the wal togidere is scatered.
[9] *Teth*. Doun piȝt in the erthe ben hir ȝatus, he loste and to-broside hir barres; his kingis and hys princes in Jentiles; ther is not lawe, and his profetis founden not viseoun of the Lord.²⁵

[(8) The Lord decided to destroy the walls of Jerusalem. He stretched out his little cord and did not stay his hand from destruction. And he cried aloud before the ramparts, and the walls were destroyed. (9) Their gates are *piȝt* into the ground. He destroyed and broke their bars. His kings and his princes are among Gentiles. There is no law, and his prophets have discovered no vision of the Lord.]

Unusually, the very place we might expect to find clarification of the meaning of *piȝt*, namely the Latin Bible, provides almost no help here. The Vulgate reads: "defixae sunt in terra portae eius." The meaning revolves around the translation of *defigere*, and, as it turns out, the semantic field of *defigere* (and its close relatives *figere* and *infigere*) closely mirrors that described by *picchen*: to fasten down or in; to drive, thrust, fix, or fasten into. We are back where we started. Although *piȝt* is undeniably a legitimate Middle English rendering of *defixae sunt*, it remains unclear exactly what St. Jerome meant by this phrase. One of the few medieval commentators on this line, Paschasius Radbertus, notes (not entirely helpfully) "Quod enim infixum est, non facile movetur" ("that which has been made fast is not easily moved"). He backs this assertion up with an illustration from Psalm 69:15: "Eripe me de luto ut non infigar" ("Draw me out of the mire, that I may not stick fast").²⁶ So in the Vulgate, at least, the city's gates have been fastened to the ground as a result of the destruction of the walls. Much like King Bathulf (mentioned above), the gates have fallen, not to be raised.²⁷

About the only way we can get *defixae sunt* to mean "thrown down" is to take it in the colloquial way used by the Roman playwright Plautus, who has one character threaten another, "Te hodie, si prehendero, defigam in terram colaphis" ("Today, if I catch you, I will drive you to the ground with blows" [*Persa* 2.4.22]). Here, *defigere* collapses the related actions of throwing, falling, and lying on the ground.

Plautus's metonymic use of *defigere* here, substituting cause for effect, may hint at the way the semantic fields of *defigere* and *picchen* expanded over time to encompass not only the acts of fixing, piercing, and embedding but also attendant circumstances or the results of those actions. Thus in the C-text of *Piers Plowman*, Reason asks Will the Dreamer about his usefulness to society:

"Canstow seruen," he seide, "oþer syngen in a churche,
Oþer coke for my cokers, oþer to þe cart picche,
Mowe oþer mowen, oþer make bond to sheues?" (C.6.12–14)²⁸

> ["Can you serve," he said, "or sing in a church, or gather hay for my laborers, or pitch it into the cart, or mow or stack, or bind sheaves?"]

Although we now associate pitching hay with the act of throwing it, the use here also recalls the primary meaning of *picchen*, to pierce, which is just what the pitchfork does.[29]

If an examination of the semantic field of *picchen* in the years before *The Knight's Tale* serves mainly to highlight Chaucer's unusual use of the word, a look at *pomel* yields similar results. With the notable exception of Donaldson, editors have been univocal in glossing "pomel of his heed" (2689) as "top/crown of Arcite's head," but again, there is no unambiguous evidence to support this usage.

As the examples amassed by both the *MED* and the *OED* suggest, the use of *pomel* in any context is rare before 1400. The most common use before the fifteenth century was to signify the knob at the end of the hilt of a sword, as in the famous episode in the life of King Arthur as related in the Auchinleck Manuscript *Arthour and Merlin*: "Þai founde / A ston stonden on þe grounde . . . / Þerin a swerd . . . / On þe pomel was ywrite: 'Icham yhot Estalibore'" (2807–17). Somewhat confusingly, *pomel* could also signify the hilt of the sword itself, as in the Wycliffite Bible: "a swerd . . . hauynge in the mydil a pomel of lengthe of the palm of an hoond" (Judg. 3.16), where *pomel* is a clear translation of the Latin *capulus*,[30] a common term in classical Latin for "hilt."[31]

One also finds *pomel* used to denote the ornamental sphere or finial placed atop an object (such as a cup or other vessel)[32] or a structure (such as a tent). The early (ca. 1300) fragment of the romance *Floris and Blancheflour* preserved in British Library MS Cotton Vitellius D.iii (fols. 6r–8v) records a description of the top of a fantastic tower: "Hondred teyse þe tour is heie . . . And þe pomel aboue the lede . . . shineþ aniht" (232) ("The tower is 700 feet high . . . and the pomel above the lead roof . . . shines at night").[33]

These few examples reflect the more common and much earlier use of the word in medieval French, which dates to the mid-twelfth century.[34] We also find in French the word used to signify the ornament on top of a helmet, as the earliest recorded example, from the *Roman d'Eneas* (ca. 1160), shows:

> Sus el pomel ot quatre esmals
> Et quatre pierres naturals,
> Et li cercles ki fu desoz
> Ert molt bien faiz a or trestoz,
> A riches pierres, a esmals.   (4437–41)[35]
>
> [On the top were four enamels
> And four gemstones,

> And the circlet that was underneath
> Was very well made of engraved gold,
> With rich gemstones and enamels.]

Interestingly, with the possible exception of line 2689 of *The Knight's Tale*, this usage does not appear in English.

Since all the medieval uses of *pomel* have something to do with "topness," one can see why editors (beginning with Manly) have glossed Chaucer's *pomel* as they have.[36] But the Italian original complicates things in that, although it says nothing about Arcite's head, it does mention what could be construed as another type of pommel:

> Sotto il qual cadde il già contento Arcita,
> e 'l forte arcione li premette'l petto
> e sí il ruppe   (9.8.1–3)[37]
>
> [Happy Arcita fell under it (i.e., the horse),
> and the hard saddlebow crushed his chest
> and pierced it.]

In the *Teseida*, Arcite's mortal wound is effected by his chest's being struck and pierced by his *arcione*, the front arch of his saddle. Although Middle English used a cognate of *arcione* to describe the saddlebow, namely *arsoun*,[38] it would by the mid-fifteeth century also use *pomel* to denote this part of the saddle. Thus in the romance *Merlin* (? ca. 1450), we read: "Theire swerdes hangynge at the pomell of theire sadeles before" (191).

And indeed, the *arsoun* or *pomel* of a medieval saddle was constructed in a way that makes Arcite's injury plausible. A common feature of the medieval saddles "was the markedly high front saddle bow, which forced the rider to hold the reins fairly high." In battle or jousting saddles (the type we can imagine Arcite would have employed), "it ran out into pommels of various shapes, often broadening into a shield, to protect the uncovered parts of the rider against thrusts directed at him straight from the front."[39] This protective feature could, however, prove deadly in the event of accident—and not just in the realm of fiction. In 1388, Sir Thomas Trivet died as the result of an incident that strikingly recalls Arcite's demise: "when riding proudly on his horse to the king's residence at Barnwell with the king [Richard II], [Trivet] spurred on his horse too harshly, causing the horse to fall and seriously injure its rider in the abdomen; in fact Sir Thomas died the following day."[40] It should be noted that Trivet did not die of a head injury nor, in fact, was his head even injured. Rather, the fallen horse "omnia pene interiora sessoris dirumpit" (literally, "ruptured nearly all the rider's bowels").

Parsing Line 2689

This mass of lexicographical and semantic data highlights the unusual and idiosyncratic diction of line 2689: "He pighte hym on the pomel of his heed." In light of currently available data, the popular readings of *pighte* as "threw" and *pomel* as "top" are necessarily based more on editorial conjecture than on linguistic evidence. The line leaves us, as readers, with some less-than-palatable options, for each of them requires assigning some degree of blame.

The first option, which has been generally exercised but not generally acknowledged, is to assign new meanings to *pighte* and *pomel* based on context and to write these off as nonce usages. In spite of Boccaccio's clear description in the *Teseida*, Chaucer is just playing free and loose with the language, making up definitions as he goes along, like Humpty Dumpty in *Alice in Wonderland*, and leaving it to his readers to intuit their meanings. Thus John Dryden, writing without the benefit of the *MED*, comes up with roughly the same interpretation that modern editors have:

> The startling steed was seized with sudden fright,
> And, bounding, o'er the pummel cast the knight;
> Forward he flew, and pitching on his head,
> He quiver'd with his feet, and lay for dead.   (701–4)

It is interesting to note that although Dryden translates *pighte* as "cast" and *pomel of his heed* as "on his head," he also includes cognates of the Middle English words in his passage ("pitching," "pummel") in their medieval senses (falling, saddlebow).

The second option is to allow the instances in line 2689 as nonce uses but also to assert that in doing so Chaucer was in complete control of his language and simply being either prescient or "too clever by half" or both. It is fascinating that although they are used in alternate senses, both *pighte* and *pomel* are standard Middle English translations of two key words in the Italian original. As we have seen, *pighte* is a legitimate rendering of *cadde* (fell) (9.8.1) and of *premette* and *ruppe* (shattered, pierced) (9.8.2, 3). Likewise, *pomel* may also have been a synonym for *arcione* (saddlebow) (9.8.2); certainly medieval Italian used *pomo* for "saddle" as early as ca. 1320.[41] The nonce usages of the words are just close enough to their established semantic fields to make them plausible. There is no great leap from the thrusting, piercing, fixing, and falling of *picchen* to the related actions of casting, crashing, and throwing. And, in fact, these are the very meanings that would eventually attach themselves to the term, superseding the medieval uses. As for *pomel*, whose meaning vexed Donaldson, the figurative analogy between the top of a tent or helmet to the top of the head (which also recalls the roundness that many decorative pommels were said to have) is not hard to see.[42] Chaucer dabbles

Lectio difficilior and All That   55

in alliteration several times in *The Knight's Tale* (and at least twice in this passage), and, if nothing else, he may have stretched the meanings of the words to serve an essentially aural purpose.

If these first two options require that we make the meaning conform to the text, the final option is much more radical and insists that we make the text conform to the established meaning in the source. If, like Donaldson, we insist that *pighte* cannot mean "thrown" and must instead mean "pierced" (as the Italian *ruppe* also suggests), then we must read the pronouns in the line as a reflexive construction: he pighte hym = he (Arcite) pierced himself. Making Arcite the antecedent of "he" in 2689 also makes sense grammatically, since Arcite is the noun nearest to "he" (having appeared on the previous line) in contrast to the horse, which last appears on line 2687.

If we insist on reading *pomel* for *arcione* (for which there is currently more evidence in medieval French and Italian than Middle English), we are forced to do something that makes many medievalists quake: emend the text. Donaldson does not even suggest doing this; he leaves the interpretation of "of his heed" to a horseman or a philologist or both. Certainly, in the face of a manuscript tradition that univocally reads "of his heed," one would hesitate to question so much scribal authority.[43] But as we have seen with the alternate readings for "furye" in line 2684, scribes are not perfect, especially if they don't understand what is going on and do not have the benefit of a copy of the *Teseida* in front of them. If we are so bold as to propose a conjectural reading for this line, we should do so with the following criteria in mind: the new reading should be orthographically possible, linguistically plausible, and easy to understand (no figurative or strained meanings).

Let me suggest, then, a word with an Anglo-Saxon pedigree and a long history in Middle English (dating back at least to 1225) and one which, I think, may meet the above-listed criteria: *stede*. Although misreading *h* for *st* is unusual, stranger orthographies have occurred in Middle English manuscripts. Likewise, the vowel in *stede* is long, just as it is in *heed* and its rhyme word *deed*. Most persuasively, however, the reading makes sense in the most literal rendering of the line and within the story's context. As such, we may emend and translate the passage thus:

> And er that Arcite may taken keep,
> He pighte hym on the pomel of his [steed],
> That in the place he lay as he were deed,
> His brest tobrosten with his sadel-bowe.
>
> [And before Arcite could take care,
> He impaled himself on the pommel of his horse,
> So that he lay in the place as if he were dead,
> His chest shattered by the saddlebow.]

Now, strictly speaking, the pommel belongs to the saddle and not to the horse, but the two entities are so closely (even metonymically) related as to render this objection nugatory. There will be, no doubt, other, sounder, objections that less foolhardy readers may propose.[44]

The principle of *lectio difficilior*, the preference for the more difficult, more obscure reading, has been dearly held by editors (and some readers) for a long time. Certainly, the scene of Arcite's mortal injury provides more than its share of *lectiones difficiliores*. Whatever option one chooses in interpreting the passage, one must ultimately acknowledge that the defining moment in Arcite's life is, paradoxically, rife with narrative and lexical ambiguities.

NOTES

Editors' note: We are grateful to be able to publish this essay, which Professor Stallcup (1970–2009) submitted to us for this volume not long before his untimely death.

1. E. Talbot Donaldson, "Arcite's Injury," in *Middle English Studies Presented to Norman Davis in Honour of His Seventieth Birthday*, ed. Douglas Gray and E. G. Stanley (Oxford: Clarendon Press, 1983), pp. 65–67.

2. Chaucer's text is cited from *The Riverside Chaucer*, ed. Larry D. Benson, 3rd ed. (Boston: Houghton Mifflin, 1987).

3. Giovanni Boccaccio, *Opere*, vol. 3, *Teseida delle nozze d'Emilia*, ed. Aurelio Roncaglia, Scrittori d'Italia 185 (Bari: Gius. Laterza & Figli, 1941), p. 259. The translation is from Giovanni Boccaccio, *The Book of Theseus: Teseida delle Nozze d'Emilia*, trans. Bernadette Marie McCoy (New York: Medieval Text Association, 1974), p. 242.

4. Dante, *Inferno* 9.43. In the *Aeneid*, Virgil describes two of the three Furies in some detail: Tisiphone (6.554–75) and Allecto (7.445–55).

5. William Coleman, "The Knight's Tale," in *Sources and Analogues of the Canterbury Tales*, vol. 2, ed. Robert M. Correale and Mary Hamel (Cambridge: D. S. Brewer, 2005), p. 191, note to the rubric of book 9 of the *Teseida*, suggests that Chaucer might have gotten the phrase "furie infernal" from this rubric, which includes the phrase "infernale furia." Dante uses the phrase "tre furïe infernal" in *Inferno* 9.38.

6. Other references to the Furies include: *LGW* 2252, *Pity* 92, *SqT* 448, *FkT* 950, 1101, *Tr* 2.436, 4.22–24.

7. John Dryden, "Palamon and Arcite," book 3, lines 699–700, in *Fables Ancient and Modern*, in *The Poetical Works of John Dryden*, ed. George R. Noyes (Boston: Houghton Mifflin, 1950), p. 778.

8. Otto Pächt and Dagmar Thoss, *Französische Schule I*, 2 vols., *Die Illuminierten Handschriften und Inkunabeln der Österreichischen Nationalbibliothek*, gen. ed. Otto Pächt (Vienna: Österreichische Akademie der Wissenschaften, 1974), 1:32–37 (description); 2:pl. 53 (image).

9. V. A. Kolve, *Chaucer and the Imagery of Narrative: The First Five Canterbury Tales* (Stanford: Stanford University Press, 1984), p. 126.

10. Roncaglia, *Teseida*, p. 259; translation from McCoy, *Book of Theseus*, p. 242.

11. Roncaglia, *Teseida*, p. 440; my translation.

12. Although Boccaccio's assigning the name "Erinis" to the Fury chosen by Venus breaks with the tradition of there being only three Furies (as popularized by Virgil and Dante), a

number of classical sources cite the name: e.g., Ovid, *Metamorphoses* 1.241, 4.490, 11.14; Virgil, *Aeneid* 7.447, 570. (It is unclear, at least in Virgil, however, whether "Erinis" is different from or simply a synecdoche for "Allecto.") Some confusion arises, however, because the plural form of the word (*Erinyes*) is frequently used to refer to the Furies as a group: e.g., Propertius (2.20.29); Ovid, *Heroides* 11.103; Statius, *Thebaid* 11.345.

13. Statius, *Thebaid* 6.495. The creature is so horrible that not even the Furies could have looked upon it without fear ("non ipsae horrore sine alto / Eumenides visisse queant" [6.499–500]).

14. Kolve, *Chaucer and the Imagery of Narrative*, p. 59.

15. Roncaglia, *Teseida*, pp. 259–60. I have preferred Coleman's translation here ("Knight's Tale," p. 192) to McCoy's (*Book of Theseus*, p. 242). His rendering of *indietro cader* as "fell over backwards" rather than McCoy's "let itself fall over backwards" seems more strictly correct. Likewise, as will become apparent in my argument, his translation of *ruppe* as "pierced," instead of "crushed," may shed some light on line 2689.

16. Donaldson, "Arcite's Injury," p. 66.

17. "Childing-pine haues te nou picht" ("Birthing-pain has now stabbed you"), in Oxford, Bodleian Tanner 169*, printed in Carlton Brown, *English Lyrics of the Thirteenth Century* (Oxford: Clarendon, 1932), Lyric 4 "Stabat iuxta Christi Crucem," p. 9, line 12. See also Laȝamon, *Brut* 6489–90: "He igrap his spere stronge, / þer he pihte hit o þon londe" ("He grasped his stout spear where he stuck it in the ground") in *Layamons Brut, or Chronicle of Britain* . . . , ed. Sir Frederic Madden, vol. 1 (London: Society of Antiquaries of London, 1847), pp. 276–77. Illustrative Middle English citations not otherwise referenced are from *MED* entries.

18. See *OED* s.v. *pitch* v² 6a.

19. *MED* s.v. *picchen* 3a; *OED* s.v. *pitch* v² 3b.

20. Donaldson, "Arcite's Injury," p. 67.

21. *The Metrical Chronicle of Robert of Gloucester*, ed. William Aldis Wright, 2 vols., Rolls Series, no. 86 (London, 1887), 1:49. Wright prints the text found in London, British Library MS Cotton Caligula A. xi.

22. *OED* s.v. *pitch* v² 12a; Donaldson, "Arcite's Injury," p. 67 n. 8. Note that the numbering system in the first edition of the *OED* (used by Donaldson) differs from that in subsequent editions.

23. All Robert's other uses of *picchen* are consistent with the standard definitions: to pierce (1174); to set up a pavilion (1116, 4155, 5526, 12005); to drive a stake (1171).

24. *Sir Ferumbras*, ed. Sidney J. Herrtage, EETS, e.s. 34 (London, 1879), p. 114. The text is edited from the unique manuscript, Oxford, Bodleian Library, MS Ashmole 33. I have reformatted the lines to conform with modern editorial practice.

25. *The Holy Bible, containing the Old and New Testaments, with the Apocryphal books*, ed. Josiah Forshall and Frederic Madden (Oxford: Oxford University Press, 1850), 3:475, col. A.

26. Paschasius Radbertus, *Threnos sive Lamentationes*, Lib. 2, *Teth* (PL 120:1122D).

27. As a nineteenth-century commentator notes, "Her gates cannot oppose the entrance of the foe into the city, for they are sunk under a mass of rubbish and earth." Robert Jamieson, Andrew Robert Fausset, and David Brown, *A Commentary, Critical and Explanatory, on the Old and New Testaments*, vol. 1 (Glasgow: William Collins, 1875), p. 562.

28. The *MED* does not give this sense for the verb *coken* (i.e., to gather hay into *cocks*) but it seems warranted here. For *coker* as laborer (also not in *MED* in this sense), see *Catholicon*

anglicanum: An English-Latin Word Book, dated 1483, ed. Sidney J. Herrtage, Camden Society, n.s. 30 (London: Trübner, 1883), p. 70 n. 6.

29. *Pitchfork* in fact, seems to antedate *picchen* by nearly seventy years. Cf. Laȝamon, *Brut* 10777: Þæ cheorles … adunriht sloȝen; Þer wes sone i-slaȝen moni cniht … wið heore pic-forcken heo ualden heom to grunden" (*MED* s.v. *picche-fork(e)*).

30. "gladium … habentem in medio capulum longitudinis palmae manus"

31. E.g., Cicero, *De fato* 3.5; Virgil, *Aeneid* 2.553, 10.536; Ovid, *Metamorphoses* 7.422, 12.133, 12.491.

32. The earliest example of this usage cited by *MED* sv. *pomel* dates from 1345–49: "j aliam platam cum j pomell," *Wardrobe Accounts of Edward III.*

33. A *teis* is a measure of length between 6 and 7.5 feet. *MED* s.v. *teis* (a).

34. I.e., referring to a candlestick at the end of the eleventh century, in A. Darmesteter and D. S. Blondheim, *Les gloses françaises dans le commentaire talmudique de Raschi* (Paris: Champion, 1929), p. 840b; referring to the hilt of a sword, before 1188: "L'espee drece, se li tent. / Li roi[s] par le pumel le prent," in *Partonopeu de Blois: A French Romance of the Twelfth Century*, ed. Joseph Gildea (Villanova, PA: Villanova University Press, 1967), line 3570; referring to a tent, ca. 1165: "Devant la tente est descenduz, / Puis est entrez el pavellion, / Dont de fin or sont li paisson, / L'estache tote e li pomeaus / E li aigles, qui trop est beaus," in Benoit de St. Maure, *Roman de Troie*, ed. Léopold Constans, Société des anciens textes français, 6 vols. (Paris: Firmin-Didot, 1904–12), vol. 2 (1906), p. 353, lines 14302–6.

35. *Eneas: Roman du XIIe siècle*, ed. J.-J. Salverda de Grave (Paris: Librairie Ancienne Édouard Champion, 1925), 1:135–36.

36. In the glossary to his edition of the *Canterbury Tales*, John M. Manly glosses *pomel* thus: "(OF *pomel*), top": *The Canterbury Tales by Geoffrey Chaucer* (New York: Henry Holt & Co., 1928), p. 690.

37. Coleman, "Knight's Tale," p. 192

38. The earliest recorded use is Laȝamon, *Brut*, ca. 1300: "He ladde bi his harsun one gisarme stronge" (2263): ed. Madden (n. 17 above), 1:96.

39. Professor Stallcup passed away before he could see the copy-edited version of his article and respond to queries with his final revisions. The editors have not been able to identify this quotation.

40. "[D]ominus Thomas Tryuet cum rege sublimis equitaret ad regis hospicium, quod fuit apud Bernewelle, dum nimis urget equum calcaribus, equus cadit, et omnia pene interiora sessoris dirumpit; protelauit tamen uitam in crastinum," *The St Albans Chronicle: The Chronica Maiora of Thomas Walsingham*, ed. and trans. John Taylor, Wendy R. Childs, and Leslie Watkiss, vol. 1, *A.D. 1376–1394*, Oxford Medieval Texts (Oxford: Clarendon Press, 2003), pp. 858–59.

41. *OED* s.v. *pommel* n[1] (no source is given for this claim).

42. Cf. a similar metaphoric usage in *Bankis of Helicon* (before 1586): "With yvoire nek, and pomellis round, / And comlie intervall" (63). Cited in *OED* s.v. *pommel*, n.[1] (3b).

43. See John M. Manly and Edith Rickert, *The Text of the Canterbury Tales*, vol. 3 (Chicago: University of Chicago Press, 1940), p. 110.

44. One phonological objection might be that ordinarily Chaucer does not rhyme close and open long *e*. See *Troilus* 5.15–19 and the note to 5.22–26 in *Riverside Chaucer*, p. 1050, and W. W. Skeat, *The Collected Works of Geoffrey Chaucer*, vol. 6 (Oxford: Clarendon Press, 1894), pp. xxxi–xxxiv. However, the purpose of suggesting this emendation is less to solve a crux and more to renew interest in this overlooked and knotty passage.

Part 2
Arthuriana Then and Now

Arthurian Bones and English Kings, ca. 1180–ca. 1550

†*Maurice Keen*

Gerald of Wales, in his *De instructione principum*, gives a vivid, probably eyewitness account of the "discovery" at Glastonbury in 1191 of what the abbot and monks (who staged the event) declared to be the bones of King Arthur and his queen, Guenevere. It was the advice of King Henry II, he says, that guided the monks as to where to dig: "Though there were certain indications in writings that they possessed . . . and others given in visions and relations to good and religious men, yet it was above all King Henry II who most clearly informed the monks, as he himself had heard from an ancient Welsh bard . . . that they would find the body at least sixteen feet beneath the earth, not in a tomb of stone but in a hollow oak."[1] Just so the body was found, "deep down in the earth and encoffined in a hollow oak," with, very conveniently by it, under a stone, a leaden cross with an inscription reading: "here lies buried the renowned King Arthur, with Guenevere his second wife, in the isle of Avalon."[2] Avalon was whither the mortally wounded Arthur was carried after his last battle against the traitor Mordred, according to Geoffrey of Monmouth, whose story of Arthur in his *History of the Kings of Britain* (completed ca. 1140) was the inspiration behind the monks' staged discovery.

Henry II died in 1189, so the discovery cannot have actually taken place in his reign, as Gerald suggests in another later work,[3] but Gerald's story that Henry had a hand in encouraging the search for the grave looks plausible. Henry was undoubtedly well acquainted with the Arthurian story. His uncle Robert of Gloucester was one of Geoffrey of Monmouth's principal patrons; Wace's Anglo-Norman poetic version of Geoffrey's *History*, the *Roman de Brut*, was presented to Henry's queen, Eleanor of Aquitaine.[4] Henry was also a munificent patron of Glastonbury, the most important of the benefactors whose generosity made possible the ambitious rebuilding of the abbey church after the disastrous fire of 1184. Though neither Geoffrey nor Wace identify Glastonbury with Avalon (Gerald is our first notice of that identification), Henry may well have known the story (which may have been the seed of the identification) told by Caradoc (d. 1156) in his *Life of St Gildas* (whom he believed to be buried at Glastonbury), of how Arthur, under the saint's influence, had come to be a major benefactor of the abbey.[5] If Henry did know of this, he would not have been displeased to be following as a benefactor in the footsteps of such an illustrious predecessor.

Arthur, in Henry II's time, had become a name to conjure with. Geoffrey's text had succeeded dramatically in bringing Arthur out of the shadows of Celtic legend, giving him a dateable place and part in soi-disant factual history as a great warrior king of the sixth century who had led the Britons in their struggles with the invading heathen Saxons. This was a career in a mold that the twelfth-century knightly world well understood and appreciated, and the story that Geoffrey told was rapidly and very widely disseminated. Within a decade of his writing, Alfred of Beverley could declare that British history was so much on everyone's lips that anyone unacquainted with it would be looked on as uncouth and uneducated.[6] In these circumstances, the potential political advantage for Henry and his dynasty of associating the authority of their kingship with that of so illustrious a forerunner as Arthur was apparent. The Arthur of the newfound history had been, like Henry, a king in England, and not of England only, but the universal over-king of the British Isles, recognized as such in Wales, Scotland, Ireland, and the Isles. Henry aspired to a comparable authority: in Wales he was acknowledged as overlord by the great Lord Rhys; in 1171 he crossed to Ireland and made himself supreme lord there; and he compelled King William the Lion of Scotland, after William's defeat and capture in 1174, to do him homage for the kingdom of Scotland.[7] Henry's royal successors in England consistently continued to aspire as he had done to an imperium over all the British Isles.

For the ambitions of Henry and of the princes of his dynasty, the victorious campaigns of Arthur outside the British Isles, as retailed by Geoffrey, and the authority they had established for him beyond the seas were of at least equal relevance. The wide extent of Henry's Angevin "empire" in France made it inevitable that the French kings should regard him and his successors as dangerous rivals for power in their kingdom, and in consequence the rulers of France and England found themselves constantly at odds. In their rivalry, Arthurian history provided for the Angevins of England the ideal foil to the history of Charlemagne, which in contemporary France was a vital element in an increasingly articulate cult of Capetian royalty and its authority throughout the French kingdom. Geoffrey's Arthur had been a ruler of comparable status to Charlemagne, operating in an earlier age on the same European-wide stage.

The territorial twist that the encomiasts of the Capetians gave to their association of contemporary French monarchy with that of the Carolingians was quite explicit. It was Philip Augustus's dream, we are told, to restore the realm of France to the ancient breadth and greatness which it enjoyed in the time of Charlemagne, and William the Breton urged Philip's son Louis to "extend the realm to the Pyrenees, where Charles had set up his tent";[8] to a breadth and greatness, that is to say, that emphatically embraced full overlordship of the continental lands of the English kings. Here once again Arthur's story, as told by Geoffrey, offered the English a nice response to aggressive French claims: from Britain, Arthur had established his authority over France; he had granted Normandy (Henry's maternal inheritance) to his cupbearer Bedevere and Anjou (his paternal inheritance) to his seneschal Kay; and his kinsman and lieutenant Hoel of Brittany had subdued for him Gascony and Poitou (the inheritance of Henry's queen, Eleanor of Aquitaine).[9] Johanek's comment that Geoffrey had recounted a history of Arthur "peculiarly well designed to be put into the service of the conception of an Angevin empire" seems amply justified, even though that was not any part of Geoffrey's intention.[10]

What Gerald of Wales tells us in the context of the 1191 exhumation is all we know for sure about Henry's personal interest in Arthur. We do, however, know a little more about some of the interpretive glosses that popular reception in England was putting on Arthur's story in the decades either side of the year 1200. Layamon, we learn, was inspired to turn the story told in Wace's *Brut* into the native vernacular by his desire "to relate the noble deeds of the English" (the English, not the British), and had thought of drawing on Bede's account of the early Anglo-Saxon kings to carry the story further.[11] In comparable spirit, the early thirteenth-century interpolations in a London text of the *Leges Eadwardi Confessoris* explained that Arthur had been ruler of the whole realm of Britain and explicitly associated the rights of the English crown with the imperium that he had exercised through all Britain. The same text also recorded that Ine, the eighth-century Anglo-Saxon king, had, by his marriage to Wala (descendent of the last British king, Cadwallader), become rightful king of Britain, and that from his time on everyone had come to refer to what had once been known as the Kingdom of Britain as the Kingdom of the English.[12] This fresh snippet of pseudohistory is of interest from an Arthurian point of view. There was a difficulty for Englishmen and their kings about appropriating to the English monarchy the glorious aura of succession to Arthur's kingship; the Arthur of Geoffrey's *History* was very explicitly a champion of the Britons in their struggle with the invading Anglo-Saxon ancestors of the English. The story of Ine's marriage to a princess of the house of Cadwallader and the consequent identification of British with English royal traditions illustrates neatly the sort of way early thirteenth-century Englishmen sought and found a means around this difficulty. The way that they found made it possible for them to use Arthurian history to buttress the dynamic coalescence of royal dynastic ambition with popular national aspiration that was the foundation of early English patriotism.

Those signs are a good deal clearer when, a hundred years on from Henry II's day, we come to the reign of Edward I. The English chroniclers of his age—Peter Langtoft, Robert of Gloucester, and Robert Mannyng—repeatedly hail him as a noble warrior-king in the image of King Arthur, whose glorious history, as told by Geoffrey and Wace, they were careful to record in detail in their opening sections on early English history. In the letter that Edward sent to Pope Boniface VIII in 1301 explaining the origin of his rights over Scotland, he himself looked back directly to that history "when King Arthur held a most famous feast at Caerleon, there were present all the kings subject to him, among them Angusel King of Scotland, who manifested his service due for the kingdom of Scotland by bearing the sword of King Arthur before him."[13] In a similar spirit Langtoft, drawing likewise on Geoffrey, explained as the basis of Edward's 1294–97 war with France the attempt of Philip IV to "withhold from him wrongfully the land which King Arthur gave to the Duke Sir Bedevere in Aquitaine."[14]

Edward clearly understood well the popular pride in Arthurian history that the chroniclers reflect and was determined to make the most of it. In 1278 (just after the end of his first Welsh war) he and his queen Eleanor journeyed to Glastonbury and there superintended the translation of the remains of Arthur and Guenevere from the tomb in the lady chapel, where they had been laid in 1191, to a new burial place before the abbey's high altar.[15] The king was plainly aware of the importance for his purposes of these bones. They were solid evidence that Arthur was dead, giving the lie to the myth that circulated in Wales (and Brittany) that Arthur had not died of his wounds and would one day return to lead the British (or Welsh) to victory over the descendants of the Saxons whom he had fought in the old days. Still more important, with their lead epitaph label, the remains were solid evidence that the king whose story Geoffrey of Monmouth recorded had been a real British king, who had lived and died and belonged to real history, and whose assertion of his rights in Britain and beyond offered an example for subsequent English kings to follow.

Edward also showed a vivid interest in other physical remains that, like the bones, helped to validate the truth and continuing relevance of the Arthur of Geoffrey's *History*. He was much excited, Rishanger records, by the discovery near Carnarvon in 1283 of the remains of the British father of the emperor Constantine, whom Arthur in Geoffrey claimed as the kinsman of his ancestors. In the same year, following the conquest of Wales, he deposited the supposed crown of Arthur, which the Welsh had surrendered to him, in Westminster Abbey "so the glory of the Welsh, by God's providence, passed to the English," the chronicler commented.[16] Edward did the same thirteen years later with the Stone of Scone, and in 1324 his son Edward II refused to consider restoring it to the Scots, since to do so "would seem basely to repudiate" the right of the English crown over Scotland, dating from the time of the earliest British kings, which "his father had lately victoriously asserted."[17]

Edward III, once he was securely in power, followed his grandfather in his enthusiasm for the cult of Arthur. In December 1331, just before Christmas, he came to Glastonbury to pay his respects in person at his great predecessor's tomb.[18] He visited Glastonbury again in May 1344, just four months after the famous January festivities at Windsor where he had announced his intention "to found a Round Table [order] of the same manner and standing as that of the lord Arthur, formerly King of England, to the number of three hundred knights."[19] This was, as it proved, the last time an English king visited the abbey, and when Edward, five years after 1344, did found an order of chivalry, the exclusive Garter companionship of twenty-six knights, it was under Saint George's patronage, not Arthur's. Edward's appropriation to England of the cult of Saint George, "whose name and protection the English people invoke as its special patron, especially in military endeavour,"[20] lent an explicit religious sanction to the English patriotism which Edward, like his grandfather before him, was seeking to harness in committed support of his warring with the French and Scots. This was a kind of sanction for national martial endeavor in the service of royal ambition that the cult of King Arthur could not offer. It could, however, give significance to another alleged Glastonbury burial that had Arthurian connections and in which Edward III was the first English king to take an interest, that of Joseph of Arimathea.

The connection of Avalon/Glastonbury with the stories both of Joseph and of Arthur's knights appears first in the Grail romances of the early thirteenth century. The earliest detailed account of Joseph's coming to Glastonbury and with his disciples building there Britain's first Christian church is given in the interpolations made at Glastonbury (pre-1250) into William of Malmesbury's *De antiquitate Glastoniensis ecclesie* (ca. 1130).[21] These stories and accounts formed the basis of the story as told by John of Glastonbury (ca. 1400?) in his similarly entitled *Cronica de rebus Glastoniensibus*, which embellished it with further details. John for instance described the two silver cruets that Joseph brought with him and that were buried with him, one containing the blood, the other the sweat, of Christ at His Passion, which is the nearest that pseudohistory gets to the Holy Grail of romance. He also recorded the prophecy of Melkin (a supposed British sixth-century soothsayer, whom John is the first to mention)[22] as to where the saint's burial place should be sought. This quest Edward III in 1345 licensed John Blome to pursue "to dig within the precincts of the said monastery for . . . those precious relics . . . the venerable body of the noble decurion Joseph of Arimathea."[23] It looks, though, as if John Blome apparently did not find what he was looking for: Joseph's remains were never found.

Yet it seems as if they very nearly were. Sometime in 1421 Henry V wrote to Abbot Nicholas Frome, asking for further information about recent excavations at Glastonbury. Abbot Nicholas's reply survives, stating that they had dug fourteen feet down in the cemetery, and had found three coffins close together, and another, a finer one, lined with linen cloth, a little way off.[24] Two of the three coffins were individual, the third housed twelve sets of bones. The abbot did not identify whose remains he thought these were, but it is clear from John of Glastonbury's *Cronica* what should be expected. His story is that Joseph (the fine coffin would presumably be his) had come with eleven companions and that a century after his coming (i.e., 166 C.E.) the missionaries Phagan and Deruvian (the two individual coffins to be claimed as theirs) restored the church that he had built and after his example ordained twelve disciples to serve it (the twelve bodies found together?).[25] Taking these details and the abbot's letter together, James Carley argues plausibly that there was a plan afoot to stage another exhumation and discovery on the same lines as that of 1191.[26] His suggestion gains added credibility from Bishop Fleming's statement of February 1424, at the Council of Siena, that he had heard that Joseph's coffin had just been found, identified by a lead label (like the one on Arthur's oak coffin) with an epitaph running: "Here lies the decurion Joseph of Arimathea, he who took Christ's body down from the Cross and who brought His faith and baptism to England."[27] Fleming's hearsay report proved in the event to be without foundation, but it sounds very like a leak of what had been part of a plan for a "discovery" that was never activated.

It is not surprising that Henry V should have been interested in the Glastonbury excavations and should have hoped to have news of a find. The general church councils of Pisa (1409), Constance (1414–18), and Siena (1424–25) actively concerned themselves with European diplomacy, vital to Henry in the war with France, as well as with church reform. The system adopted at these councils of voting by nations had moreover made the place of dignity of England among the nations of Christendom a very live issue. At Pisa Bishop Hallum claimed precedence for England over France on the ground of the seniority that Joseph's mission gave her, predating the decisive conversion of Gaul.[28] At Constance this claim became the vital strand in Thomas Polton's 1417 response for the English to the French delegation's disparagement of England as not being, as a nation, on a par with France in terms of geographical extent, the number of her churches, the saints she had nourished, or the antiquity of her Christian tradition. All these suggestions were false, Polton responded, and the last most emphatically so: "if they [the French] had noted the time when England first received the faith of Christ . . .

they would never have used that argument.... For immediately after the Passion of Christ, Joseph of Arimathea, the noble decurion who took Him down from the Cross, came with twelve disciples to labour in the Lord's vineyard, that is England, and converted the people to the faith.... they are now buried in the monastery of Glastonbury, in the diocese of Bath ... but the kingdom of France only received the faith of Christ in the time of St Denis."[29]

Polton's underlining here of England's direct connection with the very earliest apostolic age of Christianity fitted nicely into the contemporary religious tone of the propaganda of English patriotism, with the claim for England to be the "special dower" of the Virgin, and with the appeal to Saint George as the special protector of England in war. These were very live cult themes for the encomiasts of Henry V and his cause in the war with France.[30] Other points in Polton's presentation make it clear that he knew his British history per Geoffrey of Monmouth as well as Joseph's story per John of Glastonbury. In referring to the English nation, he made a point of calling it the "natio Anglicana sive Brittanica" ("the English or British nation"). He drew on Geoffrey to remind the French that Constantine the Great, emperor of Rome, was born at York, and that his mother, Saint Helena, was a British royal princess. When it came to the argument over the geographical extent of England compared with France, he enthusiastically claimed for England's crown universal lordship throughout the British Isles: that is, over "England, Scotland and Wales ... the kingdom of the Sea and four great and notable kingdoms in Ireland ... the Orkneys and other islands, about sixty in number."[31] He nowhere mentioned Arthur, but the genealogy given by John of Glastonbury showed that Arthur's father Uther was of the blood of Joseph's house.[32] The resonances of the national religious history that Polton recounted and of chivalrous Arthurian history were thus closely coupled in the mythology of late medieval English patriotism. Hardyng, writing a generation after Polton, brought Saint George too into the same framework, retailing in his chronicle Joseph of Arimathea's grant to the British king Arviragus, whom he had converted, of the same red cross arms that were later Saint George's and so England's emblem, and which Constantine and Arthur also in their day bore for Christ.[33]

Visiting Glastonbury in 1480, the antiquary William Worcester noted that "in the south side of the church are two stone crosses hollowed out where they laid King Arthur, and where in another direction lies Joseph of Arimathea."[34] Joseph's cult continued to draw pilgrims there up to the very eve of the Dissolution. The power of the name and example of the historical Arthur likewise continued to carry impact through the fifteenth century and well into the sixteenth. The Yorkist kings and Henry VII all claimed descent in blood from Cadwallader, the alleged last British king of the line of Uther and Arthur.[35]

Whether Henry VIII gave any real credence to Arthurian history has been questioned. But he was unquestionably happy to play for political purposes on continuing belief in Geoffrey of Monmouth's story and on the physical evidences for its genuine historical foundation.[36] When in 1522 the emperor Charles V visited England, care was taken to show him the Round Table hanging on the wall of the royal hall in Winchester, recently gloriously painted at Henry's order (it was probably originally constructed for Edward I, but that was now long forgotten).[37] On Henry's behalf, the Duke of Norfolk in 1531 reminded the imperial ambassador Chapuys that British Brennius had once conquered Rome and that Constantine was of British birth; and he told him also about the legend of the seal of King Arthur, preserved in Westminster Abbey, "Arthur, Emperor of Britain, Gaul, Germany and Denmark"[38] (when this seal was fabricated and by whom remains unknown). The object here was to buttress Henry's claim to be emperor in his own kingdom, and his rejection for England of the jurisdiction of Rome and of the pope. History derived ultimately from Geoffrey of Monmouth was still proving useful for royal propaganda purposes in the 1530s.

As long as that remained true, the physical evidences for Arthur's historicity retained importance for an English monarch and his servants. Caxton had conveniently listed them in his preface to Malory's *Morte Darthur*: the tomb at Glastonbury, the leaden cross with its epitaph, the Round Table at Winchester, and the imprint of Arthur's seal preserved in Westminster Abbey. Drawing on the list, John Leland, Henry VIII's loyal and learned librarian, waxed eloquent on the historical proofs that they gave in his *Assertion* of the "true life and acts" of King Arthur.[39] But skepticism was growing in the sixteenth century. Chapuys made ironically clear what he thought of the inscription on Arthur's seal that Norfolk quoted to him: "I'm surprised it doesn't call him Emperor of Asia as well."[40] Patriots, including learned patriots like Leland, clung to their belief in Arthur a little while yet, but the story of royal interest in a real historical Arthur, which started with Henry II, ends with Henry VIII.

NOTES

1. E. K. Chambers, *Arthur of Britain* (London: Sidgwick and Jackson, 1927), Record xxvi (b), p. 269; henceforward Chambers.

2. Illustrated in R. F. Treharne, *The Glastonbury Legends* (London: Cresset Press, 1967), p. 95.

3. Chambers, Record xxvi (d), p. 271.

4. R. S. Loomis, ed., *Arthurian Literature in the Middle Ages* (Oxford: Oxford University Press, 1959), p. 104.

5. Chambers, Record xx, pp. 263–64.

6. Chambers, Record xvii, p. 260.

7. W. L. Warren, *Henry II* (London: Methuen, 1973), chap. 4, esp. pp. 162–65, 184–85, 200–202.

8. G. M. Spiegel, "The *Redditus ad Stirpem Caroli Magni*: A New Look," *French Historical Studies* 7 (1971): 162, 165–66, 170.

9. Geoffrey of Monmouth, *Historia regum Brittanie*, ed. A. Griscom (London: Longmans, 1929), ix.12, p. 451; henceforward *HRB*.

10. P. Johanek, "Konig Arthur und die Plantagenets," *Fruhmittelalter Studien* 21 (1987): 346–90, 389.

11. Loomis, *Arthurian Literature*, p. 104n3.

12. F. Liebermann, *Die Gesetze der Angelsachsen* (Halle: M. Niemeyer, 1903), I, pp. 655, 658–60.

13. *Anglo Scottish Relations, 1174–1328*, ed. E. L. G. Stones (London: Nelson Medieval Texts, 1965), p. 98; *HRB* ix.9 and 12, pp. 444, 451.

14. *Chronique de Pierre de Langtoft*, ed. T. Wright (London: Rolls Series, 1866–68), 2, p. 279.

15. Chambers, Record xxxiv, pp. 280–81.

16. *Chronica Willelmi Rishanger*, ed. H. T. Riley (London: Rolls Series, 1865), p. 107; and see *HRB* ix.16, p. 463.

17. *Vita Eadwardi Secundi*, ed. N. Denholm Young (London: Nelson Medieval Texts, 1957), p. 133.

18. C. Shenton, "Royal Interest in Glastonbury and Cadbury: Two Arthurian Itineraries, 1278 and 1331," *English Historical Review* 114 (1999): 1249–55.

19. Chambers, Record xxxviii (b), p. 282.

20. D. A. L. Morgan, "The Banner-Bearer of Christ," in *St George's Chapel Windsor*, ed. N. Saul (Woodbridge: Boydell, 2005), pp. 51–61, see esp. p. 58.

21. James Carley, ed., *The Chronicle of Glastonbury Abbey* (Woodbridge: Boydell, 1985), pp. xxv–vi; henceforward John of Glastonbury.

22. Ibid., pp. lii–lix.

23. T. Rymer, *Foedera* (The Hague, 1740), 2 iv, p. 179.

24. Text printed from Vat. MS Reg. Lat. 263, in *Glastonbury Abbey and the Arthurian Tradition*, ed. James Carley (Cambridge: D. S. Brewer, 2001), pp. 296–302.

25. John of Glastonbury, pp. 46–51.

26. James Carley, "A Grave Event: Henry V, Glastonbury Abbey and Joseph of Arimathea's Bones," in *Glastonbury Abbey*, pp. 285–302, at p. 294n24.

27. Ibid., p. 295n32.

28. C. J. Hefele, *Histoire des Conciles* (Paris: Letouzey, 1907–13), vii, pp. 32–33.

29. Louise Ropes Loomis, *The Council of Constance* (New York: Columbia University Press, 1961), p. 343.

30. See, e.g., *Memorials of Henry V*, ed. C. A. Cole (London: Rolls Series, 1858), p. 121; *Gesta Henrici Quinti*, ed. F. Taylor and J. S. Roskell (Oxford: Oxford University Press, 1975), p. 145.

31. Loomis, *Council of Constance*, pp. 340–41.

32. John of Glastonbury, pp. 54–55.

33. J. Hardyng, *Chronicle*, ed. H. Ellis (London, 1812), pp. 84–86.

34. W. Worcester, *Itineraries*, ed. J. H. Harvey (Oxford: Oxford University Press, 1969), p. 299.

35. S. Anglo, "The *British History* and Tudor Propaganda," *Bulletin of the John Rylands Library* 44 (1961–62): 17–48, at pp. 22–26.

36. D. Starkey, "King Henry and King Arthur," *Arthurian Literature* 16 (1998): 171–96.

37. Ibid., p. 194; M. Biddle, ed., *Arthur's Round Table* (Woodbridge: Boydell, 2000), pp. 347, 367.

38. *Letters and Papers, Foreign and Domestic, Henry VIII*, ed. J. Gairdner (London, 1880), V, pp. 19–20.

39. J. Leland, *The Assertion of King Arthure* (printed and independently paginated [pp. 1–151] in *Middleton's Chinon of England*, ed. W. E. Mead, EETS o.s . 165 [London: H. Milford, 1925]), pp. 29, 39–40, 60; Caxton's preface in *The Works of Sir Thomas Malory*, ed. Eugène Vinaver, 3 vols., 3rd ed. rev. P. J. C. Field (Oxford: Clarendon Press, 1990), 1, p. cxliv.

40. Starkey, "King Henry and King Arthur," p. 171n35.

The *Prophecies of Merlin*: Their Originality and Importance

Geoffrey Ashe, MBE

Merlin makes his literary debut on a Welsh hill, usually identified as Dinas Emrys on the fringe of Snowdonia. He is not, of course, an old man with a long white beard. He is a youth, a teenager in fact, and he has been brought there as a human sacrifice. But he saves his life by outwitting his would-be sacrificers.

Geoffrey of Monmouth, whose *History of the Kings of Britain* introduced Merlin to the public, was (as the place-name "Monmouth" suggests) a Welshman, or possibly a son of Breton parents living in Wales. Born about 1100, he taught at an Oxford college—the university did not exist yet—from 1129 to 1151. After that, he was consecrated bishop of St. Asaph in Wales but may never have taken up the appointment. He died in 1155.[1]

The *Historia regum Britanniae* had been completed about 1138. Geoffrey's main purpose in writing it was to give the depressed Welsh a magnificent past, one they could be proud of. Elaborating a time-honored legend, he made out that they were the true Britons, descended from migrant Trojans, aristocrats of the Homeric world. Their ancestors had formerly held the whole of Britain. Invaded and almost crushed by Anglo-Saxons (ancestors of the English) in the fifth century AD, they had made a glorious recovery in the reign of King Arthur, but then lost ground till only Wales remained independent.

Geoffrey's *History* became one of the most influential books of the Middle Ages, with a readership far outside Wales. It supplied the primary framework for Arthurian romance, and it was generally accepted as factual—as real history. While that view ceased to be tenable, it can be said, even today, that Geoffrey was more conscientious in his use of sources than skeptics were once willing to admit.[2]

While he was working on the book, and had perhaps got as far as the end of Roman rule in Britain, he was turned aside by an unforeseen intervention.

There was a growing interest in the Welsh tradition of supposedly inspired bardic poetry and prophecy, with a remote ancestry in Celtic druidism. "Prophecy" could mean foretelling the future, but not necessarily. The word could apply simply to supernatural insight or vision which bards possessed. Bishop Alexander of Lincoln, who was Geoffrey's ecclesiastical superior, invited him as a well-qualified scholar to explore the topic. He was amenable and shelved the *History* for a while to do so.

Not much of this prophetic material had survived. It would be natural to suspect that when Geoffrey produced the resultant booklet—it was of modest size—he was simply obliging Alexander by fabricating bardic matter out of nothing at all. To a large extent he was, but that was not the whole story—not quite. He had noticed, for instance, a genuine and recurrent theme: the hope of a Welsh revival and a *revanche* against the English. A poem composed about 930 entitled *Armes Prydein*, "The Omen of Britain," foretold this reversal of fortune. It had turned out to be too optimistic: the English king Athelstan routed the Welsh in 937. But it was always possible to take the poem up again and reinterpret it, and it was still known in the twelfth century.[3]

Some of the Welsh matter, including the *Armes Prydein*, was associated with what appeared to be a personal name, Myrddin. Bishop Alexander had noticed this and expressed interest. "Myrddin" is linked etymologically with Carmarthen in southwest Wales. It is also, confusingly, the name or sobriquet of a semilegendary wanderer through the Forest of Celidon in Scotland, an inspired madman. At this point Geoffrey found little about its significance in either context, but since the bishop was familiar with it, he employed it as a title for the whole miscellany he had assembled. His booklet should be known as "the prophecies of Myrddin," conjuring up, with or without justification, the figure of a prophet so named. Though he had written most of it himself, to eke out the genuine items (and even those were freely paraphrased), "Myrddin's Prophecies" it should be . . . with one adjustment. "Myrddin," Latinized in his text as *Merdinus*, would suggest *merde*, a distasteful word for potential readers among the ruling Anglo-Normans. Geoffrey expurgated "Myrddin" by changing one letter, and the work that the bishop had commissioned went out to the world as *The Prophecies of Merlin*. That is how the great name originated.

In the course of his studies and speculations, Geoffrey may well have caught glimpses of a real Merlin, or rather Myrddin, but there is no certainty. He completed his assignment in 1135, and copies began to circulate. However, he had no intention of leaving it at that. Having set aside the *History* to spend time on the *Prophecies*, he now wanted to incorporate them in the *History* itself, for which a larger and more influential public could be anticipated. When he took the *History* up again, he decided to make Merlin a character in the narrative uttering the

Prophecies and to insert an episode before the *Prophecies* started, introducing him to the reader.

To contrive this episode, Geoffrey adapted a Welsh legend at least three centuries old, about a young seer in Snowdonia. He had found it in a book usually attributed to a monk called Nennius; in fact, he may have touched on this already in his draft text. At any rate, he now developed it as the prelude to Merlin's entry. The boy's name was Emrys—in Latin, Ambrosius—but Geoffrey, restructuring the story, explained that he was Merlin and was merely "also called" Ambrosius.

When Geoffrey's introduction of the prophet begins, he has already completed his account of Britain in the immediate aftermath of Rome, following Welsh tradition. The usurping king Vortigern has allowed Saxons to settle in the country as auxiliary troops, under the leadership of Hengist. But thousands more have followed without permission and ravaged the country, slaughtering the Britons and seizing their lands. Vortigern has fled to Snowdonia with a small retinue and employed workmen to build a fortress on a hill. Its foundations have repeatedly crumbled, and Vortigern's attendant magicians have told him that he must find a boy without a father, put him to death, and sprinkle his blood on the stones.

The young Merlin—this is where we now meet him—is discovered in Carmarthen. His mother was impregnated by an incubus demon, so, humanly speaking, he has no father. At the building site he confounds the magicians by revealing what they have failed to realize: that the cause of the subsidence is an underground pool. Moreover, this has two dragons in it, which, when disturbed and roused, emerge and start fighting. Vortigern perceives that Merlin has "something supernatural about him" and wants him to interpret the spectacle. The king gets more than he bargained for. Merlin is seized by a controlling spirit and pours out the whole body of the *Prophecies* in a single tremendous monologue. Here they are. Geoffrey has worked them into the *History* as planned, and it is in this passage that we can read them. They go on for fourteen pages in the standard English translation by Lewis Thorpe.

So, then, what can be said about them? First, in publishing this material, vastly inflated by his own contribution, Geoffrey was highly original. He was also, on the face of it, highly audacious. For Christians in England in his time, the legitimate scope for prophecy was restricted. Inventive authors had produced sibylline fictions looking ahead to the last days of the world: to the rise and fall of Antichrist, the Second Coming, and so on.[4] Some of these forecasts were detailed and fanciful, but they were acceptable in the church's eyes, because the essential subject matter was covered by Christian doctrine. The authors were merely elaborating what was already there, chiefly in the *Apocalypse*. With other probings of the future, it was not so: they were suspect, as belonging to the twilight world of sorcerers and astrologers. St. Augustine, who molded Christian thinking in this respect as in others, admitted that such charlatans did sometimes score, but he attributed their successes to demons, who had some knowledge of the future and communicated this to the practitioners of forbidden arts, to make it look as if their techniques were valid and to lead the gullible astray.[5]

However, Geoffrey evaded condemnation. Wales, though Augustine did not know it, was an exception. Geoffrey's compatriots had a prophetic tradition of their own, which sidestepped the demons altogether. Gerald of Wales ("Giraldus Cambrensis") gives a firsthand account of Welsh seers called *awenyddion*.[6] You could consult them on some question, and your chosen seer would go into a trance and make oracular utterances. At first these might sound irrelevant, but if you listened patiently and carefully, an answer would emerge. Afterwards, the seer had to be roused and usually recalled very little.

Such men and women might sometimes predict the future, and they did so, in Gerald's opinion, innocently. He was a churchman himself, and no one seems to have contested his view. As Geoffrey himself and others made clear, the Welsh, being of the true British stock, were descended from Trojans; Troy had prophets and prophetesses (Cassandra, for instance) long before Christianity existed to create difficulties, and without any involvement of unhallowed magic or evil spirits.

Geoffrey's concern is with greater matters than private advice, but he is a product of this milieu where prophecy can be safe, and he is clearly confident that he can give it to the world without risking ecclesiastical censure. After all, he has a bishop as sponsor. Moreover, he is careful not to endow Merlin with mantic powers of his own that might make him a suspect figure. The reader is told twice that he receives everything, like a true Welsh seer, from a controlling spirit or *numen* which he draws into him.[7] The spirit can be invited, but not commanded. When the *Prophecies* made their appearance embedded in the *History*, they reached a wide audience, and Geoffrey's inventiveness and assurance carried them along, overriding any scruples or queries, even though the author was a cleric himself. That, apparently, didn't matter.

Merlin utters the *Prophecies* in a sustained, spirit-fired ecstasy. Realistically, his performance would have taken a long time, but many speeches and sermons have been known to take longer. While a few of the *Prophecies* are more or less intelligible, most are enigmatic, and while some, as we saw, have authentic Welsh antecedents, most are (it must be repeated) Geoffrey's own work.

In composing this recital he faced a curious issue and took advantage of it. Merlin was supposed to be prophesying in the fifth century, but Geoffrey was writing about him in the twelfth. Numerous things had happened in the long period between, which Geoffrey had read about, whereas Merlin could not have, because, for him, they had not happened yet. So Geoffrey could present Merlin as a prophet indeed, by making him "foretell" some of them.

Among these pseudo-prophecies planted in the text, the most interesting concern Arthur, who, supposedly, is not yet born when Merlin speaks. The seer predicts great suffering for the Britons at the hands of the Saxons, and then introduces a mighty leader, cryptically dubbed "the Boar of Cornwall," whose victories will bring relief but who will come to a mysterious end. Having thus given a hint at Arthur, who, of course, is going to appear in the *History* later, Geoffrey continues with further pseudo-prophecies as far as the reign of Henry I, in his own lifetime. Then he can get no farther. He has to concoct imaginary predictions about the real future, through the rest of his lifetime and beyond, and attribute these also to Merlin. The prospect does not deter him. The *Prophecies* go on in lavish profusion, ending at last in a cosmic upheaval, with planets and constellations changing their positions and terrific storms raging on earth. This is not the end of the world, but it is, rather abruptly, the end of the *Prophecies*.

There is no visible transition from the first series to the second. One flows into the other without a break. A reader, noting the touches of accuracy with Henry I and others, could be excused for judging that Merlin was a true prophet and inferring that further hits must occur in the rest, after King Henry. Many readers did think like this, though the inference, of course, was fallacious. In that later and longer series, it is usually difficult to see what a prophecy is even supposed to mean. Geoffrey is being deliberately obscure.

The only prediction that makes reasonable sense is simply an expansion of the Welsh hope of a Celtic resurgence which did most to initiate the whole project: "Kambria shall be filled with joy and the Cornish oaks shall flourish. The island shall be called by the name of Brutus and the title given to it by the foreigners shall be done away with."[8] Brutus is the legendary founder of the British kingdom, and the title given by the foreigners is "England," Angle-land.

Merlin is made to foretell some very odd phenomena. Three springs will burst forth in Winchester, and streams will flow from them dividing Britain into three parts. A tree will grow on top of the Tower of London and overspread the land. The river Usk will be boiling hot for seven months, and its fish will die and give birth to serpents. A medley of symbolic creatures—at least, they seem to be symbolic—appear and vanish without explanation and go through various interactions, some of them fairly complicated. A hedgehog loaded with apples will build a palace with six hundred towers and construct hidden passages under the earth. A snow-white and gleaming giant will shed light over the land. A lion will spread havoc till he is soothed by a man carrying a drum and a lute and by swallowing a saucer of medicine brought by a girl from a former Roman city. We might expect recognizable kings and queens, but there are few. Merlin is seldom so overtly political.[9]

European literature includes another notorious body of prophecy, and the contrast is striking. Nostradamus's 942 quatrains, published in France from 1555 to 1568, contain plenty that is grotesque or opaque, but they refer to identifiable persons and places. Absurd attempts to make dozens of them "work" have done their author an injustice; but some—few, but some—interpretations have been agreed upon, showing that they do fit events long after his time quite unambiguously, whatever the explanation. No commentator could do the same with Merlin. The specifics are lacking. Whatever it is that Nostradamus does, Geoffrey does nothing similar, and hardly even tries.

Why did he go to so much trouble to produce this farrago, with bogus authentications in the first part and pointless ingenuities in the second? His performance is more than a mere outburst of exuberance. One motive is obvious—the need to provide a text ample enough to satisfy Bishop Alexander. Beyond that, the *Prophecies* can be seen as a mystification. Geoffrey calculates that by writing something very long and wholly unprecedented, with a handful of "good" prophecies to encourage his readers and a swarm of cryptic ones to set them talking, he can build Merlin up as a unique figure and give everything that he says an air of significance. Geoffrey knows he will presently be telling the tale of Arthur as the Britons' supreme hero, and a copious mass of "prophecy" can establish the status of the prophet who foretells him and prepares the way for his reign. Later, when Merlin plays a part in Arthur's story himself, the impression already made by his inspired output will be all the greater. The brief saying about the Boar of Cornwall is a first step. When the prophet masterminds Arthur's conception at Tintagel, his role in the event will give the king a more-than-mortal aura from the beginning.

If that is how Geoffrey's mind worked, his literary judgment was sound. The writers of romance not only took up his theme with enthusiasm, they enlarged Merlin's role into a supernatural sponsorship of the whole Arthurian adventure.[10] They portrayed him constructing the Round Table, advising and warning with mysterious insight, and obtaining Excalibur itself.

Geoffrey's fertility of imagination is perhaps excessive. Merlin's vaticinations often *look* as if they ought to mean something. Sometimes they recall the political cartoons of a bygone era of journalism: the Russian Bear, the American Eagle, and so on. Sometimes they are lucid yet baffling, as when Merlin foretells that the English Channel will become narrow and people will carry on conversations across it.[11] Wace, in his French verse paraphrase of the *History*, gave up on them and left them out. But others insisted on having them, and some copyists of Wace put them back. Many readers felt that some at least of the *Prophecies* must mean something, and if they were not sure what it was, that was their own fault rather than Merlin's. Attempts to make sense of them began after Geoffrey's death, when he could no longer be consulted. A commentary composed by an Arthurian enthusiast about 1170 was attributed, mistakenly but eloquently, to an eminent scholar, Alanus de Insulis. An Italian chronicler put Merlin on a level with the great biblical prophet Isaiah. His name carried so much prestige that a Spanish author attached it to prophecies actually written by himself.[12]

By breaking away from pseudo-apocalyptic confinement and writing freely about the nearer future anywhere between his own time and the Second Coming of Christ, Geoffrey affirmed an author's freedom to prophesy on a large scale about anything and everything. That affirmation was successful and lasting. Acceptance of the new possibility was beginning to stir in western Europe apart from Geoffrey. He, of course, was not solely responsible. But his contribution was real, and the widespread interest in the *History*, with its Merlin section, encouraged numerous readers to take him seriously and reflect on the future without an obsessive concentration on the End of the World.

There are already signs of this widening conception of prophecy in the phenomenal Hildegard of Bingen (1098–1179). The conception grows far wider in the hypertheology of Joachim of Fiore (1135–1202), whom Dante salutes in the *Paradiso* (12.139–41). Joachim foreshadowed a golden age by applying the doctrine of the Trinity to the movement of history. In the Old Testament era, God the Father predominated; in the Christian era, it was God the Son; and presently, Joachim announced, the Holy Spirit would come to the fore, bringing a blessed time of worldwide peace and enlightenment. Modern historians have singled Joachim out as the first person who enabled medieval Europeans to be optimistic about the earthly future.[13]

His early followers expected a clear-cut transition in 1260. When it did not happen, Joachites became, to a certain extent, politicized. Quite in keeping with Merlin, whom they quoted, they began to foretell two human inaugurators of change, not in the distant overture to the End but in the uncharted stretch of time before that, and sooner rather than later.

One was the Angelic Pope, first mentioned by the Franciscan Roger Bacon in 1267. It was foretold that he would end the church's internal dissension and cleanse it of corruption.[14] The reborn church's dedication to truth and justice would win over the schismatic Greeks, the Jews, and even the Saracens. When the Angelic Pope appeared he might be poor and unimpressive, a monk or a friar or even a hermit, but his true stature would become manifest. By the last decade of the thirteenth century, Joachite propaganda had become so effective that the election of Pope Celestine V, an aged and saintly hermit, was hailed by multitudes as fulfilling the prophecy. Celestine, however, was unequal to the huge demands made on him, and opponents soon induced him to abdicate. Dante mentions Celestine as well as Joachim, but in very different terms, condemning him to a gloomy antechamber of Hell for his "great refusal" (*Inferno* 3.58–60). However, expectation of the Angelic Pope persisted for centuries, and as late as 1555 Marcellus II became a candidate. An early death cut his pretensions short.

78   Geoffrey Ashe

The other prophesied renovator of the church and society was the Second Charlemagne, who would probably arise at the same time as the Angelic Pope and receive an imperial crown from him. The original Charlemagne had united a large portion of Europe and refounded the western Roman Empire in the year 800. His unwieldy domain fell apart, but a shrunken empire, eventually dubbed "Holy Roman," survived through the Middle Ages. Joachites foretold that it would expand again, so that a single ruler would be able to unite Christendom and establish the political groundwork for Joachim's golden age. Rival exponents of the theory discussed acrimoniously whether the Second Charlemagne would be French or German, and a few actual rulers were cast briefly in the neoimperial role. One was the French king Charles VIII in 1494. Savonarola himself took an interest, and an Italian friar tried to combine Joachim's prophecies with Merlin's. However, the excitement blew over.

George Eliot mentions the dream of the "Pope Angelico," and the Second Charlemagne fantasy, in her historical novel *Romola*, which has a Florentine setting.[15] Neither notion was inspired by Geoffrey directly, but they might not have carried the weight they did if his book validating this *kind* of prophecy (in the case of Arthur, for instance) had not become a best seller, so far as anything could be before the advent of printing.

NOTES

1. For background, see the introduction and notes in Geoffrey of Monmouth, *The History of the Kings of Britain*, trans. Lewis Thorpe (Harmondsworth: Penguin, 1966), hereafter cited as Thorpe. For further reading, see Geoffrey Ashe, *The Book of Prophecy: From Ancient Greece to the Modern Day* (London: Blandford, 1999; Orion, 2002); Geoffrey Ashe, *Merlin: The Prophet and His History* (London: Sutton Publishing, 2006).

2. John J. Parry and Robert A. Caldwell, "Geoffrey of Monmouth," in *Arthurian Literature in the Middle Ages*, ed. Roger Sherman Loomis (Oxford: Clarendon Press, 1959), pp. 72–93; and Thorpe, pp. 28–31.

3. A. O. H. Jarman, "The Merlin Legend and the Welsh Tradition of Prophecy," in *The Arthur of the Welsh*, ed. Rachel Bromwich, A. O. H. Jarman, and Brynley F. Roberts (Cardiff: University of Wales Press, 1991), pp. 136–38; Bromwich, Jarman, and Roberts, *Arthur of the Welsh*, pp. 8, 20, 35, 50, 103, 254n31.

4. The principal pseudo-sibylline texts are the *Tiburtina* and *Pseudo-Methodius*. See Norman Cohn, *The Pursuit of the Millennium* (London: Paladin, 1970), pp. 31–32, 71–74.

5. St. Augustine, *The City of God*, trans. Henry Bettenson (Harmondsworth: Penguin, 1984), 5.7, 9.22.

6. Gerald of Wales, *The Journey through Wales and the Description of Wales*, trans. Lewis Thorpe (Harmondsworth: Penguin, 1978), 1.16 in the *Description*.

7. The phrase is "Mox ille fletum prorumpens spiritum hausit prophetie" ("At once, bursting into tears, he drew the spirit of prophecy into him"). See *The Historia regum Britannie of Geoffrey of Monmouth*, Latin edition, ed. Neil Wright (Cambridge: D. S. Brewer, 1984), hereafter Wright, 7.3, 8.10, pp. 74, 90; Thorpe, pp. 171, 196.

8. Wright, p. 77; Thorpe, p. 175.

9. Hedgehog: Wright, p. 79; Thorpe, p. 178. White giant: Wright, p. 82; Thorpe, p. 182. Lion: Wright, p. 83; Thorpe, p. 183.

10. On Geoffrey's literary influence, see Parry and Caldwell, "Geoffrey of Monmouth," pp. 87–89.

11. English Channel prediction: Wright, p. 79; Thorpe, p. 179.

12. Commentators and imitators: Parry and Caldwell, "Geoffrey of Monmouth," pp. 78–79.

13. Marjorie Reeves, *Joachim of Fiore and the Prophetic Future* (New York: Harper and Row, 1977), chap. 3; and her *Influence of Prophecy in the Later Middle Ages: A Study in Joachism* (Notre Dame, IN: University of Notre Dame Press, 1993).

14. Roger Bacon and the Angelic Pope: Reeves, *Joachim of Fiore*, p. 74.

15. George Eliot, *Romola*, ed. with an introduction and notes by Andrew Brown (Oxford: Oxford University Press, 1998).

Notes toward a Reappraisal of Malory's Prose Style

D. Thomas Hanks, Jr.

Style: Jonathan Swift unhelpfully tells us that "proper words in proper places make the true definition of a style."[1] More helpful are Elizabeth Closs Traugott and Mary Louise Pratt, whose *Linguistics for Students of Literature* provides a useful approach. As they put it, "style results from a tendency of a speaker or writer to consistently choose certain structures over others available in the language . . . we can distinguish between 'style' and 'language' by saying that language is the sum total of the structures available to the speaker, while style concerns the characteristic choices in a given context."[2] Throughout this essay, I refer to Malory's "style" in the sense of his choices, especially with regard to word choice and clause structure.

Any discussion of Malory's prose style must first note the two book-length studies of that style: P. J. C. Field's magisterial *Romance and Chronicle: A Study of Malory's Prose Style*[3] and Mark Lambert's *Malory: Style and Vision in Le Morte Darthur*.[4] Many other scholars ranging from Sir Walter Scott through George Saintsbury to Eugène Vinaver himself have discussed Malory's style; limitations of space force me to leave them undiscussed here, except to note that Bonnie Wheeler herself has contributed one of the most thoughtful essays on Malory's prose, one in which she writes that Malory's paratactic style profoundly affects both his episodic plot development and his audience's sense of "gaps in causal structures" which readers are impelled to fill in.[5]

I am indebted to the scholars noted above and to their many here-unnoted colleagues; their comments on Malory's style have stimulated my own thoughts. I must note, however, that none of them has discussed Malory's style in his own terms.

One cannot fully discuss Malory's writing style without reviewing the literary culture for which and within which he wrote—a manuscript-based culture which received much of its literature through the ear rather than through the eye.

I have separated those two basic assertions into a one-sentence paragraph to emphasize them; just as Malory undeniably wrote for a readership whose reading habits he knew to be governed by manuscript conventions, likewise he wrote for an audience most of whom, he knew, would not "read" the *Morte*; they would receive it by ear (aurally) rather than by eye. That Malory's was a manuscript culture is a given; that his was an oral-aural culture is not so obvious but is indubitable. The chief recent study of his oral-aural culture is a special issue of *Arthuriana*: *Reading Malory Aloud: Then and Now*, jointly edited by Karen Cherewatuk and Joyce Coleman.[6] It contains essays by Rosamund S. Allen on syntax, Janet Jesmok on "poetic qualities" of the *Morte*, and Michael Twomey on "the voice of aurality," among others.[7] The issue, especially those three articles, fully supports the oral-aural element of the *Morte*.

In this essay, I base my argument chiefly on one fact: our earlier manuscript culture used no syntactic punctuation. Syntactic punctuation was invented by printers following Malory's time.[8] Instead of punctuation, Malory used verbal cues to syntax. His practice is now unfamiliar to us; his syntactic cues—chiefly coordinating conjunctions—may in a modern punctuated edition seem crude or unnecessarily repetitive. Then, they were essential to constructing meaning. Modern scholars have largely ignored this fact. Thus P. J. C. Field suggests that the following wording shows Malory "least at his ease" as a narrator: "And the name of thys knyght was called Balyne, and by good meanys of the barownes he was delyverde oute of preson, for he was a good man named of his body, and he was borne in Northehumbirlonde" (1:62.36–63.2).[9] This "sentence," as Field terms it, seems to him clumsily to hold "misfit clauses awkwardly tacked on late in the sentence," a result of Malory's unthinkingly applying his paratactic clause structure.[10] Note that in the manuscript, and of course in Malory's knowledge of syntactic conventions, this set of clauses could have no commas; thus the "And . . . and . . . for . . . and" construction which Field deplores results from a style based not on the modern concept of the sentence but on the concept of the clause. The conjunctions serve as markers for new clauses, and were by later conventions replaced by commas and/or by subordination of sentence elements—a replacement which fits clumsily when the two are superimposed, as they are in Vinaver's text above. Here Field criticizes an instance of the earlier convention, using a later convention as his criterion. His conclusions that "Malory finds syntactical subordination difficult" and that Malory's is therefore a style of "relentless simplicity"[11] ignore Malory's syntax and privilege his own.

Were Malory to be writing today, he would have used modern sentence markers, and the passage would have looked like this: "The name of this knight was called Balin. By good means of the barons he was delivered out of prison, for he was a good man named of his body. He was born in Northumberland." I retain the subordinating "for" but replace the coordinating "ands" with periods, as Malory would doubtless have done had he been writing in more recent centuries. Malory's "sentence," in short, is not clumsy in his manuscript context—and please recall that "sentences" were not in his repertoire of syntactical units. It appears clumsy when one judges it by the modern syntactic expectations of a print-based culture. Rosamund Allen, in her *Arthuriana* article noted above, comments on the positive effect of Malory's paratactic style for a listening audience: "the vigor and changes of pace: *and . . . and . . . and then* may look boring on the page, but work very well in creating a fast-moving, non-judgmental story-line."[12]

My explanation may sound apologetic, something like "Poor Malory: he didn't have our print-based conventions, so he had to make do with the limping syntax of his time." If so, I have given the wrong impression. Simply reading through the unpunctuated Winchester Manuscript, I find Malory's syntax fluid, articulate, and masterfully effective at communicating his story in his style. Supporting this observation, I turn to a discussion of how Malory's audience received his *Morte*.

I have mentioned that Malory wrote his *Morte* for a culture most of whose members received their texts aurally. That this was the case has been affirmed for years in studies of medieval writers in general, in such seminal articles as Ruth Crosby's and William Nelson's. Their work has been recently recapitulated and expanded by Joyce Coleman.[13] Most recently, conclusions about reading aloud and its ubiquity in medieval culture have appeared in the issue of *Arthuriana* mentioned earlier. Following upon essays in that issue, I argue here that Malory wrote what one might call "oral/aural prose," and that the chief elements of his oral/aural prose are poetic diction, rhetorical balance, and—a constant—the syntax of a culture which had yet to invent our current form of punctuation.

Oral/Aural Prose

Given that Malory wrote more for the ear than for the eye, then his style perforce becomes partly a matter of how he accommodates listeners. Listeners require certain elements in a text: wording pleasing to the ear, repetition (since they can't turn back for a missed word or phrase), and, of course, a syntax that meets their sense of the expected organization of words and clauses. I reiterate: writers of Malory's time did not have a sense of "the sentence," beginning with a capital letter and ending with a period; that syntactic construction was still in their future.[14] A listening audience grasps independent clauses much more easily than it grasps lengthy periodic sentences; Malory writes chiefly in independent clauses, with infrequent appearances of time-of-day dependent clauses and still-more-infrequent dependent clauses of other sorts. He also writes in a style containing what I call "poetic diction" and rhetorical balance.

Aurality and Poetic Diction

One might think of Malory's style much as one thinks of the style of poems intended chiefly for aural reception: the sounds of his words play a major role in his prose.[15] To be sure, how the *Morte* sounded is partly unknowable; we have no recordings of Sir Thomas reading his work aloud. We have only the surviving Winchester Manuscript, now titled BL Additional MS 59678 (ca.1475). Fortunately, Jeannette Marshall Denton—now Jeannette Marsh—has resolved the vexed question of Malory's pronunciation (markedly different from Chaucerian pronunciation).[16] Now, readers of Malory can use the Winchester Manuscript and Denton/Marsh's guide to pronunciation to come closer to reproducing the sounds of Malory's work than has been possible for centuries. Perusing the Winchester Manuscript while applying Denton's guide to pronunciation makes it clear that Malory's style was often downright poetic in its use of alliteration, assonance, and rhythm.

For an example of his oral/aural style, consider the following well-known passage wherein Bedevere falsely reports to Arthur what he saw when he supposedly threw Excalibur into the lake: "Sir he seyde I sy no thynge but watirs / wap and wawys wa*n*ne" (fol. 481; cf. Vinaver, 3:1239.25–26). The latter part of this passage—"watirs / wap and wawys wa*n*ne"—has long seemed powerful to Malory's readers. Alliteration on the "w" is the first thing one notes;[17] the assonance of the letter "a" is doubtless the second. The rhythm of the passage strikes one next; marking the natural stresses on the words shows that "but wátirs wáp and wáwis wánne" is a perfectly iambic passage. Note likewise that the rhythm mimics the sound of the water lapping against the shoreline of the lake; the passage is performative in that its sound parallels its sense. The passage is a small gem of Malory's mastery, mastery not wholly clear unless one reads the passage aloud, actually hearing the rhythm.[18]

Another example of Malory's polyphonic prose appears in the account of Elaine of Astolat's death and final journey: "Than hir fadir and hir brothir made grete dole for he[r] And whan thys was done anone she dyed And whan she was dede the corse and þᵉ bedde all was lad the nexte way vnto the te*m*mys [the Thames] And þ*er* a man & the corse and all thynge as she had devised was put in the te*m*mys and so the man th̄ [*sic*] stirred the bargett vnto Westmynst*er* and þ*er* hit rubbed and rolled too and fro a grete whyle or any man aspyed hit" (fol. 428v; cf. Vinaver, 2:1095.6–14). As this passage reminds us, Malory can be, and frequently is, succinct to the point of being laconic. When he wrote earlier about Elaine's doleful end, he wrote pathos into a lengthy account of her final days (fols. 428r–v; Vinaver, 2:1092–95). The narrator's account of her death and final journey, however, could hardly be shorter; following almost immediately after her sixteen lines of instruction to her father and brother, he writes less than one line: "And whan thys was done anone she dyed."

One notes immediately that the narrator gives a bare eight words to the clause which reports Elaine's death, while the preceding responses of father and brother ("Than hir fadir and . . . ") use eleven words. The simple presence of the death-barge at Westminster pier, on the other hand, receives seventeen words: "and þer hit rubbed and rolled too and fro a grete whyle or any man aspyed hit." No clause in the entire section is as short as the one which announces her death. I called this "succinct" earlier; looked at in context, it now seems powerfully abbreviated. Preceded by her long, affective series of comments to father and brother, this section returns to action and takes the reader through her kinsmen's compliance and sorrow to her death, then quickly to the placement of her body in a boat. The boat moves instantly to Westminster, where Malory supplies bare, but evocative, detail: "and þer hit rubbed and rolled too and fro a grete whyle." Both sound and sight are evoked in this subtly suggested image of a boat which rubs against the pier as it rolls in the waves of the Thames. The alliteration of "rubbed and rolled" is immediately apparent; less immediately apparent is the rhythmic up-and-down of "rúbbed and rólled tóo and fró," a rhythm which reproduces the wave action it describes. Malory evidently liked this sort of alliterative and assonantal onomatopoesis, as Bedevere's false report of what he saw when he did not throw Excalibur into the lake similarly indicates.

Malory's characteristic alliteration reappears in two short passages within a few pages of one another in the "Launcelot and Elaine" section of the *Morte*. The first comes from the episode wherein Dame Brusen tricks Lancelot into Elaine's bed for the second time, this time in Arthur's court (the first bed trick took place earlier, as Lancelot visited King Pelles).

In this episode, Guenevere has arranged for Lancelot to visit her on the same night of Elaine's arrival in court. She summons him chiefly owing to her jealousy of Elaine, upon whom Lancelot begot Galahad after Brusen led Lancelot to believe that he was making love with Guenevere instead of Elaine. Now—some time later—Elaine comes to court, only to find that Lancelot will have nothing to do with her. The ever-resourceful Brusen promises relief and goes to Lancelot in the night; he is expecting a lady from Guenevere, so he follows Brusen with no delay. Meeting Elaine in the dark, he goes to bed with her. Malory describes the scene thus: "And than dame Brusen . . . lad hym to her ladyes bedde dame Elayne And than she dep*ar*ted . . . And wyte you well this lady was glad and so was s*ir* Launcelot for he wende that he had had anoþ*er* in hys armys // Now leve we them kyssynge and clyppynge as was a kyndely thynge And now speke we of quene Gwenyu*er* that sente one of her women that she moste trusted vnto s*ir* launcelotys bedde And whan she cam there she founde the bedde colde" (fol. 329; cf. Vinaver, 2:804.30–805.4).

This passage of narrative, straightforward though it is, shows Malory using alliteration to underline the drama of the passage. The passage leads simply enough to its climax: "dame Brusen . . . lad hym to her ladyes bedde dame Elayne And than she dep*ar*ted." Then, after we learn that both Elaine and Lancelot are happy, we come to the stylistic climax of the passage: "Now leve we them kyssynge and clyppynge as was a kyndely thynge." The reticence of "Now leve we them" is neatly balanced against the alliteration of "kyssynge and clyppynge as was a kyndely thynge." The narrative then quickly moves to, as it were, the reverse of this alliterative kissing and clipping: Guenevere's woman "cam there" and "founde the bedde colde." This alliterative "coming" to a "colde" bed is a fitting anticlimax for Guenevere's search, and Malory ties it to the climax of Elaine's plot with the alliteration of "kyssynge," "clyppynge," "kyndely," and "cam," leading to the final "colde."

More alliteration appears just two pages later, as Agglovale and Perceval meet their mother during their search for Lancelot, recently run mad after the drama of Elaine's bedchamber. Their mother begs them to leave the Round Table and return to her. They refuse, and Malory reports her disappointment with new alliteration: "Alas my swete sonnys þa*n* she seyde for youre sakys I shall fyrste lose my lykynge & luste And than wynde and wedir I may not endure" (fol. 331–331v; cf. Vinaver, 2:818.8–10). Reading this in print, one may feel that this is altogether too much of a good thing. To a listening audience, though, the words go by quickly: "swete sonnys . . . seyde . . . sakys" lead to "lykynge & luste," immediately followed by "wynde and wedir." If one is listening instead of reading, the alliteration is not intrusive but instead serves to emphasize the dignified pathos expressed by the mother of the two knights.

Rhetorical Balance

I mentioned above Malory's rhetorical balance; it appears throughout the *Morte*.[19] One instance appears in a simple narrative explanation: King Mark has heard of Tristram's prowess, and he sends to learn more; Isode likewise sends agents. Malory balances his references to the king and queen throughout the passage: "So he sente on his party men to aspye what dedis he ded and the quene sente pryvaly on her p*ar*ty spyes to know what dedis he had done for full grete love was there be twene them So whan þe messyngers were com home they tolde þe trouthe as they herde and how he passed all oþer knyghtes but yf hit were sir launcelot than kynge Marke was ryght hevy of tho tydyng*is* and as glad was labeale Isode" (fol. 236; cf. Vinaver, 2:577.9–15). I cite this passage because it is so straightforward; one of Malory's distinctive narratorial customs is to balance his pronouncements in an envelope as he does here, opening by referring to King Mark's men, then to Isode's spies; encapsulating the messages of the two groups; and closing the passage with a report of the reception of the news first by King Mark, then by Isode. This is Malory at his most businesslike, reporting his "news" in simple but balanced prose. Note that the Mark-Isode envelope not only gives a sense of balance to the passage, it also ensures listener comprehension. The repetition with variation which moves from "he" and "the quene" to "kynge Marke" and "labeale Isode" prevents a listener's losing track of the narrative.

A more dramatic passage, still carefully balanced, appears in the early stages of the adventures of Balin (Vinaver's "The Knight with the Two Swords"). A damsel girt with a sword has come to Arthur's court; in response to Arthur's questioning, she reports that "I may nat be delyue*r*de of thys swerde but by a knyght and he muste be a passynge good man of hys hondys and of hye / dedis and withoute velony oþ*ir* trechory and w*it*houte treson" (fol. 22v; Vinaver, 1:61.33–62.2). Arthur tries and fails to draw the sword, followed by every other knight of the court except for Balin, who hangs back. Finally—as the damsel takes her leave still wearing the sword—Balin advances and asks permission to make the attempt. Seeing his poor clothing, the damsel thinks little of him and at first refuses him permission. His response—set apart as a rhetorical unit by double virgules preceding and following it—is another carefully balanced piece of rhetoric: "//A fayre damesell seyde Balyn worthynes and good tacchis and also good dedis is nat only in a raymente • but manhode and worship [is hyd] w*t*in a mannes p*er*son & many a worshipfull knyght ys nat knowyn vnto all peple and there fore worship and hardynesse ys nat in a raymente //" (fol. 23; "is hyd" supplied from Caxton, Sig. c vi. Cf. Vinaver, 1:63.23–27). The damsel agrees and allows Balin to attempt the sword; he succeeds. No wonder she is moved by so carefully balanced an argument, one wherein Balin opens by saying that worthiness, good qualities, and good deeds appear not only in "a raymente." His central message is that manhood and worthiness are interior qualities. He then closes the envelope of this statement with a comment parallel to and partly repeating his opening clause: "worship and hardynesse" are not found in "a raymente."

Such examples abound throughout the *Morte*; Malory's rhetoric, whether in narrative or in dialogue, is carefully balanced. I again point out that in an oral medium, one must repeat with variation for the sake of the audience; listeners often will not retain in memory a passage of this length without the repetition of the opening idea, which ensures that listeners retain the sense of the passage. Such repetition with variation appears in Malory's envelope structures, each of which automatically produces an instance of rhetorical balance.

❖

A longer work in progress will turn to such matters as dialogue and narrative voice. Here I discuss only Malory's oral/aural style as it appears in poetic diction and rhetorical balance. His choices in the areas of diction and balanced structure rely upon syntax, as all written expression relies upon syntax—the "rules" of a language which dictate how we arrange words and clauses (now sentences) to achieve meaning and effect. Malory's style is masterful. His mastery has been to a significant degree unrecognized by scholars who judge his style by the standards of a syntax and of a print culture which are almost irrelevant to the authorial choices Malory made as he wrote his *Morte Darthur*.

NOTES

1. Jonathan Swift, *Letter to a Young gentleman Lately Entered into Holy Orders* (1720), in *Brewer's Famous Quotations*, ed. Nigel Reese (New York: Sterling, 2006), p. 150.

2. Elizabeth Closs Traugott and Mary Louise Pratt, *Linguistics for Students of Literature* (New York: Harcourt Brace Jovanovich, 1980), p. 29.

3. P. J. C. Field, *Romance and Chronicle: A Study of Malory's Prose Style* (Bloomington: Indiana University Press, 1971).

4. Mark Lambert, *Malory: Style and Vision in "Le Morte Darthur"* (New Haven: Yale University Press, 1975). See also Eugène Vinaver, introduction to Sir Thomas Malory, *Works*, ed. Eugène Vinaver, rev. P. J. C. Field, 3rd ed., 3 vols., paginated continuously (Oxford: Clarendon Press, 1990), 1:xix–cxxvi. Hereafter cited as Vinaver.

5. Bonnie Wheeler, "Romance and Parataxis and Malory: The Case of Sir Gawain's Reputation," in *Arthurian Literature XII*, ed. James P. Carley and Felicity Riddy (Cambridge: Brewer, 1993), pp. 109–32; quotation from p. 111.

6. "Reading Malory Aloud: Then and Now," ed. Karen Cherewatuk and Joyce Coleman, special issue, *Arthuriana* 13.4 (2003).

7. Rosamund S. Allen, "Reading Malory Aloud: Syntax, Gender, and Narrative Pace," *Arthuriana* 13.4 (2003): 71–85; Janet Jesmok, "Reading Malory Aloud: Poetic Qualities and Distinctive Voice," *Arthuriana* 13.4 (2003): 86–102; Michael Twomey, "The Voice of Aurality in the *Morte Darthur*," *Arthuriana* 13.4 (2003): 103–18.

8. Malcom B. Parkes has written a history of the invention of punctuation by printers: chapter 6, "The Technology of Printing and the Stabilization of the Symbols," in his *Pause and Effect: An Introduction to the History of Punctuation in the West* (Berkeley: University of California Press, 1993), pp. 50–61.

9. In this paper, all quotations from Malory's text come from the Winchester Manuscript and/or from *The Works of Sir Thomas Malory*, ed. Eugène Vinaver, and are noted parenthetically by folio and/or by volume, page, and line numbers. Bolded text duplicates rubrication in the manuscript. I am grateful to Michelle Brown, curator of illuminated manuscripts at the British Library, and to other personnel of the British Library who have made BL Additional MS 59678 available to me several times over the past decade. I have supplemented my use of the manuscript by referring to N. R. Ker, ed., *The Winchester Malory: A Facsimile*, EETS s.s. 4 (London: Oxford University Press, 1976).

10. P. J. C. Field, "Description and Narration in Malory," *Speculum* 43 (1968): 476–86; quotation p. 478.

11. Field, *Romance and Chronicle*, pp. 479, 480.

12. Allen, "Reading Malory Aloud," p. 81.

13. Joyce Coleman, *Public Reading and the Reading Public in Late Medieval England and France* (Cambridge: Cambridge University Press, 1996); see also her "On beyond Ong: Taking the Paradox out of 'Oral Literacy' (and 'Literate Orality')," in *Medieval Insular Literature between the Oral and the Written II: Continuity of Transmission*, ed. Hildegard L. C. Tristram (Tübingen: Narr, 1997), pp. 155–76. The earlier works are Ruth Crosby's "Oral

Delivery in the Middle Ages," *Speculum* 11 (1936): 88–110, and her later "Chaucer and the Custom of Oral Delivery," *Speculum* 13 (1938): 413–32. See also William Nelson's "From 'Listen, Lordings' to 'Dear Reader,'" *University of Toronto Quarterly* 46 (1976–77): 110–24.

14. Clauses continued to be the central units of written material for well over a century. P. J. C. Field has also observed the clause phenomenon; see his *Romance and Chronicle*, pp. 40–41.

15. Janet Jesmok discusses "[a]ssonance and alliteration, word repetition, [and] silences" in her *Arthuriana* essay, "Reading Malory Aloud" (p. 87). She, too, focuses on the "watirs wap" passage for part of her discussion (pp. 88–89), as I do in the following paragraphs.

16. Jeannette Marshall Denton—now Jeannette Marsh, "A Historical Linguistic Description of Sir Thomas Malory's Dialect," *Arthuriana* 13.4 (Winter 2003): 14–47.

17. Many have commented upon Malory's use of alliteration. One must begin with N. F. Blake's "Late Medieval Prose" in *History of Literature in the English Language*, ed. W. F. Bolton, vol. 1, *The Middle Ages* (London: Barrie and Jenkins, 1970), pp. 371–403. Blake presents a stimulating example of Malory's both shortening and refining his alliterative source (pp. 397–99), and concludes that Malory's work "was magnificent, but . . . exceptional" (p. 397). P. J. C. Field comments on alliteration in several places in *Romance and Chronicle*, but see especially pp. 73–76, where he comments on alliteration as a strength in many phrases but deplores it in the "Roman Wars" section (p. 73). Terence McCarthy and Jeremy Smith have also noted Malory's alliteration; see McCarthy, "The Sequence of Malory's Tales," in *Aspects of Malory*, ed. Toshiyuki Takamiya and Derek Brewer (Cambridge: Brewer, 1981; repr. 1986), pp. 107–24 (esp. p. 111), and Smith, "Language and Style in Malory," in *A Companion to Malory*, ed. Elizabeth Archibald and A. S. G. Edwards (Cambridge: Brewer, 1996), pp. 97–113; alliteration, pp. 106–7.

18. As with his alliteration, I am not the first to comment upon Malory's sense of rhythm. One of the first must have been George Saintsbury, in his *History of English Prose Rhythm* (London: Macmillan, 1912; repr. Bloomington: Indiana University Press, 1965). Saintsbury shows how much Malory changes and adapts the stanzaic *Morte Arthur* in his own recounting of Guenevere's opening speech in her last meeting with Lancelot. Malory's process here, as throughout his *Morte*, says Saintsbury, was to weave "a quite new rhythm, accompanying and modulating graceful and almost majestic prose of the best type. There had been nothing in English prose before like [this]" (p. 85). Most recently, Jeremy Smith, in "Language and Style in Malory," comments lucidly upon Malory's sense of rhythm (p. 107).

19. For a fuller treatment of Malory's rhetorical balance, or envelope structure, see D. Thomas Hanks, Jr., and Jennifer L. Fish, "Beside the Point: Medieval Meanings vs. Modern Impositions in Editing Malory's *Morte Darthur*," *Neuphilologische Mitteilungen* 98.3 (1997): 273–89.

The Scottish *Lancelot of the Laik* and Malory's *Morte Darthur*: Contrasting Approaches to the Same Story

Edward Donald Kennedy

> This storie is also trewe, I undertake,
> As is the book of Launcelot de Lake,
> That wommen holde in ful greet reverence.[1]

The Scots-English *Lancelot of the Laik*, found in Cambridge University Library Kk.1.5.vii, is an incomplete mid-to-late fifteenth-century verse adaptation of the noncyclic Prose *Lancelot do Lac*'s account of the love of Lancelot and Guenevere and of the knight Galehot's war against Arthur. A better known and quite different account of Lancelot in English is in Sir Thomas Malory's *Morte Darthur*, completed in 1469/70 and published by William Caxton in 1485. *Lancelot of the Laik* is based upon a source with a happy ending: the *Lancelot do Lac* ends with Lancelot establishing his reputation as Arthur's greatest knight and winning the love of Guenevere. Malory, however, drew upon the Vulgate (Lancelot-Grail) Cycle's account of the love of Lancelot and Guenevere, which includes most of the noncyclic *Lancelot do Lac* but also tells of the results of the adulterous love: it causes Lancelot's failure on the Grail Quest and contributes to the destruction of Arthur's kingdom before reaching its resolution through the lovers' penance and salvation. The different sources that the author of *Lancelot of the Laik* and Malory used give contrasting interpretations of the love story, and although Malory apparently had access to the material found in *Lancelot do Lac*, he chose not to use it. The author of *Lancelot of the Laik* may have been moved to write his version as a reaction against Malory's version, but since there is no proof that he had read Malory's account, he simply may not have seen the tragic potential of the story.

Although *Lancelot of the Laik* breaks off at line 3487, with an estimated three thousand additional lines needed to complete the story,[2] a summary at the beginning indicates how it was to end: the author's subject is "the weirs . . . Of Arthur in defending of his lond / Frome Galiot"; how Lancelot came to Arthur's defense; how, thanks to Lancelot, Arthur and Galiot made peace; and how Venus rewarded Lancelot by granting him his lady's love.[3] It was intended as a partial adaptation of its French source. Its author, like Chaucer in the *Knight's Tale*, uses the rhetorical device of *occupatio* to tell us in eighty lines (214–94) what he is not going to discuss, that is, he is not going to tell us about Lancelot's birth, his being brought up by the Lady of the Lake, his falling in love with Guenevere, his vowing to avenge a wounded knight, his being sent to defend the lady of Noralt, his conquest of Dolorous Garde, or his rescue of Gawain and others. The list continues, and he probably added this for those in his presumably aristocratic audience familiar with the source. Any one of the omitted adventures, he admits, "mycht mak o gret story" (296), but he will leave the task of adapting them to others.

The work is framed as a love vision in which the narrator, like Chaucer in the *Legend of Good Women* and Gower in *Confessio Amantis*, wanders into the woods on a spring morning, falls into a trance, and dreams. In his dream a bird tells him that the god of love wants him to write "for thi lady sak" a declaration of love based upon "sum trety . . . / That wnkouth is" (145–47). The narrator recalls a story "boith of loue, and armys" (200), the story of Lancelot, and prays for inspiration from an anonymous "flour of poyetis" (320), probably Chaucer. In fact, the choice of subject may have been inspired by Chaucer's statement that the tale of Launcelot de Lake is one that "wommen holde in ful greet reverence" (even though Chaucer's relegating it to the equivalent of today's supermarket romances is hardly complimentary).[4]

Sally Mapstone, contrasting *Lancelot of the Laik* with the tragedy that Malory produced, describes the former as optimistic.[5] Mapstone is concerned primarily with the part of the romance focused on Arthur, and she points out that although in this romance a wise man severely criticizes Arthur, his kingdom will not be destroyed as it is in Malory's account, and Arthur learns to become a better king. To this I would add that the romance also presents optimism concerning the love of Lancelot and Guenevere. The author of *Lancelot of the Laik*, like the author of the French *Lancelot do Lac*, gives no indication that he saw that the story of the adultery of a queen and the king's greatest knight could lead to tragedy.

The Scottish romance is an example of a reader's response to the non-cyclic French prose *Lancelot* that contrasts sharply with that of the "architect" who planned the Vulgate version or of Dante.[6] The Vulgate architect must have believed that a story that glorified the adulterous love of the queen and the king's best knight should not have a happy ending; he consequently incorporated most of the *Lancelot do Lac* into his series of romances that would tell the disastrous consequences of that love.[7] Dante, who, like the Scottish author, probably knew the *Lancelot do Lac* rather than the Vulgate version, similarly saw possibilities for tragedy in the story along with the irresponsibility of an author who would write a work that might encourage marital infidelity. The noncyclic romance would have probably been the version that caused Paolo and Francesca to commit adultery and go to hell (*Inferno*, canto 5). Such speculation about the version Dante had read is tempting since, although he knew the Vulgate *Mort Artu*, his references to the *Lancelot* refer to the part covered by the noncyclic version[8] (one of the surviving copies of which is a thirteenth-century manuscript in Florence[9]). Although there is no evidence that Dante read that particular manuscript, its existence indicates that this version was in circulation in Italy.

To the modern reader, one of the peculiarities of the Scottish version is that although the author omits a great deal of the *Lancelot do Lac*, he devotes about a fourth of the extant romance to an adaptation of the French source's account of a wise man's lecture to Arthur on his shortcomings as king. This would have seemed less unusual to a Scottish audience since a number of writers of the period treated traditional subject matter (legends of Troy and Alexander as well as of Arthur) from "the perspectives of kingly conduct."[10] Although most of the advice about Arthur's failings is in the French source, it is similar to advice found in *speculum regis* literature that, judging from the number of surviving manuscripts in Latin and vernaculars, appealed to readers interested in moral edification. Contemporary Scottish examples of the genre include Gilbert Haye's translation of *Secreta secretorum* (1456) and John Ireland's *Meroure of Wysdome* (1490). As R. J. Lyall points out, such advice could be paralleled in other English and Scottish literature written between 1450 and 1580 intended for "the moral and political edification of successive kings."[11] Although political content in a love poem might now seem strange, medieval readers familiar with Gower's *Confessio Amantis*—a work ostensibly about love but whose seventh book is a manual for princes—would have found it less so. This part of *Lancelot of the Laik* probably appealed to whoever compiled its manuscript, which also includes moral treatises such as *Ratis Ravyng* and *Craft of Dying* and political treatises like *Ye Grete Lawis of Scotland* and Christine de Pizan's *Body of Polycye*.[12]

The political content appears prominently shortly after the lovesick narrator concludes his prologue and falls into a trance. He dreams of Arthur, who has had two dreams that involved not love but visions of his hair and intestines falling out. Arthur soon learns that Galehot, son of the fair giant, is about to invade his kingdom with one hundred thousand men and that his own men will fail him. A counselor, Amytans, says that God will destroy him for his wickedness. Amytans berates Arthur for his failings as a king; the list of these failings includes neglecting the poor, being avaricious, and failing to be just and merciful (1320–88).

To some, this portrait of Arthur as a weak king who must be lectured on his duties seems appropriate for a Scottish Arthurian romance. Although references to Arthur in some works like Barbour's *Bruce*, Hary's *Wallace*, and the chronicle of Andrew of Wyntoun are positive, the attitude toward him in many others, beginning with the fourteenth- and early fifteenth-century Latin chronicles of John of Fordun and Walter Bower, is critical and at times hostile.[13] These chroniclers were reacting against the English who since the late thirteenth century had used Geoffrey of Monmouth's account of Arthur's hegemony over Scotland to bolster their own claims to Scotland. Although the catalogue of Arthur's shortcomings in *Lancelot of the Laik* corresponds somewhat to the negative attitude toward Arthur found in these chronicles, anti-Arthurian bias is probably not a major factor in accounting for the selection of this material from the French prose *Lancelot*: Arthur nevertheless has great knights like Gawain and Ywain, and Lancelot, the hero of the poem, supports him. Moreover, Arthur heeds the wise man's advice and becomes a better king. The Scottish author is also less severe in his criticism of Arthur than the French source, where the wise man calls Arthur the worst of all sinners.[14]

Furthermore, the narrator says that he is going to tell how Lancelot makes peace between Arthur and Galehot, and thus Galehot will further enhance the court by swearing loyalty to Arthur. Another indication that the author did not wish to present a purely anti-Arthurian romance is indicated by his apparently not planning to present the account of Arthur's failings found in the conclusion of *Lancelot do Lac*. At that moment—before Guenevere and Lancelot consummate their relationship—Arthur commits adultery with the Saxon Camille. Arthur later believes that the false Guenevere is his wife and plans to have the real Guenevere scalped, her palms skinned, and then have her dragged through the town and burned alive.[15] The Scottish author does not mention either of these episodes in his prologue, either among the stories he will not discuss or among those he will.

It is tempting to speculate that *Lancelot of the Laik* might have been written as an alternative to Malory's *Morte Darthur*, as an Arthurian comedy where all turns out well in opposition to Malory's tragedy. The date of *Lancelot of the Laik*, however, is uncertain, and nothing indicates that its author had read Malory's work. Any date of composition between the mid-fifteenth century and the date of the copying of *Lancelot of the Laik* (near the end of the century) is possible. Suggested dates range from ca. 1460 to ca. 1490. Scholars have tried to associate the political advice given to Arthur with the reign of the weak James III,[16] but the problem with attempts to find allusions to James's reign is that much of the advice corresponds to what is in the French source and the rest, as mentioned above, is typical of *speculum regis* literature. Nevertheless, *Lancelot of the Laik* could have been written late in the century, after the publication of Malory's book in 1485. This is possible even if one accepts the theory that it reflects concern with the reign of James III, since Caxton's edition of Malory appeared three years before James's death in 1488. The narrator, by indicating at the outset that he is going to tell "sum trety . . . / That wnkouth is" (145–47), could be making an oblique reference to his romance's being part of Lancelot's story that Malory omits.

Malory's third (and shortest) tale, the "Tale of Lancelot," concerns, like *Lancelot of the Laik*, Lancelot's establishing his reputation as a knight; however, this tale fails to include much of the content of the Vulgate *Lancelot*, which runs to eight volumes of text in Alexandre Micha's edition.[17] It does not draw for its adventures upon parts of the Vulgate based upon the noncyclic version. Its few episodes are derived from the third and final part of the Vulgate *Lancelot* and from another French romance, the *Perlesvaus*. Lancelot sets out because "he thought himself to preve in straunge adventures."[18] Characters in it mention rumors of Lancelot's love for Guenevere (1:257, 270, 281), which he denies, and it has been argued that his denial indicates that the tale takes place before Guenevere loves him.[19] There is, however, little basis for such an argument: Lancelot, to protect his lady's honor, would have denied the love whether it were true or not, as he later does in tale 8 when he returns Guenevere to Arthur's court (3:1197). Within the context of the Vulgate *Lancelot*, the events in Malory's tale take place after Lancelot and Guenevere have consummated their relationship. Later in his seventh tale, Malory returns to the Vulgate Lancelot for the story ultimately derived from Chrétien's *Chevalier de la Charrette*. The source for this episode also occurs later than the adventures in the first part of the Vulgate *Lancelot* that were based upon *Lancelot do Lac*.

However, although Malory did not adapt episodes from the first part of the Vulgate *Lancelot*, he had at some point read it. In the "Poisoned Apple" episode of Malory's seventh tale, when Arthur thanks Lancelot for rescuing Guenevere, Lancelot replies: "My lorde . . . y ought . . . ever [to be] in youre quarell and in my ladyes the quenys quarell to do batayle, for ye are the man that gaff me the hygh Order of Knyghthode, and that day my lady, youre queen, ded me worshyp. And ellis had I bene shamed, for that same day that ye made me knight, thorow my hastynes I loste my swerde, and my lady, youre quene, founde hit . . . and gave me my swerde whan I had nede thereto" (2:1058). That is not in Malory's major sources for that tale, the Vulgate *Mort Artu* and the English stanzaic *Morte Arthur*: Lancelot is recalling an event from the first part of the prose *Lancelot* when he was made knight. Admittedly it does not happen quite like that in the French romance, for Arthur is there a bungler who forgets an important part of the knighting ceremony, the belting on of the knight's sword.[20] This difference could be due to Malory's forgetting the details, to his presenting Lancelot as being too courteous to mention a mistake that his king had made, or to Malory's wishing to present Arthur more favorably than he appears in the French *Lancelot*. Moreover, descriptive details from Lancelot's fight with giants in Malory's "Tale of Lancelot" in which the giants are armed "with two horryble clubbys" (1:271) were probably drawn from the first part of the Vulgate *Lancelot*.[21] These references suggest that Malory had at some point read the part of the Vulgate *Lancelot* that corresponds to the noncyclic version but chose not to use it.

Malory would not have liked much of the early part of the French *Lancelot*. Judging from Malory's general expressions of admiration for Arthur—"the moste kynge and nobelyst knyght of the worlde" (3:1229), for one example—he probably would not have cared to reproduce a lecture on Arthur's inadequacies as a king or tell of his adultery with Camille or of his cruelty and stupidity in the false Guenevere episode. Moreover, he would have been unlikely to celebrate as the Scottish Arthur did Lancelot's success in winning his lady. Malory never condemns the lovers, and he apparently sympathized with them since he blames Mordred and Aggravaine for the civil war rather than Lancelot and Guenevere (see 3:1154, 1161); however, their actions helped destroy the kingdom, and, judging from the ending in which both Lancelot and Guenevere acknowledge their sins, he also realized, as Dante and the authors of the Vulgate cycle did, that it would have been best if they had never fallen in love.

What is evident from *Lancelot of the Laik*'s emphasis on Amytan's lecture to Arthur is that the author was interested in politics, and as Mapstone points out, it is optimistic in that Arthur learns from his mistakes.[22] What is surprising, however, and what critics have missed, is that an author so interested in politics failed to see that an ending in which Lancelot wins Guenevere's love could not have been satisfactory or optimistic from a political point of view: in betraying the king the lovers were committing treason. Dante interpreted this as morally wrong, and the authors of the Vulgate Cycle, Malory, and (probably) Chrétien saw its political dimension as well. In *Lancelot of the Laik*, however, although Arthur will become a better king and his kingdom will be strengthened through Lancelot's help, Lancelot is rewarded with Guenevere's love. There is no indication that the author saw any problem with this. Near the beginning of the romance, he explains that "to translait the romans of that knycht" is beyond his ability: "Myne ignorans may it not comprehende" (211–13). This is, of course, a conventional modesty topos. However, in this case one might wonder if there is not some truth in the statement and if, in fact, the author failed, like the author of his French source, to understand the implications of a happy ending that involved the betrayal of a king.

NOTES

1. Geoffrey Chaucer, *The Nun's Priest's Tale*, lines 3211–13, in *The Riverside Chaucer*, ed. Larry D. Benson, 3rd ed. (Boston: Houghton Mifflin, 1987), p. 258.

2. Elizabeth Archibald, "*Lancelot of the Laik*: Sources, Genre, Reception," in *The Scots and Medieval Arthurian Legend*, ed. Rhiannon Purdie and Nicola Royal (Cambridge: D.S. Brewer, 2005), pp. 71–82, at p. 73.

3. *Lancelot of the Laik and Sir Tristrem*, ed. Alan Lupack (Kalamazoo, MI: Medieval Institute Publications, 1994), lines 299–314. Subsequent references to this edition will appear within parentheses within the text. For a general discussion of the romance, see Flora Alexander, "*Lancelot of the Laik*," in *The Arthur of the English*, ed. W. R. J. Barron (Cardiff: University of Wales Press, 2001), pp. 146–50. The source is *Lancelot do Lac: The Non-Cyclic Old French Prose Romance*, ed. Elspeth Kennedy, 2 vols. (Oxford: Clarendon Press, 1980).

4. Chaucer may have been referring to the Vulgate version of this romance but probably not to Chrétien de Troyes's romance, usually identified in medieval manuscripts as *Le Chevalier de la Charrette*. See my "Gower, Chaucer, and French Prose Arthurian Romance," *Mediaevalia* 16 (1993 [for 1990]): 62–69.

5. Sally Mapstone, "The Scots, the French, and the English: An Arthurian Episode," in *The European Sun*, ed. Graham Caie, Roderick J. Lyall, Sally Mapstone, and Kenneth Simpson (East Linton: Tuckwell, 2001), pp. 138, 142–44; Sally Mapstone, "Kingship and the *Kingis Quair*," in *The Long Fifteenth Century*, ed. Helen Cooper and Sally Mapstone (Oxford: Clarendon Press, 1997), pp. 61–62.

6. For discussion of the "architect," see Jean Frappier, "The Vulgate Cycle," in *Arthurian Literature in the Middle Ages*, ed. Roger Sherman Loomis (Oxford: Clarendon Press, 1959), pp. 315–17.

7. Similarly Chrétien must have realized that a happy ending to his *Chevalier de la Charrette* was impossible since he turned it over to Godefroi de Leigni to complete. See Chrétien de Troyes, *The Knight of the Cart*, in *Arthurian Romances*, trans. William W. Kibler (London: Penguin, 1991), pp. 207–94, at p. 294.

8. Daniela Delcorno Branca, "Dante and the *Roman de Lancelot*," in *Text and Intertext in Medieval Arthurian Literature*, ed. Norris J. Lacy (New York: Garland, 1996), pp. 133–45, at 135–36.

9. Kennedy, *Lancelot do Lac*, 2:7.

10. A. S. G. Edwards, "Contextualizing Middle Scots Romance," in *A Palace in the Wild*, ed. L. A. J. R. Houwen, A. A. MacDonald, and S. L. Mapsone (Leuven: Peeters, 2000), pp. 61–73, at p. 72; also Mapstone, "Kingship," p. 62.

11. R. J. Lyall, "Politics and Poetry in Fifteenth and Sixteenth Century Scotland," *Scottish Literary Journal* 3.2 (1976): 5–29, at pp. 20, 25.

12. For the content of the manuscript, see Archibald, "*Lancelot of the Laik*," pp. 79–80.

13. Karl Heinz Göller, "King Arthur in the Scottish Chronicles," trans. Edward Donald Kennedy, in *King Arthur: A Casebook*, ed. Edward Donald Kennedy (New York: Garland, 1996), pp. 176–80 (Göller's date for Bellenden's chronicle—1591—is a typo for 1531; I reproduced the error in my translation). Also see Flora Alexander, "Late Medieval Attitudes to the Figure of King Arthur: A Reassessment," *Anglia* 93 (1975): 17–34; Nicola Royan, "'Na les vailyeant than ony uthir princis of Britane': Representations of Arthur in Scotland, 1480–1540," *Scottish Studies Review* 3.1 (2002): 9–20; Royan, "The Fine Art of Faint Praise in Older Scots Historiography," in Purdie and Royal, *Scots and Medieval*

Arthurian Legend, pp. 43–54. Steve Boardman contrasts positive accounts of Arthur in vernacular texts and negative ones in Latin texts ("Late Medieval Scotland and the Matter of Britain," in *Scottish History: The Power of the Past*, ed. Edward J. Cowan and Richard J. Finlay [Edinburgh: Edinburgh University Press, 2002], pp. 47–72); the vernacular *Scottis originale*, however, is an exception to Boardman's thesis.

14. Mapstone, "Scots, the French, and the English," p. 142; Alexander, "Late Medieval Attitudes," pp. 25–28.

15. Kennedy, *Lancelot do Lac*, pp. 546, 591–608; *Lancelot of the Lake*, trans. Corin Corley (Oxford: Oxford University Press, 1989), pp. 379, 415–17 (summary).

16. For a survey see Mapstone, "Scots, the French, and the English," pp. 135–37; also Mapstone, "Kingship," p. 61; Bertram Vogel, "Secular Politics and the Date of *Lancelot of the Laik*," *Studies in Philology* 40 (1943): 1–13, at p. 10; Karl Heinz Göller, *König Arthur in der englischen Literatur des späten Mittelalters* (Göttingen: Vandenhoeck & Ruprecht, 1963), p. 130n58; Alexander, "Late Medieval Attitudes," p. 28. Mapstone tentatively favors a date early in the reign of James III—late 1460s, early 1470s, when he was young and the advice might have done some good.

17. See *Lancelot*, ed. Alexandre Micha, 9 vols. (Geneva: Droz, 1978–82). The ninth volume consists of notes and glossary. The brevity of Malory's "Tale of Lancelot" could have been due to the influence of the brief *Lancelot* section of the post-Vulgate *Roman du Graal*; see my "Malory's 'Noble Tale of Sir Launcelot du Lake,' the Vulgate *Lancelot*, and the Post-Vulgate *Roman du Graal*," in *Arthurian and Other Studies Presented to Shunichi Noguchi*, ed. Takashi Suzuki and Tsuyoshi Mukai (Cambridge: D. S. Brewer, 1993), pp. 107–29, at pp. 111–19.

18. Sir Thomas Malory, *The Works of Sir Thomas Malory*, ed. Eugène Vinaver, 3rd ed., rev. P. J. C. Field, 3 vols. (Oxford: Clarendon Press, 1990), 1:253. Subsequent references to Malory will appear within parentheses in the text.

19. See R. M. Lumiansky, "'The Tale of Lancelot': Prelude to Adultery," in *Malory's Originality*, ed. R. M. Lumiansky (Baltimore: Johns Hopkins, 1964), pp. 91–98.

20. Kennedy, *Lancelot do Lac*, 1:164–65; Corley, *Lancelot*, pp. 79–82.

21. See Kennedy, *Lancelot do Lac*, 1:270; Corley, *Lancelot*, p. 221. See my discussion of the fights with giants in Malory's version and the first part of the Vulgate *Lancelot* ("Malory and His English Sources," in *Aspects of Malory*, ed. Toshiyuki Takamiya and Derek Brewer [Cambridge; D. S. Brewer, 1981], pp. 27–55, at pp. 33–35).

22. Mapstone, "Kingship," p. 61.

"The Strength of Ten": The Cultural Resonance of Tennyson's "Sir Galahad"

Alan Lupack

Tennyson's poem "Sir Galahad," written in 1834 and first published in 1842, opens with lines whose impact far exceeded their quality:

> My good blade carves the casques of men,
>   My tough lance thrusteth sure,
> My strength is as the strength of ten,
>   Because my heart is pure.

In the author's preface to her novel *Blessed Bastard* (1997), Ruth P. M. Lehmann quotes this passage and comments that "in four lines [Tennyson] makes an inhuman monster of [Galahad]."[1] But that was not the view of nineteenth- and early twentieth-century readers. Though Tennyson's "Sir Galahad" can hardly be considered a masterpiece of Victorian verse or of Arthurian literature, it was nevertheless widely known in its day and has had a resonance in British and American culture greater than that achieved by poems that are much more highly prized by critics. Frequently published in editions of Tennyson's works, the poem was also the subject of a couple of notable illustrations. Dante Gabriel Rossetti (1828–82) provided one such illustration for the 1857 Moxon Tennyson (see figure 1),[2] which depicts Galahad at the altar of a "secret shrine." Beneath the altar are two ladies, one ringing the bell mentioned by Tennyson. Perhaps they are the source of the "solemn chaunts" that Galahad hears; and perhaps they remind viewers of the ladies whom Galahad saves "from shame and thrall" but whose sweet looks mean little to him since "all my heart is drawn above."

Tennyson's poem also inspired an 1858 drawing by Edward Burne-Jones (1833–98), which "portrays a dreamy, contemplative youth, naïve rather than stalwart in his dedication."[3] As Marilynn Lincoln Board has observed, this Galahad

Figure 1. Dante Gabriel Rossetti's illustration for Tennyson's "Sir Galahad" in the 1857 Moxon Tennyson.

"is oblivious to the temptations of youth that surround him," temptations represented by ladies and musicians, as he pursues his quest.[4] For Burne-Jones, Galahad was an inspirational ideal. Early in his life, in fact, Burne-Jones planned to found an Order of Sir Galahad, "a small conventual society of cleric and lay members working in the heart of London." And he recommended to one correspondent and potential member that he "Learn 'Sir Galahad' by heart."[5]

But the artwork most closely associated with "Sir Galahad" was the painting *Sir Galahad* (1862) by George Frederic Watts (1817–1904)—though Watts denied that he had Tennyson's poem in mind when he painted the picture.[6] Despite "a substantial quantity of circumstantial evidence that suggests otherwise," his second wife "claimed that he had not read [Tennyson's] poem at the time he conceived *Sir Galahad*"; and when a version of the painting was exhibited in 1881–82, "instead of a quotation from Tennyson's poem Watts requested that it be accompanied by a passage from Chaucer's Canterbury Tales describing the Squire who was 'a lover and a lusty bachelor,' though 'courteous and serviceable.'"[7] Watts's *Sir Galahad* was well known and widely reproduced, largely because of the moral qualities that it evoked. One art critic has asserted that "Watts's picture was eventually to take Sir Galahad out of the private, esoteric world of Burne-Jones and his circle and present him to a wider public as an ideal type, a model for young manhood."[8] But it may be that this effect was possible only because the painting was linked to Tennyson's poem, the opening lines of which were often quoted because they seemed to epitomize a view of chivalry that appealed to the Victorian era and the early twentieth century. In fact, in this period there was a symbiotic intertextual relationship between the painting and the poem, each of which had a greater popularity and cultural resonance because of its association with the other. They combined to offer a moral view of chivalry that allowed young men to imagine themselves living in the spirit of Arthurian knighthood.

The intertwining of Tennyson's poem and Watts's painting in the popular mind, as well as the understanding of both as inspirational, can be seen in *Sir Galahad: A Call to the Heroic* by James Burns.[9] Burns evokes a version of the Watts painting[10] presented by the artist to Eton College and the quotation from Tennyson's "Sir Galahad" (as well as quotations from the *Idylls*) to encourage and inspire the young soldiers who would be called to the "great purpose" of fighting in defense of Britain in World War I.[11] Burns uses the two lines from Tennyson as an epigraph on the title page, facing the frontispiece reproduction of Watts's *Sir Galahad* (see figure 2). He also refers to them in the body of his treatise as he comments on the fact that the Galahad of the painting seems too frail for the task he has undertaken, which Burns defines not as seeking the Grail but rather as contending with "the relentless and implacable forces of evil at work in the world," an obviously revisionist reading of the Grail story to make Galahad a suitable model for his audience. His conclusion is that Watts's vision was correct because "the mighty things of life are not the physical but spiritual." Burns continues his inspirational rhetoric as he explains the advantage British youth will have against their enemies:

> "Fervour," said Napoleon, "counts against numbers on the field of battle as three to one." But there is something which, when the human heart possesses it, more than trebles that ratio. It is the pure heart, flaming with a lofty ideal, and conscious of the righteousness of its cause. Nothing in this world can compare with the impetuous valour of men thus possessed.
>
> "My strength is as the strength of ten,
>   Because my heart is pure,"
>
> cries Sir Galahad with radiant joy, and right at the entrenched forces of evil he hurls himself, fearing God and knowing no other fear. And at

SIR GALAHAD

A CALL TO THE HEROIC

BY

JAMES BURNS, M.A.

Author of "The Happy Warrior," etc., etc.

"My strength is as the strength of ten
Because my heart is pure"

LONDON
JAMES CLARKE & CO.
13 & 14, FLEET STREET

Figure 2. Frontispiece and title page of *Sir Galahad: A Call to the Heroic* (1915) by James Burns.

the flash of his sword the legions of darkness roll back, for no cohorts, however consolidated, can stand against the impetuous rush of those whose hearts are set on fire by God, who have seen the Vision, and whose spears are levelled against iniquity.[12]

Burns is sure that in the face of the barbarism and cruelty of the enemies who threaten "national existence" and who oppose "the cause of God," the young "Galahads" of Britain will not prove "recreant" since they "listen to the voice within" and are "of the pure in heart." He concludes that "their strength is as the strength of ten; for they fight not for love of conquest, but for love of God, for the eternal rights of man, and for the precious things of peace."[13]

Tennyson's familiar lines appear again in a very different context. In an advertisement for Michelin tires that was published in *The Sphere* on March 13, 1915, "we see the Michelin Man lying in the English Channel pushing away a German torpedo and surrounding a mine as enemy U-boats sail away and a Zeppelin flies overhead, as he states, 'My strength is as the strength of ten, because my rubber's pure'" (see figure 3).[14] The slogan had appeared earlier on a poster created in 1905 to mark the introduction of Michelin tires into Britain. In that image, Sir Bibendum (the name given to the Michelin Man because Michelin tires drink up road obstacles) was depicted as a knight, with helmet, spurred sabatons, a lance, and a shield.[15] Thus the Michelin marketers appealed to the Tennysonian notions of purity and purpose to suggest the superiority—indeed the uniqueness—of their product.

But the commercial uses were secondary to the social. The Galahads of Tennyson's poem and Watts's painting were inseparably linked as the epitome of youthful virtue and dedication. Christine Poulson has demonstrated that the figure of Watts's Galahad was often used in memorial stained-glass windows to commemorate young men who had died in World War I as well as some who had died in peacetime. These windows were occasionally, though not always, accompanied by Tennyson's lines about the strength of ten.[16] In addition, "Watts' painting hung in nurseries and schoolrooms throughout England and the British Empire. Like Tennyson's poem, its popularity was based upon its capacity to inspire boys toward masculine virtue" and toward the defense of British imperialism.[17] So essential did the Tennysonian concept of Galahad become that when Eleanor Boss retold the Grail story in 1930, largely through quotations from the "Holy Grail" idyll, she wrote of Galahad's singing that his strength is "as the strength of ten" not out of pride but rather in "praise and thanksgiving to God."[18]

As widely known as Watts's painting and Tennyson's poem were in Britain, they seem to have been even more prevalent in America where the moral view of knighthood they proposed allowed young boys from any class to identify with and imitate the heroes of chivalry. In fact, the notion of the strength of ten echoes throughout American culture of the late nineteenth century and the twentieth century.

Figure 3. Advertisement for Michelin tires published in *The Sphere* on March 13, 1915.

Tennyson's lines are repeated in a number of nineteenth-century American literary works. Elizabeth Stuart Phelps (1844–1911), who reshapes and deliberately deconstructs the romantic Arthurian images created by Tennyson and other male writers, treats Galahad in her poem "The Terrible Test."[19] She describes Galahad as a person "whose strength was the strength of ten" and who is recognized as "the eidolon of holiness" because he is "pure in deed, and word, and thought." But she refers to Christ's taking on flesh and suggests that only this one perfect model is necessary. Thus Galahad's "test" is terrible not because of its difficulty but because it has cost him his humanity. African-American poet Eloise A. (Alberta) Bibb, in "In Memoriam Frederick Douglass" (1895), makes an implicit comparison between Galahad and abolitionist Frederick Douglass, who labors "With zeal increased and strength of ten / To ameliorate the ills of men."[20] In the novel *Iola Leroy, or, Shadows Uplifted* (1893), by another African-American writer, Frances Ellen Watkins Harper, the title character Mrs. Leroy observes that "we must instill into our young people that the true strength of a race means purity in women and uprightness in men; who can say, with Sir Galahad:—'My strength is the strength of ten, / Because my heart is pure.'"[21] In each of these works, Tennyson's lines represent an ideal—even though Phelps believes that the human is not meant to be ideal. And in Harper's view, the ideal of Galahad is a model for both young men and young women.

Knowledge of Tennyson's poem and Watts's painting increased through the Arthurian youth groups that became widespread in America. The club with the largest membership and the greatest geographic range was the Knights of King Arthur, founded in 1893 by William Byron Forbush, a minister concerned about what he called "the boy problem."[22] An important part of these clubs was a program of reading tales of chivalry and viewing appropriate pictures. A number of the manuals for the Knights of King Arthur specifically recommended that the boys read Tennyson's "Sir Galahad" and that "Every castle hall should be adorned with beautiful pictures. The most familiar and easily obtained is Watts's Sir Galahad. You can buy this for one-half cent, or one, two, or five cents each. You ought to give one to every member of the castle. An artotype size 22x28, large enough for your wall, costs 75 cents. Or a really fine print . . . in permanent colors, in various sizes, may be had at prices from $5 upwards."[23] Similarly, the manual for another youth group, the Order of Sir Galahad, opens with three stanzas, including the first, from Tennyson's poem. Though the frontispiece illustration facing these verses is of Galahad from the Edwin Austin Abbey murals in the Boston Public Library, the manual speaks of Watts's painting as depicting the "young knight of chivalry whose 'strength was as the strength of ten because his heart was pure'" and who represented "a working ideal to interest and transform" the boys.[24] Thus many thousands of boys who belonged to these clubs came to see the Tennyson/Watts Galahad as a model of modern chivalric behavior, and that view was encouraged by the rituals and the imagery associated with the clubs (see figure 4 from Forbush's *The Boys' Round Table*).

In addition to the references in instructional manuals for the youth groups, there is a body of literature inspired by these groups in which Galahad figures prominently. Some of these works are retellings of Arthurian stories, but other more original fiction relies heavily on the notion of the strength of ten. For instance, in the didactic novel *Little Sir Galahad* (1904) by Lillian Holmes, a boy named Arthur Bryan and his friends play at being King Arthur and his knights; he laments to his mother that his friend David cannot play with them because he is crippled. But Mrs. Bryan offers the example of Galahad and quotes from Tennyson's poem "Sir Galahad" about "the strength of ten."[25] In another novel with the same title, *Little Sir Galahad* (1914) by Phoebe Gray, there is also a strong didactic bent, one of the chief messages being the dangers of alcohol. As in Holmes's story, the little Sir Galahad of the title, a boy named Charlie, is crippled, a condition that occurred when his "jovially stimulated" father dropped him. Charlie is enrolled by a young friend, Mary Alice Brown, in a group called the Galahad Knights and is dubbed "little Sir Galahad" by a doctor who finds Charlie's "fidelity to his quest for the Grail ... infinitely fine and touching" and who observes, in a sentiment reminiscent of the inspiration for the Arthurian clubs, that "the development of these rare little souls is the vital problem of our country."[26]

Two other Tennysonian young Sir Galahads appear in a novel in the "Little Colonel" series by Annie Fellows Johnston, one of the most popular turn-of-the-century American authors of children's literature. In her epigraph to the tale of *Two Little Knights of Kentucky* (1899), she sets the tone for her Americanization of chivalry: "knighthood has *not* passed away. The flower of Chivalry has blossomed anew in this new world, and America, too, has her 'Hall of the Shields.'"[27] The New World chivalry is exemplified by Keith and Malcolm MacIntyre when they befriend a boy named Jonesy, who is abandoned by the tramp with whom he has been traveling. To raise money so Jonesy can stay in the care of a kindly but poor old professor, the two boys want to organize a benefit. Their Aunt Allison pleads with her mother, the boys' grandmother, to allow them to hold the benefit by pointing out that it is a way for them to learn the lesson of *The Vision of Sir Launfal*, that what is important is "Not what we give, but what we share, / For the gift without the giver is bare." Feeling that "If this little beggar at the gate can teach them where to find the Holy Grail, through unselfish service to him, I do not want to stand in the way,"[28] the grandmother agrees. The benefit itself takes the form of a pageant in which "the old days of chivalry" will live again through readings from *The Vision of Sir Launfal* and Tennyson's *Idylls*, accompanied by tableaux in which the children don the garb of knights and ladies. The boys exhibit the New World chivalry not by dressing up as knights but by performing an act of charity. As the professor tells Keith, because of his good intentions, "thy shield will never be blank and bare. Already thou hast

Figure 4. A young Galahad is central in the struggle between good and evil in an image from William Byron Forbush's *The Boys' Round Table: A Manual of Boys' Clubs* (1907).

blazoned it with the beauty of a noble purpose, and like Galahad, thou too shalt find the Grail."[29] And when Keith says that if he and Malcolm could keep Jonesy from growing up to be a tramp, that would be "as good a deed as some the real knights did," their aunt calls them "my dear little Sir Galahads." Later she tells them of Tennyson's Sir Galahad, "whose strength was as the strength of ten because his heart was pure." The symbolic nature of the boys' knighthood is underscored when Aunt Allison gives them a badge of knighthood, a white enamel flower with a small diamond in the center. Though they "can't wear armour in these days," wearing "the white flower of a blameless life," like the badges Forbush's Knights of King Arthur wore, reminds them that they "are pledged to right the wrong wherever you find it, in little things as well as great."[30]

Largely under the influence of the Arthurian youth groups, other authors produced collections of didactic tales, often combining Arthurian and other heroes, both medieval and modern. One of these collections, *Pan and His Pipes and Other Tales for Children* (1916) by Katherine Dunlap Cather, incorporated the story of the Holy Grail.[31] Published by the Victor Talking Machine Company, Cather's book had a commercial purpose reminiscent of the use of Tennyson's lines to promote Michelin tires. Each tale is followed by a list of related Victor records. For "The Holy Grail," the list includes recordings of selections from Wagner's *Parsifal* and *Lohengrin*. But it is not from these operas that the Galahad of the story sings. In the course of the story, the opening page of which faces a reproduction of Watts's *Sir Galahad*, Galahad sings the first stanza from Tennyson's "Sir Galahad" as he leads the knights from Arthur's court to the quest.

For Winfield Scott Hall, in the treatise *The Strength of Ten: Telling What Manhood Is and How a Boy May Win It* (1910), Galahad—along with other young heroes—is once again a model for boys. Obviously influenced by chivalric youth groups and a concern for what he perceives as one particular "boy problem," Hall discusses a fictional prehistoric youth named Ab, who invents the bow and arrow; David, who slays Goliath; and Arthurian knights, especially Galahad, whose purity gives him the strength of ten.[32] The treatise is typical, to a point, of the collections of stories that offer models for adolescent behavior; but when Hall speaks of discoveries in European and American laboratories of two fluids produced in the testicles when boys begin to mature, he shifts gears and shows that his primary interest is in his conception of sexual "purity" and not Galahad's purity of heart. Loss of one of these fluids, he contends, prevents proper development into "the high estate of young manhood"—just as, to use Hall's metaphor, a gelding does not develop the same power and indomitable will as a stallion—and so "the highest type of young men never play with their reproductive organs."[33]

The popular perception of Tennysonian moral chivalry can be found again in somewhat secularized fashion in a number of short stories. "The Strength of

Ten" by William H. Hamby, published in 1914 in *Redbook*, tells of Curtis Gilbert, a young lad who displays "chivalry" by confronting his stepbrother, who has made vulgar comments about a young woman.[34] The phrase "the strength of ten" does not appear in the text of the tale, but the title makes it obvious that Curtis is an example of the modern, moral knight. An even less specific allusion to Tennyson's notion of knighthood occurs in another story, Mary S. Cutting's "The Strength of Ten" (1902), in which a man named John Atterbury is struggling to support his family. After being betrayed in a business deal, he does not despair. Instead he asserts himself to obtain a business opportunity that will allow him to pay off his debts and care for his wife and child. As a result, "The current of a mighty strength was in him, dominant, compelling, that strength which in some mysterious way has a volition of its own, apart from him who possesses it, bending men and events to his uses."[35] Though Atterbury's newfound strength seems a far cry from Galahad's "strength of ten," it is clear that Tennyson's phrase has passed so far into the popular consciousness that no other allusion to "Sir Galahad" is needed beyond the title of the story, and that the phrase has come to represent virtually any strength of character. Science fiction writer Algis Budrys is another author to use the theme. In his short story "The Strength of Ten" (1956), that strength is found not in the physical might and abilities of a robot but rather in the conviction, drive, and passion that only a human being can display.[36]

The Tennysonian phrase appears as well in works by better-known twentieth-century writers. In one of T. H. White's great intertextual links in *The Once and Future King* (1958), Lancelot, not his son Galahad, believes that people could have the strength of ten only if their hearts are pure. For this reason Lancelot tries to resist his love for Guenevere. And when he is tricked into sleeping with Elaine, he is distraught because she "had stolen his strength of ten."[37] Some other novelists also use the phrase self-consciously and with a good deal of irony. Such is the case with John Steinbeck, in *The Winter of Our Discontent*, a novel influenced by T. S. Eliot's *The Waste Land* and abounding in Grail allusions. One of Steinbeck's characters, the alcoholic Danny, proclaims that his strength "is the strength of ten because the bottle's here."[38] Another American novelist, Thomas Berger, employs the phrase in his novel *Reinhart in Love* (1962). When Reinhart makes love to his new wife, "the conviction that for the first time in his life he was doing what everybody everywhere approved, gave him the endurance of Galahad, who had the strength of ten because his heart was pure."[39] In a later novel, *Vital Parts*, Berger's Reinhart says that his son "Blainey's favorite [knight] was Sir Galahad, the pure, the dedicated, whose strength was that of ten because his heart was squeaky clean." But Reinhart had considered Galahad too sexless, priggish, obsessive-compulsive; he preferred Launcelot, "who carried about him an aura of stain even in the bowdlerized versions for children."[40]

What is significant about these modern literary allusions to Tennyson's poem is that they depend upon and indeed assume a familiarity with Tennyson's Galahad and the source of his moral strength. The same may be said of the numerous popular allusions. All sorts of men from radically different walks of life are praised for various achievements by the suggestion that they had the strength of ten. An 1883 article on the Confederate dead in the Baltimore *Sun*, for example, calls one soldier killed rushing into gunfire in an attempt to take a hill "that young Galahad . . . whose 'strength was as the strength of ten because his heart was pure.'"[41] A 1926 article in the *Chicago Daily Tribune* records that a politician complains about a decline in political integrity by asking, "Where are the old leaders in shining armor? The trouble today is that we have no Galahad, whose strength is as the strength of ten because his heart was pure."[42] And a 1998 article on the legendary basketball coach John Wooden says that he had "the strength of ten because his heart was pure" (though the article erroneously cites "the good book" rather than Tennyson's poem as the source of the quotation).[43]

The strength of ten even makes its way into cartoons. A 1978 political cartoon in the *Christian Science Monitor* uses Tennyson's lines as a caption to a picture of "Sir Galahad Carter" (President Jimmy Carter) charging the castle of Congress.[44] And a 1998 cartoon in the *New Yorker* depicts a businessman saying to a colleague, "My strength is as the strength of ten, because I'm rich."[45]

These and other examples that could be cited indicate the extent to which the notion of moral knighthood articulated in Tennyson's "Sir Galahad" and transformed into a more general sense of what is good has become a part of popular culture. Galahad's near-unique virtue mirrors the fate of the Grail itself, the unique object which has become a cliché referring merely to something highly desirable in any field or endeavor.

Tennyson's own notion of the quest for the Grail and of Galahad's visionary virtue changed considerably by the time he published "The Holy Grail" idyll in 1869, but his lines about the strength of ten continued to be frequently quoted and widely known because they epitomized a view of knighthood that captured the Victorian imagination. The democratic nature of a chivalry that depended on virtue rather than wealth or social class also appealed to Americans who adapted the concept of moral chivalry in literature and life. At a time when only the wealthy few, like Lord Eglinton and his friends, could even play at being knights—and that rather ingloriously, as accounts of the Eglinton Tournament confirm—Tennyson's Galahad offered a new paradigm, which was the culmination of developments in concepts of chivalry as it was viewed by the postmedieval world and which offered a model for modern men, especially young men, to follow as they attempted to be knights of the nineteenth and twentieth centuries.

NOTES

1. Ruth P. M. Lehmann, *Blessed Bastard: A Novel of Galahad* (San Antonio: Wings Press, 1997), p. vii.
2. This image is reproduced in other editions, such as *The Poetical Works of Alfred Tennyson* (New York: Harper & Brothers, 1870), p. 75.
3. Debra N. Mancoff, "'Because My Heart Is Pure': Sir Edward Burne-Jones and Tennyson's *Sir Galahad*," *Avalon to Camelot* 1.2 (Fall 1983): 26.
4. Marilynn Lincoln Board, "Art's Moral Mission: Reading G. F. Watts's *Sir Galahad*," in *The Arthurian Revival: Essays on Form, Tradition, and Transformation*, ed. Debra N. Mancoff (New York: Garland, 1992), p. 138.
5. G B-J [Georgiana Burne-Jones], *Memorials of Edward Burne-Jones*, 3 vols. (London: Macmillan, 1906), 1:77–78.
6. Christine Poulson, *The Quest for the Grail: Arthurian Legend in British Art, 1840–1920* (Manchester: Manchester University Press, 1999), p. 114.
7. Board, "Art's Moral Mission," pp. 134–35.
8. Poulson, *Quest for the Grail*, p. 114.
9. James Burns, *Sir Galahad: A Call to the Heroic* (London: J. Clarke, 1915). The full text of *Sir Galahad: A Call to the Heroic* is available through *The Camelot Project* (http://www.lib.rochester.edu/camelot/burngala.htm).
10. Board, "Art's Moral Mission," p. 152n1 discusses the four versions of Watts's *Sir Galahad*. The third version (1897) was the one given to Eton College.
11. Burns, *Sir Galahad*, p. 30.
12. Ibid., pp. 17–20.
13. Ibid., pp. 24–27.
14. I am grateful to Peter Harrington of the John Hay Library at Brown University whose excellent online exhibition "Selling in Wartime: Advertisements in *The Sphere*, 1914–1918" first alerted me to this image and who kindly provided me with a scan of it.
15. For a reproduction of the image, see Pierre-Gabriel Gonzalez, *Bibendum: 100 Years of the Michelin Man in Posters* (Paris: Michelin, 1998), p. 144.
16. Poulson, *Quest for the Grail*, pp. 110–13.
17. Board, "Art's Moral Mission," pp. 132–33.
18. Eleanor Boss, *In Quest of the Grail* (London: Marshall, Morgan & Scott, 1930).
19. Elizabeth Stuart Phelps, "The Terrible Test," *Sunday Afternoon* 1 (Jan. 1878): 49. Reprinted in *Songs of the Silent World* (Boston: Houghton Mifflin, 1891), pp. 92–93.
20. Eloise A. Bibb, "In Memoriam Frederick Douglass," in *Poems* (Boston: Monthly Review Press, 1895), pp. 8–9.
21. Frances Ellen Watkins Harper, *Iola Leroy, or, Shadows Uplifted* (Philadelphia: Garrigues Brothers, 1893), p. 254. The Tennysonian allusions in Bibb's poem and Harper's novel were first noted in Barbara Tepa Lupack's essay "King Arthur in Black American Popular Culture," in *New Directions in Arthurian Studies*, ed. Alan Lupack (Cambridge: D. S. Brewer, 2002), pp. 105–21.
22. For a full account of Arthurian youth groups in America, see my essay "Arthurian Youth Groups in America: The Americanization of Knighthood," in *Adapting the Arthurian Legends for Children*, ed. Barbara Tepa Lupack (New York: Palgrave Macmillan, 2004), pp. 197–216.
23. William Byron Forbush and Frank Lincoln Masseck, *The Boys' Round Table: A Manual of the International Order of the Knights of King Arthur* (Potsdam, NY: Frank Lincoln Masseck, 1908), pp. 131 and 139.

24. *The Manual for Leaders of the Order of Sir Galahad Incorporated: A Club for Boys and Men of the Episcopal Church* (Boston: The Order of Sir Galahad, 1921).

25. Lillian Holmes, *Little Sir Galahad* (Chicago: David C. Cook, 1904), pp. 27–28, 35–36.

26. Phoebe Gray, *Little Sir Galahad* (Boston: Small, Maynard, 1914), p. 222.

27. Annie Fellows Johnston, *Two Little Knights of Kentucky: Who Were the "Little Colonel's" Neighbours* (Boston: L. C. Page, 1899). The epigraph repeats a passage that appears on p. 116.

28. Ibid., pp. 96–97.

29. Ibid., p. 109.

30. Ibid., pp. 120–22.

31. Katherine Dunlap Cather, *Pan and His Pipes and Other Tales for Children* (Camden, NJ: Victor Talking Machine Company, 1916). "The Holy Grail" appears on pp. 64–71.

32. Winfield Scott Hall, *The Strength of Ten: Telling What Manhood Is and How a Boy May Win It* (La Crosse, WI: B. Steadwell, 1910), p. 36.

33. Ibid., pp. 54–60.

34. William H. Hamby, "The Strength of Ten," *Redbook*, February 1914, p. 831.

35. Mary S. Cutting, "The Strength of Ten," in *Little Stories of Married Life* (New York: McClure, Phillips, 1902), pp. 66–67.

36. Algis Budrys, "The Strength of Ten," *Fantastic Universe* 5.4 (May 1956): 42–49.

37. T. H. White, *The Once and Future King* (New York: Ace Books, 1987), pp. 368 and 376.

38. John Steinbeck, *The Winter of Our Discontent* (New York: Viking, 1961), p. 134.

39. Thomas Berger, *Reinhart in Love* (New York: Delacorte/Seymour Lawrence, 1962), p. 204.

40. Thomas Berger, *Vital Parts* (New York: Delacorte/Seymour Lawrence, 1970), p. 257.

41. "The Confederate Dead: A Tribute to Their Memory," *Baltimore Sun*, June 7, 1883, p. 1.

42. "Bewails Passing of the Galahad Days in Politics: 'Senator' Recalls When Hearts Were Pure," *Chicago Daily Tribune*, March 14, 1926, p. 14.

43. Herman L. Masin, "Wooden, 28 Years Later," *Coach and Athletic Director* 67.10 (1998): 10.

44. Editorial Cartoon, *Christian Science Monitor*, August 30, 1978, p. 24.

45. *New Yorker*, February 2, 1998, p. 51.

Googling the Grail

Donald L. Hoffman and Elizabeth S. Sklar

> "The power of the Grail, even today, comes from its obscurity."
> —Dean Jacques, chivalrynow.net/grail

> "The Birkin is the holy grail of handbags."
> —unusualthreads.com

> "The Grail is an empty signifier."
> —Marty Shichtman

> "It's only a cup."
> —Urban Dictionary

Our quest, to Google "The Holy Grail" and see what popped up, proved to be a more arduous and daunting undertaking than we had anticipated.[1] What "popped up" was more than fourteen million hits, and we found ourselves adrift in a chaotic and alien environment, forced to blunder about in a Perilous Forest littered with cultural junk, signs without signification, the detritus of an abandoned allegory: vintage motorcycles, baseball cards, and fishing lures, slasher flicks, designer grunge, invisibility cloaks, booze bottles, severed fingertips, genuine titanium sporks, iPhones, and the Holy Handbag of Bottega Veneta. We also experienced a series of bewildering encounters with a variety of indigenous creatures, some beneficent, some obsessed, others representing a range of threats to our pocketbooks, our self-esteem, or, indeed, our very sanity: on the one hand, serious scientists grappling with cutting-edge developments in physics and neurobiology or hackers and professional techies proposing ingenious solutions to problems we never knew existed; on the other, hawkers shamelessly peddling the secret of infinite wealth for a mere pittance, madmen serving up what we might call a psychedelic/schizophrenic stew of pseudoscience and

Dan Brown, and creepy alchemical revelations of Satan's plan for derailing the Second Coming.

Like King Arthur's knights of old, we had no map to guide us through this surrealistic terrain (and nary a Handy Hermit in sight). Because the objective of our quest was to explore the ways in which the Holy Grail has been appropriated by contemporary culture outside the academy, we chose to limit our investigation to the areas of science, technology, business (broadly construed), and marketing. We deliberately excluded academic sites and their scions, medievalist or Arthurian enthusiast sites that replicate, in however imperfect or abridged form, canonical accounts of the Grail Quest. Of necessity, because they are so prolific and quirky, we also eschew detailed discussion of those sites devoted to spiritualism, alternate religion, and alternate history.[2]

Defining the Googled Grail

Contemporary concepts of the Grail in what passes for the "real world" are easy enough to come by. Many sites such as "The Straight Dope" and numerous fantasy, alternative-religion, and SCA-related pages predictably present a potted canonical history of the Grail for popular consumption, while others like "Your Dictionary.com" provide a simple definition that seems to encapsulate popular understandings of the term: the Grail is "any ultimate, but elusive, goal pursued as in a quest." A similar, albeit fuzzier, rendition is found on wordreference.com: "a 'holy grail' is the ultimate goal of someone"—lots of wiggle room here. That these reference sites provide a reasonable approximation of common understanding of nontraditional grails is affirmed by definitions on websites devoted to specialized fields, such as marketing or technology, where we find "grail" defined as something "greatly desired, often sought after, but not attainable" (sandhill.com) or as "a very desired object or outcome that borders on a sacred quest" (techweb.com). Numerous nonce-definitions are available as well: "The Holy Grail of business application development is to be able to develop application code once and reuse it for many different . . . applications" (*Bill Clementson's Blog*, bc.tech.coop/blog); "FeatureServer+AreSDE Data Store=Holy Grail" (spatiallyadjustedl.com); "I suppose all css developers . . . have already stumbled upon 'the perfect layout' dubbed *the holy grail*" (dnevnikeklektika.com); the hydrogen-powered automobile is "the holy grail for automakers, environmentalists, political leaders" (rd.com); "For some years now bringing down the cost per kWh of photovoltaics to a more manageable level has been the holy grail of the solar power industry" (dailyack.com).

We must confess at the outset that this particular episode of our grail adventure was not without its whimsical moments. Who would have guessed, for example, that "'Holy Grail' is a song performed by the Australian band Hunters and Collectors" (Wikipedia), or that "the cup or chalice which Jesus used at the

Last Supper . . . was made from the stone which fell from Lucifer's crown as he plunged to earth" (experiencefestival.com)? The sassy "Urban Dictionary" is notable for providing the only obscene usage of the phrase (which we tactfully resist replicating here), along with the deadpan, "A cup. That's it, it's just a cup." One of our favorite discoveries was the "Uncyclopedia," a kind of anti-Wikipedia site devoted to dysinformational absurdities, which informs us that "The Holy Grail was made up by a French writer named Chuck Norris, in an attempt to slay Great Britain's legends of King Arthur. As soon as the Knights of the Round Table left Camelot and rode off in all directions to find this stupid cup, the golden era of Camelot was over." The other was a classically ironic Google moment: heading the search results was the invitation to "Find What Is the Holy Grail and Compare prices at Smarter.com" and "Find Bargain Prices on Holygrail." Galahad should have had it so easy.

Parsing the Googled Grail

With respect to the canonical Holy Grail, there are several points to note here, the first of which is that Googled grails do, in theory at least, retain certain features of their prototype: whatever its nature, the grail is still an obscure object of desire. It must be actively sought—the idea of quest is paramount. The grail is compelling, ever beckoning, ever elusive. Surprisingly, we were mistaken in our initial assumption that—given the often blatantly promotional nature of many of our websites—the majority of the Google questers would be laying claim to having actually "encheved" their grails.[3] This was not always the case, particularly on scientific, technical, and business websites, where the unattainability of the originary Grail is sustained by a variety of tactics, amongst them:

1. The Fudge-Factor: "aligning IT with business objectives is *often seen as* the Holy Grail by many CIO's" (search.techrepublic.com); "For designers, a font manager that can activate and deactivate fonts on-the-fly is the Holy Grail of the GNU/Linux desktop. . . . So far, the *closest candidate* is *Fonty Python*" (linux.com, italics ours).
2. The Mark Interrogatory (or The Hedged Claim): "The Holy Grail of Online Advertising?" (ReadWriteWeb); "KDE 4.0 the holy grail of Desktops?" (linux.slashdot.org); "Is this the holy grail of gadgets?" (globeandmail.com); "VOIP in the Call Center: Have We Found the Holy Grail?" (goliath.ecnext.com); "Could MacOS X be the 'Holy Grail'?" (linux.com), "The holy grail of photography?" (commentisfree.guardian.co.uk).
3. The Disclaimer Indirect (use of quotation marks around the operant phrase): "'Holy Grail' of Nanoscience" (sciencedaily.com); "A 'Holy Grail' of Healing" (freerepublic.com); "'Holy Grail' of Hearing" (medicalnewstoday.com); "The 'Holy Grail' of physics" (bbc.co.uk).

4. The Disclaimer Direct: "The Holy Grail of CSS is to separate the content of a web page from the instructions that control what it looks like. . . . However, reality is different and *here in the real world CSS does not do all these things*" (websitenotes.com); "The *design does not work*, at least for me" (deal-times.com); "Trusted or trustworthy computing has long been a goal of both industry and government, but attaining it remains *elusive*" (William Jackson, washingtontechnology.com, italics ours).

To a certain extent, as well, the communal aspect of the canonical grail still pertains, insofar as the varied grails of, say, the IT, the scientific, the medical, and the business communities share objectives and desired outcomes.

Still, the differences between Googled grails and the canonical Holy Grail impressively outnumber the similarities. In the first place, Googled grails have gone generic. Unlike the canonical Grail, for example, Googled grails are not singular or unique; as the approximately nine million hits for "holy grail *of*" might suggest, there appear to be as many grails as there are professional objectives, personal desires, or grailers. Often as not, "holy grail" is preceded by an indefinite article, a tacit acknowledgment that this particular grail is but one of countless members of the same set (a proposition supported by one technician's assertion that "There are several Holy Grails in the Computer Business"—technoweb): "We can see why the formulation of a set of actions, like rules, has become *a holy grail* of educational research" (your dictionary.com); "The ship has remained *a holy grail* for maritime archeologists [*sic*] ever since" (yourdictionary.com); "For years this . . . market has been *a 'holy grail'* for many enterprise technology firms" (sandhill.com); "*A 'Holy Grail'* of Healing" (cbsnews.com, italics ours). A corollary to this newly acquired genericity is that unlike their canonical predecessor, which could be achieved only by an elect few, Googled grails have been democratized, put up for grabs: they are potentially attainable by anyone and everyone. Indeed, we can go haring off after "our own personal grail" (yourdictionary.com), the contemporary quester's equivalent, perhaps, of the monogrammed pillowcase.

More significantly, Googled grails have lost contact with their religious and cultural origins. Whatever the contemporary quest object might be, the spiritual element of the canonical grail has suffered almost total eclipse (despite almost universal retention of the modifier "holy")—a dispiriting if unsurprising phenomenon, given the current association with hard science, technology, business, marketing, and assorted products.[4] Additionally, Googled grails have become completely unmoored from Arthurian narrative. Unlike other popularly invoked Arthurian icons (the Round Table, Excalibur, Camelot, Merlin), which trail in their wake some echoes of the legend, however Disneyoid, Googled grails are devoid of Arthurian resonance. Thematization is as scarce as the proverbial hens' teeth.[5] In fact, Googled grails have for the most part devolved into disposable commodities: having been emptied of spiritual, ideological, and legendary content, they rarely, except in the cases of product or project names, survive beyond the headline or the first sentence of text, serving merely as code words, come-ons, or rhetorical flourishes. In sum, the semantic field for "grail" is now null; the *signifié* has all but gone AWOL, and the grail stands shivering in its naked denotative state, not much more than a convenient shorthand that eliminates the need for descriptors, adjectives, and other such boring grammatical paraphernalia: at best, a demotic stand-in for *nec plus ultra*.[6]

Selling the Grail

It becomes clear, then, that most people who invoke the Holy Grail have a remarkably dim idea of what they are talking about—the kind of semantic deterioration you see in student references to "a doggy dog world" or the common contemporary understanding that "hoi polloi" refers to the elite. It also becomes clear that the modern grail operates as a sort of semiological McGuffin: like its Hitchcockian prototype—a seemingly significant device deployed to fuel the plot and subsequently ignored—the modern grail evokes an illusion of meaning, and having served its purpose, is promptly abandoned. But if our grail is an empty signifier, it is simultaneously and paradoxically a capacious container, a kind of cosmic trash bin into which we have permission to toss any and all of our cultural garbage. And, it should be noted, much of our capital—symbolic and literal—as well. Like everything else these days, grails don't come cheap: Grail/Unholy Grail clothing, for example, retails from between $59 for a T-shirt to $168 for a pair of skimpy jeans. The Holy Grail of Calendars will set you back by $1,000, while a Holy Grail handbag costs anywhere between $10,000 and $50,000. And the Holy Grail of Baseball Cards (a 1909 Honus Wagner card) recently went at auction for a whopping $2.36 million.

Which brings us to one of the least appealing features of our quest. If any spiritual dimension is irrelevant on scientific, business management, and IT sites, it becomes unthinkable in some of the marketing and promotional sites. Grail references promoting sporks (combination utensils), cookbooks, sports lenses, or combination kites involve a degree of puffery, but create a slightly comic disconnect. One begins to imagine Sir Gawain riding past wodwoses and sleeping at night in armor rusting in the blizzard in order to find a really terrific combination kite, or fighting at Maiden Castle to rescue a sports lens or a white-hot crocodile Bottega Veneta, "The Holy Grail of Handbags."

The use of the Grail to promote bags and lenses, speed training and fish breeding, is a little tacky, but mildly amusing. There are, however, marketing sites that vary from the merely tedious (e.g., "Best Practice: The Holy Grail of Project Management or Fallacious Argument?" and "Midmarket: The Holy Grail"), to the triumphantly capitalist (e.g., "The Celebrated Stock Option: A Holy Grail for Tech?"), to the truly offensive unabashedly promotional sites. While some of these sites may actually convey information with the grail as a benign McGuffin, some resort to snake-oil tactics, like the promotion of Forex Holy Grail, a product that promises to deliver investment "secrets from a group of self-made FOREX millionaires," at a sale price of only $39.95 for a lifetime of riches, or the Grail Indicator, which purportedly provides "a simple, 4 step method you can use to make up to $1,000 a day" in stock trading (tradestars.com). A few, like the relentless "Holy Grail of Marketing" (holygrailnetworkmarketing.com), are nothing short of aggressively irritating. There is always the consistent ideological unpleasantness of the Grail being adapted to such antithetical purposes, but in this case the insistent audio of the sleazy yammering of one Mark Yarnell pushing a dubious product magnifies the ideological unpleasantness with a deeply visceral one. And then there is the simple moral unpleasantness of the appeal to a desire for enormous wealth with little expenditure of time or effort, except for the outlay of $600 for the set of Holy Grail CDs with, of course, the come-on of a free DVD, which we are assured is worth the great sum of $29.95. At that price it seems, alas, holiness is not included. One might argue that as the medieval Grail satisfies dreams of gluttony, these pitches satisfy dreams of cupidity, but the desires are qualitatively different; dreaming of a good meal, for example, is not the same as dreaming of a scheme to sell delusions to your neighbors. These sites exploit the semiotic vacuity of the contemporary Grail to evoke a completely decontextualized referent that serves exclusively as a marketing gimmick. The meaning of the Grail here is as irrelevant as it is unknown to the promoter and the consumer, for whom it serves less as an ornament than as a lure, perhaps as a poison McGuffin.

On the other hand, there remain far happier instances of a marketing or even marketed Grail. The most audacious and pugnacious is that created by rock journalist Christopher Dawes and his friend Rat Scabies, from the punk rock band The Damned. These two entrepreneurs are, in fact, offering the Grail itself. Having followed the story of Rennes-le-Chateau and its suspiciously wealthy priest, they have undertaken to propose a new Quest for the Grail with a truly modern twist. They have put shares of the Grail up for auction on eBay. If they succeed in finding the Grail, and it turns out to be a cup after all, a 2 percent share brings the following entitlements, according to the contract: "The Grail shareholder will be allowed one sip from the vessel of a beverage of the Grail Stakeholder's choosing, which beverage to be provided by the Grail Stakeholder at the Grail Stakeholder's expense. The Grail Stakeholder may thereby gain eternal life and the healing of all physical ailments. However, because the Grail Finders cannot be held responsible for the mysterious powers of the Grail and all that, the Grail Finders shall not be held responsible for a failure on the part of the Holy Grail to give eternal life to the Grail Stakeholder" (boingboing.net/2006/05/08/your-chance-to-own-2.html)

With this descent into the promotional abyss, sort of a Grail Degree Zero, we return to the silliness that has infused the Grail ever since Monty Python got their hands on it. Christopher Dawes and Rat Scabies do, however, refer to two of the salient properties of the Grail: its association with healing and with drinking. The Grail as a miraculous healing vessel underwrites the hope that haunts the medical Grail sites. At the most basic level, the Grail is merely an acronym: GRAIL = Galen Representation And Integration Language—this in a site which magisterially links the scientific and thaumaturgic origins of medical science. Other sites deliver holy grails of regeneration (a man regrew his thumb by means of an extracellular matrix made from pig bladders), a new practice in chiropractic manipulation of a particularly tricky body part, or the breakthrough in medical marijuana (the Holy Grail of which seems to be a marijuana that produces medical benefits without the downside of euphoria—a dubious Grail, indeed), and, to cite one more example, the grail of fetal nucleated erythrocytes, which allows for efficient and early diagnosis of prenatal diseases. These sites seem to echo the dream of the Grail's miraculous healing properties. Modern methods are more secular, but the goal of perpetual health and eternal life is a constant, and remains as elusive as ever. And a reminder of the heroic quest surely remains in these scientists who labor at least as intensively as the legendary monks to provide comfort, healing, and life, extended, if not yet eternal.

On a less noble register, there is an occasion memorialized on several sites, when modern Pythonesque silliness actually confronted traditional Catholic spirituality—or at least its contemporary incarnation: Pope Benedict XVI. In early 2008, the archbishop of York visited the pope along with Tony Blair and King Abdullah of Saudi Arabia. Tony Blair, Catholic convert that he is, presented the pontiff with a painting of John Henry, Cardinal Newman. King Abdullah presented him with a jeweled scimitar. But the archbishop of York presented the pope with a gift of Grail Ale brewed by the Black Sheep Brewery located in Masham in the diocese of York.[7]

In this gift, spirituality and celebration join and we are led to consider our last Grail category, which addresses the nurturing of body and soul and some of the venues where much of this activity joyously takes place. The hungry travel enthusiast may find the Holy Grail of Hamburgers in Chicago, the Holy Grail of Chips [a.k.a. french fries] in Great Britain, and the Holy Grail of Chocolate in France. For the more sophisticated palate, Indo-Chinese fusion is "the holy grail of ethnic dining" (columbusunderground.com), while the fitness addict may pump up on Carb Slam, "the holy grail of pre-workout pump stimulators" (nutraplanet.com). The Grail has been celebrated (or traduced) in song as well. Pop singers and rock bands have gone a-grailing, one way or another, over the years, among them: the aforementioned Aussie postpunk Hunters and Collectors (whose 1992 "Holy Grail" was adopted as the theme music for Channel Ten's rugby broadcasts in 2002 and has since "become an Australian anthem"); the Norwegian death metal/Goth band Unholy Grail, whose titles include "Carrying the Cross" and "Ashes of Human," and whose album motto reads "Schlechter Tod für halb tote Leute"; and Iain Ashley Hersey, who seems to have found the Grail in the trunk of a hollow tree, in which he apparently dwells. On a more cheerful and markedly less countercultural note, several sites promote The Brobdingnagian Bards, who have issued "The Holy Grail of Irish Drinking Songs," which includes such favorites as "Beer, Beer, Beer" and "Seven Drunken Nights." This is a far cry from a spiritual quest, but it does capture some of the jollity at Camelot, when the Grail produced abundant food and drink. Finally, calling upon the Grail, but not waiting for its divine appearance, several taverns in different parts of the world have named themselves after the holy object. There are two Holy Grail Taverns in the Cincinnati area, another pair in Canberra, Australia, one in New Zealand, and another in Tokyo; and best of all (because we, the authors of this article, have actually been there), O'Reilly's Holy Grail Tavern in San Francisco, which provides cakes and ale and high-end pub fare in an evocative setting of stained glass saints and grail images.

In conclusion, we are tempted to say that the Grail is alive and well and living on Google. But we must qualify. References to the Grail are plentiful, but few of them are meaningful and many evoke the Grail with only the haziest recollection of its original significance and context. Most suggest that the Grail is now merely a cliché and a marketing gimmick ("Have I got a Grail for you"). The general impression is that the Grail Quest is over, our capitalist prayers have been answered, and, if you want a Grail, I can sell it to you. And yet vague memories of youthful pastimes linger in the technological cyberworld, and some echo of healing still resounds in the medical sites. Perhaps, as with the film that inspires many of these sites, laughing at and with the Grail gets us closest to it, if only by reminding us of what has been lost. It may, finally, be in the Holy Grail taverns that the meaning of the Grail is best preserved in celebration and companionship.

NOTES

1. All the sites discussed here were accessed between April and July 2008.

2. These sites account for a not insignificant portion of Googleable Grails, but we have chosen to disregard them for a number of reasons, primarily because they are each highly idiosyncratic and many offer systems of clearly schizophrenic complexity. They are united only in their virulent anti-Catholicism and their deeply held belief that the Truth is out there but has been taken hostage by some evil organization (usually the Roman church) intent on preventing the mass of humanity from reaching enlightenment and/or power. While Google makes it easy to access these sites, we find them peripheral to

the tendencies we find in the mass of material we understand to be what we are calling "the Googled Grail."

3. Although they are in the minority, we do find companies and individuals claiming to have found their Grails: "iCal Server—The Holy Grail Has Arrived" (techsuperpowers .com); "This is the Holy Grail" (Andrew Stone, software developer, quoted on wired.com); "The holy grail—found!" (inkjet paper, blog.charlesbandes.com); "The Holy Grail of Private Banking Has Been Found" (Aoureliou Televko, ezinearticles.com). Claim to achievement of the Grail is implicit in some product or company names as well, such as Holy Grail Reverb ("a compact digital reverb guitar pedal"), Grail Sports ("represents the quest to understand the mysteries that make certain athletes seem to perform so effortlessly," 8boardtennis.com), or GRAIL, "the Graphics and Imaging Laboratory" at the University of Washington, for example.

4. There are, of course, those for whom the Grail is still meaningful and the quest an ongoing adventure, particularly amongst those who espouse alternative belief or mystical systems. These range from GAGUT (the God Almighty Grand Unified Theorem), which has been touted as "The Holy Grail! World wide enquiries jam the website of Nigerian professor [Professor Gabriel Oyibo], who discovered the secrets of the universe" (Sola Fanawopo, sunnewsonline.com), to revelations of the demonic Grail Kings from Cain to Jesus who were fed on Anunnaki Star Fire until about 2000 BC when they switched to a diet featuring "high-spin" metal supplements (graal.co.uk). Except for the rather simple self-help sort of versions, in which the Quest for the Grail is a search for inner peace and wholeness, the mystical sites are bound together primarily by common paranoid visions bolstered by schizophrenic structures and often involve, à la Dan Brown and *Holy Blood, Holy Grail* (pervasive influences on these sites), revelations, discoveries, and codes. (One of the most transparent of these codes is the one that interprets "Grail" as an inversion of "L'Arc" which, of course, is the Ark and somehow links up with proving that the Merovingians transported the Grail/Ark of the Covenant to Baton Rouge, Louisiana [watch.pair .com/ark-grail]). With less madness, but equally dubious logic, many sites locate the Grail in Valencia, perhaps, or Hertfordshire, and produce objects (chalices, cups, or enigmatic inscriptions) to bolster their claims.

5. A few exceptions inevitably pertain here. The Gene Recognition and Assembly Internet Link (GRAIL) for the division of computational biology at Oak Ridge National Laboratory (compbio.ornl.gov/) has a software package that includes modules called Perceval, Galahad, and Gawain. Unlike biologists, IT folks seem more heavily influenced by Monty Python and the Holy Grail than by Malory; Pythonesque allusions regularly seep into technological article titles and product names, such as "Green Nano and the Holy Grail," Fonty Python (a font manager for Linux), and Python, a programming language that enables use of the Grail Internet Browser. Perhaps the most endearing invocation of MPHG occurs in "The Holy Grail of Infosecurity," a brief essay in which a sequence of information security concepts is elucidated by alternating brief scene summaries from the film itself with a neopatristic technological explication de texte (Jason Holloway, infosecurity-magazine.com).

6. Indeed "the holy grail" has become the standard identifier of the top of the line in a given type of product or brand: "Vodka right now is a big badge product.... If you can get the bottle on the table, then you've got the brand associated with the experience, which is the brand's Holy Grail" (Roberto Cavalli, cited on iconocast.com).

7. One wag, citing Holy Grail Ale's promotional blurb, commented, "It has a distinctive taste with plenty of fruity hops, which is about how I'd describe the movie it commemorates" (grailcode.com).

Part 3
Joan of Arc, Then and Now

"Because It Was Paris":
Joan of Arc's Attack on Paris Reconsidered

Kelly R. DeVries

"She wished to attack such a strong town and so well stocked with men and artillery, simply because it was the city of Paris." So rationalized the author of the *Journal du siège d'Orléans* at the conclusion of his account of the failure of Joan of Arc to take Paris in September 1429.[1] Joan of Arc's attack on Paris had lasted for only one day before she was wounded and her soldiers withdrew. Most historians, myself included, have blamed the failure to take Paris on Charles VII, whose disinterest in the endeavor initially delayed and then precipitously ended it. But is that a fair assessment of events in September 1429? Could Paris actually have been captured as Joan planned? This article will discuss the siege of Paris and compare it to a successful conquest earlier in the fifteenth century, that of John the Fearless in 1418. His success seems only to have come when a sizeable part of the Parisian population rose up in favor of the attackers. This is what Joan counted on in taking the city but what others, including the king, did not believe would happen and so they chose to retreat rather than expend any more lives and energy.

Paris's geography does not lend itself well to defense. Split by a major river, the Seine, with the royal administration and, at least in the early Middle Ages, a large proportion of the population living on an island, it was difficult to keep river-borne invaders, such as the Vikings, at bay. Nor could Paris be effectively walled in the early Middle Ages, especially as it continued to grow at a rate unsurpassed by other northern European cities. "Suburbs," areas built outside of the defensible "urbs," meant that expensive fortification plans were often scrapped, or outgrown, before they were begun. Only when the very confident and extremely wealthy Philip II Augustus occupied the royal throne did the city acquire its first circuit of walls (ca. 1200).[2]

By the fifteenth century the Parisian walls measured about eight meters in height, topped with wall walks, crenellations, and arrow slits. Every 110 to120 meters along the walls stood strong rectangular towers which rose high above the walls. Six gates pierced the walls into the city, and these were all protected by massive gatehouses—the Saint-Honoré gate (which would receive Joan of Arc's most determined assault) is known from archaeological reports to have measured 18.5 meters by 8.34 meters—with angular towers, arrow slits, gunports, machicolations, murder-holes, portcullises, and drawbridges built into them, their chambers capable of garrisoning a large number of soldiers. Outside these gatehouses in the later Middle Ages were boulevards, earthen fortifications filled with soldiers, archers, and gunners. All along the walls and throughout the towers, gatehouses, and boulevards were mounted a large number of gunpowder weapons. Also around the Paris city walls was a moat, three meters deep and thirty-two meters in width in some places (again confirmed by archaeology) and, depending on the level of the Seine River, filled with water. The entire fortification was a formidable defensive structure, built as much to intimidate any enemy attacker into *not* attacking it as it was to defend against any of their attacks.[3]

John the Fearless was also the only fifteenth-century attacker of Paris who succeeded in conquering the city. Despite being the cousin and chief baronial advisor of the French king, the all-but-incapacitated Charles VI, John had been forced from his side, and from the city of Paris, when he was implicated in the murder of yet another cousin who vied for control of the throne, Louis, Duke of Orléans, on November 23, 1407. This prompted the Armagnac-Burgundian civil war which raged within France at the very time that England was planning to return to the Hundred Years War.[4] There is little doubt that John undertook this assassination planning to take advantage of what he anticipated would be a weakened Armagnac side to extend his own lands and political power.[5] Later, he paid Jean Petit, a theologian at the University of Paris, to write a *Justification* for the murder, claiming that it was done only to put a stop to Louis of Orléans's "tyrannicide."[6] Such maneuvers were able to convince or pacify some French, but only a few in Paris, and John was forced to flee the city.

For the next eleven years John fought against the Armagnacs.[7] Early on, the two sides traded victories and defeats but eventually the Burgundians began to gain the upper hand. During this time John made frequent trips to Paris, usually in secret, to gauge his ability to return to the city. By August 22, 1412, after he had signed a peace treaty at Auxerre with the Armagnacs, which granted him a pardon for the assassination of Louis of Orléans, it seemed as if he had won this civil war. However, the Treaty of Auxerre's provisions were not heeded for long, and throughout the remainder of 1412 and all of 1413, Armagnac factions worked to undermine John's victories, while a popular rebellion in Paris—known as the Cabochien revolt—turned against the duke. Once more, the Burgundian leader was forced to flee from Paris.[8] The Armagnac-Burgundian war resumed. Then came the English victory at Agincourt where many Armagnac nobles lost their lives—as did many Burgundian nobles, including John's brother, Antoine, the Duke of Brabant—and John again became poised to enter Paris, this time by force.

John's strategy in 1417 was simple: he would surround Paris with Burgundian holdings. Since John's ouster in 1413, the Parisians had been split on whether to give their allegiance to the Burgundians or to the Armagnacs. During 1416–17, several Parisian rebellions even tried to force the city to accept John's rule. These had always been harshly quelled by the Armagnacs. But when Burgundian soldiers—so numerous that Enguerrand de Monstrelet claimed their large number of tents "was a good sized city"[9]—stood outside of the city's walls from late 1417 into early 1418, firing their cannons against and over the city walls, the intensity of these rebellions increased. Finally, on May 29, 1418, the citizens of Paris, being attacked from without and persuaded from within, opened their town's gates to John the Fearless.[10] A massacre of Armagnacs ensued, with more than two thousand killed, and the unstable King Charles VI welcomed John as "protector" of France.

The difference between John's and Joan's attacks on Paris was their ability to bring the citizens to their side. After Joan successfully raised the siege of Orléans (May 7, 1429) and crowned the dauphin as Charles VII (July 17, 1429), other French cities began declaring themselves for the French king: Laon, Soissons, Château-Thierry, Provins, Coulommiers, Crécy-en-Brie, Senlis, Lagny, and Compiègne.[11] It is certainly plausible that Parisians would have done the same, especially if given some incentive to do so, like an attack on the city by Joan and others loyal to the king.

Joan arrived at Paris from Compiègne on August 15.[12] She camped for the next several days at Saint-Denis, frequently visiting the basilica to ask for God's aid in the presence of the many earlier French kings and queens buried there. Later she relocated her camp to La Chappelle, a small village nearer Paris.[13]

On August 26, Joan and the other French leaders began to try and discover where the walls were weakest. According to Perceval de Cagny, an eyewitness, she sent out skirmishers "each day, two or three times a day," riding or marching up to the base of the gates or walls, "one time in one place, and then another." This practice continued daily, and by this Joan "very willingly studied the situation of the town of Paris, and with this which place seemed to her to be the best for making an assault."[14] Jean Chartier adds that during this time the French also continually bombarded the walls with their gunpowder artillery.[15] This was done, however, with little hope of breaching the walls or killing the soldiers defending them but to weaken the resolve of the Parisians.

Yet, by the beginning of September no assault had been made on the walls, as such an action could not be done without the presence or permission of Charles VII. He was still at Compiègne, where he had lodged since his crowning, and he had not permitted such an action to take place. Finally, on September 1, the Duke of Alençon rode north to ask when the king could be expected at Saint-Denis so that the attack could proceed.[16] Alençon was told that Charles would leave the following day for Saint-Denis, but when he had still not arrived by September 5, Alençon again rode to find him. The king had in fact moved from Compiègne to Senlis, but he seemed to have no intention of proceeding farther. However, Alençon was steadfast in his resolve and refused to leave without the king. So, two days later, Charles VII finally arrived in Saint-Denis, where he and the military leaders determined that the army would attack Paris the following day.[17]

Thus on the morning of September 8 Joan led her soldiers—knights, men-at-arms, and archers, according to contemporary sources—to an assault of the Saint-Honoré gate. The attack began with a bombardment of the walls by gunpowder weapons and the filling of the moat with bundles of sticks, wood, carts, and barrels. Cagny writes that Joan then "took her standard in her hand and was the first to enter the moat." "The attack was hard and long," he continues,

> and it was a marvel to hear the sound and noise of the cannons and couleuvrines which those inside fired at those outside, and all manners of missiles in such a great multitude as to be innumerable. And although the Maid and a great number of knights, squires, and other soldiers had descended into the moat at the edge or around there, very few were wounded. And there were many on foot and on horse which were struck and knocked to the ground by blows from cannon stones, but by the grace of God and the presence of the Maid, not any man was killed or was wounded who was not able to return to his side and his tent without aid.[18]

But that was not the view from inside the city, as Clément de Fauquembergue, who was in Paris at the time, insists that many French soldiers were wounded and killed by gunfire at Saint-Denis.[19] Likely the number of casualties were between Cagny's and Fauquembergue's reports.

As the day wore on, the French began to tire, and then came a major blow to their morale: Joan was wounded. Cagny writes:

> And after sunset, the Maid was struck by a crossbow bolt in the thigh. And since she was so struck, she forced herself to cry more strongly that each man should approach the walls and that they should take that place. But because it was night and she was wounded and the men-at-

arms were fatigued from the long assault which they had made, the lord of Gaucourt and others came and took the Maid, and, against her will, they took her out of the moat. And thus the assault ended. And she had very great regret to have thus departed, saying "by my Martin, the place should have been taken." They put her on her horse and took her to her tent in La Chapelle.[20]

Fighting for the day ended.

On the morning of September 9 the French army arose early and prepared for another attack on the walls of Paris. Even Joan of Arc, though wounded, intended to carry on the battle. Cagny reports that she "sent for the fair Duke of Alençon, by whom she would be led, and asked him to sound the trumpets and mount the horses to return to Paris. And she said … that she never wanted to leave there until she had taken that town."[21] She was also delighted to hear of the arrival of the Count of Montmorency and fifty to sixty "gentlemen" who had defected from the city, wishing to fight with her and the French army against their former allies.[22] It looked as if her plans for igniting an uprising in Paris were beginning to take effect.

But just as the French army was preparing to renew its assault of the walls, René of Anjou, Duke of Bar, and Charles, Count of Claremont, appeared with a summons for Joan to speak with the king in Saint-Denis. She was notably miffed by this delay, but this was nothing compared to the anger she felt when she was told that rather than pursuing the assault Charles VII had ordered the destruction of a bridge built across the Seine River to allow for another section of the Parisian walls to be attacked.[23] Joan's anger increased even more when she was also told that Charles was postponing any further military action against the city until the royal council met to discuss whether they should continue the attacks.[24] The council, over the vehement objections of Joan, Alençon, and others, decided to end the siege, and the French army left Paris.

The official reason given for the retreat, found in the *Chronique* of Jean Lefèvre de Saint-Rémy, was that "the king saw that the town of Paris was too strongly fortified" to risk any more assaults.[25] However, most historians put the blame on the influence of Joan's rival at court, Georges de la Trémoïlle, following contemporary Jacques Bouvier's suggestion that "the Lord of La Trémoïlle had caused the soldiers to return to Saint-Denis."[26] Since Charles's coronation, Joan's favor had been declining at court, chiefly due to two councillors who opposed her actions, Regnault of Chartres and Georges de la Trémoïlle. They had been speaking against Joan almost since she had first appeared at Chinon, although they had only limited influence while she was delivering victories. As Paris did not fall after the September 8 attacks, and as she was wounded in them, they were able to foment considerable doubt about her continued warfare. This was not out of malice or treason, however, but because they preferred diplomacy to fighting, wanting a settlement that would convince Duke Philip the Good of Burgundy to break his alliance with the English, which they reckoned would end the war faster than a prolonged reconquest. (In this they would be proven correct, as most historians conclude that it was the Burgundian abandonment of the English at the 1435 Congress of Arras which ultimately ended the Hundred Years War—although not until 1453.)[27]

Why did Joan fail at Paris? Was she to blame for the loss there, overconfident in her military abilities? Or does the blame lie elsewhere? With the quote that begins this article the anonymous author of the *Journal du siège d'Orléans* seems to wonder if she had overreached, "simply because it was the city of Paris."[28] The suggestion here and in other narrative sources, that Joan should have been content with the relief of Orléans and the crowning of the king, presupposes that Paris could not have been conquered. But clearly she did not feel this way, and there seem to have been many who agreed with her. Joan believed the city was vulnerable, and after reconnoitering the walls, the French military leaders as an entire command council agreed, making a plan of attack which they were confident would succeed. But then the king failed either to come to the battlefield when he said he would or to allow an assault of the walls without his permission. The Duke of Alençon was eventually able to gain this, but after only one day of fighting Charles stopped the attack and ordered a retreat, swayed by advisors not interested in pursuing war as a means of forcing the English to leave France. Paris did not fall in a day, so Charles decided to pursue more diplomatic means of attaining this goal.

Still, what could have been expected after only a day? As John the Fearless had proven more than a decade previously, Paris would not fall without the help of the Parisians themselves. Where did they stand in 1429? Some certainly supported the French in their efforts, as was proven by the arrival of the Count of Montmorency and others after the first day of the siege. But, at least at this point, they seem to have been but a small minority. The account of the Bourgeois of Paris, who was after all a *bourgeois of Paris*, suggests that a completely different opinion was held by many if not most in the city:

> On the eve of the Nativity of Our Lady in September [September 8], the Armagnacs came to attack the walls of Paris, which they hoped to take by assault. But what they won by conquest was only sadness, shame, and mischief, because many of them were wounded for the rest of their lives, who, before the assault, were quite healthy. But a fool does not fear so long as he is successful. I say that to those who were filled with such a large amount of bad luck and such evil belief. I say that to a creature who was with them in the form of a woman, who they called the Maid. Who was it? God knows.

> On the day of the Nativity of Our Lady, they came together, all of one accord, to attack Paris on that day. And they assembled at least twelve thousand or more, and came around the hour of High Mass, between eleven and twelve, their Maid with them, and a large number of wagons, carts, and horses, all filled with great bundles of sticks in three lines, to fill the moat of Paris. And they began to make their attack between the Saint-Honoré gate and the Saint-Denis gate, and they made a very savage attack, and during the attack they said many vile insults to the Parisians: "You must surrender to us quickly, for Jesus' sake, for if you do not surrender yourselves before it becomes night, we will invade you by force, willing or not, and you will be put to death without mercy." "See here," said one [of the Parisians], "bawd! wench!" And he shot a bolt from his crossbow right at her, and it pierced her leg straight through, and she fled. . . . A little after four o'clock, the Parisians became confident in themselves, so that they fired their cannons and other artillery so many times that the army charging at them recoiled and stopped their attack, and they left. As they were leaving, it became even more disastrous, for the Parisians had a large cannon which fired from the Saint-Denis gate as far as all the way to Saint-Lazare [about a kilometer]. This they fired into their backs, which was very terrible. Thus was it put to an end.[29]

Perhaps these feelings would have changed had more assaults been carried out, but it is just as likely that the Parisians might have steeled themselves even more against the French who were trying to take their city by force and/or deprivation. On two previous occasions the Bourgeois had written in his diary that rumors of Joan's "atrocities" had been spread throughout the city.[30] No doubt the rumors would have continued.

The citizens of Paris needed a lot of convincing before they would rise up on Joan's behalf. It was certainly not going to come after only a single day of attack upon the very strong city fortifications. Despite being in the middle of intense warfare for the majority of the fifteenth century, only once was the city taken, by John the Fearless in 1418. And he had the citizens of Paris behind him. Without them he would not have been successful. Joan of Arc did not have their favor, and it does not appear that she would have it even if she had been able to besiege the city for several months. This largest city of northern Europe could be captured, but not without substantial help from inside the walls as well as a lengthy siege waged against them on the outside.

NOTES

After hearing me deliver a paper on Joan of Arc, "A Woman as Leader of Men: Joan of Arc's Military Career," at the Twenty-eighth International Congress on Medieval Studies, Western Michigan University, on May 6, 1993, and then agreeing to publish it in her and Charlie Wood's *Fresh Verdicts on Joan of Arc*, Bonnie Wheeler encouraged me to write a more complete military history of the Maid of Orléans. This led to my book *Joan of Arc: A Military Leader* and to my eternal gratitude. No one has more spirit and enthusiasm for the Middle Ages than does Bonnie!

    1. *Journal du siège d'Orléans*, in *Procès de condamnation et de réhabilitation de Jeanne d'Arc dite La Pucelle*, ed. Jules Quicherat, 5 vols. (Paris, 1841–49) [hereafter Quicherat], 4:199–200. All translations are my own.

    2. Alain Erlande-Brandenburg, "L'architecture militaire au temps de Philippe Auguste: Une nouvelle conception de la défense," in *La France de Philippe Auguste: Le temps des mutations; Actes du colloque international organisée par le C.N.R.S. (Paris, 29 septembre–4 octobre 1980)*, ed. Robert-Henri Bautier (Paris: C.N.R.S., 1982), pp. 595–604.

    3. Henri Couget, *Jeanne d'Arc devant Paris* (Paris: Éditions Spes, 1925), pp. 21–23, 76–77, and Ferdinand de Liocourt, *La mission de Jeanne d'Arc*, 2 vols. (Paris: Nouvelles Éditions Latines, 1974–76), 2:221, 223–24.

    4. Richard Vaughan, *John the Fearless: The Growth of Burgundian Power* (London: Longmans, 1966), pp. 43–48; Bertrand Schnerb, *Jean sans-Peur: Le prince meurtrier* (Paris: Payot, 2005), pp. 205–32; and Bernard Guenée, *Un meurtre, une société: L'assassinat du Duc d'Orléans, 23 novembre 1407* (Paris: Gallimard, 1992). The Armagnacs were so named after Louis's son-in-law, Bernard, Count of Armagnac, who took over the leadership of those opposing John the Fearless.

    5. Vaughan, *John the Fearless*, pp. 46–48, and Schnerb, *Jean sans-Peur*, pp. 235–45.

    6. Vaughan, *John the Fearless*, pp. 68–74, and Schnerb, *Jean sans-Peur*, pp. 247–56. An edition of the full document can be found in Enguerrand de Monstrelet, *Chronique*, ed. L. Douët-d'Arcq, 6 vols. (Paris, 1857–62), 1:177–242.

    7. See Kelly DeVries, "John the Fearless' Way of War," in *Reputation and Representation in Fifteenth Century Europe*, ed. Douglas L. Biggs, Sharon D. Michalove, and A. Compton Reeves (Leiden: Brill, 2004), pp. 39–55.

    8. Vaughan, *John the Fearless*, pp. 98–102; Schnerb, *Jean sans-Peur*, pp. 541–72; and A. Coville, *Les cabochiens et l'ordonnance de 1413* (Paris, 1888).

    9. Monstrelet, *Chronique*, 3:216.

    10. Ibid.; *Chronique du religieux de Saint-Denys*, ed. L. Bellaguet, 6 vols. (Paris, 1839–52), 4:85, 127–29; Vaughan, *John the Fearless*, pp. 221–27; and Schnerb, *Jean sans-Peur*, pp. 666–70.

    11. Jean Chartier, *Chronique de Charles VII*, in Quicherat, 4:78.

    12. Kelly R. DeVries, *Joan of Arc: A Military Leader* (Stroud: Sutton, 1999), pp. 142–44.

    13. Ibid., pp. 145–49.

    14. Perceval de Cagny, *Chronique des ducs d'Alençon*, in Quicherat, 4:25. See also Chartier, *Chronique de Charles VII*, in Quicherat, 4:86; and the *Journal du siège d'Orléans*, in Quicherat, 4:197.

    15. Chartier, *Chronique de Charles VII*, in Quicherat, 4:86–87.

    16. Cagny, *Chronique des ducs d'Alençon*, in Quicherat, 4:24–25.

    17. Ibid., 4:25–26.

    18. Ibid., 4:26–27.

19. Clément de Fauquembergue, *Journal*, in Quicherat, 4:457.
20. Cagny, *Chronique des ducs d'Alençon*, in Quicherat, 4:26–27.
21. Ibid., 4:27.
22. Ibid., 4:27–28.
23. Ibid. Germain Lefèvre-Pontalis confirmed this part of Cagny's chronicle when he discovered a letter written by Henry VI in 1431 which reminds Denisot Doe, a citizen of one of the villages surrounding Paris, of the bridge's existence during the time of Joan's attacks. See Germain Lefèvre-Pontalis, "Un détail du siège de Paris par Jeanne d'Arc," *Bibliothèque de l'écoles des chartes* 46 (1885): 5–15.
24. Cagny, *Chronique des ducs d'Alençon*, in Quicherat, 4:27–28.
25. Jean Lefèvre de Saint-Rémy, *Chronique*, in Quicherat, 4:436.
26. Jacques (or Gilles le) Bouvier, the Herald of Berry, *Chroniques du roi Charles VII*, in Quicherat, 4:48.
27. On the Congress of Arras see Joyceline Gledhill Dickinson, *The Congress of Arras, 1435: A Study in Medieval Diplomacy* (Oxford: Clarendon Press, 1955).
28. *Journal du siège d'Orléans*, in Quicherat, 4:199–200.
29. Bourgeois de Paris, *Journal*, in Quicherat, 4:464–66.
30. Bourgeois of Paris, *Journal d'un bourgeois de Paris, 1405–49*, ed. A. Teutey (Paris, 1881), pp. 243, 245. This is a more complete edition than that found in Quicherat, who does not include either of these comments.

"They want us to think she is Joan of Arc, not some warmonger."
—*The Impostor* (2002)

Warrior not Warmonger: Screen Joans during World War I

Kevin Harty

Gary Leder's 2002 film, *The Impostor*, based on a short story by Philip K. Dick, is set on a war-ravished Earth in the year 2079. Decades of conflict with invading Alpha Centauri have reduced large parts of the planet to rubble as the human race fights for survival. Global leadership is vested in someone simply referred to in the film as "the Chancellor," whose carefully scripted appearances and pronouncements are designed to convince everyone that she is, in the words of the film's central female character, Maya Olham (played by Madeline Stowe), "Joan of Arc, not some warmonger."

Neither Dick's original short story nor Leder's film have any connection to the life or legend of Joan of Arc; indeed, the reference to Joan that occurs in the film's opening segment is not even in the Dick short story.[1] But what is clear from this casual reference to Joan is that Joan of Arc has become someone to be invoked in film (and elsewhere) to lend legitimacy to various causes in times of war. The origins of this invocation can be found during World War I, when film Joans were used to advance a decidedly pro-war agenda designed to rally at times reluctant supporters to the cause of saving France and her allies from the German onslaught.

By the mid-1910s advances in filmmaking made it possible to produce feature-length screenplays rather than simply cinematic pageants and tableaux, and filmmakers soon turned to the story of the life and legend of Joan of Arc for reasons other than hagiography. Co-opting the image of Joan on film became a convenient way for directors to advance an agenda related to the Great War. In these films, Joan is no longer seen simply as a candidate for canonization;[2] she becomes instead the archetype of the warrior maiden.[3]

In late September 1915, the French launched an attack on the Germans at Artois, with the British doing the same at nearby Loos in what was to be the major Allied offensive on the western front that year. The Allies had the initial advantage at Loos, yet the French and the British were eventually routed. British casualties alone at Loos were a staggering sixty-one thousand, more than three times those of the Germans.[4] In the face of this disaster, the popular press in both France and England seized upon the memoirs of a seventeen-year-old hero, Émilienne Moreau, who not only survived the occupation and bombardment of her hometown but valiantly aided the French in their attempts to drive the German occupiers out of Loos and the surrounding areas. For her bravery, she would later be awarded the Croix de guerre.

Moreau's account of the siege of Loos was serialized in both *Le Petit Parisien* and *Lloyd's Weekly News* in late 1915 and early 1916.[5] The advertisement announcing the English translation of Moreau's memoirs left no doubt in the minds of *Lloyd's* weekly Sunday readers that the French teenager had been conscripted into the Allied propaganda campaign:

THE HEROINE OF LOOS.

French Girl of Seventeen Who Killed Five Germans.

STORY OF HER LIFE IN
"LLOYD'S"
NEXT SUNDAY.

"SHE IS THE JOAN OF ARC OF MODERN TIMES."[6]

Moreau's story soon found its way to the screen in Australia in George Willoughby's 1916 *The Joan of Arc of Loos* with Jane King in the title role.[7] To the account found in the memoirs Willoughby's film adds a love interest for Moreau (a captured British soldier played by Clive Farnham) and the appearance on the battlefield of an armor-clad figure who is identified in the film's credits simply as "the angel" (Jean Robertson) but whose presence is clearly meant to suggest that the real Joan of Arc has sanctioned Moreau's exploits as a latter-day re-creation of her own. The angel is a woman in full medieval battle armor brandishing a sword, *the* image of Joan of Arc used throughout World War I for purposes of stirring up pro-Allied sentiment.

Initial critical reaction to the film was mixed. *Australian Variety* praised the film, especially for its technical qualities, but Sidney's *Theatre Magazine* worried that Moreau's father was perhaps too much of a hawk looking forward to war. Still, the magazine found much to praise in the film's invocation of the idea that God was on the side of the Allies.[8]

In the film, Moreau stands out because of her courage, her ingenuity, and her unflappability. The men around her are decidedly less courageous, ingenious, and unflappable. Her father does seem a windbag and throwback to a former age. The Germans are cruel, almost ridiculously caricatured villains—their elaborate mustaches making them look like buffoons. The local parish priest is more timid than saintly, and Moreau's love interest seems more inept than heroic—indeed, she, not he, is decorated after the battle. Throughout the film, then, Moreau's role seems to be to inspire men. When they falter, she is there to set them on the right path again. She is fearless, resourceful, and just plain clever in her encounters with the Germans, who in turn are cruel, dull, and almost comically inept.

Moreau's soldier love interest is a disaster as a courier of top secret information, riding by mistake right into the middle of a German gun emplacement. Moreau herself ends up delivering the information to the Allied command. Subsequently captured, imprisoned, and ordered to be shot, the unnamed soldier love interest is able to escape from his German prison only because of Moreau's assistance. Single-handedly, she steals a German uniform and motorcycle for him and manages to drug the German soldiers guarding him in prison.

As the Allies initially attack, they find themselves pinned down by snipers. Moreau abandons the safety of a barn in which she is hiding to kill two German snipers with a pistol. After the Allied advance is then halted by further sniper fire, Moreau ventures forth into the woods surrounding the now-destroyed town and lobs hand grenades at the three additional snipers, thereby killing them and facilitating the continued Allied advance. Moreau then rushes back to the Allied troops to tend to the wounded and dying. When an Allied rout seems all but certain, Moreau abandons her nursing duties, grabs a bullet-ridden French tricolor, intones the French national anthem, and all but leads the Allied rally that initially halts the advancing German hordes.

The Joan of Arc of Loos conveniently avoids the final disastrous outcome of the battle of Loos—a disaster that is the work of men;[9] the focus here is on a latter-day Joan of Arc, who succeeds where men fail, no matter what the circumstances. Moreau's real activities during the siege and subsequent battle of Loos are genuinely heroic. Willoughby's film emphasizes and expands upon them to advance an agenda that would counter any opposition to the just cause that was the Allied role in World War I and to inspire men to fight the good fight.[10]

During World War I, Australian filmmakers seemed rather taken with christening women heroes as latter-day Joans of Arc. On October 12, 1915, a British nurse, Edith Cavell, was shot to death in Belgium by a German firing squad for allegedly assisting Allied prisoners of war to escape. News of her execution shocked the world, and Cavell instantly became a flash point for anti-German propaganda among the Allies. Within months of her death, three

Australian films competed to tell her story. John C. Gavin and C. Post Mason's *Martyrdom of Nurse Cavell* was released in Australia in early 1916 and subsequently screened in the United States and England to great critical and commercial success. A rival Australian film, W. J. Lincoln's *Nurse Cavell*, was released almost simultaneously but was quickly withdrawn when Gavin and Mason charged Lincoln with copyright infringement. Undaunted, Lincoln released another film about Cavell in April, *La Revanche*, expanding upon the screenplay for his earlier film and casting wounded and battle-scarred Australian and New Zealand Army Corps (ANZAC) veterans in a number of minor roles. Interestingly, Lincoln's first Cavell film had the telling subtitle *England's Joan of Arc*.[11]

While Cavell makes a sympathetic and compelling rallying point for anti-German propaganda, she is more problematic on one level than Moreau. Moreau triumphs in her ordeal and goes on to continue to fight the good fight; Cavell dies a martyr who can nonetheless inspire others. The men Cavell aids, not Cavell herself, go on to fight the good fight. As the review of *La Revanche* in *Argus* points out, "if you turn a deaf ear to your country's call and still STAY AT HOME it may not be long before you find yourself under the domination of these despoilers and barbarians."[12] Perhaps, though, as William D. Routt speculates, for Australians at least, "this particular story about a heroic British woman [Cavell] martyred in a foreign land may have had a special resonance for those still trying to come to terms with what had happened to the ANZACs at Gallipoli."[13]

But real historical figures such as Moreau and Cavell were not the only women linked to Joan of Arc by filmmakers. Even young children could be inspired by Joan of Arc to do their part to help the Allied cause, as William Bertram's 1917 film *The Little Patriot* makes clear. One day, Marie Yarbell, the title character played by Hollywood's first well-known child star, Baby Marie Osborne, goes to school where her teacher reads her class the story of Joan of Arc.

Marie is inspired by the story to undertake various patriotic and preparedness activities, including organizing her male playmates into a kind of home watch, which attracts the attention and support of a wealthy neighbor, Mr. Mulhouser (Herbert Standing), who is financing the development of a new aerial torpedo. When Marie's mother (Marian Warner) unwittingly rents a room to a German spy named Hertz (Frank Lansing), it is Marie who sneaks into his room to discover his plans and unmasks him. Marie then stops Hertz from destroying the aerial torpedo project by retrieving a lit bomb that Hertz has thrown into the Mulhouser torpedo factory and then tossing it into the street. Though stunned by the concussion from the bomb's explosion, Marie and her little companions capture Hertz and his coconspirators and hold them prisoner until the authorities arrive.

Marie is rewarded for her patriotism when it is revealed that the financier is actually her grandfather. Mulhouser had been estranged from Marie's parents since her mother married her chronically unemployed father. But, once the war is over, she will be able to live happily ever after with Mulhouser and her parents in the Mulhouser mansion.

Earnest orphans too could do their part to root out German spies, especially if they were young girls much cleverer than the men with whom they fell in love. In 1918, George Loane Tucker cast the noted comedienne Mabel Normand against type as the title character in *Joan of Plattsburg*.[14] An orphan named Joan (Normand) passes the time reading about Joan of Arc and soon becomes convinced that she is the reincarnation of her namesake. In a dream sequence in the film, Normand even imagines she is the armor-clad Joan of Arc. The orphanage, which it turns out is run by German spies, is located near a major military training camp.

Like Joan of Arc, Normand's Joan hears voices, though the voices she hears are those of German spies plotting against the government to steal the secret plans for a new wireless device that will turn the tide of the war in the Allies' favor. When Joan realizes what the Germans are up to, she reports them to the commander of the camp, Captain Lane (Robert Elliott), with whom she is in love. Lane initially does not believe Joan, but he eventually realizes that the plot is real. Then, with Joan's help, Lane captures the spies and secures the secrecy of the wireless project. Lane next ships out to the front but returns safely after the war to marry Joan.

The patriotic agenda of *Joan of Plattsburg* is clear from the start. *Moving Picture World* quotes Porter Emerson Browne, who wrote the film's photoplay, explaining that *Joan of Plattsburg* was "meant to typify the American woman's desire to do her share in the great war."[15] But Normand's Joan does more than simply her part. Not only does she thwart German spies as the Little Patriot had done but she also proves herself cleverer than her boyfriend as Moreau had been. Normand's Joan, unlike Moreau, is, however, able to inspire her boyfriend to feats of bravery rather than simply rescue him from failed acts of heroism. At the end of *The Joan of Arc of Loos*, Moreau seems set to marry her soldier love interest. In *Joan of Plattsburg*, Normand does marry Lane but only after he proves himself on the battlefield. Moreau's bravery remains her own; Normand's is shared with and emulated by Lane.

The story of Joan of Arc inspired yet another young screen hero to aid in the defeat of the Germans in World War I. In Joseph De Grasse's 1918 film for Universal, *The Wild Cat of Paris*, Collette, a prostitute and apache dancer played by Priscilla Dean, leads her fellow apaches to the defense of France after she sees a painting of Joan. Collette's apache troupe repels the Germans when they reach the outskirts of Paris. Eventually, Collette even abandons her wildcat past totally to become a nurse at the front, where she meets, saves the life of, and eventually marries the American artist whose painting of Joan was her original inspiration.

Mabel Normand as Joan of Arc in the dream sequence from George Loane Tucker's 1918 film *Joan of Plattsburg*. (Still courtesy of the British Film Institute.)

Robin Blaetz takes a decidedly different view of Collette's activities than I do. According to Blaetz, Collette ultimately surrenders to the control of a man, the painter whom she will marry.[16] (Interestingly, the painter's name is Jean, the masculine form of Joan/Jeanne.) Collette can, however, also be seen as one with other latter-day World War I screen Joans—active participants in the world of war whose accomplishments reaffirm the value of women's contributions to the war effort, often when the contributions of the men in their lives pale by comparison. Jean is, after all, wounded and nursed back to health by Collette.

The most commanding screen Joan to appear during World War I was the legendary opera singer Geraldine Farrar in the title role of Cecil B. DeMille's first film spectacle, the 1916 *Joan the Woman*. Two different versions of the film were released, one in the United States and one in France. The original American version is much longer and more diffuse, emphasizing an overly romantic—in several senses of the term—view of Joan. A shorter French version, based on a reedited version of the American original, streamlines the plot substantially to emphasize Joan's mythic role in the French national consciousness.[17]

The film's screenplay borrows from Friedrich Schiller's 1801 stage drama *Die Jungfrau von Orleans* in its retelling of the familiar events of Joan's life, especially in giving Joan a love interest, but it does not have her die in the dauphin's arms, as she does in Schiller's play. The American version of the film can be read as a call to arms for the United States to come to the aid of a France in desperate need of American assistance. The film twice shows Farrar's Joan with her arms outstretched silhouetted against a fleur-de-lis that slowly morphs into a cross. Farrar herself has said that "Joan of Arc is the woman Christ of all ages."[18]

Framing the traditional story of Joan in DeMille's film is a story involving Eric Trent (Wallace Reid), an English soldier in the trenches in France during World War I. In the film's prologue, Trent discovers an old sword in the walls of his trench bunker. That sword conjures up the image of Joan of Arc and a memory of one of his ancestors, an English commander in France during the fifteenth century who met, fought against, fell in love with, and finally abandoned Joan to her executioners. As Trent contemplates the sword, Joan of Arc appears to him, challenging him to right the wrongs done to her by his ancestor. In the film's epilogue, Trent resolves to accept Joan's challenge by going on a suicide mission against the Germans, France's new invaders and would-be conquerors. Trent's sacrifice counters his ancestor's personal betrayal of Joan and England's long history of geopolitical betrayal.

DeMille's reading of the life of Joan is unique on both a personal and a more general political level. The initial title cards announce that the film is "founded on the life of Joan of Arc, the Girl Patriot, Who Fought with Men, Was Loved by Men, and Killed by Men—Yet withal Retained the Heart of a Woman." The film becomes a commentary about the battle of the sexes with a possible suffragist context as well as a pro-war, less-than-subtle social and political agenda. Nativist, anti-Catholic, and isolationist sentiments were at odds with DeMille's hawkish posture before and during the war: "DeMille's epic was in fact part of public discourse enlisting support for an embattled France symbolized by Joan of Arc rather than the modernist aesthetic so alienating to Protestant middle-class sensibility. Patriotic appeals associated with the maid of Orléans were useful in overcoming American prejudice against Parisian avant-garde movements that contravened sacrosanct notions of genteel culture. An ad, for example, addressed the reader as follows: 'Would Joan of Arc Be Burned Today? . . . Is the World Freed of the Arch-Enemies of Truth—Ignorance and Superstition?'"[19]

In one of the film's more original and jarring touches, a scene that stirred protests against the film in Catholic circles, Joan appears before a court of Ku Klux Klan–like white-hooded accusers who torment her at Bishop Cauchon's behest. The Klan had organized itself in 1915 in what would turn out to be a rising tide of nativism that swept across the country and that DeMille obviously viewed with some alarm.[20]

But, most importantly, *Joan the Woman* presents a woman who is willing to sacrifice all for the greater good and the rescue of France. The film's introduction of Trent's fifteenth-century ancestor, with whom he shares a surname, reminds film audiences that Joan herself gave her life for France and advances a familiar enough gendered agenda for a World War I film Joan. Joan's own personal happiness must not interfere with her greater public duty and destiny. When she decides to embrace that destiny, Joan provides a role model for the initially reluctant Trent to undertake what will prove a suicide mission to dislodge the German forces from their secure bunker. In turn, Trent becomes the doughboy as Everyman; his mission, the film not so subtly argues, needs to be replicated by the still officially neutral American forces. The times call for Americans bravely to risk all, as Joan had, to save France. The screen Joans of World War I are then role models for those at the front and inspirations for those at home in the great battle to defeat the Germans—these Joans are warriors not warmongers.[21]

NOTES

1. Dick's story, also called "The Impostor," first appeared in 1953 and is reprinted in *The Selected Stories of Philip K. Dick* (New York: Pantheon Books, 2002), pp. 101–15.

2. Joan was burned to death at the stake in Rouen on May 30, 1431. The first inquiry into the validity of Joan's sentence was held in 1450, the second in 1452. In 1455–56, the formal process of nullifying the verdict of 1431 was begun, and the verdict was finally rescinded. The case for Joan's canonization was not, however, placed before the Vatican until 1869. Joan was declared venerable in 1903, she was beatified in 1909, and she was finally canonized in 1920.

3. The earliest surviving film about Joan of Arc is the 1895 Edison *The Execution of Joan of Arc*. This film was quickly followed by Georges Hatot's 1898 *Jeanne d'Arc* for the Lumière Brothers; Hatot's 1899 travelogue-documentary *Domremy: La Maison de Jeanne d'Arc*, also for the Lumière Brothers; Georges Meliès's 1900 *Jeanne d'Arc*; Mario Caserini's 1900 *La Vita di Giovanna d'Arco*; Caserini's 1905 *Giovanna d'Arco al rogo* and *La Vita di Giovanna d'Arco*; Albert Capellani's 1908 *Jeanne d'Arc*; and Nino Oxilia's 1913 *Giovanna d'Arco*. Each of these films is simply a brief exercise in cinematic hagiography. For further information on these and other films about Joan of Arc, see variously Michelle Aubert and Jean-Claude Sequin, *La Production cinématographique des Frères Lumière* (Paris: Bibliothèque du film, 1996); Robin Blaetz, *Visions of the Maid: Joan of Arc in American Film and Culture* (Charlottesville: University Press of Virginia, 2001); François Amy de la Bretèque, *L'imaginaire médiéval dans le cinéma occidental* (Paris: Honoré Champion, 2004), pp. 777–833; Kevin J. Harty, "Jeanne au cinéma," in *Fresh Verdicts on Joan of Arc*, ed. Bonnie Wheeler and Charles T. Wood (New York: Garland, 1996), pp. 237–64; Kevin J. Harty, *The Reel Middle Ages: American, Western, and Eastern European, Middle Eastern and Asian Films about Medieval Europe* (Jefferson, NC: McFarland, 1999); Judith Klinger, "Jeanne d'Arc" in *Mittelalter im Film*, ed. Christian Kiening and Heinrich Adolf (Berlin: Walter de Gruyter, 2006), pp. 135–70; Nadia Margolis, *Joan of Arc in History, Literature, and Film* (New York: Garland, 1990), pp. 393–406; and Charles Musser, *Edison Motion Pictures, 1890–1900: An Annotated Filmography* (Washington, DC: Smithsonian Institution Press, 1997), p. 190.

4. The most thorough account of the battle of Loos remains that in Liddell Hunt, *A History of the World War, 1914–1918* (London: Faber and Faber, 1930), pp. 255–68.

5. See *Le Petit Parisien*, January 2–16, 1916, for the French version of Moreau's memoirs; news stories about her bravery appear in the same publication on October 1, 1915; October 16, 1915; October 17, 1915; and October 28, 1915. An article on November 15, 1915, refers to her as a "seventeen-year-old heroine"; another on December 5, 1915, dubs her "the heroine of Loos." *Lloyd's Weekly News* ran an English translation of Moreau's memoirs from December 12, 1915, until February 6, 1916.

6. See *Lloyd's Weekly News*, December 5, 1915. Moreau remained an inspiration even after the battle of Loos. In the final paragraph of the last installment of her memoirs, she urged the French and their allies to strike back at German oppression, to liberate those still in occupied territories, and to embrace the divinely ordained destiny of France to mete out "the implacable punishment of Germany." See *Lloyd's Weekly News*, February 6, 1916.

7. All copies of Willoughby's *Joan of Arc of Loos* were thought to be lost until the mid-1990s when about eighteen hundred of the original five thousand feet of the film were discovered. For information about the film and a copy of the surviving footage on videotape, I am grateful to the staffs of the Australian National Film and Sound Archive in Canberra and of Screen-Sound Australia.

8. *Australian Variety*, May 3, 1916, and *Theatre Magazine*, May 1, 1916.

9. Heads rolled in the British command after a series of disasters on the western front in 1915, the worst of which was at Loos. See John Keegan, *The First World War* (New York: Knopf, 1999), p. 268–89, and Hunt, *History of the World War, 1914–1918*, pp. 255–68, for further details.

10. The disaster at Gallipoli, in which Australian and New Zealander forces suffered especially heavy losses, also occurred in 1915. On Gallipoli and the ANZAC role on the Turkish front, see Keegan, *First World War*, pp. 234–44.

11. On the three Australian films about Cavell, see Andrew Pike and Ross Cooper,

Australian Film, 1900–1977: A Guide to Feature Film Production (New York: Oxford University Press, 1998), pp. 59–62. Cavell has been the subject of a number of films, although the first British film about her was not made until 1928, Herbert Wilcox's *Dawn*, starring Sybil Thorndike as Cavell. Wilcox made a second film about Cavell in America in 1939, *Nurse Edith Cavell*, which had the misfortune (or good luck) to premiere the week that World War II broke out. An earlier American film about Cavell, *The Woman the Germans Shot*, directed by John G. Adolfi, was released in late 1918 coincidental with the Armistice.

12. *Argus*, April 8, 1916. Lincoln's *La Revanche* avoided copyright problems by billing itself as a sequel to *Nurse Cavell* that focused on the revenge her Belgian friends exacted on her executioners. See Pike and Cooper, *Australian Film*, p. 61.

13. "The Martyrdom of Nurse Cavell," in *The Oxford Companion to Australian Film*, ed. Brian McFarlane et al. (New York: Oxford University Press, 1999), p. 284.

14. While reviews of *Joan of Plattsburg* were generally positive, critics expressed some uneasiness with Normand's having been cast in a serious role, given her long career in screen comedies. See *The Bioscope*, October 31, 1918; *Motion Picture News*, May 18, 1918; *The Moving Picture World*, May 11, 1918 and May 18, 1918; *Variety*, May 3, 1918; *Wid's Daily*, May 12, 1918; and William Thomas Sherman, *Mabel Normand: A Source Book to Her Life and Films* (Seattle: Cinema Books, 1994). Incongruously, the film's original title was *Joan of Flatbush*. See Agnes Smith, "'Glad to Come Back,' Says Mabel Normand," *New York Morning Telegraph*, September 9, 1917. Plattsburg, the site of a major Army training camp, was a more appropriate setting for the film than Flatbush.

15. *Moving Picture World*, May 18, 1918. See also *Wid's Daily*, May 12, 1918.

16. Blaetz, *Visions of the Maid*, p. 73.

17. For a comparison of the different versions of the film, see Robin Blaetz, "Cecil B. DeMille's *Joan the Woman*," in *Medievalism in North America*, ed. Kathleen Verduin (Cambridge: D. S. Brewer, 1994), pp. 109–22.

18. Quoted in "'Joan of Arc' Ambitious Lasky Production," *New York Dramatic Mirror*, September 30, 1916.

19. Sumiko Higashi, *Cecil B. DeMille and American Culture: The Silent Era* (Berkeley: University of California Press, 1994), p. 140.

20. See Higashi, *Cecil B. DeMille and American Culture*, pp. 136–38.

21. My thanks again to David Sharp, former Librarian, and the staff of the Library at London's British Film Institute for their generous, professional, and continuing support of my research on medieval-themed films in general and on the films discussed in this essay in particular.

The Drama of Left-Wing Joan: From "Merlin's Prophecy" to Hellman's *Lark*

Nadia Margolis

Joan of Arc has functioned as an important political symbol for all manner of factions and causes within and outside France, although her most frequent appropriation in modern times has been by the right in France, most recently Jean-Marie Le Pen's National Front Party (1990s).[1] But when the so-called "Merlin's Prophecy" cited by Geoffrey of Monmouth in the twelfth century, and then marshaled by Joan as she was garnering support for her mission, declared "ex nemore canuto puella eliminabitur ut medelae curam adhibeat" ("from out of the oak forest would come a maiden to give care to healing"), it portended a future for what we might call the "people's Pucelle" as well as for the already well-documented royal-imperial political-symbolic structures. Her simple, pure qualities—she actually did frequent the neighboring oak forest around Domremy—would overshadow even the dauphin's ennoblement of her family, particularly in the romantic nineteenth century, as praised by Jules Michelet in his highly influential Republican (centrist), anticlerical history of her (1841).[2]

Returning to Joan's era, we might possibly interpret Christine de Pizan's *Ditié de Jehanne d'Arc* (Song of Joan of Arc) (1429)—the first nonanonymous work honoring Joan in French during the heroine's lifetime—as the poet's sole populist piece, which accordingly differs from her other writings in its simple, spontaneous style and unabashedly patriotic tone. That it survives in only two complete manuscripts, neither elaborately produced, also suggests a work aimed more at the masses than at her usual royal patrons. The occasion may have been a celebration of Charles VII's coronation as rightful king and his victory over the English, for which Christine penned her poem to reassure the populace, including the *menu peuple*,[3] that Joan was divinely—not diabolically, as the pro-English propagandists argued to explain their humiliation at Orléans—inspired.[4] The poet thereby also contributes toward establishing three key facets of Joan's persona that would inform her future incarnations throughout world literature: her heroism, her piety, and her link to the supernatural.[5]

Among several manifestations since the French Revolution, during which various political wings defined themselves according to their placement around the *hémicycle* of the National Assembly, her left-wing presence occurs most strikingly during the early mid-twentieth century, not long after her canonization in 1920: a time when right-wing totalitarianism in the form of the Nazis and their allies threatened to dominate Europe and thus also soon affected the United States after the ill-wrought Treaty of Versailles ended World War I. This era (1920s–50s) also interests us because it involves three very distinct major authors of different nationalities: the German playwright Bertolt Brecht, the French dramatist Jean Anouilh, and the American woman of letters Lillian Hellman.[6]

❖

Bertolt Brecht (1898–1956), throughout his career, ended up writing—or, more accurately, cowriting or adapting—three plays on Joan: with Emil Burri and Elisabeth Hauptmann, *Die Heilige Johanna der Schlachthöfe* (Saint Joan of the Stockyards) (1928–29); with Lion Feuchtwanger, *Die Gesichte der Simone Machard* (The Visions of Simone Machard); and adapting, with Benno Besson, Anna Seghers's radio play *Der Prozess der Jeanne d'Arc zu Rouen 1431* (The Trial of Joan of Arc at Rouen 1431) for the stage in 1952.[7] The first proved to be the most important, since, by itself, coming right after his sensational *Dreigroschenoper* (Threepenny Opera), it displays Brecht's most characteristic and significant ideas on several levels: the Marxist-philosophical, the sociohistorical, and the theoretical. As one of his deliberately Marxist-didactic plays or *Lehrstücke*, it renders Joan's story not so much a model to be emulated as an entire, disturbing moral fable of what happens to a virtuous, sincere, but naively idealistic, nonviolent individual locked within a brutal class struggle; it depicts his view of a Depression-era United States ruled by bankers (the same who preyed upon impoverished post–World War I Germany), as portrayed by the muckrakers such as Upton Sinclair. Theoretically, the play puts into practice Brecht's pioneering notion of "epic theater": alternatingly detaching and engaging the spectators from the action on stage so as to incite them finally to social action via knowledge accumulated as the play progresses, rather than through conventional "bourgeois" emotional involvement with the characters and plot suspense.[8] Most pointedly influenced by Shaw's *Saint Joan* (1924) and *Major Barbara* (1905), which Brecht admired, *Heilige Johanna* mercilessly parodies Schiller's then-revered *Die Jungfrau von Orleans* (The Maid of Orleans) (1801) and, to a far lesser extent, Goethe's *Faust* as examples of classical form (based on harmony and balance) and romantic fabrication (most strikingly, Schiller has Joan die in the dauphin's arms on the battlefield rather than at the stake), which made classicism and romanticism such effective vehicles for the bourgeois values Brecht despised in his brazen youth.[9]

However, despite *Heilige Johanna*'s undeniable theatrical historical value, its Joan, so dated by ideological circumstance and deliberately dissociated from the spectator by Brecht's theoretical dogma summarized above, may appear no more credible to us than Schiller's force-of-nature Joan of over a century earlier. A verse drama set in Chicago's meatpacking district (he had originally considered setting it in the city's wheat market but chose the meat industry for its irresistible metaphor of the class struggle as slaughterhouse), *Heilige Johanna* tells the story of Joan Dark (her last name betokening her well-meaning inability to see the world clearly, like Oedipus: both figures suffering tragic ends when they finally do see the truth of their lives). Joan belongs to a Salvation Army–like group, the Black Straw Hats, who attempt to aid the miserable unemployed or underpaid workers whose suffering results from the ruthless business practices of Pierpont Mauler, a meatpacking magnate trying to undercut his competitors. Joan identifies and approaches Mauler (the cynical dauphin figure) to convince him to help the poor. Mauler counters that the poor are also fundamentally wicked and unworthy of her compassion, but she perseveres in her sympathies, even after being expelled by the Black Straw Hats. Then the Communists, organizing a general strike, appoint her as a messenger to inform the workers of the strike—her mission, spurred on by her voices—but they alienate her by advocating violence, which she opposes. During the violent confrontation from which Mauler emerges victorious by corrupting all factions and averting the strike, Joan, now mortally injured, in her dying words espouses violence as necessary to progress: she has seen the light. Simultaneously overshadowing this speech, the story of her martyrdom (as in Schiller's play, on the battlefield, not the stake) is canonized by her betrayers—workers and Black Straw Hats alike—in a litany of religious clichés, led by Mauler, who then canonizes her as "St. Joan of the Stockyards." Thus the play's Marxist attack shifts from capitalist economics to religion, the infamous "opiate of the people."[10] In all, Brecht engages Joan's three key qualities—heroism, piety, and association with the supernatural—to deflate them and destroy her. At least one critic reads this, Brecht's first full-length Marxist play, as "to a certain degree, the autobiographical story of the bourgeois author's involvement with the proletariat and his gradual acceptance of violence."[11]

Brecht, unable ever to stage *Heilige Johanna* beyond a radio performance in 1932, moved on. Despite his unfavorable portrayal of the United States, he visited there in the 1940s in hopes of breaking into its theater scene (and thus benefiting from capitalist munificence himself) particularly with a play devoted to another illustrious victim of the church's intolerance, *Galileo* (1947).

This play premiered in Beverly Hills and New York, but its author soon found himself before another audience, the HUAC (House Un-American Activities Committee), because of his Communist affiliation. Although he cleverly succeeded in convincing the bumbling committee to release him, even cordially, this did not prevent Brecht from comparing HUAC to Hitler's persecution of un-German activities.[12]

❖

Jean Anouilh (1910–87), a prolific and artistically innovative playwright, proves by example that right-wing authors were also capable of experimentation in Shaw's and Brecht's wake. Interested in existentialism—though less affected by "isms" than the other writers treated here—as well as in honing his artistic talents, Anouilh favored courageous heroes, often taken from history or myth, and depicted them grappling with mid-twentieth-century sociopolitical questions but in a more transcendently philosophical or human way than one finds in the political theater of Brecht or French contemporaries. Indeed, he always labeled himself as apolitical, even in his *Antigone*, in whose heroine many readers saw a resistance fighter and in Creon, Vichy. However, if Vichy served as the traumatic backdrop for leftist authors, the right received its comeuppance promptly after the 1944 liberation, in a purge during which the defeated pro-Nazi collaborators, including journalists and artists, were hunted down and executed by the newly empowered leftists. For artists and writers of either side, the most appalling event was the trial and execution of Robert Brasillach, one of France's most gifted men of letters, who had written abundantly for the Vichy press. As it so happens, he spoke reverently of Joan (and, like Brecht, also dramatized her trial), with whom he identified as he bravely faced the firing squad in 1945. Brasillach was pardoned by the literati, if not by General de Gaulle, because he had acted on patriotic principles (i.e., Nazi ideals would benefit a France gone soft) from which he never wavered, not even to save himself. Anouilh also wrote for pro-German papers but more innocuously, on literature and the arts; he consorted with other similarly passive, even naïve, right-wing writers and artists, since he had always considered himself a "penseur artisanal"[13] (artistic thinker) rather than the overtly committed, political-esthetic polemicist Brasillach could be.[14] After the latter's execution jolted Anouilh out of his apolitical delusions, he wrote at least one play that even he avowed as political: *Pauvre Bitos* (Poor Bitos) in 1956, attacking the liberation purge. Moreover, throughout de Gaulle's regime, Anouilh, by now the most esteemed French playwright of his time, refused to allow his plays to be staged by any state-run theater (including the Comédie-Française) and furthermore refused nomination to the Académie Française.

Within the evolutionary progression bridging *Antigone* and *Pauvre Bitos*, Anouilh's Joan play, *L'Alouette* (The Lark) of 1952, also addresses the problem of the individual versus political fanaticism and intolerance. But he himself (typically innocently, or disingenuously) labeled it one of his *Pièces costumées*, or "costumed plays": the "costume" in Joan's case involved not only a medieval backdrop and garb but also an engaging restructuring of her fate. He was first encouraged to write it by the leading Joan scholar of the day, the pro-Pétain Jesuit priest Paul Doncoeur, who extolled her as the "Christian Antigone."[15] Anouilh at first balked at the idea out of the usual fear of overexploitation of the Maid and then accepted because it offered a new chance to redramatize her story.

As this one-scene-only play opens in the courtroom, Warwick and Cauchon, before actually condemning her—which they are eager to do—ask Joan to replay the great moments of her life, for which rearrangement Anouilh uses the cinematic technique of the flashback to construct clever, sometimes poignant or amusing, historical and cultural parallels between the two time frames. This technique thrusts the modern spectator into Joan's life and times while projecting Joan into the present, thereby inviting a positive reinterpretation of Joan's fate. The chronology now scrambled, the characters try to regain control of the story, each in his or her own way. Anouilh thus injects a sort of intelligent anarchy rather than any one political stance. As a prime example, here the dauphin's coronation supersedes the stake as the apogee of her mission, and Joan is saved from burning by Beaudricourt; her story has a "joyous ending," as the dauphin exults, organs play, trumpets sound, and the sacred doves soar. Yet despite this happy ending, Anouilh never sacrifices the elements of her heroism, piety, and relationship to the supernatural: he manages to reinforce her physical, political, and religious purity, as one critic notes,[16] and effects the third aspect as author—the playwright as prime mover—while she herself offers to act the role of her voices, since she confuses heaven's voice with her own anyway.

Shaw's influence is obvious when she calls the dauphin "Charlie"; like Shaw, Anouilh achieves powerful characterizations and expresses profound ideas with much wit and deftness, more than we find in Brecht. As in Schiller's play, but treated differently, the anachronistic presence of Agnès Sorel, the dauphin's later mistress, affords an intriguing comparison of herself and Joan as opposite female legends. Anouilh associates Joan with the lark because she flutters over the soldiers' heads, singing her "chant joyeux et absurde d'une petite alouette immobile dans le soleil pendant qu'on lui tire dessus" (joyous and absurd song of a little lark transfixed in the sunshine, while they try to shoot her down).[17] The play was so well received in Paris that Anouilh decided, like Brecht, to try to conquer the American public. For this enterprise his agent, Dr. Jan van Loewen, approached one of the foremost American dramatists in 1955, Lillian Hellman.

Lillian Hellman (1905–84) was born and bred in a country never ruled by a monarch nor occupied by a foreign power, and one that believed, among other national myths, its society to be devoid of class boundaries. Hellman consequently exemplifies the most idealistic, comfortable style of Marxism, as she herself knew. She could visit such beleaguered locales as Russia and sincerely sympathize with and write about its people's struggle with far greater perceptiveness than they themselves, because she could afford to, and then could return to her home in New York or to a country retreat among her celebrity friends. Even in her moments of greatest suffering for her beliefs—and this, the McCarthy era, was admittedly a horrible time, personally and professionally, for her and other artists and intellectuals—she was at least allowed to live and recoup her life. Financially ruined by the McCarthy-era blacklist, Hellman first confirms that money was the motive for accepting the invitation to adapt *L'Alouette*, only to disavow that and ascribe it instead to "feeling mischievous" as she sat negotiating with van Loewen, in that unlikely Marxist bastion, the Ritz Hotel in London.[18] In sum, although there was some squabbling later on between van Loewen and Hellman, Anouilh appears to have been very cooperative, entrusting any revisions to Hellman's sense of what would please the American public.[19] Hellman's adaptation, *The Lark*, premiering in November 1955 and starring Julie Harris in the title role, with music by Leonard Bernstein, was enormously acclaimed by critics and attained box-office success, with 229 performances.

The Anouilh-Hellman *Lark* has received much insightful critical attention over the years. Yet very few American critics and scholars seem aware of the potential ideological clash between the two authors, not to mention the motives behind and the effect of Hellman's changes.[20] Despite Hellman's openly labeling her work an "adaptation" rather than a "translation," various critics profess to be analyzing Anouilh's Joan when actually they are innocently reading Hellman's English version for convenience, or claim to be examining Hellman versus Anouilh, but the latter via Christopher Fry's moderately successful 1955 translation of the French. Uncomprehending others wonder why Hellman bothered, in light of Fry's translation.[21]

Nor did Anouilh and Hellman seem aware of their political differences, probably because each author was pursuing a more pressing agenda: new horizons in their respective careers. Hellman did not use Fry's translation after seeing its 1955 London performance, which left her cold.[22] She instead based her adaptation—the second and most successful of her career threesome—on an unpublished rendering, by two no-less-accomplished translators of French literature, Lucienne Hill and Jane Hinton, which Hellman went over very thoroughly, to judge by the number of annotations.[23] Hellman also admired Shaw's *Saint Joan*, and her notes reveal such sources as Willard Trask's then already classic *Joan of Arc—A Self-Portrait,* based on rearranged excerpts from Joan's trial testimony, plus correspondence with a certain Father Rover concerning Inquisition details.[24] Hellman's feminism was also a factor, coupled with her leftist politics: "I was convinced that Joan was history's first modern career girl, wise, unattractive in what she knew about the handling of men, straight out of a woman's magazine. The wonderful story lay, as Shaw had seen it, in the miraculous self-confidence that carried defeated men into battle against all sense and reason, forced a pious girl into a refusal of her church, caused the terrible death that still has to do with the rest of us, forever, wherever her name is heard."[25] These words also convey how she would handle Joan's heroism, piety, and supernatural aura.

Hellman's emendations to the play would subtly yet forcefully incorporate these beliefs, especially since, as she confesses, after working halfway through Anouilh's play she decided she didn't like it much after all.[26] She "scaled down the play" and omitted the comparisons to the Occupation and "tributes to the French spirit," since she had her doubts about the French spirit and also suspected Anouilh did as well. She also eliminated the "fake" doves at the end.[27] Scholar Henry Knepler has more thoroughly discussed Hellman's modifications, too numerous and complex to list here,[28] which most American critics consider an improvement, since her play is tighter, uses drama rather than discourse, and thus moves along more briskly than either Fry's or Anouilh's.[29]

So was Joan another vehicle or did Hellman really identify with her, especially during her McCarthy-era troubles?[30] Hellman never says as much outright, perhaps because, as a skillful author, she feared it would sound too obvious, even trite, on the part of a politically militant woman writer to state explicitly: "I felt like Joan of Arc."[31] Neither does Christine de Pizan, arguably Joan's literary doppelgänger, maybe for the same reasons. But as Ann Astell, among others, has demonstrated in analyzing Hellman's third memoir, *Scoundrel Time*, this account, by invoking mysterious voices that inspired her during her HUAC ordeal, appears to set up such parallels so as to facilitate equating the two and thus making herself a heroine, if not a saint.[32] But this is not hollow narcissism on Hellman's part. Joan is one of several characters either created or adapted by the playwright to underscore her ideal of personal dignity via unflagging moral commitment in the face of active or passive evil.

❖

To conclude: for all three authors, Joan was only one historical character on whom they would write who appealed to their personal political philosophies. Brecht's *Heilige Johanna* is both sociopolitical fable and theoretical vehicle. Anouilh used her as a pretext for rewriting a certain moment in the history of the individual against collective persecution. Hellman adapted Anouilh's Joan to express very similar themes to those of Brecht and Anouilh but in an American vein, despite the opposing political affiliations of each author.

NOTES

Earlier versions of this article were given at an international colloquium, "Pucelle: Ne s'emploie qu'avec Orléans," at the University of Montpellier, September 22, 2006, and also in a seminar, French 515: "Jeanne d'Arc," at Mount Holyoke College, fall semester 2007. My thanks to both institutions for their hospitality and feedback, from which the current work has greatly benefited.

1. See Michel Winock's survey of Joan's many political appropriations, "Jeanne d'Arc," in *Les Lieux de Mémoire*, vol. 3, *Les France*, part 3, *De l'archive à l'emblème*, ed. Pierre Nora (Paris: Gallimard, 1992), pp. 675–733.

2. Jules Michelet, "Jeanne Darc, Charles VII," occupies vol. 5 of his *Histoire de France* (Paris: Hachette, 1841). Michelet's republican, post-Revolutionary (i.e., without the particle) spelling of her last name may have influenced Brecht's spelling of "Dark."

3. That is, the lower classes, whom she sympathetically treats in vv. 6413–6580 in her *Mutacion de Fortune* (Fortune's Transformation), quite exceptional for a court poet of her time. See the edition by Suzanne Solente, Société des anciens textes français (Paris: Picard, 1959), 2:73–79.

4. Christine de Pizan, *Ditié de Jehanne d'Arc: Christine de Pisan*, ed. Angus J. Kennedy and Kenneth Varty, Medium Ævum Monographs, n.s. 9 (Oxford: Society for the Study of Mediæval Languages and Literature, 1977), vv. 393, 198. For the Merlin prophecies and others, see notes to this edition, esp. pp. 68–69.

5. See Christine de Pizan, *Ditié*, e.g., for heroism: vv. 218–19, 265; piety: vv. 249–53; relationship with the supernatural: vv. 225–28, 274.

6. For "the Marxist Joan of Arc" in Shaw, Brecht, and Hellman, citing directly from Marx and Engels, see Ann W. Astell, *Joan of Arc and Sacrificial Authorship* (Notre Dame, IN: University of Notre Dame Press, 2003), pp. 109–45, to which the above discussion is indebted while pursuing a different track.

7. For all three texts, see *Bertolt Brecht, Die Drei Johanna-Stücke* (Frankfurt: Fischer Bücherei, 1964); and in English, *Saint Joan of the Stockyards*, translated by Ralph Manheim (New York: Arcade, 1991).

8. For Brecht's "epic theater," see notes to Manheim, *Saint Joan of the Stockyards*, pp. 118–20; also Claude Hill, *Bertolt Brecht*, Twayne's World Authors Series 331 (Boston: Twayne, 1971), pp. 140–59.

9. Martin Esslin (*Brecht: A Choice of Evils*, 4th rev. ed. [London: Methuen, 1984], p. 49) deems *Die Jungfrau* "one the silliest plays in the German classical canon." However, it was Schiller's *Die Jungfrau* that reawakened the world, including the French, to the heroine's mythic potential. See, e.g., Claude Foucart, "'Cette vivante énigme': Jeanne d'Arc," *Cahiers de recherches médiévales* 11 (2004): 19–29.

10. See Esslin, *Brecht*; Hill, *Bertolt Brecht*; and Astell (who in *Joan of Arc and Sacrificial Authorship* persuasively compares her to Sophocles's Oedipus, whose production Brecht had seen in 1929, pp. 114–21; for Brecht as inspired by Shaw and Schiller; see also Gundula M. Sharman, *Twentieth-Century Reworkings of German Literature* (Rochester, NY: Camden House, 2002), pp. 16–44.

11. Hill, *Bertolt Brecht*, p. 71.

12. Esslin, *Brecht*, pp. 71–73, quotes from and comments upon *Hearings Regarding the Communist Infiltration of the Motion Picture Industry . . .* (Washington, DC: U.S. Government Printing Office, 1947), pp. 491–504.

13. See Anouilh's interview with Nicolas de Rabaudy, "Jean Anouilh," *Paris-Match*, Oct. 21, 1972, pp. 86–89.

14. Mary Ann F. Witt, *The Search for Modern Tragedy: Aesthetic Fascism in Italy and France* (Ithaca: Cornell University Press, 2001), pp. 228–29, details Anouilh's Fascist undercurrents, even in *Antigone*, and his open sympathy with Brasillach.

15. Elie de Comminges, *Anouilh, littérature et politique* (Paris: Nizet, 1977), p. 19. Doncoeur had served as consultant to Hollywood director Victor Fleming to help his film *Joan of Arc* (1947) avoid the violent, artistically stifling, conflicts with the French right endured by Carl Dreyer during the making and premiere of *La Passion de Jeanne d'Arc* (1927–28). Doncoeur later recanted his allegiance to the Vichy government out of disillusionment with its leader, Marshal Pétain.

16. Anne Régent, "*L'Alouette* de Jean Anouilh," *Études Médiévales* 2.2 (2000): 349–57.

17. Jean Anouilh, *L'Alouette* (Paris: Table Ronde, 1953; repr. Paris: Folio, 2006), p. 111.

18. Lillian Hellman, *Pentimento* (Boston: Little, Brown, 1973), p. 200.

19. Letter from van Loewen to Hellman, May 21, 1955, described by Manfred Triesch in *The Lillian Hellman Collection at the University of Texas* (Austin: University of Texas Press, 1966), p. 96, item C20.

20. The sole instances I have found are Dominique Goy-Blanquet's review of Astell in *Medium Aevum* 74 (2005): 337, and Claude Grimal, "The American Maid," in *Joan of Arc, a Saint for All Reasons: Studies in Myth and Politics*, ed. Dominique Goy-Blanquet (Aldershot: Ashgate, 2003), pp. 136–38.

21. See, e. g., Sandra Lee, "*The Lark*, Lillian Hellman's Adaptation of Jean Anouilh's *L'Alouette*, directed by Kirsten Kelly," online review (2000) at <http://www.artscope.net/PAREVIEWS/TheLark0800.shtml>, p. 2: "That Lillian Hellman wrote an adaptation of *L'Alouette* only two years after its original production is more difficult to fathom." For Hellman's text, see Jean Anouilh, *The Lark*, adapted by Lillian Hellman (New York: Random House, 1956).

22. Hellman, *Pentimento*, p. 201.

23. These typescripts (items A9d–A9f) are housed along with Hellman's drafts of the play and other papers related to *The Lark* at the University of Texas Harry Ransom Collection, items A9–A9r. See Triesch, *Lillian Hellman Collection*, pp. 56–62.

24. Willard Trask, *Joan of Arc: A Self-Portrait* (New York: Stackpole, 1936); Triesch, item C21.

25. Hellman, *Pentimento*, p. 202.

26. Interview with John Phillips and Anne Hollander, *Partisan Review* 33 (1965): 64–65; reprinted in *Conversations with Lillian Hellman*, ed. Jackson R. Bryer (Jackson: University Press of Mississippi, 1986), pp. 58–59.

27. Hellman, *Pentimento*, p. 202.

28. Henry Knepler, "*The Lark*: Translation vs. Adaptation: A Case History," *Modern Drama* 1 (1958): 15–28.

29. For a critical overview of the play, see Barbara Lee Horn, *Lillian Hellman: A Research and Production Sourcebook* (Westport, CT: Greenwood Press, 1998), p. 48.

30. In fact, her HUAC interrogation itself lasted only just over an hour and ended with

her release, thanks to shrewd legal counsel—something Joan certainly lacked. For her dealings with HUAC and her writing of *The Lark*, see Deborah Martinson, *Lillian Hellman: A Life with Foxes and Scoundrels* (New York: Counterpoint/Perseus, 2005), chap. 6; for her HUAC testimony, FBI file, and other records, see Martinson's notes, pp. 406–10. Hellman's personal memoir of the McCarthy era is *Scoundrel Time* (Boston: Little, Brown, 1976).

31. Whereas, by contrast, an utterly unlikely author such as Arthur Rimbaud need have no qualms about such a self-comparison to Joan, as in "Mauvais sang," in *Une Saison en Enfer* [1873] in *Oeuvres complètes*, ed. Roland de Renéville and Jules Mouquet (Paris: Gallimard/Pléiade, 1967), p. 223.

32. Astell (*Joan of Arc and Sacrificial Authorship*, pp. 142–44) adds much to the previous critics whom she cites on the Joan-Hellman parallels.

Part 4
Nuns and Spirituality

A Letter to the Abbess of Fontevrault from the Abbot of Clairvaux

Giles Constable

Most medieval letters survive in collections, and comparatively few are known from isolated copies.[1] The letter published here from Stiftsbibliothek Admont MS 446, fol. 110v was written probably in the middle of the twelfth century by the abbot of Clairvaux to the abbess of Fontevrault. The text breaks off in the middle (not the end) of a line, which suggests that the scribe copied all that he had before him and that the text was taken from an incomplete copy rather than that a page of the manuscript is missing. It was apparently written by two scribes, of whom one copied the first twenty-five lines, up to *sanctuario*, and the second the remaining eleven words.[2] The handwriting resembles those in other manuscripts from Admont in the second half of the twelfth century, but it does not match that of any known scribe.

The abbess is identified by the initial M, which may stand for Mathilda I of Anjou, abbess from about 1149 to 1155, or for Mathilda II (1189/90–94), Mathilda III (1194–1207), or Mary of Champagne (1207–8).[3] The abbot is identified as P, but neither of the two possibilities whose names begin with P, Pontius of Polignac (1165–70) and Peter Monoculus (1179–86), coincided with an abbess whose name starts with M. It is possible that P is an error for R and refers to Robert of Bruges, who was abbot of Clairvaux from 1153 to 1157, which would date the letter 1153/5.[4] The initials may be fictitious, however, as indeed may be the entire letter.

The letter shows the abbot's respect and affection for the abbess, whom he had met before, since he said that they were already united by "a single and pure grace" and that their love for one another was subsequently (*deinde*) augmented. Most of the letter is a paeon of praise to "the grace of the eternal bridegroom," that is Christ, which brought them together and is the source of their love. The

155

abbot lists the many benefits bestowed on mankind and himself by grace, which he addresses as "you," though in places this may refer to the abbess. It is owing to grace, he writes, that he exists, lives, knows, and adores the saints and that he deserves to see and adore grace "in the temple of your holy name [and] in the sanctuary of your glorification." These are strong words, even making allowance for rhetorical exaggeration, and they reflect both his confidence in the efficacy of grace and the warmth of his feelings for the abbess. The comparative grade of the last word—*sanctius* "more holy"—after which the text breaks off, suggests that it went on in the same vein, but unless another manuscript comes to light the continuation remains unknown.

The letter was probably one of those medieval letters which, to the despair of hardheaded scholars, includes more sentiments than facts. The sentiments are not without interest, however, and constitute a fact in themselves. That the head of the most important reformed monastic order of the twelfth century wrote in such terms to the abbess of the motherhouse of an influential female order is not without significance, and that he apparently already knew the abbess and planned another meeting adds a small but interesting fact to the history of the relations between male and female religious orders in the twelfth century.

The letter is printed here as it is found in the manuscript, including the capitals, the repeated *ex* at the break of the fourth and fifth lines of the manuscript, and the spelling *obsura* (presumably for *obscura*) in line 22. Both V and U are used at the beginnings of the third and fourth sentences. The capitals H and S at the beginnings of lines 13 and 20 are placed in the left-hand margin. The punctuation follows that of the manuscript, with a few additions, aside from replacing the periods with commas and in one case a semicolon. The translation poses a few problems, including the occasional ambiguity of *te* and *tuus*, which may refer to grace or the abbess, and the use of some unusual words. An effort has been made to reflect the style of the original, but much of it, such as the wordplay on *aufert*, *confert*, *defert*, and *refert* in reference to grace, is lost.[5]

[V]enera[bile] abbatisse
fontis erbaldi, M. P. clareuallensis, abbas suus in christo
amicus, gratiam et gloriam sponsi eterni. Inspector conscientiarum
deus et testis. Nouit quibus dignationem uestram precordiis exceperim,
quia incomprehensibiliter ad considerationem mutui amoris ex [*sic*] 5
exultauerim quiaque incomparabiliter omni auro familiaritatem
uestram pretulerim. Vnica siquidem et pura me uobis prius conciliauit
gratia, tamen deinde ampliandam amoris multiplex superuenit
causa. Ubi non nulla causa operum preludia, nulla precederint offi-
ciorum blandimenta, unde amorem dixerim precedere, nisi a gratia? Hec 10
non operatur motibus propriis et spontaneis in corde hominum, sine peni-
tentia, cum multa reuerentia, et absque inuidorum calumpnia.
Hec aufert suspicionem, confert affectionem, defert honorem,
refert pudorem; hac interuentione soluuntur malignantia uel su-
surria, consolidatur bonorum concordia, et prorsus adimuntur insidi- 15
antium machinamenta. Hec spirituum coagulum, ac indissolubi-
le bitumen animarum, diuersitates morum, ad unam consonantiam reducit,
et meritorum inequalitates, ad equalitatis contemperantiam proportionaliter
recolligit. O gratia generosa, sine te omnia mala, tecum omnia bona.
Sine te inquam inanis uniuersa creatura, et a te repletur angelica cum hu- 20
mana creatura. Tu reformas deformia, lapsa reparas, confirmas
debilia, clausa reseras, congregas dispersa, et obs[c]ura illumi-
nas. Tuum est quod sum, quod uiuo, quod sapio, quod sanctorum uestigiis procumbo de-
uotus. Tuum inquam, tuum est quod te in templo sancti tui nominis, quod in
sanctuario tue glorificationis uidere et adorare te me- 25
rui. Si enim sanctius

Abbot P. of Clairvaux, her friend in Christ, [sends] the grace and glory of the eternal bridegroom to the venerable abbess M. of Fontevrault. God, the inspector and witness of consciences, knows with what heartfelt emotions I have received your honor, because I have immeasurably rejoiced in considering [our] mutual love and because I have incomparably preferred your friendship to all gold. A single and pure grace previously brought us together, but then [grace as] a multiple cause came to increase love. Whereas some cause [is] the prelude of works [and] no favors of offices would come first, wherefore would I say that [our] love comes first, if not by grace? This [grace] does not work in the hearts of men by their own and spontaneous movements without penitence, [but] with great reverence and without the tricks of envious men. This [grace] removes suspicion, confers affection, bestows honor, revives shame; by its intervention malignancies and complaints are dissolved, the agreement of good men is strengthened, and the machinations of deceitful men are entirely removed. This [grace] brings back into a single harmony the bond of spirits and the indissoluble solidity of souls, [and] the diversity of manners, and it gathers in proportion the inequalities of merits into a tempered mixture of equality. O generous grace, without you all [is] bad, with you all [is] good. Without you, I say, all creation [is] empty, and by you angelic [creation] is replenished with human creation. You reform deformities, repair lapses, strengthen weaknesses, open what is closed, assemble what is dispersed, and illuminate what is dark. It is owing to you that I exist, that I live, that I know, that I prostrate myself in devotion before the remains of the saints. It is owing to you, I say, to you, that I have deserved to see and adore you in the temple of your holy name, in the sanctuary of your glorification. For if more holy . . .

NOTES

1. Giles Constable, *Letters and Letter-Collections*, Typologie des sources du Moyen Âge occidental 17 (Turnhout: Brepols, 1976), pp. 55–56.

2. I owe this and the following observation to Professor Alison Beach of Ohio State University, who pointed out among the differences between the two hands the connection of *o* and *r* and the formations of the *c-t* and small *d*.

3. Some of these dates are approximate: see Honorat Nicquet, *Histoire de l'ordre de Font-Evraud* (Paris: Chez M. Soly, 1642), pp. 392–430 (for this reference I am indebted to Jacques Dalarun); Edouard Biron, *Fontevrault et ses monuments*, 2 vols. (Paris: Grande imprimerie catholique de France, 1873–74), vol. 1, pp. 201–44; J. Daoust in *Dictionnaire d'histoire et de géographie ecclésiastiques*, vol. 17 (Paris: Letouzey et Ané, 1971), p. 969.

4. J.-M. Canivez in *Dictionnaire d'histoire et de géographie ecclésiastiques*, vol. 12 (Paris: Letouzey et Ané, 1953), p. 1053.

5. I am grateful for assistance on some points in the translation to Professor Janet Martin of Princeton University.

The Nuns of Bival in the Thirteenth Century

William Chester Jordan

Even the best scholars of the history of medieval Normandy have had little to say on the Cistercian nunnery of Bival.[1] The exception was Joseph Strayer, who in the 1950s discovered a late twelfth-century forged charter pertaining to the abbey, whose text he edited and whose circumstances of production he explained in an article in *Speculum*.[2] Other authentic twelfth- and thirteenth-century charters for the nunnery came to his attention while his article was in proof, and he summarized some of the information in these materials in a brief appendix. Otherwise, he did not further exploit the charters. Since then, however, his photostatic reproductions of the manuscripts along with his working notes have come into my possession and, together with other available information, they provide the bulk of the data for this study.[3]

The *Speculum* article of 1959 identified a manuscript in the Scheide Collection of Princeton's Firestone Library, box 206, no. 6992, as a forgery purporting to come from 1177. It represented a lost set of originals that had a great deal of authentic information about the house and its possessions.[4] Since little is known of Bival from unimpeachable records, it was useful to separate the truth from the falsehoods of the forgery. For, as Strayer remarked, "[t]here is more information about Bival's possessions in this supposed charter of [King] Henry II [of England, the Duke of Normandy,] than in all the printed sources." The nuns of Bival, originally of the Congregation of Savigny before their affiliation with the Cistercians, were trying to assert a measure of control over the abbey of Bondeville, whose first residents probably included nuns sent from Bival. The situation was compounded by the fact that Bival itself was trying to secure its autonomy from another house, Beaubec, from which its original nuns had migrated. Bondeville found a willing ally in Beaubec in trying to counter Bival's claim.[5]

Despite the forgery, which embedded its supposed lordship over Bondeville in a list of authentic rights, Bival's claim was never accepted, and the nuns of the thirteenth century ultimately let it drop. For a while in the late twelfth and early thirteenth century, Bival managed to command modest grants from aristocrats living in its vicinity. In 1185, one Hugues d'Oiry, for example, donated to the nuns the revenue of half the tithes in a small territory he possessed.[6] In 1220 Gérard de Caigni, out of love and for the salvation of his soul and the souls of his ancestors, endowed the nuns with half the patronage of the church of Saint-Lucien of Caigni (the present-day Crillon) and the sixth part of the tithes of the parish of Caigni.[7] He also attested the grant of other tithes to the nuns by his wife Isabelle the same year.[8] (This grant led to a dispute in 1228, but this was resolved amicably *pro bono pacis* by the co-owners, Saint-Lucien of Beauvais and, now, Bival.)[9] There is a record of one Aveline de Beaussault granting the nuns a tithe on a mill at Hodeng in 1222.[10] Bival's claim to patronage rights in the same place, however, became a source of dispute in 1231.[11] Finally, in 1240 Barthélemy de Fontaines, for his soul and those of his ancestors, granted the tithes pertaining to part of his lands and rights for a barn to store the produce collected.[12]

The surviving charters recording grants to Bival then peter out for a while, reflecting a likely decline in oblations, but another source kicks in from the 1240s, the *Register* or record of daily travels and episcopal visitations of the Franciscan archbishop of Rouen, Eudes Rigaud.[13] Male Cistercian monasteries were exempt from episcopal visitation. The nunneries were not.[14] Eudes visited Saint Mary Magdalene of Bival, to give the house its original patronal designation, at least fourteen times from 1248 to 1269.[15] What he found on his first visit on August 7, 1248, may explain why gifts were not forthcoming to the monastery, if the pattern of surviving deeds is not misleading. A few of the nuns were *diffamati*, that is, had been reported to him or to his administration as in some form of rebellion against authority or their vows. In this case the accusations levied involved sexual misconduct, although Eudes's *Register* does not go into specifics. The charges were sufficiently serious that the archbishop demanded and received the resignation of Eleanor, the abbess. He then took the governance of the house into his own hands and instructed the nuns to elect a new abbess.[16] The election, scheduled for two days later, took place while Archbishop Eudes visited other establishments in the area. He received word by letter as to what they did.[17]

They used the method known as "delegation," a method employed where the Holy Spirit did not immediately inspire consensus on a candidate. The nuns designated three nuns to come to consensus for them. "They," the record says, "taking counsel together, have canonically with one heart and one mind provided Marguerite of Aunay for our monastery." They asked for Archbishop Eudes's confirmation and blessing. Eudes granted them the confirmation, commended their work, committed the temporalities to the new abbess, and enjoined obedience on the nuns. "And be it known," he wrote to them, "that if any shall be disobedient or rebellious, we shall punish them in such a manner that the punishment of one shall be a terror to the rest."[18]

We do not know how many nuns were at Bival in 1248, but when Archbishop Eudes visited on August 28, three years later, he noted that there were thirty-three.[19] He was disturbed that some of them left the cloister without the license of the abbess or other superior authority, and he reminded them of their duty to remain cloistered. He was also disturbed at the reverse porosity of the walls. Lay folk entered the cloister, kin of the nuns, including some of their brothers, a potentially scandalous situation. He sought to remedy this situation but cautioned the nuns not to apply his proscription against all laypeople, some of whom might be required, though under careful supervision, to attend to the nuns' needs. Forbidding such people might be a scandal in itself, he pointed out.[20] The nuns had a small debt they were carrying, not anything to worry about. But they talked too much, he discovered, when more silence was, in his view, to be preferred. Finally, they also had small chests where they kept personal belongings. The archbishop was wary of this, but he noted that it was the abbess who permitted the practice and even granted the sisters the privacy of their personal possessions by allowing them to have their own individual keys to the chests.

Little over a year later Eudes visited again.[21] Thirty-two nuns greeted him. The problems, as he constructed them, were the same. Most of the nuns were proving to be obedient inmates, though there were two exceptions, including a Sister Isabelle of Tarines. Certain of the nuns had personal goods, including food, which they prepared as separate meals. He ordered the food removed to the common stock. He noted again the chests and keys. He was also again reassured, however, by the fact that the abbess from time to time took possession of the keys in order to inspect the chests. She made sure that the personal goods in the chests did not include forbidden materials or frivolities, which might have come to the nuns through gifts from their lay friends. To his displeasure Eudes discovered that some of the inmates of the house were receiving such gifts without permission. He heard that some of their lay friends and other inappropriate laypeople continued from time to time to enter the cloister, eat with the nuns, and even stay overnight (the nuns wrongly adjusted religious services to accommodate them). A few nuns also persisted, despite his prohibition, in leaving the cloister to do errands, one supposes, or to visit friends and relatives. In the cloister, silence was, in his words, "not well observed."[22] Debts were still relatively low, forty French pounds and six measures of wheat. He found out more this time about the workings of the nuns. For example, they were bringing up ten young boys, orphans possibly, who doubled, again possibly, as servants.

The archbishop told them to bring the practice to an end and ordered them to return the boys to their home villages.

During 1254 Archbishop Eudes, breaking his usual routine, visited in winter (February 27).[23] The number of nuns had held more or less steady at thirty-three. He affirmed that this should be the upper limit, the house being too poor to shelter more.[24] Debts had grown to a sum above fifty pounds, more than a 25 percent increase. He instructed the nuns to have two nonprofessed girls returned to their homes. (Typically Eudes railed against taking girls into nunneries for rearing and for fees.)[25] Eating with men (seculars) from outside the cloister had not ceased, and he turned his wrath on the abbess for this lapse. He threatened to impose on her the penalties detailed in the Benedictine rule, namely, exclusion from the common table and common prayer, if she proved negligent in the future. The fact that a Sister Isabelle had borne a child by a local priest helps explain the archbishop's loss of temper. Eudes appears at least to have been pleased that the community was taking communion appropriately and confessing regularly, seven times a year and more. He was less pleased, however, that the nuns were allowing girls not yet fourteen years old to profess and that there were some internal disputes so bitter that the parties refused to greet one another. The archbishop forced these women to reconcile and symbolize their reconciliation by kissing on the lips, and he imposed silence on them—on pain of excommunication—if they dared to mention the original cause of their falling out.[26]

The attempts at reconciliation and the archbishop's threats did not have the desired effect in his eyes. A few months later (November 1255) he returned to Bival.[27] A few of the nuns had been confined to cells and were brought before the archbishop in a cart, like criminals, for his chastisement. The abbess got her come-uppance, too, from the visiting prelate: she was to obey the instructions already issued in his name by his archdeacon, and these included stopping the nuns from leaving the cloister and from smuggling letters out to friends and relatives complaining about conditions and relations at Bival, letters that had not first been submitted to the abbess for approval. As the archbishop's ire grew, he came close to deposing her.

Eudes clearly reached the conclusion that visitation annually, let alone less frequently, was inadequate for Bival. So, less than two months later he returned.[28] Thirty-four nuns were in residence, one of whom was a visiting or retired prioress. The community was still confessing and taking communion as regularly as ever. But other matters had degenerated or at least not been ameliorated: the occasional breach of cloister, the sending of unapproved letters, and the pregnancy of a sister or perhaps a servant which had put the house in bad odor. The father? Possibly it was the parish priest who ministered to the nuns' sacramental needs, although this could not be proved. Nonetheless, Eudes dismissed him.[29] Debts had now also risen to 140 pounds; and even taking into account outstanding sums owed the house, the shortfall or deficit was eighty pounds, a 60 percent increase in two years and double the debt burden since the early visitations of his archiepiscopate. The nuns had also begun to lease out property (in this case, holdings at Pierrement) at a poor rate of return, approximately 35 percent of annual value. Transactions of this sort were useful to get a large amount of money quickly, and they guarded against the vagaries of unfavorable market conditions. Sometimes it was better to receive fifty pounds up front from a lessor of a manor that typically produced an income of 140 pounds than to keep the manor in one's own hands and suffer a bad harvest and no income. But sometimes is not always; such leasing could have very negative long-term effects.[30]

The nuns in February 1257 received their archbishop's visitation in a state of less trepidation than the year before.[31] No moral offenses came to light, and they continued their regular communion (seven times a year) and confession (more than seven times a year), which was mandated by the rule. They were adhering to the thirty-three nun limit on inmates. The service staff, if the numbers provided by the visitation record represent the full extent, was small: two maidservants and three *conversae* or lay sisters. Two of the latter were not present, being on a mission for the abbess to purchase goods for those who were ill. The annual pittance for clothes for each nun was noted as twelve shillings. Any money not spent on clothing could be used individually by the nuns for their other needs. Eudes would have learned these things either from oral testimony to that effect or from consulting Bival's fiscal accounts, which, the *Register* notes, were written out in a parchment roll. Debts were down from eighty to sixty pounds, but grain reserves were low. It was not foreseen that they would last the nuns until the next harvest. This was not their fault; the years 1257–58 were bad for harvests all over northwestern Europe.[32] The difficult rural situation contributed, for example, to the tensions in England when barons accused King Henry III of squandering the royal fisc while increasing financial demands on them. This contributed to the baronial uprising against King Henry III.[33]

What seems to have occurred in the wake of the subsistence crisis of these years was an ephemeral stability at Bival. When Eudes visited in July 1259, he wrote a memorandum that, although not fully favorable to the nuns, was upbeat.[34] Thirty-three nuns, three maidservants, and one *conversa* constituted the community. The problem of leaving the cloister illicitly appears to have become less acute. The nuns were reminded that this was forbidden, but the archbishop permitted the abbess to authorize an occasional visit to family, perhaps in times of sickness, but only for brief intervals and not unaccompanied. The nuns were still enrolling their accounts (he wanted a few more nuns to take part in their systematic review, however), had further reduced their debts—to somewhat over fifty-six pounds—

and were regularly distributing their twelve-shilling yearly clothing and personal allowances. Communion and confessional practices remained stable.

At last, in August 1261, the archbishop wrote down some fully positive things about Bival in the record of his visitation. Pleased that there were still only thirty-three nuns (one of whom was a novice) and three maidservants, and that the sisters were abiding by their rule with regard to communion and confession, he also commended the further reduction of their outstanding debts to forty pounds. Their larders were not overflowing, but they did have provisions. And, as Eudes wrote, "[w]ith God's grace we found everything else to be in a satisfactory state."[35] There was one disturbing note. The priest, whom he had dismissed for being suspected of impregnating one of the inmates four years before, even though the evidence against him was inconclusive, was receiving from the nuns a rather large annual pension of thirty pounds. He was living quite far away from them at the time, in Amiens in Picardy. Eudes noted his displeasure without confiding to his *Register* what he did or intended to do about this.

However far the archbishop thought Bival's nuns had come in their journey toward perfection in August 1261, he was shocked to learn during his visitation slightly more than two years later, in September 1263, that they had backslid.[36] They had breached the limit of their approved numbers, rising to thirty-five nuns and one *conversa*. They were making money from selling bread that they had. Vending the bread to outsiders in undersupervised venues created occasions for scandal. Sales were being made even though their own stores were low and their seed corn probably insufficient for the winter wheat planting. But what really galled him was that they had taken a chaplain under their wing, in a fraternity of prayer presumably, but also, it is implied, with a monetary annuity of some amount. Eudes fulminated against the arrangement, stripped the chaplain of any other sources of income in the archdiocese and prohibited his saying Mass anywhere in the province of Rouen, which is to say, basically all of Normandy.

It is possible that an otherwise blameless lack of vigilance on the old abbess's part was at fault in this rapid degeneration of conditions at Bival. Marguerite of Aunay had been elected in 1248. By 1263 she had served fifteen years, a considerably lengthy headship. One may guess that she was quite ill, possibly debilitated, for she soon retired from the headship or died in office. Less than two months after the visitation of September 16, 1263, when the arrangements for the chaplain were discovered, Eudes was asked to confirm the election of a new abbess, Marguerite of Cristot. In fact, the archbishop rejected her election as uncanonical. A plausible reason, since he liked and respected Marguerite of Cristot, is that the nuns had not informed him, as was required, of their intention to hold an election. Nonetheless, despite their breach of procedure, he invoked the "utility" of Marguerite's election and permitted her installation on November 8, 1263.[37]

For a while Marguerite of Cristot turned things around.[38] Natural attrition brought the number of nuns back down to thirty-three by the time Archbishop Eudes visited in July 1265. The new abbess may even have cut the number of servants, at least temporarily, from three to one. There was also still one *conversa*. Eudes reminded the abbess to keep a sharp eye on the individual nuns' chests and to inspect them more often for forbidden possessions. And he wanted no reversion to private meals with special delicacies for some and not others. Marguerite of Cristot managed to keep debts from increasing, although she was still faced with the prospect of recurrent inadequate levels of stores and seed corn. She was emphatic when Eudes wanted to associate a monk with the nuns in a fraternity of prayer. The monk was known to the nuns from laxer times, and they wanted to have no truck with him. Eudes was insistent but then yielded "at the request of the abbess and by reason of her supplication."[39] He had come to be persuaded that it was worse to have this monk nearby rather than at a distance, spatially and conceptually.

Archbishop Eudes's faith in Marguerite of Cristot continued over the next few years. The visitation of August 2, 1266, found the nuns in what he called a "sufficiently good state."[40] Debts were no worse. Thirty-two nuns were in residence and one *conversa*. Reminders were issued all around about proper behavior and obedience. The archbishop listened favorably to the nuns' complaint that a pension assigned against them for a priest was unnecessarily burdensome, and he began the procedure to reduce the financial onus.

Undoubtedly Archbishop Eudes's faith in Marguerite of Cristot was based on the latter's firmness. This firmness had its darker side, which manifested itself in several ways. To her nuns the abbess could seem cold and arbitrary. Eudes cautioned her at his next visitation, September 13, 1268, "to make an effort to conduct herself towards the nuns in all things in a more clement and solicitous manner than she had done."[41] What brought this admonition on? The archbishop found evidence of the abbess appropriating (for the common chest) whatever the nuns were not spending on clothes from their yearly pittances. She was putting together the fiscal accounts without including other older nuns in the process. She was not paying an aged predecessor of hers the pension to which she was entitled. And, curiously, she was doing some sort of favor for someone by seeing to the rearing of a child at a nearby village, Pierrement, where the nunnery had rights.

The admonitions did not have the desired effect. During the last visitation to Bival recorded in the *Register* (October 24, 1269), Eudes noted that the number of nuns was down to twenty-nine plus the *conversa* and three maidservants.[42] Had word got out that the abbess and regime at Bival were overly harsh and was the house therefore not receiving novices? The archbishop, as was his routine, reissued ordinances about common eating and guests. He was disappointed with his protégée's failure to pay the aged former abbess's pension. This was a sin, and Eudes ordered Marguerite of Cristot to do unspecified penance for her lapse. She also had not taken care to rid herself and the house of the burden of rearing the boy in Pierrement. Moreover, when the archbishop found out that she had not redeemed a chalice that her immediate predecessor had pawned in another scheme to get ready money during a crisis (probably over low stores of seed corn), he commanded her to do so by the next All Saints, that is, within a week. Even Abbess Marguerite's skills at keeping down debt may have been slipping. Eudes recorded the debt as twice what it had been at the last visitation (120 pounds rather than sixty). This may have been an accounting fluke; the precise doubling is suggestive. But Eudes recorded it and presumably regarded it and bemoaned it as a genuine doubling of the abbey's debt.

Although Eudes's *Register* can no longer guide research after 1269, a few charters allow us to bring the story of Bival to a tentative conclusion. They demonstrate that over the next thirty years a very small number of local notables showed interest in the house, confirmed some of its rights and endowed it with small-ish clusters of properties, but nothing very spectacular and not always without accompanying disputes.[43] Bival, in Strayer's words, was never "to become a wealthy and famous house."[44] Of course, very few nunneries did; they were notoriously underendowed.[45] What is significant, however, throughout Strayer's narrative of the twelfth-century vicissitudes of the monastery and my attempted reconstruction of some of its thirteenth-century history, is that Bival was *almost always* on the brink of bankruptcy.

Bival could never clear its deficits, and every time it reduced them, some problem intervened that made them shoot up once more. This in turn led the nuns to expedients in raising money that antagonized the archbishop—pawning a chalice, leasing out demesnes at too low rates of return, and the taking in of children for money. The pattern is similar to that of other economically precarious female monasteries.[46] It also led to divisions in the house between the haves and have-nots, those who could get support from their families and friends through gifts and those who could not. Vigilant abbesses fought against and controlled this, but this in turn could undermine the monastery's attractiveness, making it seem too strict, too oppressive, to the minor aristocratic parents who wanted to place some of their daughters in monasteries. A certain kind of easygoing headship, on the other hand and ironically, could encourage local elites to put their daughters in the nuns' care and endow the house. The porousness of the cloister walls under permissive leadership may actually have bound Bival more firmly to the wider community.

Permissive leadership, however, had its downside, in that the human porosity of the cloister could provide opportunities for behaviors that brought scandal on the house. One need not accept all of Eudes Rigaud's judgments as fair. He was a censorious archbishop, and he was probably too quick to credit the gossip that some nuns laid against others. Yet he did not invent the pregnancies, and even if the nuns were slurring one another in telling salacious tales, the very fact that they did so to the archbishop was a scandal in itself. In short, Bival's economic precariousness made it almost impossible to command the respect that it needed to overcome that precariousness. It was a catch-22 situation, which was not mastered before the house faced far more debilitating traumas in the fourteenth and fifteenth century—famine, incessant wars, the plague cycle. It is a wonder Bival survived, but the story of its endurance through these later troubles will have to await another historian.

NOTES

1. Penelope Johnson, *Equal in Monastic Profession: Religious Women in Medieval France* (Chicago: University of Chicago Press, 1991), pp. 267–69; Adam Davis, *The Holy Bureaucrat: Eudes Rigaud and Religious Reform in Thirteenth-Century Normandy* (Ithaca: Cornell University Press, 2006), pp. 74, 76–77.

2. Strayer, "A Forged Charter of Henry II for Bival," *Speculum* 34 (1959): 230–37; repr. in *Medieval Statecraft and the Perspectives of History: Essays by Joseph R. Strayer*, ed. John Benton and Thomas Bisson (Princeton: Princeton University Press, 1971), pp. 28–38. Subsequent page citations are from this reprint.

3. A word on how these papers came into my possession is in order. Following Strayer's death, his widow, Sylvia Thrupp, gave them to me as his friend and successor at Princeton.

4. A conclusion accepted by Daniel Power, *The Norman Frontier in the Twelfth and Early Thirteenth Centuries* (Cambridge: Cambridge University Press, 2004), p. 488n3.

5. The quotation is from Strayer, "Forged Charter," p. 28. The paragraph above summarizes his article, pp. 28–36.

6. I will be identifying the charters I am citing from Archives Départementales (AD): Seine-Maritime, 51H, by the first words. The original 1185 record is "Universis Sancte Matris Ecclesie filiis." A vidimus of the original begins "Tous ceulx qui ces lettres verront ou orront."

7. AD: Seine-Maritime, 51H, MSS of 1220, "Omnibus ad quos presens scriptum pervenerit" and "Sciant omnes presentes et futuri quod ego Girardus de Kaigni."

8. AD: Seine-Maritime, 51H, MS of 1220, "Ego Gerardus de Kaigni."

9. AD: Seine-Maritime, 51H, MS of 1228, "In nomine domini et filii et spiritus sancti amen" and MS of 1229 (Saint-Lucien's agreement "for the good of peace"), "R. [?] divina permissione abbas sancti Luciani belvacensis."

10. AD: Seine-Maritime, 51H, MS of 1222, "Sciant omnes quod ego Avelina."

11. AD: Seine-Maritime, 51H, MS of 1231, "Universis Christi fidelibus."

12. AD: Seine-Maritime, 51H, MS of 1240, "Omnibus Christi fidelibus."

13. References to the *Register* in English are to Sydney Brown, trans., *The Register of Eudes of Rouen* (New York: Columbia University Press, 1964). The Latin edition, which the English truncates, is rare: Th[éodose] Bonnin, *Registrum visitationum archiepiscopi rotomagensis / Journal des visites pastorales d'Eude Rigaud, archevêque de Rouen, MCCXLVIII–MCCLXIX* (Rouen: A. Le Brument, 1852).

14. Davis, *Holy Bureaucrat*, p. 69; Brown, *Register*, p. 6n23.

15. For the patron, Brown, *Register*, p. 6n25; for the number of documented visitations, Johnson, *Equal in Monastic Profession*, p. 269.

16. Brown, *Register*, p. 6.

17. Ibid., p. 7.

18. Ibid., p. 8.

19. Ibid., p. 131.

20. Cf. Davis, *Holy Bureaucrat*, p. 77.

21. Brown, *Register*, p. 165.

22. Ibid., p. 165.

23. Ibid., pp. 226–27.

24. See Davis, *Holy Bureaucrat*, pp. 100, 148.

25. Ibid., p. 100.

26. The mandate is addressed in ibid., p. 76.

27. Brown, *Register*, p. 252

28. Ibid., p. 300.

29. See Davis, *Holy Bureaucrat*, p. 74.

30. William Chester Jordan, *The Great Famine: Northern Europe in the Early Fourteenth Century* (Princeton: Princeton University Press, 1996), pp. 71, 75, 81.

31. Brown, *Register*, p. 339.

32. Derek Keene, "Crisis Management in London's Food Supply, 1250–1500," in *Commercial Activity, Markets and Entrepreneurs in the Middle Ages: Essays in Honour of Richard Britnell*, ed. Ben Dodds and Christian Liddy (Woodbridge: Boydell Press, 2011), pp. 50–57.

33. William Jordan, *A Tale of Two Monasteries: Westminster and Saint-Denis in the Thirteenth Century* (Princeton: Princeton University Press, 2009), p. 9.

34. Brown, *Register*, p. 386

35. Ibid., p. 462.

36. Ibid., p. 532.

37. Ibid., p. 541.

38. Ibid., pp. 596–97.

39. Ibid., p. 597.

40. Ibid., pp. 629–30.

41. Ibid., p. 702.

42. Ibid., p. 732.

43. AD: Seine-Maritime, 51H, MSS of 1269, 1279, 1306 (n.s.), 1325, "Omnibus hec visuris," "Noverint universis presentes," "Tous ceus qui," and "In nomine dei amen."

44. Strayer, "Forged Charter," p. 36.

45. Davis, *Holy Bureaucrat*, pp. 99–100.

46. William Chester Jordan, "The Cistercian Nunnery of La Cour Notre-Dame de Michery: A House That Failed," *Revue bénédictine* 95 (1985): 311–20; Anne Lester and William Chester Jordan, "La Cour Notre-Dame de Michery: A Response to Constance Berman," *Journal of Medieval History* 27 (2001): 43–54.

The Sonic Presence of Mary Magdalene at the Last Supper: The Maundy of the Poor at Barking Abbey

Anne Bagnall Yardley

In the wake of Dan Brown's phenomenally popular book *The DaVinci Code*, several humorous representations of DaVinci's *Last Supper* have made the rounds of the Internet with Mary Magdalene inserted into the scene. While these were intended primarily as jests, the chants accompanying the *Mandatum pauperum* as practices by the nuns at Barking Abbey in the fifteenth century do more than insert Mary Magdalene as one figure in this picture—they make her sonic presence the defining characteristic of the rite. In this essay I argue that the popularity of the legend of Mary Magdalene in the later Middle Ages influences the ritual of the *mandatum* throughout English monastic circles and that it finds special resonance at Barking Abbey, a large and influential Benedictine nunnery just outside of London.[1]

The Ritual of the *Mandatum*

The *mandatum*, or footwashing, is a central monastic ritual, celebrated weekly according to the Benedictine rule and with special solemnity on Maundy Thursday as a reenactment of Christ's final meal with his disciples (John 13).[2] In many medieval monasteries both male and female, this ritual evolved into two distinct ceremonies: one the Maundy of the Poor and the other the Conventual Maundy. In the English monastic tradition, the dual celebration of the *mandatum* on Holy Thursday dates back at least to the tenth-century *Regularis concordia*, where explicit instructions are given for the Maundy of the Poor before the office of *none* and the Conventual Maundy after vespers and a meal. The *Regularis concordia* instructs the monks and nuns to sing the antiphons proper to this ceremony, although the actual antiphon incipits are not listed.[3] Similarly, in the description of the Maundy of the Poor in Lanfranc's eleventh-century constitutions, only one chant is explicitly mentioned: "Abbas uel cantor incipiat antiphonam *Dominus Ihesus*, et alias que conueniunt" (The abbot or cantor shall then intone the antiphon *Dominus Ihesus* and others suitable).[4] The use of the *Dominus Ihesus* chant as first in the series offers an indication of a possible source of its popularity in later English sources, many of which start the *mandatum* with that chant instead of the more widely used *Mandatum novum*.[5] Neither source, however, provides any more extensive knowledge about which particular chants were part of the ritual.

A later English medieval source, the ordinal and customary from the Abbey of Saint Mary in York, offers a very clear theological understanding of the reasons for the Conventual Maundy. "Hoc ergo mandatum quod fit a prelatis representat factum Christi. Unde notandum quod tres sunt cause quare Dominus lavare voluit discipulorum pedes: primum in signum dilectionis; secundo in exemplum humilitatis; tercio ratione misterii, quia lotio pedum signat lotionem affectum" (This mandate therefore that is instituted by the prelates, manifests the deed of Christ. Whence it is noted that there are three motives wherefore the Lord wanted to wash the feet of the disciples. The first as a sign of love. The second as an example of humility. The third reason for this service is that by the washing of feet, it signals washing with affection).[6] Clearly at York the *Mandatum fratrum* is completely focused on Christ's actions. Yet in this description we can see the seeds of the connection to Mary Magdalene. Love, humility, and affection are all major elements of the medieval conception of Mary Magdalene.[7]

Despite this Christological emphasis, by the twelfth century English processionals and customaries already indicate some inclusion of images of Mary Magdalene in the Maundy.[8] Bukofzer comments that "Strictly speaking, the Mary Magdalene episode does not belong to the *mandatum*; the point of the latter is precisely that Jesus washes the feet of others, but the similarity of the subject accounts for the association."[9] In this essay I argue that it is the rise of the legend of Mary Magdalene in the later Middle Ages that creates this strong connection between the *mandatum* and Mary Magdalene made audible in the chants sung during the ritual washing of feet.

Mary Magdalene in the Middle Ages

The medieval understanding of Mary Magdalene was shaped in large part by Pope Gregory the Great. In the late sixth century, he issued an influential sermon on Mary Magdalene that artfully conflates Luke's sinful woman, John's Mary, and Mark's Mary while avoiding other references.[10] This understanding of Mary Magdalene, expressed in the telling of her story in the *Golden Legend* and in the liturgy for her feast day, develops out of such conflations as Gregory's. The fusion of several women into the one legend of Mary Magdalene creates a character that embodies several different characteristics. Mary is the sensual and extravagant lover who anoints Jesus's feet; she is the penitent sinner who bathes Jesus's feet with her tears; she is the disciple who sits at the feet of Jesus while her sister Martha prepares the meal; and she is the person who first sees the resurrected Christ and falls at his feet. As Susan Haskins notes, "to the extent that Mary Magdalene was subsequently identified with these figures, she also inherited their characteristics in her composite form, so that through the centuries she was to become the symbol of the contemplative life and model of repentance, while the significance of her actual role in the New Testament as disciple and primary witness to the resurrection receded into the background."[11] Images of Mary Magdalene as lover, sinner, disciple, and witness to the Resurrection are present in the texts for the chants sung during the *Mandatum pauperum* at Barking Abbey. Mary Magdalene, in her multiple roles, is present at the great *mandatum* through her songs.

Peter Jeffery suggests that the presence of references to Mary Magdalene in the *mandatum* connect it to a more penitential understanding of the rite: "The penitential interpretation of the footwashing, connecting it with the forgiveness of sins committed after baptism, also made its appearance in medieval chant texts. . . . The penitential interpretation is also expressed in some medieval antiphons that retell the story of the woman who anointed Jesus's feet."[12] The rise of the importance of Mary Magdalene in the Middle Ages corresponds to the greater emphasis on the sacrament of penance following the Fourth Lateran Council in 1215. Katherine L. Jansen explicates a four-step process of penance in the Middle Ages: *compunctio* (compunction), *compassio* (compassion), *contritio* (contrition), and *amor* (love). She cites the work of Jacobus de Voragine in classifying Mary Magdalene's tears: "those of compunction in keeping with the memory of her sins; those of compassion for her dead brother Lazarus; those of contrition at the Crucifixion; those of love, wept while standing outside the sepulcher."[13] Thus, even in her tears, Mary Magdalene is more than a penitent—she is a complex symbol of lover and sinner, compassionate woman and contrite reprobate.

Music during the *Mandatum* in English Monastic Sources

Among extant evidence, both customaries and processionals provide indications of the chants sung at the *mandatum*. To gather some context for the Barking Ordinal, I consulted the list of chants compiled by Floyd in his article on English monastic processionals as well as several published customaries and the processionals from Chester, Wilton, and Aldgate.[14] Of the eighteen sources thus consulted, all included the chant *Mandatum novum*. Several other chants are included in at least half of the sources (see table 1).

Table 1. Chants Commonly Sung at the Monastic *Mandatum* in Medieval England

Chant incipit	Scriptural source	# of uses
Mandatum novum	John 13:34	18
Diligamus nos		15
Dominus Ihesus postquam cenavit	John 13:12, 13, 15	13
In diebus illis mulier	Luke 7:37–38	13
Postquam surrexit dominus	John 13:4, 5, 15	10
Maria (ergo) unxit	John 12:3	9
Ante diem festum pasche	John 13:1	9

Two of these chants are also sung commonly at the feast of Mary Magdalene: *Maria ergo unxit* and *In diebus illis mulier*.[15] *In diebus*, the Magdalene chant most commonly associated with the *mandatum*, focuses on the penitential nature of Mary the *peccatrix*, who weeps tears in order to wash Jesus's feet. This connection between the story in the Gospel of Luke and the *mandatum* corresponds to Jeffery's assertion of a more penitential approach to the ritual in the later Middle Ages. In contrast, the short chant *Maria unxit* offers the anointing of Jesus's feet by Mary of Bethany in John's gospel and specifically names the importance of the fragrance of perfume, a beautifully sensual image. (The appendix lists the full sequence of chants in several medieval sources.) Only three of the eighteen sources had neither of these chants. So Mary Magdalene clearly made at least a brief appearance at most English monastic Maundys. Thus unlike the visual typology of footwashing described by Von Daum Tholl which appears to draw upon Old Testament sources as well as the Last Supper and St. Benedict,[16] the aural typology draws upon the sounds of Mary Magdalene and holds up the images of incense filling the air as a penitent sinner dries Jesus's feet. These images take their place alongside those of Jesus at the Last Supper as an important part of the soundscape of monastic footwashing on Maundy Thursday in medieval England.

The *Mandatum pauperum* at Barking Abbey

In contrast to the ritual described above, the picture provided by the Barking Ordinal shows two distinctly different rituals: the Maundy of the Poor with Mary Magdalene as the sole focus and the Conventual Maundy which connects the nuns to Jesus and the Last Supper. Thus instead of celebrating two very similar rituals, Barking uses the two strands to provide two entirely different foci for these parallel rituals.

The first reference to the Maundy of the Poor in the Barking Ordinal occurs immediately preceding the instructions for the Mass of the day. There, a brief reference suggests that the poor are brought into the abbess's chapel and the chapter house before the Mass and considerably before the Maundy itself.[17] It appears that the poor wait for some time before the actual Maundy. Are they fed a midday meal as the nuns eat in the refectory? That is not clear from any of the following rubrics.

The instructions for the ritual Maundy of the Poor follow upon those for the midday meal:

> Cumque uenerit abbatissa contra ostium capituli seruitrices lintheis precingantur. Et incipiat abbatissa Ant. *Mandatum nouum*, ps. *Beati immaculati*, et Ant. *Rogabat*. Tunc uadat abbatissa in capellam suam et priorissa intret capitulum ad lauandum pedes pauperum, et ministrentur ab illis quas ad hoc ipsemet elegerint; reliquas antiphonas et responsoria cantrix incipiat, Ant. *Rogabat Ihesum*, Ant. *Recumbente Ihesu*, Ant. *Cum discubuisset*, Ant. *Emit Maria*. Ant. *Sinite mulierem* Ant. *Mittens hec mulier* R. *Accepit Maria*. Ant. *Maria ergo* R. *Felix Maria* R. *O mirum et magnum*. Ant. *Symon autem* Ant. *Dixit autem*. Interea lauantur pedes pauperum hoc modo. Omnes per ordinem sicut sunt priores coram pauperibus prosternantur humi breuem facientes oracionem. Deinde surgentes lauant pedes illarum, quatuor sororibus, in capitulo premonitis, aquam et tersoria sibi deferentibus. Postquam autem pedes abluerint; lintheis detergent et tunc deosculentur. Lotis omnium pedibus, det unaqueque aquam pauperum manibus: et ministre teneant manutergia. Post manuum detercionem, tribuant pauperibus nummos a cameraria sibi commendatas manus earum deosculando. Si autem alique infirme in lecto decubuerint: introducantur pauperes ad illas et ibi ab eis abluentur.[18]

> (And when the abbess has come opposite the doorway of the chapter house, the servers should encircle (gird) her with linen. And let the abbess begin the antiphon *Mandatum nouum*, ps. *Beati immaculati* (Ps. 118), and the antiphon *Rogabat*. Then the abbess should go into her chapel and the prioress should enter the chapter house to wash the feet of the paupers and they should be attended to by those who have themselves been chosen for this; the cantrix should begin the rest of the antiphons and responsories: Ant. *Rogabat Ihesum*, Ant. *Recumbente Ihesu*, Ant. *Cum discubuisset*, Ant. *Emit Maria*. Ant. *Sinite mulierem* Ant. *Mittens hec mulier* R. *Accepit Maria* Ant. *Maria ergo* R. *Felix Maria* R. *O mirum et magnum*. Ant. *Symon autem* Ant. *Dixit autem*. Meanwhile, the paupers' feet should be washed in this way: all those in order as they were previously should prostrate themselves on the ground in front of the paupers, making a brief prayer. Then, rising, they should wash their feet, with four sisters, having been forewarned in the chapter, carrying water and towels to them. After the feet have been washed, however, they should be wiped with the linens and then kissed. After the feet of all have been washed, let water be placed on the hands of the poor and attendants should hand them a towel. After

the drying of the hands, let the money be divided among the poor by the cameraria entrusting it to their kissed hands. If, however, any infirm nuns are bedridden, the paupers should be led in to them and there they should be washed by them.)

Although there are no specific instructions in the ordinal on the number or identity of the paupers, these women were presumably "outsiders,"[19] brought within the enclosure for the specific purposes of the ritual. In washing their feet, the nuns reenact the conflated Mary Magdalene's washing of Jesus's feet. Although the entire liturgy begins with Jesus ("Mandatum novum"—a new commandment I give to you—John 13:34), the rest of this rite draws upon all four Gospels in presenting the composite portrait of Mary Magdalene. The chants depict scenes in which Mary Magdalene anoints Jesus's head (Matthew 26) as well as ones that reference the feet (see table 2). They do not present a sequential narrative but rather a bathing in the sounds that reference Mary Magdalene and that nuns would associate with the celebration of the Feast of Mary Magdalene on July 22.

Table 2. Chants in the Maundy of the Poor at Barking Abbey[20]

Text incipit	Scriptural source	Use in Mary Magdalene liturgy	Chant type
Mandatum novum	John 13:34	[Maundy only]	Antiphon
Rogabat ihesum	Luke 7:36	Matins or vespers	Antiphon
Recumbente Ihesu	Mixture	Matins, vespers, or lauds	Antiphon
Cum discubuisset	Luke 7:37	Matins or vespers	Antiphon
Emit maria	Matthew 26:7–11		Antiphon
Sinite mulierum	Mark 14:6–9	Palm Sunday/Maundy	Antiphon
Mittens hec mulier	Matthew 26:12	Variety of times[21]	Antiphon
Accepit maria	John 12:3 and Luke 7:38	Matins 3:1	Responsory
Maria ergo	John 12:3	Matins or lauds	Antiphon
Felix maria	John 12:3	Matins or vespers	Responsory
O mirum et magnum		Matins	Responsory
Symon autem	Luke 7:39	Matins 2:1 or vespers	Antiphon
Dixit autem	Luke 7:44, 46	Feria 5 de Passione	Antiphon

The Barking manuscript does not include musical notation, but we can see that the chants include both short antiphons and lengthy matins responsories. The latter offer a form of aural incense, a musical intensification and elaboration on the

The Sonic Presence of Mary Magdalene 175

text that is both as aesthetically pleasing and as impractical as incense. Consider *O mirum et magnum miraculum*:

[Musical notation with text underlay:]

it mul - - tum.

℣. Vi -dit Ma - ri - a do - mi - num et cre - di -

dit et cum gau - di - o sus - ce - - pit il - lum gau - dens

et flens qui - a cog - no - vit se pec -

ca - - - tri - - - - - - - cem.

> O mirum et magnum miraculum quia peccatrix femina audebat redemptorem mundi tangere lacrimando et capillis tergendo crimina sua abluebat ideo remissa sunt ei peccata multa quoniam dilexit multum.
>
> V. Vidit Maria dominum et credidit et cum gaudio suscepit illum gaudens et flens quia cognovit se peccatricem.
>
> (O strange and great miracle that a sinful woman dared to touch the redeemer of the world with her tears, wiping her sins away with her hair; therefore her many sins are forgiven because she loved much.
>
> V. Mary saw the Lord and believed and with joy received him joyfully, crying because he recognized a sinner.)

Textually the chant asserts, in the verse section, Mary's primacy as a witness to the Resurrection—the one thing the Gospels do agree on but that medieval depictions regularly ignore. This chant foreshadows the Barking version of the *Visitatio sepulchri* enacted at dawn on Easter when Mary sees the risen Lord. To my knowledge, the only other English manuscript that includes *O mirum et magnum* at the Maundy is the Wilton Processional which is also the only other known source of the Easter drama from an English nunnery.[22] Musically the verse section ("Vidit Maria") of *O mirum* is the most syllabic and hence narrative portion of the chant. The initial response section, in contrast, is highly melismatic, from the early melisma on "magnum" to the great prolixity of the final phrase "quoniam dilexit multum"—"because she loved much."

Jesus admonishes us that our treatment of the poor, widows, and other marginalized people is analogous to our treatment of him (Matthew 25:31–46). Thus, theologically, for the nuns to offer this rite to the poor is to wash the feet of Jesus just as Mary Magdalene did. Simultaneously there are resonances with Jesus's actions as a servant leader in the Johannine account. What better way to reinforce this concept than through the beautiful ornate sounds of this responsory chant? The resonance of liturgical occasion, ritual action, and the soundscape are compelling.

Reflections and Conclusions

Is the Barking Maundy an isolated ritual or one that reflects a broader late medieval understanding of the *mandatum* as reflective of both Jesus and Mary Magdalene? As noted earlier, two chants from the Feast of Mary Magdalene are incorporated quite widely on Maundy Thursday. The processional from the Benedictine nunnery at Wilton includes four Mary Magdalene chants; the Abbey at Fécamp (Normandy) includes five in its thirteenth-century customary.

The thirteenth-century ordinal from the French nunnery Origny Ste-Benoîte offers a clear theological statement of this connection. This ordinal instructs the nuns that their weekly *mandatum* should be one in remembrance of Mary Magdalene: "The Maundy which is prepared every Saturday was established in honor of the Blessed Magdalene and in remembrance of the hour when she bowed completely so that she served the world from her heart of sin."[23] Thus these nuns understand their basic conventual Maundy, done weekly, to be a remembrance of Mary Magdalene's penitence, an extreme form of the interpretation of the act as penitential rather than commemorative. In other words, the nuns at Origny are to identify with Mary Magdalene the penitent sinner rather than with Jesus the humble master.

The *Mandatum pauperum* at Barking Abbey proffers a more complex incorporation of Mary Magdalene imagery, however, than the merely penitential. While it appears that virtually all English medieval monastic celebrations of the rite on Maundy Thursday had some tinge of resonance with the penitent sinner identified as Mary Magdalene in medieval liturgy, the liturgy at Barking Abbey expressed a much fuller and more nuanced understanding of Mary's role in Holy Week. The inclusion of so many chants from the liturgy for Mary Magdalene leads directly into their portrayal of Mary in the Easter drama that is part of their liturgy just three days later. Through the adoption of a unified focus on Mary Magdalene during the Maundy of the poor, the nuns of Barking bring Mary Magdalene— sensual lover, pentitent sinner, disciple, *and* witness to the Resurrection—into the rite through the sounds of her chants filling the chapter house.

Appendix

Lists of Chants in Selected English Sources of the *Mandatum*
[Underlined chants are those from the liturgy for Mary Magdalene]

Sarum
1. Mandatum novum
2. Diligamus nos
3. <u>In diebus illis</u>
4. <u>Maria ergo unxit</u>
5. Postquam surrexit
   [If necessary:]
6. Vos vocatis me magister
7. Si ego Dominus
8. Ante diem festum
9. Venit ad Petrum

Chester Processional
1. Mandatum novum
2. Si ego Dominus
3. Postquam surrexit
4. <u>In diebus illis</u>
5. <u>Accepit Maria</u>
6. Ante diem festum
7. Venit ad Petrum
8. Tellus ac aethera [hymn]
9. Congregavit nos Christus
10. Congregavit nos in unum
11. Domum istam

Barking Ordinal
[Maundy of the Poor]
1. Mandatum novum
2. <u>Rogabat Ihesum</u>
3. <u>Recumbente Ihesum</u>
4. <u>Cum discubuisset</u>
5. <u>Emit Maria</u>
6. <u>Sinite mulierem</u>
7. <u>Mittens hec mulier</u>
8. <u>Accepit Maria [R.]</u>
9. <u>Maria ergo</u>

10. <u>Felix Maria [R]</u>
11. <u>O mirum et magnum [R]</u>
12. <u>Symon autem</u>
13. <u>Dixit autem</u>
    [Conventual Maundy]
1. Mandatum novum
2. Ante diem festum pasche
3. Congregavit nos Christus
4. Maneant in nobis
5. Diligamus nos
6. Caritas est summum
7. Caritas paciens est
8. Ubi fratres
9. Ecce quam bonum est
10. Tellus ac ethera [hymn]
11. Surgit Ihesus a cena
12. Misit denique aquam

Aldgate
1. Mandatum novum
2. Postquam surrexit Dominus
3. <u>In diebus illis mulier</u>
4. <u>Maria ergo</u>
5. Vos vocatis me magister
6. Diligamus nos
7. Ubi [est] caritas et dilectio
8. Congregavit nos Christus
9. <u>Mulier que erat in civitate</u>
10. Domine tu michi lavas pedes
11. Si ego Dominus
12. In hoc cognoscent omnes
13. Maneant in nobis
14. Benedicta sit sancta trinitas
15. Ubi caritas et amor

Wilton
   [Maundy of the Poor]
 1. Mandatum novum
 2. Si ego Dominus
 3. Diligamus nos
 4. Maneant in nobis
 5. In hoc cognoscent omnes
 6. Ubi sorores [same as ubi fratres with word change]
 7. <u>In diebus illis mulier</u>
 8. Caritas est summum
 9. <u>O mirum et magnum [R]</u>
10. <u>Emit Maria</u>
11. <u>Dilegebat Dominus Mariam et Martham</u>
   [Conventual Maundy]
 1. Dixit autem
 2. Domine tu michi lavas pedes
 3. Ante diem festum pasche
 4. Venit ad Petrum
 5. Tellus ac ethera [hymn]
 6. Surgit Ihesus a cena
 7. Misit denique aquam

St. Mary's York
   [Maundy of the Poor]
 1. Dominus Ihesus postquam
 2. Surgit Ihesus a cena
 3. Mandatum novum
 4. Dominum istam protege
      [Conventual Maundy]

 1. Mandatum novum
 2. Diligamus nos
 3. Ubi [est] caritas et dilection
 4. Ante diem festum pasche
 5. Domum istam protege
 6. Circumdederunt
 7. Dominus Ihesus postquam
 8. Tellus ac ethera [hymn]

Bury St. Edmunds
 1. Dominus Ihesus postquam
 2. Surgit Ihesus a cena
 3. Vos vocatis me magister
 4. Postquam surrexit Dominus
 5. Mandatum novum
 6. <u>Maria ergo</u>
 7. Diligamus nos
 8. Maneant in nobis
 9. Tellus ac ethera [hymn]
10. Ubi fratres

Abbey of Fecamp (Norman)
 1. Dominus Ihesus postquam cenavit
 2. Ante diem festum pasche
 3. Venit ad Petrum
 4. <u>Rogabut Ihesum</u>
 5. <u>In diebus illis mulier</u>
 6. <u>Dixit autem</u>
 7. <u>Mittens hec mulier</u>
 8. <u>Maria ergo</u>
 9. Tellus ac ethera [hymn]

NOTES

I am delighted to contribute to this volume in honor of Bonnie Wheeler, who is both mentor and friend to me. I left the bounds of the music department at Columbia to study Arthurian literature with her during my PhD study in 1973. Since that time she has continued to challenge me to think more broadly and more deeply in my work. I treasure her immense generosity as a scholar and a friend.

1. I am indebted to my colleague Melanie Johnson-DeBaufre, associate professor of New Testament, for her careful reading of this manuscript.

2. The word *maundy* derives through French from Latin *mandatum*: "The ceremony of washing the feet of a number of poor persons on the day before Good Friday was instituted as a way of recalling and following the example of humble service given by Jesus who, at the Last Supper, washed the feet of his disciples and exhorted them to wash one another's feet (John 13:4–14). The words 'A new commandment (*mandatum novum*) I give to you, that you love one another' (John 13:34), from the discourse which followed the washing of the disciples' feet, were adopted as the first antiphon sung at the ceremony, which hence acquired the name of *mandatum*" (OED, s.v. *Maundy*, n).

Few studies exist of the monastic *mandatum* in the later medieval period. The most complete study is Thomas Schäfer, *Die Fusswaschung im monastichen Brauchtum und in der lateinischen Liturgie: Liturgiegeschichtliche Untersuchung*, Text und Arbeiten, 1: Abteilung 47 (Beuron: Beuroner Kunstverlap, 1956). Manfred F. Bukofzer offers several observations on the musical chants of the *mandatum* in his study of the *Caput* chant in *Studies in Medieval and Renaissance Music* (New York: Norton, 1950), pp. 217–310. In a more recent article, Peter Jeffery traces the history of the rite and especially women's participation in it: "Mandatum novum do vobis: Toward a Renewal of the Holy Thursday Footwashing Rite," *Worship* 64:2 (March 1990): 107–41.

3. Thomas Symons, trans. and ed., *Regularis Concordia Anglicae Nationis Monachorum Sanctimonialumque* (London: Thomas Nelson and Sons, 1953), pp. 39–41.

4. David Knowles, trans. and ed., *The Monastic Constitutions of Lanfranc*, rev. ed. Christopher N. L. Brooke (Oxford: Clarendon Press, 2002), pp. 48–49 (translation and original from this edition).

5. See Bukofzer, *Studies*, pp. 235–36, where he indicates that in the Sarum rite *Dominus Ihesus* is the *communio* of the preceding Mass. At Barking Abbey the chant is indeed found listed for the Mass of the day but not at either *mandatum*.

6. J. B. L. Tolhurst and the Abbess of Stanbrook, *The Ordinale and Customary of the Abbey of Saint Mary, York*, vol. 2 (London: Henry Bradshaw Society, 1937), pp. 280–81. Translations are by the author throughout unless otherwise noted. I am grateful to my colleague Jesse Mann for his assistance with the translations.

7. On Mary Magdalene three very helpful books are: Susan Haskins, *Mary Magdalen: Myth and Metaphor* (Old Saybrook, CT: Konecky and Konecky, 1993); Jane Schaberg, *The Resurrection of Mary Magdalene: Legends, Apocrypha, and the Christian Testament* (New York: Continuum Press, 2002); and Jane Schaberg and Melanie Johnson-DeBaufre, *Mary Magdalene Understood* (New York: Continuum Press, 2006). For insight into artistic depictions of monastic footwashing, see Susan E. von Daum Tholl, "Life according to the Rule: A Monastic Modification of Mandatum Imagery in the Peterborough Psalter," *Gesta* 33:2 (1994): 151–58. None of the artistic representations she cites depict Mary Magdalene. She does note the close connection between the chants and the liturgical actions (p. 154).

8. Bukofzer (*Studies*, p. 233) lists the chants from an eleventh-century French source from Saint Yrieux that also includes some chants for Mary Magdalene.

9. Ibid., p. 236.

10. For the text of his remarks, see Pope Gregory the Great, Sermon 33, PL 74, col. 1239, as cited in Haskins, *Mary Magdalen*, p. 96. For more detailed discussions of the various women in the New Testament, see Schaberg, *Resurrection of Mary Magdalene*.

11. Haskins, *Mary Magdalen*, p. 26. See also Schaberg and Johnson-DeBaufre, *Mary Magdalene Understood*, pp. 32–66.

12. Jeffrey, "Mandatum novum do vobis," p. 123.

13. Katherine L. Jansen, "Mary Magdalen and the Mendicants: The Preaching of Penance in the Late Middle Ages," *Journal of Medieval History* 21 (1995): 1–25. This citation is specifically from page 6 and is extracted from the writings of Jacobus de Voragine.

14. The sources tabulated are:

Aldgate Priory (Franciscan, 15th century)—Reigate Parish Church, Cranston Library MS. 2322, fols. 88v–97v.

Barking Abbey (Benedictine, 15th century)—taken from Tolhurst and the Abbess of Stanbrook, *Ordinale and Customary*, pp. 94–96.

Breamore (Augustinian, 13th century)—in Malcolm Floyd, "Processional Chants in English Monastic Sources," *Journal of the Plainsong & Mediaeval Music Society* 13 (1990): 1–48.

Bury St. Edmunds (Benedictine, 15th century)—Ibid.

Castle Acre Priory, Norfolk (Benedictine, 14th century)—Ibid.

Cathedral Priory Church, Norwich (Benedictine, 13th century)—J. B. L. Tolhurst, *The Customary of the Cathedral Priory Church of Norwich*, Henry Bradshaw Society (London: Harrison and Sons, 1948), pp. 85–87.

Chester Priory (Benedictine, early 16th century)—J. W. Legg, *The Processional of the Nuns of Chester*, Henry Bradshaw Society, vol. 18 (London: n.p., 1899), pp. 9–11. (I have also consulted the manuscript itself and a microfilm.)

Christ Church Canterbury (Benedictine, late 11th century)—in Floyd, "Processional Chants."

Durham (Benedictine, 14th century)—Ibid.

Guisborough (Augustinian, late 13th century)—Ibid.

Haughmond (Augustinian, late 12th century)—Ibid.

Hyde Abbey (Benedictine, ca. 1300)—J. B. L. Tolhurst, *The Monastic Breviary of Hyde Abbey, Winchester*, Henry Bradshaw Society (London: Harrison and Sons, Ltd., 1932), vol. 1, fols. 94–94v.

Sarum rite (16th century)—W. G. Henderson, *Processionale ad usum insignis ac praeclarae Ecclesiae Sarum* (Leeds, 1882), pp. 64–66.

St. Mary's Abbey, York (Benedictine, 15th century)—Tolhurst and the Abbess of Stanbrook, *Ordinale and Customary*, 2:278–82.

St. Peter's, Gloucester (Benedictine, 12th century)—Floyd, "Processional Chants."

Tynemouth Priory (Benedictine, 12th century)—Ibid.

Wilton Abbey (Benedictine, 13th–14th century)—copy of the now-lost manuscript at Solesmes Abbey, fols. 36v–44v.

Worcester Cathedral (Benedictine, 13th century)—Floyd, "Processional Chants."

15. The full texts for these two chants are: "In diebus illis mulier que erat in civitate peccatrix ut cognovit quod ihesus recubuit in domo Symonis leprosi attulit alabastrum

unguenti et stans retro secus pedes domini Jesu lacrimis cepit rigare pedes ejus et capillis capitis sui tergebat et osculabatur pedes ejus et unguento ungebat" (In those days a woman in the city, who was a sinner, having learned that Jesus was eating in the house of Simon the leper, brought an alabaster jar of ointment and standing behind him at his feet, weeping she began to moisten his feet and with the hairs of her head she wiped them and she kissed his feet and anointed them with the oil). And: "Maria (ergo) unxit pedes ihesu et extersit capillis suis et domus impleta est ex odore unguenti" (Maria (therefore) anointed Jesus's feet and wiped them with her hair and the house was filled with the fragrance of the perfume.)

16. Von Daum Tholl, "Life according to the Rule."
17. Tolhurst and the Abbess of Stanbrook, *Ordinale and Customary*, p. 92.
18. Ibid., p. 94.
19. Although "pauperes" does not indicate gender, the use of "illarum" and "earum" would indicate that the paupers are women.
20. These are taken from the passage in the Barking Ordinal cited above.
21. Based on the listings in CANTUS, this chant appears to have been used on several liturgical occasions, including matins for the Feast of Mary Magdalene, Palm Sunday, Passion Sunday, and weekdays during Holy Week.
22. See Anne Bagnall Yardley, *Performing Piety: Musical Culture in Medieval English Nunneries* (New York: Palgrave Macmillan, 2006), pp. 146–55 for a discussion of these two versions of the *Visitatio sepulchri*.
23. Saint-Quentin, Bibliothèque de Saint-Quentin, MS. 86, *Le Livre de la tresorye de l'abbaye d'Origny Saincte Benoite*, p. 36, lines 12–17:

12 Il mandes confait tous les samedis
13 fue estores en l'onneur de le beneoicte
14 magdelainne et en la ramembrance
15 de leure quelle fu cornitie tout ensi
16 ame elle servi le munde de sen cors
17 a pechier:

The Royal Purple Mantle of El Greco's *Espolio*

Annemarie Weyl Carr

Bonnie Wheeler's keen, capacious intellectual imagination enveloped our years of shared teaching like a protean mantle, measured to an ever more demanding body of insight. In our last semester it reached to envelop the very spaces of Southern Methodist University's Meadows Museum of Spanish Art in a course drawing personnel from all of the university's six schools and attracting students to the museum in droves. As in every preceding semester, her radiant faith forced me to examine my own reticence. My very life as a Byzantinist had been consecrated to images that were not in museums but in use. Not long before that course, however, the Meadows Museum had acquired a painting that seemed to place her ardor and my interests in convergence: it had acquired its first El Greco.[1] El Greco, in reality Domenikos Theotokopoulos (1541–1614), was a master icon painter before leaving his native Crete around 1567. The following essay endeavors to define the kind of convergence I sensed in that acquisition. At the same time, it suggests how vital, indeed how integral, the mantle of Bonnie's imagination was to my own life at SMU.

The role of El Greco's Greek background in the formation of his mature art is a perennial question,[2] debated already long before it was established that he had been a master icon painter before leaving Crete,[3] and in no sense resolved since. The question is fueled by the spiritual intensity of his paintings, and though the residual hold of Cretan painting upon his visual imagination is most often explored through the quest for compositional parallels between his images and icons, the affective force that makes such parallels compelling is hard to dissociate from his style.[4] By his "style" is meant the manner that emerged in Spain, where he is seen for the first time in works of grand scale, beginning with his great *Espolio* of 1577–79 in the cathedral sacristy in Toledo. Here Theotokopoulos abandoned almost absolutely the receding proscenium spaces that had preoccupied him in Venice, focusing his attention on the human figure and on issues of style. Theotokopoulos's faith in style, as Manoles Chatzedakes has argued, is what most clearly binds him to his Cretan background.[5] Yet the style that he evolved on the basis of this faith was more alien to that of the Cretan icon painters than it was to the art of his Counter-Reformation contemporaries in the West. More crucial may have been the focus on the human body, above all his heightened attention to the sacramental body of Christ. It is to this dimension of El Greco's art that the present article turns. It seeks the image-legacy of his Greek background less in his style or composition than in his use of images of Christ's sacramental humanity that were steeped in the art and poetry of Greek Orthodoxy. It turns for this purpose to the *Espolio* itself (see figure 1).

The *Espolio* is a curious painting for this purpose, because its theme—the stripping of Christ before his crucifixion—is not attested in Byzantine art.[6] With few and sporadic exceptions, the Orthodox tradition presents Christ fully clothed throughout the scenes leading up to his crucifixion; only when his body is stripped of life is it exposed to view.[7] The *Espolio* was commissioned for the sacristy of the cathedral of Toledo, where the clergy robed for the Mass, and its theme was surely chosen in conjunction with its setting, evoking both the robes of the clergy and the work of sacrifice accomplished in them.[8] The stripping of Christ had seen a phase of extensive popularity in the wake of Franciscan spirituality in the fourteenth century, but it was rare as a theme in Renaissance painting, little attested after the early fifteenth century and seen more often in northern than in Mediterranean art.[9] Thus the sources that inspired Theotokopoulos's conception of the scene are a matter of some interest.

That there is something Byzantine about the *Espolio* has long been acknowledged. Even Harold Wethey, who most firmly resisted the idea of Theotokopoulos as an icon painter, wrote that "the *Espolio* is the first major work in which El Greco's iconography is derived from Byzantine sources. Its most obvious prototype is the Arrest of Christ whether by the Italian Duccio or by one of innumerable anonymous Byzantine masters, as Byron and Rice and others have previously observed."[10]

The painting certainly has a generic kinship with Cretan icons of the Betrayal, as exemplified by the paintings of Theotokopoulos's somewhat older Cretan contemporary, Theophanes Stretlitzas Bathas.[11] Theophanes, too, shows a hectic crowd piling up in a clamor of brandished weapons over Christ, who is being seized from the left. But as Chatzedakes points out, the kinships with Theophanes are no more compelling than they are with Albrecht Dürer's *Betrayal* in the Little Passion of 1509–11, where one sees the gesture of the man seizing Christ's robe.[12] Nicos Hadjinicolaou offers a yet closer parallel in Dirk Bouts's

Figure 1. Domenikos Theotokopoulos (El Greco). *The Disrobing of Christ.* 1577–79. Cathedral, Toledo, Spain. Photo: Erich Lessing / Art Resource, New York.

Figure 2. *Christ Drawn to the Cross.* Church of the Holy Cross, Pelendri, Cyprus. Photo: Athanasios Papageorgiou.

Betrayal of the 1450s, in which a reticent Christ is engulfed by armed aggressors who surge above him and snatch at the neck of his robe.[13] In its compressed verticality and fierce play upon the varied physiognomies surrounding Christ's face, the Bouts is more akin to the *Espolio* than the icons by Theophanes. But neither accounts for the theme itself, for the presence of the Cross and the women who gaze at it, or for the intense blood red of Christ's robe. These features suggest that Theotokopoulos had in mind not the Betrayal but a different icon, evoking a different moment in the Passion story: the icon known as the *Helkomenos epi Stavrou*—Christ drawn to the Cross.

The *Helkomenos epi Stavrou* combines both significances of "drawn." Christ's hands are bound and he is pulled by his captors to the foot of the Cross. But he also does not resist—he is drawn to it as if seduced by love. Named from a phrase in the hymn by Kosmas the Melode (d. ca. 740) sung on Good Friday,[14] the image was established in Byzantine art by the late twelfth century, when the emperor Isaac II Angelos (1185–95) sequestered a great icon of this theme from the church bearing the same name in Monemvasia in southern Greece.[15] A poetic epigram composed by John Apokaukos after the icon's arrival in Constantinople describes it as showing Christ at the foot of the Cross, crowned with thorns and surrounded by Jews. The contemporary mosaic at Monreale probably gives a good impression of its composition. Christ, wearing a short-sleeved red colobium, his hands bound and head crowned with thorns, stands to one side of a huge, central cross; a Pharisee faces him from the other side as soldiers eddy around them and a worker pounds stakes into the ground around the cross's foot.[16] The late twelfth-century enameled *Esztergom Staurothek* enriches the composition, showing the colobium-clad living Christ led to the Cross on one side of the cruciform relic cavity and his lifeless body, wearing only a loincloth, being removed from the Cross on the other.[17] The earliest known panel painting of the theme, a large icon of the late twelfth century in the church of the Holy Cross at Pelendri, Cyprus, makes a crucial addition to the scene (see figure 2): the Mother of God balances Christ on the other side of the Cross, her anguished alarm contrasting sharply with his submissive passivity.[18] These works in varied media make it clear that the image had assumed an established identity by the end of the twelfth century.

The theme evolved as Passion cycles expanded in Byzantine mural programs and the West alike. Briefly in the thirteenth and early fourteenth centuries, Byzantine painters showed the figure of Christ on the way to the Cross wearing an elaborate garment adorned with embroidery and pearls;[19] this must have been adopted to distinguish the royal robes placed on Christ at his mocking from his own, simpler red garment seen in the *Helkomenos epi Stavrou* at the foot of the Cross.[20] This brief period of sensitivity serves to underscore the consistency with which the late Byzantine Christ retains the short-sleeved or sleeveless royal red colobium, the garment first assigned to him in pre-Iconoclastic images of the Crucifixion, when he was still shown open-eyed and living on the Cross.

In thirteenth-century versions, the scene at the foot of the Cross acquired a ladder, propped against the Cross as a visual metaphor for Christ's ascent. From here, the scene evolved in two directions. On the one hand, it became activated, showing Christ in willing condescension climbing the ladder to ascend the Cross. Only briefly attested in Byzantium, this elaboration was eagerly embraced in Italy, where an episode was added showing Christ stripped of his garments at the foot of the Cross.[21] The stripping may have been current already in Europe—it appears in an English manuscript of about 1250 by William de Brailes, and a related scene of Christ stripped as he ascends the Cross adorns a German Zackenstil manuscript.[22] But it was in Italy that the event with its full complement of Jews and anguished women was taken up. Franciscan authors expanded upon its details, and Bonaventure introduced the poignant vignette of the Virgin Mother tying her own headscarf around Christ's nudity. A richly detailed version—though without the vignette of Mary's scarf—is still seen in Lorenzo Monaco's predella of 1409, with the Cross, Christ divesting himself of his red robe, and Mary watching in anguish.[23] By this time, the episodes of stripping had begun to multiply in the Passion narrative, and Christ was shown being stripped on at least three occasions: after the trial and after the mocking, as well at the foot of the Cross.[24] By the end of the fifteenth century there were many versions of the stripping, especially in print sequences on the Passion. Essential in all of them is the nakedness of Christ: his robe has been taken off, and his pale body is bare of all but his loincloth.

In Byzantium itself, by contrast, the Helkomenos took a different course. Rather than being elaborated, it was compressed. As Vassilike Foskolou has shown, murals in a number of thirteenth-century churches in Greece itself and the islands show the slender figure of the red-clad Christ, hands bound and head crowned with thorns, before the Cross and ladder—or even before the ladder alone.[25] Soldiers or a Pharisee may confront him from the other side of the Cross; more often he is alone, though the command "ἀνάβηθι"—"go up!"—at the base of the scene may imply the others' presence. A similar, stark composition in the famous thirteenth-century illuminated gospel book Iviron 5 is severely abraded, suggesting that its poignant content may have attracted especially intimate acts of devotion.[26] Some decades later, a particularly evocative variant of the theme was adopted in the full-page frontispiece to the gospel lectionary London, British Library, Add. 37006.[27] Beneath the right arm of a huge frontal cross stands the slender Christ, hands bound before his royal red robe and bent head crowned with thorns; beneath its left arm stands the imperially clad Andronikos II Palaiologos. Vassilike Foskolou suggests that the book might have been an imperial gift to Monemvasia, which Andronikos particularly favored.

Toward the end of the fifteenth century, the Helkomenos assumed its final, post-Byzantine form, as a single-figure icon (see figure 3).[28] Showing Christ frontal and alone, usually in half-length, without the Cross or any narrative elements, the image retains nonetheless its identity though its title, *Helkomenos epi Stavrou*. Though closely akin to the half-length *Ecce Homo* that became widespread in both Western and Cretan painting at much the same time, it addresses a different moment and shows Christ not nude but clothed. In stark contrast to Western images of Christ at the foot of the Cross, the Byzantine image of the Helkomenos retains the long-canonical crimson colobium; it does not show him stripped.

Byzantium, then, never developed an imagery of the stripping of Christ: there was no Byzantine counterpart to the scene of the *Espolio*. The reticence to develop such an image may well have been rooted in the substantial burden of content given in Orthodox thought to the robe that Christ wore to the Cross. Revered as one of the Passion relics preserved in the Pharos Chapel in the imperial palace, it had been linked already very early in Byzantine thought with the body of Christ itself. This is nowhere more potent than in John of Damascus's three treatises on the images, in which he states as a veritable creed that "I venerate together with the King and God the purple robe of his body, not as a garment, nor as a fourth person (God forbid!), but as called to be and to have become interchangeably equal to God, and the source of anointing."[29]

The metaphor of Christ's flesh as a purple robe is a recurrent one, but other metaphors developed, too. In his famous "On Mary at the Cross," the early sixth-century hymnographer Romanos has Christ speak of his stripped flesh to his Mother as he goes to the Cross:

> Bear up for a short time, O Mother, and thou shalt see
> How like a physician I strip and come where they lie dead
> And cure their wounds . . .
> And when I have opened up the cut with the surgical lance of the
> nails, I shall use my cloak as dressing.[30]

Here Christ strips—that is, divests himself of his body—so he can descend to Hades to heal the wounds of sin, using his cloak—his own flesh—to bind humankind's wounds. Mary's presence on the way to the Cross was deeply rooted in Byzantium. Already the *Acta Pilati* had placed her in the crowd, lamenting the violence to Christ's body. Seeing him stripped she cries: "My lord, my son, where is the beauty of your form?" Absent his robe, he does not gain bodily presence; he loses it. These early Byzantine metaphors of Christ's body as a robe which is stripped from him in the Passion, and Mary's engagement in the scene,[31] remained as a legacy in later periods. The lament attributed to St. Epiphanios of Salamis has Christ say to Adam at the Anastasis: "Thou didst put on the skin-coat

Figure 3. *Christ Helkomenos*. Monastery of St. John the Theologian, Patmos. Photo: with permission of His Reverence Abbot Antipas of the Holy Monastery of St. John the Theologian, Patmos.

made of shame (see Gen. 3:24), but being God I put on the haematic coat of thy flesh. Wherefore, arise, let us go hence, from death into life, from corruption into incorruption."[32] And the red cloak placed on the throne prepared for the Last Judgment at Decani retains the form of a living body, as Aleksandra Davidov pointed out.[33] Though verbal exegeses of the Passion included pungent descriptions of Christ stripped of his robes, visual ones retained the ancient colobium unchanged as a pungent iconographic sign.

Icons of the lone Christ Helkomenos are not numerous, but most surviving examples come from the period of Theotokopoulos's own life.[34] We know from Cretan inventories that they were being made in Candia during his youth.[35] John Gripiotis, a teacher of painting, produced one that so pleased the abbot who commissioned it that he paid off Gripiotis's debts so it would not be impounded with the painter's possessions.[36] Another Christ Helkomenos from this period is preserved with its original, richly gilded frame in the monastery of Patmos, where it is specially venerated in Holy Week.[37] Chrysanthe Baltoyianne has attributed it to the young Theotokopoulos himself, proposing that this was the image of the Passion by him that was evaluated at an exceptionally high price just before he left Crete.[38] Among surviving examples of the Helkomenos, this one stands out especially for the vibrant blood-red of Christ's red robe—of all images of the theme, this is the one most evocative of the *Espolio* itself. Like the *Espolio*, and in keen visual contrast to Western images of Christ stripped, the sacramental character of Christ's body is displayed through the purple mantle of his flesh and not the pallor of his bare skin. Whether El Greco himself produced the painting on Patmos or not, it exemplifies an iconic image of a kind that he surely knew. I submit that the Christ Helkomenos lies behind the enveloping, blood-red mantle of the *Espolio*.

The red color of the robe of the Helkomenos in Cretan icons contrasts sharply with the robe of Christ stripped in European painting. We have already contrasted the red robe of the *Espolio* with the violet robe in Dirk Bouts's image of the Betrayal; this same violet runs though almost all of the sixteenth-century images of Christ stripped.[39] The red of the Toledo painting stands out vividly. No less vivid is the contrast between the Byzantine view of the robe, as emblematic of Christ's own flesh, and the European view of the stripping, exemplified by a Franciscan text: "But let us come now to the final events. Our most loving Lord Jesus Christ is stripped of his clothes. Why? So that you may be able to see the ravages done to His most pure body. Therefore is this supremely good and sovereign Jesus despoiled."[40] The Franciscan text sees the clothing removed to reveal the flesh; the Byzantine image retains the clothing as the very image of the flesh.

The figure of Christ clothed, in John Damascene's words, in the "royal purple mantle of his flesh" was a legacy of Byzantine art, passed on in the figure of the Helkomenos. The introduction of the Christ Helkomenos with his royal purple mantle of human flesh into the scene of the disrobing enables Theotokopoulos to play upon the stripping of Christ with unprecedented, visceral intensity, for the hand at the neck of his robe is poised to tear the mantle of flesh from Christ. Thanks to Luba Freeman, we know the searing purity of El Greco's nudes.[41] In this case the hand on the mantle would flay him.

The theme of flaying was a live one in 1577. In some sense, it had had a persistent presence throughout the High Renaissance, for the myth of Apollo and Marsyas was a favored allegory, representing art's preeminence over nature.[42] But in this sunny privileging of art and culture, flaying had functioned only subliminally—the bestial fate of the bestial. Thus the two antique statues of Marsyas stretched for his flaying that flanked the entrance to Lorenzo de Medici's famous garden must have elicited only a frisson of enthusiastic transcendence in its Neoplatonically inclined visitors as they crossed the threshold.[43] Certainly in Raphael's *Stanza della Segnatura* the myth presented the rightful preeminence of culture over nature, of learned art over intuition.

In the third quarter of the sixteenth century, however, the fate of Marsyas saw a kind of restless problematization. The theme eddied especially around the late Michelangelo. His catafalque was adorned with images of Marsyas in honor of his anatomical mastery. The Florentine academy, of which he was the honorary head, required its artists to attend anatomical dissections, symbolized by the Marsyas figures. But rebels against such codified training soon set the surgical brilliance of the dissecting Sun god in contrast to the integrating capabilities of passionately inspired art, thus challenging the logic of the myth.[44] Michelangelo himself had cast far fiercer light upon the theme of flaying. He placed his own face on the flayed skin of St. Bartholomew in the Sistine *Last Judgment*. Turning attention forcibly from flayer to flayed, he focused upon the sheer ferocity of transcendence, the violent surgery that enabled the self to shed its s(k)in. The Marsyas myth followed his lead, its emphasis shifting from the sunny self-assurance of the all-exposing Sun god to the dark harshness of his discipline. Ottavio Farnese used Marsyas on his impresa as a warning of the futility of challenging the gods;[45] Giulio Romano and Lelio Orsi depicted Apollo performing the flaying himself with explicit and sexual violence,[46] while Guglielmo della Porta produced a Marsyas of almost Christ-like suffering.[47] The figure of Bartholomew, in turn, found vivid currency in the Jubilee of 1575, his flayed and bloody skin flaunted over the backs of bleeding flagellants.

Not art but life, however, brought the theme to its most violent reality. In 1571, just after Theotokopoulos had left Venice for Rome, Marcantonio Bragadin, the Venetian general defending the island of Cyprus, was flayed alive by his Ottoman adversaries and his stuffed skin sent in triumph to Istanbul. This event is often linked with Titian's famous *Flaying of Marsyas*.[48] Among Titian's very last works and a painting of imposing size and intensity, the *Flaying* was the first full-scale treatment of Marysas's myth in Renaissance art.[49] Here in a canvas with the scale and format of an altarpiece portraying a martyrdom, Titian seized a theme already deeply embedded in late Renaissance culture and thrust it into a wholly new artistic and emotional frame of reference, focusing on its cruelty in a way that was both fiercely topical and disturbingly cultural. Flaying took center stage.

In its relentless visuality, displaying violence in a dazzling veil of virtuosity, Titian's *Marsyas* has riveted recent viewers, and its current bibliography is rife with interpretations.[50] Recurrent throughout, however, is the theme of art itself. Be it in the surgical concentration of Apollo's attention to Marsyas's flesh or the keen vitality of Titian's brushwork that rivets yet horrifies the eye, one's attention is drawn to the artistry of the surface. The artist, like Apollo, is relentlessly demanding of the form. But what then of the paradox and violence packed within? The painting is a brooding reflection on art itself and its adequacy to address the remorseless reality of human pain. Be it in the elegant terminology of cultural theory, the earnest challenge of Reformation faith, or the deadly confrontation of empires in the Mediterranean, the theme of flaying was recurrent. The iconography of the Helkomenos allowed Theotokopoulos to use that same theme here, but now on a sacramental level, as a meditation on the sacramental body of Christ. It is a meditation that verges on the transfigurative, for we know that if the royal purple robe of Christ's flesh were torn away, the bone-white brilliance of his body would blind like a theophany.

Theotokopoulos knew Michelangelo's *Last Judgment*; he knew Ottavio Farnese; he knew the admiral Don Juan of Austria, whose triumph at Lepanto repaid the Porte for Bragadin's ghastly death;[51] he surely knew the myth of the Marsyas as an intricate allegory of art's fierce and focused discipline. We do not know whether he had an opportunity to see Titian's haunting meditation on Marsyas. Harold Wethey's argument that Theotokopoulos remained in Rome until he left for Spain continues to be questioned by scholars who believe he must have seen Venetian works of the 1570s.[52] It is hard to believe that Theotokopoulos was unaware of the *Flaying of Marsyas*. It was one of Titian's last and profoundest paintings, a meditation upon his own work as a painter in which, as Sidney Freedberg said, he used his sheer brilliance to turn an intolerable image into an experience of art.[53] El Greco presented his *Espolio*, too, as a work of transcendent and intensely self-conscious artistic skill. As Richard Kagan has shown, he did not engage in a lawsuit, but he did set an impossibly high monetary value on it, proclaiming in his price its value as a work of the highest art.[54] Through the theme of the Helkomenos with its royal purple mantle of flesh, Theotokopoulos laid claim to the allegory of flaying and its message of transcendent artistic ambition.

With great sophistication the Orthodox content of the Helkomenos is made to resonate with themes of political and art-theoretical concern that were current in El Greco's Europe in the 1570s. The contemporaneity of the content shows that Theotokopoulos himself did not regard the image-legacy of his own tradition as incompatible with European art. This legacy was not a style. Rather than in style, or even in iconography in the art-historical sense of a codified composition, the Orthodox heritage that one sees in the *Espolio* lies in the potent visual use of certain images steeped in meaning by Greek liturgical painting, poetry, and performance.

NOTES

1. *St. Francis in Meditation*. 76 x 63.5 cm (30 x 25 inches); attributed to 1605–10; from the collection of Marquèz de Amurrio in Madrid; first published by Harold E. Wethey, *El Greco and His School*, 2 vols. (Princeton: Princeton University Press, 1962), 2:227–28, no. X-300.

2. For recent insights into the question see on the one hand Nicos Hadjinicolaou, "Δομήνικος Θεοτοκόπουλος· 450 χρόνια από τη γέννηνή του / Domenicos Theotocopoulos 450 Years Later," in *Δομήνικος Θεοτοκόπουλος Κρης. El Greco of Crete*, exhibition catalogue, Basilica of St. Mark, Irakleion, 1 September–10 October 1990 (Iraklion: Municipality of Iraklion, 1990), pp. 66–75, 90–97, with pungent quotations from Manoles Chatzedakes, and on the other hand Lydie Hadermann-Misguich, "Permanence d'une tradition byzantine dans l'oeuvre espagnole du Greco," in *El Greco of Crete: Proceedings of the International Symposium, Irakleion, Crete*, 1–5 September 1990, ed. Nicos Hadjinicolaou (Iraklion: Municipality of Iraklion, 1995), pp. 397–407; Hadermann-Misguich, "Le byzantinisme du Greco à la lumière de découvertes récentes," *Bulletin de la classe des beaux-arts*, 5th ser. 69 (1987): 42–64.

3. Konstantinos D. Mertzios, "Σταχυολογήματα από τα κατάστιχα του Νοταρίου Κρήτης Μιχαήλ Μαρά (1538–1578)," *Κρητικά χρονικά* 15–16 (1961–62): 228–308.

4. Wethey (*El Greco*, 2:52) sums up the elements identified to that date as Byzantine, and though he speaks of them as iconographic, the features he cites—frontality, lightshot and jagged landscape forms, and the framing of a figure against a brighter or darker neutral ground—are as readily seen as stylistic. Similarly Pál Kelemen (*El Greco Revisited: Candia—Venice—Toledo* [New York: Macmillan, 1961], p. 158b) sums up his presentation of El Greco's art as deeply Greek by speaking of "his unique way of painting, the Byzantine compositional method."

5. Manoles Chatzedakes, "Greco entre la peinture byzantine et la peinture occidentale," in *Δομήνικος Θεοτοκόπουλος Κρης, Κείμενα 1940–1990* (Athens: Cultural Foundation of the National Bank of Greece, 1990), pp. 98–99, where he writes "La predominance en peinture des lois de l'esprit exprimée par le style, qui met à un plan secondaire l'imitation de la nature, constitue une leçon importante que le peintre Crétois n'oubliera jamais pendant son exil à l'autre bout de la Méditerranée."

6. The frieze Gospel Paris, gr. 74, includes on folio 205v a dramatic image of Christ stripped for the Flagellation, his arms held out as if in the Crucifixion and his body clothed only in a perizoma. See Henri Omont, *Évangiles avec peintures byzantines du XIe siècle*, 2 vols. (Paris: Berthaud, 1908), vol. 2, fig. 176 (2). The yet more densely illustrated frieze

Gospel in Florence, Laur. VI 23 does not repeat the image, and it remains exceptional, paralleled only by sporadic mural paintings of the Flagellation in the late thirteenth and fourteen centuries in Serbia, Cyprus, and Crete, areas in close contact with Western European traditions.

7. Thus the Flagellation is only rarely included in Byzantine cycles of the Passion; the stripping as such is not known; and the scene of Christ ascending the Cross, in which he is stripped to his loincloth, is exceptional, appearing only for a brief period in the art of Serbia and—in one instance—in Cyprus in the church of the Panagia, Choulou, in the Paphos District. On imagery of the Passion in Byzantium see especially Anne Derbes, *Picturing the Passion in Late Medieval Italy: Narrative Painting, Franciscan Ideologies, and the Levant* (New York: Cambridge University Press, 1996), and Gabriel Millet, *Recherches sur l'iconographie de l'évangile aux XIV, XV, et XVIe siècles,* 2nd ed. (Paris: E. De Boccard, 1960), pp. 362–93.

8. Wethey, *El Greco,* 2:51.

9. Wethey (ibid.) cited twenty-two instances of Christ despoiled of his garments in the Princeton Index of Christian Art, of which eighteen were from the fourteenth century. The numbers today are larger, with twenty-eight in all, but the proportions are the same. Just three are Byzantine: the image in Paris, Bibliothèque national de France, gr. 74, fols. 58r and 205v (Omont, *Évangiles avec peintures byzantines,* 1:49 [2] and 2:176 [2]); Florence, Biblioteca Medicea Laurenziana, Laur. VI 23, fol. 58r (Tania Velmans, *Le tétraévangile de la Laurentienne, Florence, Laur. VI. 23* [Paris: Éditions Klicksieck, 1971], figs. 118–19); and the Lectionary in San Giorgio dei Greci in Venice. All of these except Paris, gr. 74, 205v, cited in note 6 above, show Christ fully clothed.

10. Wethey, *El Greco,* 2:52. The same association had been made by Robert Byron and David Talbot Rice, *The Birth of Western Painting* (London: Routledge, 1930), notes to pl. 46.

11. Theophanes used much the same composition for the Betrayal in a panel now at Iviron Monastery on Mount Athos, reproduced in color in José Álvarez Lopera, ed., *El Greco: Identity and Transformation; Crete, Italy, Spain*, exhibition catalogue, Museo Thyssen Bornemisza, Madrid, 3 February–16 May 1999 (Milan: Skira, 1999), p. 219, cat. no. 2; and in the mural at the Athonite monastery of Stauronikita, reproduced in color in Hadjinicolaou, "Δομήνικος Θεοτοκόπουλος· 450 χρόνια από τη γέννηνή του," fig. 11.

12. Manoles Chatzedakes, "Ο Δομήνικος Θεοτοκόπουλος και η κρητική ζωγραφική," *Κρητικά Χρονικά* 4 (Sept.–Dec. 1950): 85, repr. in Chatzedakes, *Δομήνικος Θεοτοκόπουλος Κρης, Κείμενα 1940-1990* (Athens: Cultural Foundation of the National Bank of Greece, 1990), p. 85.

13. In color in Hadjinocolaou, "Δομήνικος Θεοτοκόπουλος," fig.10.

14. Andromache Katselake, "Ο Χριστός Ελκόμενος επί Σταυρού, Εικονογραφία και τυπολογία της παράστασης στη βυζαντινή τέχνη (4ος αι.–15ος αι.)," *Δελτίον τῆς χριστιανικῆς ἀρχαιολογικῆς Ἑταιρείας* 19 (1996–97), pp. 169, 195 [English summary on p. 200 as "*The Way to Calvary*: The Iconographic Development of the Representation of Christ Elkomenos in Byzantine Painting (4th cent.–1435)"]. The hymn is still part of the Lenten Triodion: see *The Lenten Triodion*, trans. Mother Mary and Archimandrite Kallistos Ware (London: Faber and Faber, 1978), p. 593. In painting the theme survives for the known first time in a sequence of tiny Passion scenes on an eleventh-century icon on Mount Sinai: Vassilike Foskolou, "Αναζητώντας την εικόνα του Ελκομένου της Μονεμβασίας. Το χαμένο παλλάδιο της πόλης και η επίδρασή του στα υστεροβυζαντινά μνημεία του νότιου ελλαδικού χώρου," *Σύμμεικτα* 24 (2001): 238, fig. 8 [English summary on p. 256

as "Tracing the Monemvasia Icon of Christ Helkomenos: The City's Lost Palladium and Its Influence on the Late Byzantine Mouments of Southern Greece"]; George A. Soteriou and Maria Soteriou, *Εἰκόνες τῆς Μονῆς Σινᾶ*, 2 vols. (Athens: Institut français d'Athènes, 1956), 1:145, 2:123–25.

15. Haris Kalligas, *Byzantine Monemvasia: The Sources* (Monemvasia: Akroneon, 1990), pp. 69–70. Though removed by Isaac to his new church of the Archangel Michael in Anaplous near Constantinople, the icon remained embedded in local legend for centuries: see Foskolou, "Ἀναζητώντας την εικόνα του Ελκομένου της Μονεμβασίας," p. 231.

16. Otto Demus, *The Mosaics of Norman Sicily* (London: Routledge and Kegan Paul, 1949), fig. 71A.

17. Derbes, *Picturing the Passion*, fig. 86.

18. Athanasios Papageorgiou, *Icons of Cyprus* (Nicosia: Holy Archbishopric of Cyprus, 1992), pp. 22–25, fig. 14; Annemarie Weyl Carr, "Thoughts on Seeing Christ Helkomenos: An Icon from Pelendri," in *Byzantinische Malerei: Bildprogramm–Ikonographie–Stil. Symposium in Marburg vom 25.–29. 6. 1997*, ed. Guntram Koch (Wiesbaden: Reichert Verlag, 2000), pp. 405–20, reprinted in Carr, *Cyprus and the Devotional Arts of Byantium in the Era of the Crusades* (Aldershot: Ashgate, 2005).

19. The example at the Panagia Phorbiotissa in Asinou, Cyprus, is well reproduced in Andreas Stylianou and Judith A. Stylianou, *The Painted Churches of Cyprus: Treasures of Byzantine Art*, 2nd edition (Nicosia: A.G. Leventis Foundation, 1997), fig. 67. See also St. Nicholas, Prilep, of 1298, in Gabriel Millet, *La peinture du Moyen Âge en Yougoslavie (Serbie, Macédoine et Monténégro)*, 4 vols. (Paris: E. De Boccard, 1954–59), vol. 3, fig. 24, 3; and the church of the Panagia at Spilies, Euboia, of 1311, in Katselake, "Ὁ Χριστός Ἑλκόμενος ἐπί Σταυροῦ," fig. 2.

20. As in Matt. 27:28–31: "And they stripped him, and put on him a scarlet robe.... And after that they had mocked him, they took the robe off from him, and put his own raiment on him, and led him away to crucify him" (King James Version).

21. On the imagery of the stripping of Christ, see Derbes, *Picturing the Passion*, pp. 138–45.

22. Ibid., p. 140 and fig. 84.

23. Marvin Eisenberg, *Lorenzo Monaco* (Princeton: Princeton University Press, 1989), pp. 11, 98–99, fig. 11. It is one of two predellas in Florence, Accademia, no. 438, showing the Agony in the Garden. Similar motifs recur in the second half of the fifteenth century in a large painting of the Stripping of Christ in the style of Francesco di Giorgio Martini in Siena: see Gertrud Schiller, *Iconography of Christian Art*, vol. 2, *The Passion of Jesus Christ*, trans. Janet Seligman (Greenwich, CT: New York Graphic Society, 1972), fig. 318.

24. Derbes, *Picturing the Passion*, p. 142.

25. Foskolou, "Ἀναζητώντας την εικόνα του Ελκομένου της Μονεμβασίας," pp. 231–34.

26. Ibid., p. 242; Katselake, "Ὁ Χριστός Ἑλκόμενος ἐπί Σταυροῦ," fig. 15.

27. Foskolou, "Ἀναζητώντας την εικόνα του Ελκομένου της Μονεμβασίας," fig. 15.

28. Chryssanthe Baltoyianne, "The Place of Domenicos Theotocopoulos in Sixteenth-Century Cretan Painting and the Icon of Christ from Patmos," in Hadjinicolaou, *El Greco of Crete*, p. 86.

29. Andrew Louth, trans., *St. John of Damascus: Three Treatises on the Divine Images* (Crestwood, NY: St Vladimir's Seminary Press, 2003), pp. 22, 86.

30. Romanos the Melode, "On Mary at the Cross," in *Kontakia of Romanos, Byzantine Melodist*, vol. 1, *On the Person of Christ*, trans. Marjorie Carpenter (Columbia: University

of Missouri Press, 1970), pp. 202–3. The hymn was composed for Good Friday and is still extensively quoted in the Lenten Triodion.

31. Amy Neff, "The Pain of Compassio: Mary's Labor at the Foot of the Cross," *Art Bulletin* 80 (1998): 254.

32. *The Lamentations of Matins of Holy and Great Saturday, and also an Homily by Our Father among the Saints Epiphanius, Bishop of Cyprus*, trans. Holy Transfiguration Monastery (Boston: Holy Transfiguration Monastery, 1981), p. 50.

33. Aleksandra Davidov, "Ciklus Strašnog suda," in *Zidno slikarstvo manastira Dečana / Mural Painting of Monastery of Dečani*, ed. Vojislav Đurić (Beograd: Srpska akademija nauka i umetnosti, 1995), fig. 1 [English summary as "Cycle of the Last Judgment"]. I am very grateful to Dr. Davidov Temerinski for drawing my attention to this striking image and for her discussion of it.

34. There is the one in Patmos cited just below; one of similar date in the State Hermitage Museum in St. Petersburg reproduced in Manoles Chatzedakes, ed., Εικόνες της κρητικής τέχνης (από τον Χάνδακα ως την Μόσχα και την Αγία Πετρούπολη) (Iraklion: Vikelaia Public Library, 2004), pp. 340–41, no. 8; one of 1552 in the Monastery of Great Meteora reproduced in Myrtali Acheimastou-Potamianou, *Greek Art: Byzantine Wall Paintings* (Athens: Ekdotike Athenon, 1994), fig. 186; an early seventeenth-century one in the Loverdos Collection in Athens reproduced in Nicos Hadjinicolaou, ed., Δομήνικος Θεοτοκόπουλος Κρης, *El Greco of Crete* (cited in n. 2 above), p. 89, fig. 7; and the late seventeenth-century one in the church of the Helkomenos in Monemvasia itself, reproduced in Nikos A. Bees, "Ὁ Ἑλκόμενος Χριστὸς τῆς Μονεμβασίας μετὰ παρεκβάσεων περὶ τῆς αὐτόθι Παναγίας Χρυσαφιτίσσης." *Byzantinisch-neugriechische Jahrbücher* 10 (1932/33 and 1933/34): pl. Γ'.

35. Baltoyianne, "Place of Domenicos Theotocopoulos," p. 90.

36. Ibid., pp. 85, 90.

37. Ibid., pp. 86–95 and fig. 5; Manoles Chatzedakes, *Icons of Patmos: Questions of Byzantine and Post-Byzantine Painting* (Athens: National Bank of Greece, 1985), p. 89, no. 41, fig. 100. It measures 68.5 x 53.5 x 3 cm. Though he labels it an Ecce Homo, Chatzedakes distinguishes it from the customary Ecce Homo because it is clothed and associates it throughout his discussion with the Helkomenos instead. The icon is processed in Patmos on Maundy Thursday and called "the Bridegroom," echoing the Triodion's appellation of the sacrificed Christ as the bridegroom of the church.

38. Baltoyianne, "Place of Domenicos Theotocopoulos," p. 95. The painting is cited in Georgio Klontzas's evaluation of 1566 as "quadro della Passione del Nostro Signor Giesu Christo, dorato."

39. This is exemplified by the miniatures in the sixteenth-century manuscripts from Princeton University Library reproduced in color in the Index of Christian Art at http://ica.princeton.edu/index.html. See Princeton, Garrett 53, fol. 70r of ca. 1490; Garrett 55, fol. 56r of ca. 1475–85; Garrett 57, fol. 14r of ca. 1500; and Garrett 63, fol. 86r of the first quarter of the sixteenth century.

40. Derbes, *Picturing the Passion*, p. 150.

41. Luba Freedman, "El Greco's Approach to Nudity," *Konsthistorisk Tidskrift* 69: 3–4 (2000): 197–209. I am indebted to Professor Freedman for sending me an offprint of this article.

42. See especially Edith Wyss, *The Myth of Apollo and Marsyas in the Art of the Italian Renaissance: An Inquiry into the Meaning of Images* (Newark: University of Delaware Press, 1996).

43. The statues have an ample recent bibliography: Fredrika Jacobs, "(Dis)assembling: Marsyas, Michelangelo, and the Accademia del Disegno," *Art Bulletin* 84 (2002): 426–48; Charles Burroughs, "Monuments of Marsyas: Flayed Wall and Echoing Space in the New Sacristy, Florence," *Artibus et Historiae* 22, no. 44 (2001): 44nn20, 24; Shigetoshi Osano, "Due 'Marsia' nel giardino di Via Larga: La ricezione del 'décor' dell'antichita romana nella collezione medicea di sculture antiche," *Artibus et Historiae* 71, no. 34 (1996): 95–120. Lorenzo also, of course, owned the famous Roman gem with the theme of Marsyas that influenced so many Renaissance renditions of the theme: see Melissa Meriam Bullard and Nicolai Rubinstein, "Lorenzo de' Medici's Acquisition of the Sigillo di Nerone," *Journal of the Warburg and Courtauld Institutes* 62 (1999): 283–86.

44. Jacobs, "(Dis)assembling," pp. 434–35.

45. Wyss, *Myth of Apollo and Marsyas*, p. 125, fig. 97.

46. Ibid., pp. 97–100, fig. 64; p. 126, fig. 97.

47. Ibid., p. 128, fig. 101.

48. Sidney Freedberg, "Titian and Marsyas," *FMR* 4 (1984): 52–64; Christopher Hitchens, *Hostage to History: Cyprus from the Ottomans to Kissinger*, 2nd ed. (London: Quartet Books, 1989), pp. 1–2.

49. Wyss, *Myth of Apollo and Marsyas*, pp. 133–40; Philipp P. Fehl, "The Punishment of Marsyas," in *Decorum and Wit: The Poetry of Venetian Painting. Essays in the History of the Classical Tradition* (Vienna: ISRA, 1992), pp. 130–49; Frank Stella, *Working Space* (Cambridge, MA: Harvard University Press, 1986), pp. 99–103.

50. See Jodi Cranston, "Theorizing Materiality: Titian's *Flaying of Marsyas*," in *Titian: Materiality, Likeness, Istoria*, ed. Joanna Woods-Marsden (Turnhout: Brepols, 2007), pp. 5–18; Una Roman D'Elia, "Titian's Mute Poetry," in ibid., pp. 113–24; Thomas Puttfarken, *Titian and Tragic Painting: Aristotle's Poetics and the Rise of the Modern Artist* (New Haven: Yale University Press, 2005), p. 196; Joanna Nizynska, "Marsyas's Howl: The Myth of Marsyas in Ovid's Metamorphoses and Zbigniew Herbert's 'Apollo and Marsyas,'" *Comparative Literature* 53 (2001): 151–69.

51. Manoussos Manoussacas, "Lepanto e I Greci," in *Il Mediterraneo nella seconda metà del '500 alla luce di Lepanto*, ed. Gino Benzoni (Florence: Olschki, 1974), p. 231.

52. Harold E. Wethey, "El Greco in Rome and the Portrait of Vincenzo Anastagi," in *El Greco: Italy and Spain*, ed. Jonathan Brown, *Studies in the History of Art* 13 (1984):171–80; Wethey, *El Greco*, 2:87–88, no. 130. See by contrast Lionello Puppi, "Η διπλή παραμονή του Γκρέκο στη Βενετία," in *Ο Γκρέκο στην Ιταλία και η ιταλική τέχνη*, ed. Nicos Hadjinicolaou, exhibition catalogue, Athens, National Gallery, 1995 (Athens: National Gallery and Museum of Alexander Soutzos, 1995), p. 38 (English translation, "El Greco's Two Sojourns in Venice," p. 393); Nicos Hadjinicolaou, "Ο Γκρέκο στην Ιταλία," in ibid., p. 58 (English translation, "El Greco in Venice," p. 405).

53. Freedberg, "Titian and Marsyas," pp. 63–64.

54. Richard L. Kagan, "El Greco and the Law," in "Figures of Thought: El Greco as Interpreter of History, Tradition, and Ideas," ed. Jonathan Brown, special issue, *Studies in the History of Art* 11 (1982): 84–86.

Part 5
Royal Women

Signed, Sealed, and Delivered: The Patronage of Constance de France

William W. Clark

In late July or early August 1165, Constance, Countess of Toulouse, Duchess of Narbonne, and Marquise of Provence, was suddenly repudiated and "divorced" by her second husband, Raymond V, Count of Toulouse, et cetera. Shortly thereafter, she likely managed to join her brother, Louis VII, in the Auvergne for the journey to Paris, where she subsequently lived as a single woman, the self-styled Countess of Saint-Gilles, for the rest of her life.[1] One indication of her presence in Paris, and possibly of her acceptance within the royal family, is that she was named the principal godmother of the new heir, Philip, born August 21, 1165. According to a letter of Abbot Ernis of Saint-Victor, the newborn prince was baptized the following day in the church of S. Michaelis de Platea (the new chapel dedicated to Saint Michel built in the Cité palace by Louis VII), by Maurice de Sully, bishop of Paris, as he was held by his principal godfather, Abbot Hugh of Saint-Germain-des-Prés, accompanied by his two other godfathers, Abbot Ernis and Eudes, the recently retired abbot of Sainte-Geneviève (then living in the community of Saint-Victor), and the principal godmother, Constance (identified as "sister of the king, wife of Raymond, count of Saint-Gilles"), and two Parisian widows.[2]

Constance de France, the only daughter among the nine children of Adelaide de Maurienne and Louis VI, was twice described by Père Anselme as always carrying herself like a queen because of her first marriage to Eustace, heir presumptive to King Stephen of England.[3] Born a princess and trained to be queen by two remarkable women—first, her mother and subsequently her mother-in-law, Mathilda of Boulogne, queen of England—Constance was never a crowned queen.[4] The birth and death dates of her six brothers and two husbands are recorded, but hers are hardly mentioned and are subject to a certain degree of conjecture.[5] Yet Constance outlived her brothers and husbands and is as deserving of scholarly attention as any of them.[6] This exceptional woman was probably born in 1124 and, after two marriages and a long period as an active single woman within the royal family, was still alive in 1190.[7]

While Constance's personal seal, first used ca. 1165, identifies her in legal terms as Countess of Toulouse, Duchess of Narbonne, and Marquise of Provence, she identified herself (and the documents always identify her) as sister of the king and Countess of Saint-Gilles for the remainder of her life, which suggests that she constructed her political identity, in legal terms with the seal and in personal terms as the Countess of Saint-Gilles. But it is also possible that she did not accept the validity of the "divorce." The well-known impression of Constance's still intact seal (see figure 1) is affixed to a charter in the Archives nationales.[8] Since the 1850s, this charter in favor of Saint-Victor has been dated "after 1194." The donation was made, however, while Ernis was abbot (1161–72) and after Constance returned to Paris in 1165, so the charter and the seal attached to it must be dated between 1165 and 1172.[9] Given the presence and participation of both Constance and Ernis in the baptism of Philip on August 22, 1165, together with the troubles that marred the later years of Ernis's abbacy, a date closer to 1165 seems more plausible.[10] This suggests that she began using the seal almost immediately after she returned to Paris, rather than at the end of her life.

Constance was pregnant with her fourth child when she arrived in Paris. Her third son with Raymond V, Baudouin, was probably born in February or March 1165. We know little else about the events in Constance's life in the next years. In 1168, she tried to claim the county of Boulogne as the widow of Eustace, according to letters from Pope Alexander III to northern French bishops rather ineffectually supporting her claim, but this was most likely an effort to obtain a position and an inheritance for Baudouin.[11]

Living as a single woman in Paris, Constance flatly refused to consider reconciliation with Raymond even though Pope Alexander III strongly advocated it in 1174.[12] She is known to have gone to the Holy Land, perhaps on a pilgrimage mandated by the pope after she refused to rejoin her husband. In 1176 she purchased the *casal* (castle or citadel) of Bethduras on the plain of Ascalon for 5,800 *byzantios* from John Arrabit and his brothers, Peter and Henry.[13] Shortly thereafter, she granted the Christian inhabitants of Bethduras the right to farm the land in return for one quarter of their crops as rent.[14] In late 1178 or early 1179 Constance joined the order of the Hospitalers of Saint John in Jerusalem and presented Bethduras, together with most of its income, to the grand master of the order, Roger de Moulins.[15] Some of the funds were specifically reserved for the hospital itself. The charter makes it clear that, at that time, Constance planned to spend the rest of her life there and to be buried in the hospital cemetery.[16]

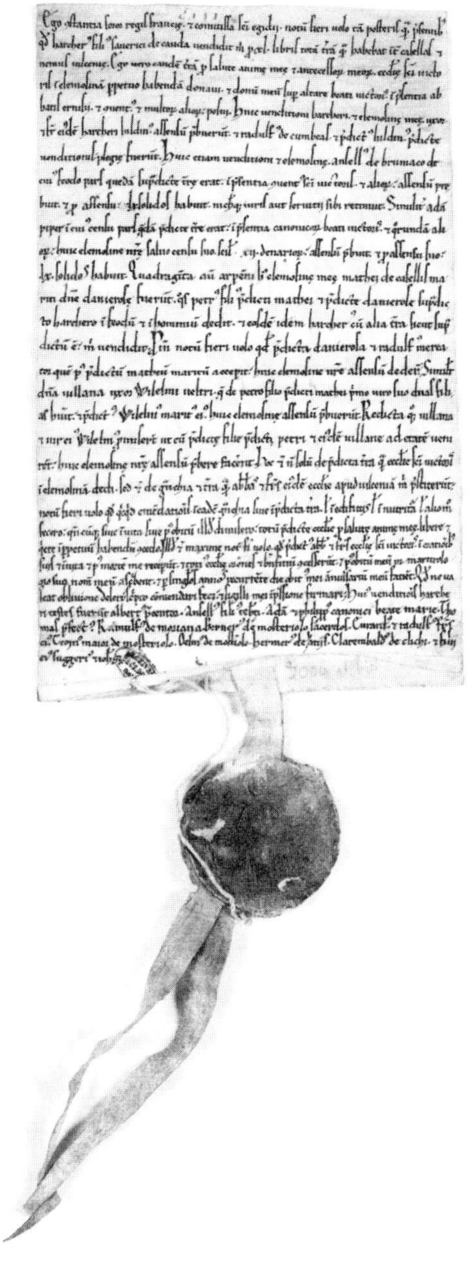

Figure 1. Constance's Donation Charter to Saint-Victor, Paris, with seal, here dated 1165, AN S 2139, no. 17. Paris, Archives nationales, photo courtesy of T. G. Waldman.

Her anniversary was to be remembered every year. However, as Luc Sery noted, incorporated in the wording of the charter was the possibility of her leaving the order.[17] In fact, Constance was back in Paris in 1180, probably shortly after the death of Louis VII on September 18, and remained there for the rest of her life. Sery believed that Constance died in Paris about 1190 and was buried at Saint-Victor.[18] So far as we know, the place of burial is correct, because Constance's anniversary was entered in their martyrology on September 3 (3 Nonas Sept.). The final donation charter to Saint-Denis (listed below as no. 9) was dated 1190, but this does not prove that she died in that year, nor that she had decided to be buried at Saint-Denis.

The Seal of Constance

The personal seal of Constance is a rare example of a round, double-sided seal used by a woman in the twelfth century.[19] The obverse, or front face (see figure 2), is well known. Brigitte Bedos-Rezak has identified and analyzed the image of Constance in majesty, seated on a rectangular throne with a chairlike back, the corners of which are festooned with fleurs-de-lys.[20] She holds the orb topped by another fleur-de-lys in her left hand and the small cross of Toulouse in her right, held in front of her breast. The sun and the moon are displayed above her. Unusual too is her skirt, decorated with two vertical panels of richly ornamented textile.[21] The inscription reads: *Sigillum Constancie Ducisse Narbone Marchesie* (the Seal of Constance, Duchess of Narbonne, Marquise [of Provence]).[22]

The reverse (see figure 3) shows Constance on horseback, riding sidesaddle but facing the viewer, wearing the same costume, including the decorated skirt panels, as on the obverse. She holds a long, leafy branch in her right hand.[23] The sun and crescent moon are again visible above her. The inscription reads: *Sigillum Constancie Comitisse Tholose* (the Seal of Constance, Countess of Toulouse).

Round seals used by women in the twelfth and early thirteenth centuries are highly unusual.[24] The preferred shape of seals for women of all ranks, from queens to the minor aristocracy, including abbesses, was an elongated, frequently pointed, oval. This type was used by Constance's mother, mother-in-law, and all other French and English queens.[25] The exception was the round seal of Empress Mathilda,[26] which was based on that of her first husband, the German emperor Henry V, right down to the crown type, although, as expected, the emperor's seal was larger. The empress used this single-sided seal from the time of her marriage to Henry, in 1114, until her death on September 10, 1167. It is doubtful that Constance considered the seal of her first father-in-law's enemy as a suitable model for her own seal, although that has been proposed.

Constance's seal should be understood as a deliberately created image that reflected her social position, as well as her political persona.[27] The front face, with its majesty image, establishes Constance's royalty, both as princess of France and "designated" queen of England, while the back face is the mark of her aristocratic status as wife of the Count of Toulouse.

Without question, the seal of Louis VII (see figures 4 and 5) accounts for the majesty pose and the presence of the sun and the moon. But Louis is seated on the throne of Dagobert, as Bedos-Rezak has demonstrated,[28] while Constance is seated on a rectangular chair-throne with a back, for which there are no identified French or English royal precedents. An important source that has not been previously considered is the seal of Raymond V (see figures 6 and 7).[29] No complete example of Raymond's seal has been located, so the imagery was "re-created" for Laurent Macé by making photo montages of fragments, identified from the descriptions given by Peiresc;[30] by considering the titles used in his charters; and by comparing the images on the seals of his successors, Raymond VI and Raymond VII.

The front face of the first seal of Raymond V (see figure 6), based on that affixed to charters dated between November 1163 and November 1165, shows a short-haired Raymond in the majesty pose, incongruously seated on a "copy" of the throne of Dagobert, with his sword laid across his knees and holding an orb in his raised left arm. He wears long aristocratic robes, including a cloak fastened at the shoulder of the sword arm. Above his right shoulder is a crescent moon. The inscription, of which only fragments remain, would have read: *Sigillum Raimundi Dei Gracia Comitis Tolose, Ducis Narbone, Marchionis Provincie* (the Seal of Raymond, by the Grace of God, Count of Toulouse, Duke of Narbonne, Marquis of Provence).[31] The reverse (see figure 7) shows Raymond in full armor galloping left with a standard in his right hand and, in his left, a large shield emblazoned with the cross of Toulouse. In the field above him is the sun. The inscription would have read: *Raimundus Dei Gracia Comitis Tolose Marchionis Provencie* (Raymond, by the Grace of God, Count of Toulouse, Marquis of Provence). As Macé observed, the latter title is a deliberate territorial pretension because Raymond was never the Marquis of Provence. Raymond also never used the title Count of Saint-Gilles that figures so prominently in all but one of Constance's donation charters.[32]

After Raymond married Constance, the daughter and sister of kings, in 1154/5, he adopted royal iconography for his seal, particularly the majesty pose with the sun and crescent moon and a folding throne.[33] In fact, she gave him, as it were, the right to royal symbolism; a right that was bequeathed to their son, Raymond VI, and to his heir, Raymond VII, and that was adopted by the counts of Barcelona and the kings of Aragon, as Robert-Henri Bautier demonstrated.[34] Raymond even took the unusual step of using a double-sided seal—the back bearing the traditional equestrian image of him holding a shield displaying the cross of Toulouse—a reference to Louis VII, who still used an equestrian reverse image (as Duke of Aquitaine) as late as 1154, fully two years after his divorce from Eleanor.[35]

Figure 2. Seal of Constance de France, obverse. Photo: author, from a cast.

Figure 3. Seal of Constance de France, reverse. Photo: author, from a cast.

Figure 4. Seal of Louis VII, obverse. Photo: author, after a cast.

Figure 5. Seal of Louis VII, reverse. Photo: author, after a cast.

Figure 6. Seal of Raymond V, reconstruction of obverse. Photo: author, after Bacqué.

Figure 7. Seal of Raymond V, reconstruction of reverse. Photo: author, after Bacqué.

Figure 8. Seal Matrix of Joanna, Queen of Sicily, obverse. Photo: author, after Pottier.

Figure 9. Seal Matrix of Joanna, Duchess of Narbonne, Countess of Toulouse and Marquise of Provence, reverse. Photo; author, after Pottier.

While it is clearly the seal of Louis VII that brought the royal imagery to the seals of both Raymond and Constance, it is equally evident that the seal of Constance was based as much, if not more, on Raymond's double-sided seal. There is only one other known example of a woman shown in the majesty pose, the seal matrix of Joanna, queen of Sicily and countess of Toulouse (see figures 8 and 9).[36] Joanna, the daughter of Eleanor of Aquitaine and Henry II, became, as the fourth wife of Raymond VI, Countess of Toulouse in 1196. The young widow of William II, king of Sicily, continued styling herself queen of Sicily, as her seal-die was inscribed. While the double-faced, pointed oval seal-die shows the standing image of Joanna wearing the royal crown on the obverse, the reverse has Joanna seated in majesty on a folding throne, a clear reference to the seal of Constance, as Abbé Pottier recognized immediately in 1875. Finally, the memory of Constance lived on in Languedoc: as soon as he became count in 1197, Raymond VI began identifying himself in his charters as "Raymond, son of Queen Constance."[37]

The Patronage of an Independent Woman

Nine surviving charters illuminate Constance's patronage during this third period of her life, from 1165 until 1190. Constance was neither a queen nor an abbess, and while the number of her surviving charters is impressive, her donations seem appropriate to her status as a lesser member of the royal family. As a princess, Constance was a political pawn in the hands of her brother, who twice sold her into marriage for what he perceived as both monetary and political gain. On the occasion of her first marriage to Eustace she received a sizable cash payment and dower lands centered on the city of Cambridge. After his death she surrendered the city to King Stephen. We do not know the financial terms of the second marriage, but we do know that she received the city of Toulouse as dower and was much beloved by its municipal council. However, after ten or eleven years of marriage to Raymond, and barely a month before her arrival in Paris, in the latter of two letters to Louis VII she complained of being impoverished.[38] She did not retain control over her dower lands in the Languedoc, which included the city of Toulouse. There is no surviving information about how she supported her household in Paris, nor where she lived in the city.[39] The only surviving documents that shed light on her activities are the charters recording her donations to religious institutions, mostly associated with her family. In fact, they involve some relatively complex financial transactions that were intended as ongoing, income-producing gifts based on property rather than outright money. In most cases she either already had, or bought, property, then assigned the rents to her favored institutions. In short, her transactions were deliberately intended to maximize resources over time, the mark of a prudent donor. The pattern is evident in the earliest identified gift she made in Paris, a donation to Saint-Victor (no. 1) described in the surviving charter, S 2139, no. 17 (see figure 1), and is still seen in the last gift, made to Saint-Denis and dated 1190 (no. 9).

In the list that follows, the charters are given in order of date, recipient, amount of rent, and source of rent, with citations in the notes:

1. ca. 1165. Abbey of Saint-Victor. Gift of land valued at 40 l. located near the chateau in the forest at Vincennes, bought from Harcher.[40] For the observance of her anniversary.
2. 1171, between March 28 and November. Infirmary at the nunnery of Saint-Denis and Notre Dame, Montmartre. 10 s. and 8 d. in annual rent on land at Aubervillers acquired from Hugh de Chailly. Annual revenue from a mill at Clichy, with 18 *seriers* of flour annually reserved for her niece, Elizabeth; fishing rights from the mill, with half reserved for the niece, during her lifetime.[41]
3. 1172 (between April 16, 1172, and April 7, 1173). The Knights Templar. Income from a house in the markets (Champeaux) that no one wanted. She paid 8 l. to have the house torn down and rebuilt and another 14 l. and 6 s. on it.[42] The Templars received the house on her death.
4. 1173. Hospitalers of Jerusalem. 6 s. in rent annually from property at Montreuil-sous-Bois.[43]
5. 1178–79. Hospitalers of Jerusalem. Constance joined the community and gave Bethduras, together with its property and income, to Roger of Moulins, grand master of the order, for the perpetual commemoration of the anniversaries of herself, her parents, her brother, her nephew, and her sons.[44]
6. 1180/81. Nunnery of Montmartre. 25 s. 6 d. annual rent for food for the nuns from property at Montreuil-sous-Bois bought from Symon de Perruchei.[45]
7. 1181. Nunnery of Montmartre. 100 s. annual rent as income for the chaplain in the Martyrium Chapel from a house on the Grand Pont, for which she gave the Hospitalers the purchase price of 145 l.[46]
8. 1184. Nunnery of Montmartre. 120 l. annual rent to support the nuns, and for the observance of the anniversary of her son, William Taillefer (d. 1183); plus the land named "fief Bataille" at Montreuil-sous-Bois, in exchange for property at Chaumontel held by the nuns.[47]
9. 1190. Abbey of Saint-Denis. 60 s. annual rent for the observance of her anniversary.[48]

Besides the donations made to Saint-Victor and Saint-Denis for the commemoration of her anniversary, her major gifts were made to two institutions, the Knights Hospitalers of Jerusalem and the nuns of Montmartre. Given her personal associations with the Hospitalers, the donations (nos. 4 and 5) to the Knights of Jerusalem are understandable.[49] The final donation to the Hospitalers (no. 7), in which she gave them 145 l. to buy a house (and then to pay 100 s. annually to support a chaplain in the Martyrium Chapel at the convent on Montmartre) should probably be understood as gratitude for being released from her earlier vows (no. 5) in Jerusalem.

The most significant gifts (nos. 2, 6, 7, and 8) were those made to the nuns of Montmartre. The first was made six years after her return to Paris and might have been a gift in memory of her mother, who, in 1154, was buried in the abbey church she had founded. The later three, made after the death of Louis VII on September 18, 1180, were dramatically larger and represented her reactions to his decision, made between March 24, 1174, and April 12, 1175, to limit the number of nuns in the abbey of Montmartre to sixty.[50] His stated aim was to stem the rapid depletion of the financial resources of the abbey caused by its dramatic growth. When the number reached sixty nuns, no more were to be admitted until a vacancy, resulting from the death of one of the sisters, occurred. On the surface, this act, which was agreed to by the abbess and confirmed by Pope Alexander III in 1178, must have appeared to be a reasonable solution.[51] In reality, it doomed the abbey to constant financial problems because it eliminated the other most lucrative income source, namely, the dower given by the family of each young woman joining the nunnery, funds that were intended to help support her in the community.

Because the exact date of Constance's departure for the Holy Land is not known, we cannot determine if she was still in Paris when Louis's act was promulgated. But we can see her reaction to it almost immediately upon her return. Two donations, nos. 5 and 6, were made in rapid succession; while the third and largest, no. 7, was probably intended as opposition to Philip's reaffirmation of the act of his father in 1183.[52] These three acts should be recognized as the efforts of a strong woman to counter male attempts to hinder or even to close down a female institution.[53]

Conclusion

Although raised to be a queen under the tutelage of two great queens, namely, her mother and her first mother-in-law, Constance never became a crowned queen. What is remarkable is what she was able to achieve in the last phase of her life, living alone in Paris without having the status of a husband in a male-dominated political landscape. Armed with a unique personal seal, Constance became a skilled "real estate agent," buying and trading property and donating the rental income, and ultimately, the property, to religious institutions associated with her family. Her patronage of her mother's foundation, the nunnery on Montmartre, consisted of several valiant, even heroic, attempts to oppose the decisions of her brother and nephew and, thereby, to avert the mounting financial crises faced by the nuns. The result was the first significant matrilineal patronage in the Capetian dynasty, and a record unequaled in dynastic history.

NOTES

This article is part of a larger study of Constance de France being readied for publication. The present analysis of the last phase of the life of this spirited independent woman in the twelfth century is lovingly offered to another independent, spirited, and dynamic woman whose achievements span many disciplines: For Bonnie from Big Brother. Parts of this material have been presented at annual meetings of the Medieval Academy and of the International Congress of Medieval Studies at Kalamazoo. I owe thanks to a number of people for their comments and advice, most especially to Tom Waldman and to another dynamic woman, Vivian Cameron. All remaining errors are my responsibility.

1. The best recent assessment is given by Laurent Macé, *Les comtes de Toulouse et entourage, XIIe–XIIIe siècle* (Toulouse: Privat, 2000). Dom Claude Devic and Dom Joseph Vaisette (*Histoire Générale de Languedoc*, 3rd ed., 8 vols. [Toulouse: Privat, 1872–75], 6:7–8), suggest that Constance might have joined Louis VII in the Auvergne for the hasty trip to Paris for the birth of the heir.

2. The letter of Abbot Ernis is Epistole Ervisii [*sic*] Abbatis, no. 1. in J.-P. Migne, *Patrologia cursus completus: Series latina* [hereafter PL], vol. 196 (Paris: Migne, 1855), cols. 1381–83. See also Dietrich Lohrmann, "Ernis, abbé de Saint-Victor (1161–1172): Rapports avec Rome, affaires financières," in *L'Abbaye parisienne de Saint-Victor au moyen âge*, ed. Jean Longère, Bibliotheca Victorina, vol. 1 (Turnhout, Brepols: 1991), pp.181–93. On the chapel, see Jean Guerot, "Le Palais de la Cité Paris des Origines 1417: Essai Topographique et Archéologique," *Paris e* 1 (1949): 57–212, esp. p. 145. It is worth noting that in no known surviving document did Raymond V ever use the title, or refer to himself as, Count of Saint-Gilles.

3. Père Augustin Déchaussé Anselme de Sainte Marie, *Histoire Genealogique et Chronologique de la Maison Royale de France* (Paris: Compagnie des Libraires, 1726), 2:75, and 2: 687. The first marriage (1140–53) was to Eustace, Count of Boulogne, son of Stephen, king of England. Although he was declared king by Stephen, he was never crowned, and died before his father. It seems to have been an unhappy marriage, with Constance neglected by Eustace and virtually abandoned at Canterbury because he preferred incessant warfare. The literature on the reign of King Stephen is vast; among the best assessments are David Crouch, *The Reign of King Stephen, 1135–1154* (Harlow: Pearson Education, 2000); ibid., *King Stephen and Northern France: King Stephen's Reign (1135–1154)*, ed. Paul Dalton and Graeme J. White (Woodbridge: Boydell, 2008), pp. 44–57; Luc Sery, "Constance, Fille de France, 'Reine d'Angleterre,' Comtesse de Toulouse," *Annales du Midi* 63 (1951): 193–209. Sery presents a thorough analysis of Constance's two marriages, citing all of the chronicle references and pointing out the inconsistencies between them. He did not investigate the charters detailing her patronage in Paris. The assessments by Hélène Débax, "Les Comtesses de Toulouse: Notices biographiques," *Annales du Midi* 100 (1988): 215–34, and "Stratégies Matrimoniales des Comtes de Toulouse (850–1270)," *Annales du Midi* 100 (1988): 131–51, ignore Constance's life after 1165, save to repeat the error that she died in 1176.

4. Still, as many have observed, Constance always carried herself as a queen and was often so styled in the charters of Raymond V and Raymond VI. See Macé, *Les comtes de Toulouse et entourage*, for a discussion of the charters of both Raymond V and Raymond VI. For the charters of Raymond V, see Emile G. Léonard, *Catalogue des Actes de Raymond V de Toulouse* (Nimes: Chastanier Frères, 1932). Léonard includes eight charters (nos. 8, 11, 12, 16, 18, 19, 21, and 22), issued by Raymond V between 1156 and 1160/61, that include Constance's participation. Four of these (nos. 11, 12, 18, and 22) identify her as queen (*Constantia*

regine); three (nos. 8, 12, and 22) characterize her as sister to the king (*regis Francorum sororis*); and three (nos. 8, 18, and 22) as the count's wife (*comitis uxor*). The full text is not given for nos. 16, 19, and 21, although Constance is mentioned in the summaries. In addition, it is likely that all of the charters including Constance were issued from the castle at Saint-Gilles. Examples of the charters of Raymond VI are found in François Delaborde, *Recueil des Actes de Philippe Auguste*, vol. 1 (Paris: Imprimerie Nationale, 1916). Additional examples are given in J. Delaville le Roulx, *Cartulaire de l'Ordre des Hospitaliers de Saint-Jean de Jérusalem*, 4 vols. (Paris: Leroux, 1894–1906), vol. 1, no. 884; vol. 2, nos. 1179, 1334, 1612, and 1617. Raymond VI identified himself as the son of Queen Constance.

5. For example, the French Wikipedia entry gives her dates as 1128–76 and refers to her as "dame de Montreuil-sous-Bois." See http://fr.wikipedia.org/wiki/Constance_de_France,_fille__de_Louis_VI.

6. See, most recently, Jim Bradbury, *The Capetians: Kings of France, 987–1328* (London: Hambledon, 2007), and Patrick Van Kerrebrouck, *Les Capétiens, 987–1328*, Nouvelle Histoire Généalogique de l'Auguste Maison de France 2 (Villeneuve d'Ascq: van Kerrebrouck, 2000). Constance is barely mentioned in both, yet Kerrebrouck devotes many pages to the genealogy of the brothers who were not ecclesiastics. Achille Luchaire (*Louis VI le Gros: Annales de sa vie et de son règne* [Paris: Picard, 1890], p. xxxiv, n. 4) and Andrew W. Lewis (*Royal Succession in Capetian France: Studies on Familial Order and the State* [Cambridge, MA: Harvard University Press, 1981]) both stated that Louis VI and Adelaide had nine children, whereas Anselme (*Histoire Genealogique et Chronologique*, 1:75) listed only eight. Constance, the only girl, was the fifth child, but Anselme lists her as the last because she was female! According to Lewis (*Royal Succession*, pp. 51 and 58), Constance was named after her father's sister, who, in turn, was named for Queen Constance of Arles, wife of Robert the Pious.

7. Her last donation, no. 9, is dated 1190; see below.

8. The seal is catalogued in Louis-Claude Douët-d'Arcq, *Collection de Sceaux. Inventaire et documents publiés par Ordre de l'Empereur sous la direction de M. Le comte de Laborde, directeur des Archives de l'Empire*, 1/1 (Paris: Henri Plon, 1863), 1:381, no. 741 and 741bis. The charter is paraphrased by Fourier Bonnard (*Historie de l'abbaye royale et de l'ordre des chanoines réguliers de St.-Victor de Paris*, 2 vols. [Paris: A. S va te, 1904–9], 1:218–19) and listed among his sources (1:xxv), although they are not linked in the text.

9. Special thanks to Tom Waldman for calling my attention to the role of Ernis in the charter. It is, of course, possible that the seal of Constance was made in Languedoc after her marriage to Raymond. The first seal of Raymond V, discussed below, appears to be smaller (ca. 6 cm) than that of Constance (6.3 cm). If that is the case, then I suspect the seal was created for Constance shortly after her arrival in Paris.

10. I am preparing an edition of this charter and publication of the three other originals (nos. 3, 5, and 9). The citations are given below. Lohrman ("Ernis, abbé de Saint-Victor") discusses Ernis's "avarice" in "strong-arming" donations to Saint-Victor.

11. Philip Jaffe, *Regesta Pontificum Romanorum*, vol. 2 (Leipzig: Veit, 1888), nos. 11417 and 11418, letters to Henry, archbishop of Reims (brother of Constance), and to several of his suffragan bishops. See also *Alexandri III Opera Omnia*, PL 200, cols. 497–99, letters 496 and 497; and *Recueil des Historiens de la France* [hereafter *RHF*], ed. Michel-Jean-Joseph Brial (Paris: Victor Palmé, 1878), 40, nos. 231 and 232. Having no prospects in the north, although his name comes from his maternal grandmother's family, Baudouin turned to his older brother, now Raymond VI, in Toulouse. Eventually he became head of the cadet family, known as Toulouse-Lautrec. See Macé, *Les comtes de Toulouse et entourage*, pp. 74–86.

12. Jaffe, *Regesta Pontificum Romanorum*, 12343, PL 200, cols. 794–95; and *RHF*, 40:942, no. 370. Constance refused the reconciliation on two grounds, infidelity and polygamy, claiming that Raymond had too many women around him. Only two of Raymond's illegitimate children have been identified, Indie and Peire Raymond. The name "Peire" suggested to Macé (*Les comtes de Toulouse et entourage*, p. 177) that his mother was a member of the Rabasten family, a lineage very close to the counts of Toulouse.

13. Delaville le Roulx, *Cartulaire de l'Ordre des Hospitaliers*, 1, nos. 495, 516, and 517.

14. Ibid., 1, no. 491.

15. Ibid., 1, nos. 551 and 557 (the papal confirmation). "... ego Constancia, me in consoror in prefate sancte domus communi capitulo, in manus magistri R[ogerio] di Molinis..."

16. Ibid., 1, no. 551. "Post obitum vero meum corpus meum Hospitalarii accipiant, et in cimiterio suo, ut consororis sue, honorifice acceptum sepeliant, et annuale meum celebrari faciant."

17. Sery ("Constance, Fille de France," p. 208) quotes the relevant passages from Delaville le Roulx, *Cartulaire de l'Ordre des Hospitaliers*, 1, no. 551.

18. Sery, "Constance, Fille de France," p. 208 and n. 93.

19. The study of seals, sigilography, has generated an enormous and specialized bibliography. That assembled by René Gandilhon and Michel Pastoreau in their *Bibliographie de la Sigillographie française* (Paris: Picard, 1982) has over twenty-five hundred entries and many more have appeared since then. The great catalogues consulted during the preparation of this study are all cited there.

20. Brigitte Bedos-Rezak, "Women, Seals and Power in Medieval France, 1150–1350," in *Women and Power in the Middle Ages*, ed. Mary Erler and Maryanne Kowaleski (Athens: University of Georgia Press, 1988), pp. 61–82, esp. p. 70, fig. 7; Frederic L. Cheyette, *Ermengard of Narbonne and the World of the Troubadours* (Ithaca: Cornell University Press, 2001), p. 259.

21. Janet E. Snyder discusses the taste for rich oriental fabrics in twelfth-century costumes ("Cloth from the Holy Land: Appropriated Islamic *Tiraz* in Twelfth-Century French Sculpture," in *Medieval Fabrications*, ed. E. Jane Burns, The New Middle Ages [New York: Palgrave Macmillan, 2004], pp. 147–64).

22. See Douët d'Arcq, D741 (not illustrated). It must be noted that Constance was not Marquise of Provence; rather her seal repeats what Macé, *Les comtes de Toulouse et entourage*, pp. 288–89, refers to as Raymond's territorial pretension. See below, n. 32.

23. The branch is most likely either laurel (victory) or olive (peace), more or less following antique precedents.

24. Susan M. Johns (*Noblewomen, Aristocracy and Power in the Twelfth-Century Anglo-Norman Realm* [Manchester: Manchester University Press, 2003]) catalogued 142 women's seals from the later twelfth and early thirteenth centuries. Of these, only seventeen were round and only one had anything in common with the seal of Constance. Pierre Bony (*Un siècle de Sceaux Figurés (1135–1235)* [Paris: Le Léopard d'Or, 2002]) has fourteen examples, in addition to that of Constance, out of a total of 582 illustrations.

25. For images of Adelaide and her seal, see Kathleen Nolan, "The Tomb of Adelaide de Maurienne and the Visual Imagery of Capetian Queenship," in K. Nolan, ed., *Capetian Women*, The New Middle Ages (New York: Palgrave Macmillan, 1993), pp. 45–76. The seal of Queen Mathilda is described in Johns, *Noblewomen, Aristocracy and Power*, p. 204, no. 4, and illustrated in Kathleen Nolan, *Queens in Stone and Silver: The Creation of a Visual Imagery of Queenship in Capetian France* (London: Palgrave Macmillan, 2009). See most

recently Philippe Plagnieux, "Le Tombeau de la Reine Adélaïde de Maurienne (d. 1154) à Saint-Pierre de Montmartre: entre célébration mémoriale et béatification," *Les Cahiers de Saint-Michel de Cuxa* 42 (2011): 143–52.

26. Johns, *Noblewomen, Aristocracy and Power*, p. 203, no. 3.

27. Jean-Luc Chassel discusses the use of the seal in "L'Usage du sceau au XIIe siècle," in *Le XIIe siècle: Mutations et renouveau en France dans la 1er moitié du XIIe siècle*, dir. Michel Pastoureau, special issue, *Cahiers du Léopard d'Or* 3 (1994): 61–102. *Recueil des actes de Louis VI, Roi de France (1108–1137)* (ed. Jean Dufour, 4 vols. [Paris: Boccard, 1992–94], 3:219–21) demonstrated that Adelaide de Maurienne only began using a seal as the widow of Louis VI and continued to use it during her second marriage in the administration of her dower lands.

28. Brigitte Bedos-Rezak, "Mythes monarchiques et thèmes sigilaires de sceau de Louis VII aux sceaux de Charles VII," *XV Congresso Internacional Genealogia y Heráldica* (Madrid: Instituto Salazar y Castro, 1982), pp. 199–213; Bedos-Rezak, "Suger and the Symbolism of Royal Power: The Seal of Louis VII," in *Abbot Suger and Saint-Denis*, ed. Paula L. Gerson (New York: Metropolitan Museum of Art, 1986), pp. 95–103. See, in particular, Martine Dalas, *Les Sceaux des Rois et de Régence*, Corpus des Sceaux Français du Moyen Âge 2 (Paris: Archives nationales, 1991), pp. 146–49.

29. Macé (*Les comtes de Toulouse et entourage*, pp. 287–314) discusses the "image" of the count, including the seal (pp. 295–96) in a broad context. Raymond V used two different seals, both of which have been "re-created" by Patrick Bacqué, illustrated in Macé, *Les comtes de Toulouse et entourage*, pp. 432–433. He used the second seal dated ca. 1171–89.

30. Léonard (*Catalogue des Actes*, pp. lxix–lxx) quotes in full the two descriptions by Peiresc of the first seal, dated 1163 and 1165. Peiresc believed these two were different seals, but the descriptions speak of such minor differences as could be observed in two damaged impressions of the same seal; see Macé, *Les comtes de Toulouse et entourage*, p. 432. The only important difference is that the November 1163 impression has the equestrian image as the front and the majesty image as the reverse; the August 1165 impression, probably made after the divorce from Constance, has them in the other order with the majesty on the recto, as though Raymond was now expressing the image of royalty on his own. The second seal, in use from 1171 to 1189, confirms this with two significant changes to the majesty image. The throne is now a high-backed chair and the orb is replaced by a model of the Château Narbonnais, the count's fortress and palace at Toulouse. In short, the second seal emphasizes his power in Toulouse, formerly held by Constance. Raymond is the only great lord to use the majesty image.

31. The phrase in the inscription, *Dei Gracia*, normally associated with royalty, is frequently used by Raymond in his charters. See Léonard, *Catalogue des Actes*, nos. 11 and 12, for example.

32. Macé, *Les comtes de Toulouse et entourage*, pp. 288–89.

33. Macé (ibid., pp. 319–20) considers the influence of Constance in determining the royal iconography of the first seal of Raymond and her own later adoption of such details as the chairlike throne (with the addition of the Capetian fleur-de-lys) from traditions she would have seen and known in Languedoc.

34. Robert-Henri Bautier, "Echanges d'influences dans les chancelleries souveraines du Moyen Age, d'après les types des sceaux de majesté," *Académie des Inscriptions et Belles-Lettres: Comptes rendus des séances*, 1968: 192–220.

35. Dalas, *Les Sceaux des Rois et de Régence*, p. 147.

36. Abbé Pottier, "Sceau inedit de Jeanne d'Angleterre, Comtesse de Toulouse," *Bulletin Archéologique et Historique de la Société Archéologique du Tarn-et-Garonne* 5 (1877): 261–70; John Evans, "Seal of Joanna Queen of Sicily," *Proceedings of the Society of Antiquaries*, 2nd ser., 8 (Jan. 1879–June 1881): 34–39; Alec Bain Tonnochy, *Catalogue of British Seal-Dies* (London: British Museum, 1952); Débax, *Les Comtesses de Toulouse*, pp. 229–30; Macé, *Les comtes de Toulouse et entourage*, pp. 60–61, 320–21; and Johns, *Noblewomen, Aristocracy and Power*, p. 204, no. 5. Pottier recognized the reliance of the majesty pose on Joanna's seal to that image on Constance's, but the reference was not repeated in the later literature, until Macé.

37. Macé, *Les comtes de Toulouse et entourage*, pp. 289–90. It survived another way as well. Raymond VI had five wives but only two children. With his second wife, Beatrice of Béziers, there was a daughter, appropriately named Constance; with his fourth wife, Joanna, there was a son, the future Raymond VII. See Macé, *Les comtes de Toulouse et entourage*, p. 434.

38. There are three letters of Louis VII in *RHF*, vol. 16, ed. Michel-Jean-Joseph Brial (Paris: Victor Palme, 1878), pp. 126–27, letters 389–91. Sery ("Constance, Fille de France," p. 195 and n. 14) dated the middle letter, 390, to the 1140s, during Constance's first marriage, and reversed the dating and order of the other two: 389 is dated 1165 and 391 is dated 1164. Cheyette (*Ermengard of Narbonne*, p. 262) gives a good modern translation of letter 389.

39. She seems to have owned properties in Montreuil-sous-Bois, which figure in her donation charters discussed below, but that is no indication that she resided there. The first charter also suggests the possibility that she might have lived in the chateau at Vincennes.

40. Original: Paris, Archives nationales, S 2139, no. 17. Constance bought a piece of property, located near the chateau in the forest at Vincennes, valued at forty pounds from Harcher, son of Savari de Cauda. She placed the charter as a donation on the high altar of the church of Saint-Victor in the presence of Abbot Ernis and the canons. She asked to be included in their prayers and remembered in perpetuity. Her name was to be entered in the martyrology and remembered every year on her anniversary, September 3. Included is a lengthy list of fourteen witnesses, one, Bernerius, deacon of Montreuil-sous-Bois (Mosteriolo) is listed as a witness in three additional charters (nos. 3, 4, and 5); while Claremboldus of Clichy and his son, Suggerius, are found again as witnesses in no. 3. The charter (AN, S 2139, no. 17) has the original seal attached to it, as noted by Douët d'Arcq, 1:381, 741. The reference, repeated from the Archives nationales, is the source of the erroneous post-1194 date.

41. Paris, Archives nationales, LL 1030 (cartulary, fols. 16–17); Edouard de Barthélemy, *Recueil des chartes de l'Abbaye Royale de Montmartre* (Paris: Champion, 1883), pp. 107–9; Robert de Lasteyrie, ed., *Cartulaire général de Paris* (Paris: Imprimerie Nationale, 1887), no. 497; Ferdinand François, Baron de Guilhermy, *Montmartre* (Paris: Société le Vieux Montmartre, 1906), pp. 46–47; Maurice Dumoulin, "Notes sur l'Abbaye de Montmartre," *Bulletin de la Société de l'Histoire de Paris et de l'Ile-de-France* 58 (1931): 145–238, 244–325, esp. p. 158. The niece in question would have been Elizabeth of Dreux, the daughter of Constance's brother, Robert, Count of Dreux, and his third wife, Agnes of Braine. See Anselme, *Histoire Genealogique et Chronologique*, 1:424–25. There are no witnesses listed in the charter.

42. Original: Paris, Archives nationales, S 5077, no. 87, now K 25, no. 5³. Jules Tardif, *Monuments Historiques: Archives de l'Empire; Inventaires et Documents* (Paris: J. Claye, 1866),

no. 640; Lasteyrie, *Cartulaire général de Paris*, no. 507. The names of twenty-one witnesses are listed.

43. Original: Paris, Archives nationales, K 25, no. 5[8]. Tardif, *Monuments Historiques*, no. 646; Sery, "Constance, Fille de France," p. 27. This has been incorrectly interpreted to indicate that Constance gave them her house before departing for the Holy Land, but she donated only the rent. There are three witnesses listed, and the charter is said to be sealed, but it is not noted if the actual seal impression survives.

44. Original: Malta, Archives of the Order, div. 1, vol. 3, no. 7 (original lost) and no. 9 (notification of the donation by the donor); vol. 46 (papal confirmation). Delaville le Roulx, *Cartulaire de l'Ordre des Hospitaliers*, 1:373–74, no. 551; 377–78, no. 557 (papal confirmation). The names of twenty-one witnesses are included.

45. Barthélemy, *Recueil des chartes*, pp. 112–13; Dumoulin, "Notes sur l'Abbaye de Montmartre," p. 159. There are eight witnesses listed.

46. Barthélemy, *Recueil des chartes*, pp. 123–24; Lasteyrie, *Cartulaire général de Paris*, no. 578; Delaville le Roulx, *Cartulaire de l'Ordre des Hospitaliers*, 1, no. 868 (1189 confirmation); Guilhermy, *Montmartre*, p. 51; Dumoulin, "Notes sur l'Abbaye de Montmartre," pp. 159.

47. Guilhermy, *Montmartre*, pp. 51–52; Dumoulin, "Notes sur l'Abbaye de Montmartre," pp. 159–60. Constance built a chapel and funded a priest at Chaumontel. On her death the abbess received the right to name the priest. The son, William Taillefer, died in 1183 or 1184; see Anselme, *Histoire Genealogique et Chronologique*, 2:687.

48. Original: Paris, Archives nationales, K 26, no. 11. Tardif, 1866, no. 700; Sery, "Constance, Fille de France," p. 208.

49. This analysis omits the details of her activities in the Holy Land, discussed above in the text.

50. Barthélemy, *Recueil des chartes*, pp. 109–10; Luchaire, *Louis VI le Gros*, p. 315, no. 686; Lasteyrie, *Cartulaire général de Paris*, pp. 434–35, no. 529; Dumoulin, "Notes sur l'Abbaye de Montmartre," p. 158.

51. Barthélemy, *Recueil des chartes*, pp. 113–14; Lasteyrie, *Cartulaire général de Paris*, p. 453, no. 553.

52. The editors and compilers of the *Gallia christiana*, 7, cols. 614–15, were obviously taken by these three donations to the nunnery, since they carefully quoted them all; they are the only documents so cited after the foundation charter, col. 612. *Recueil des actes de Philippe Auguste, Roi de France*, ed. Henri-François Delaborde et al., 6 vols. (Paris: Imprimerie nationale and Boccard, 1916–2005), 1:89–90, no. 69, dated 1183.

53. After the death of Louis VI in 1137, Adelaide de Maurienne married—likely at the instigation of Louis VII, who would have wanted to lessen her influence at court—Matthew de Montmorency, who was promptly made Constable of France. They had a daughter, Adele or Adelaide de Montmorency, who married at least three times. During her second marriage, the queen founded another women's religious house in her dower lands, St.-Jean-aux-Bois. There are no recorded donations from either daughter to this house. Later examples of Capetian matrilineal patronage are cited in the longer version of this study. While this article was in press an important new study of seals has been published: Marie-Adelaide Nielen, *Les sceaux des reines et des Enfants de France*, Corpus de sceaux français du Moyen Age 3 (Paris: Archives nationales, 2011), p. 140, nos. 51 and 51bis.

The Testamentary Strategies of Jeanne d'Évreux: The Endowment of Saint-Denis in 1343

Elizabeth A. R. Brown

Before her death at Brie-Comte-Robert on March 4, 1371, Jeanne d'Évreux spent forty-three years as a very rich widow after losing her husband, King Charles IV of France (1294–1328) on February 1, 1328.[1] The couple had been married since July 5, 1324. Jeanne had had two daughters (one of whom predeceased her father) and was pregnant with a third when Charles died. During her long widowhood, Jeanne worked to promote peace between France and Navarre out of dedication to her nephew, Charles of Navarre (known as "the Bad"). Her chief concerns, however, were her two daughters Marie (1326–41) and Blanche (1328–93), their property rights, the lands she herself held in dower, her impressive collection of relics and holy images, the elegant books and jewels she owned, and, principally, the welfare of her soul—and her husband's. She made a cult of widowhood and philanthropy. To advance her husband's salvation and her own, she herself created a multitude of charitable institutions. Clearly aware of the power the living exercised over the dead and of the special vulnerability of royal widows, Jeanne came to devise imaginative and extraordinary testamentary strategies to protect herself against the pitfalls of will-making. Distrustful of postmortem provisions, Jeanne would eventually obtain special royal approval of her novel and extraordinary design to execute her testament herself. To be sure, many wills contained clauses specifying the fulfillment or completion of projects the testator failed to carry out while alive,[2] but, as will be seen, Jeanne's plan was far more sweeping and dramatic than any such provision.

As queen and young widow, Jeanne took a traditional, conservative approach to matters testamentary, which were of considerable concern to her. She drew her first will in October 1326, five months after her coronation at the Sainte-Chapelle, while she was awaiting the birth of her second child.[3] The will does not survive,[4] but her husband endorsed it in an act dated October 18, 1326, preserved in many exemplifications, that ordered its execution and assigned the revenues of Champagne for this purpose. After her husband's death, as she awaited the birth of her third child, Jeanne obtained the authorization of the regent, her cousin Philip of Valois, to draw a new will containing bequests up to the sum of 16,000 l.par. (20,000 l.t.). Philip granted his approval on March 28, 1328, four days before Jeanne had the daughter whose birth catapulted him to the throne of France.[5] Whether Jeanne actually had a will drawn up is unknown. She may not have done so, since scarcely more than a year later, on October 3, 1329, Philip (now Philip VI) renewed his act of 1328, again authorizing Jeanne to change her will.[6] Once more, Jeanne may or may not have availed herself of the king's permission. Not until May 1349 is she known to have issued another will[7] (which, like the others, no longer exists). Only her final testament and two codicils (dated, respectively, March 1366/67 and October 1370) are preserved, in imperfect copies made in the seventeenth century by Jacques Menant (d. 1699), auditor of the Chambre des comptes.[8] Still, abundant traces of her testamentary activities are found in royal acts that reveal her preoccupation with death and the afterlife.

Having in August 1338 obtained from Philip VI clarification and modification of the sources of revenue that would be available for executing her testament,[9] Jeanne grew more ambitious. By the beginning of 1339 she had decided to launch an endowment campaign to benefit a host of institutions and individuals. She began by securing the king's permission to dedicate to "piteables vsages" 500 l.par. (625 l.t.) of annual revenue—roughly equivalent to assets worth 5000 l.par. On February 15, 1339, granting her request, Philip VI amortized the property that would provide the revenue, so that donees would receive her gifts tax-free.[10] The king also stipulated that, should Jeanne not dispose of all this property before she died, her executors might do so for her soul's welfare.

At this stage Jeanne was in all likelihood contemplating the novel project for which she secured royal authorization later in the year: to execute her testament herself, during her lifetime, without jeopardizing the 16,000 l.par. repeatedly guaranteed for the execution of her bequests. Acknowledging her project's unusual nature, the king granted his approval on August 7, 1339.[11]

After this date Jeanne made a host of charitable gifts, some of them clearly testamentary, others not. Although just a few of her surviving acts explicitly mention anticipatory execution,[12] a number of individuals and institutions, ecclesiastical and lay, profited from her pre-mortem bequests.[13] Between 1343 and 1354 four formal auditing sessions were held to review her disbursements.[14] Further, on September 23, 1366, to permit her to continue anticipatory execution after war with England had curtailed her resources, King Charles V granted her 15,000 *frans d'or* outright, in place of the 16,000 l.par. that had regularly been promised to her executors.[15]

I hope soon to recount the complex story of Jeanne's testamentary adventures in detail. Here, in homage to a lady as shrewd and determined as Jeanne herself, I would like to present an edition of Jeanne's grandest anticipatory endowment: her donation of three precious objects and a substantial annuity to the abbot and monks of Saint-Denis on August 1, 1343.[16] The two acts describing the endowment have been published once before,[17] but besides being difficult of access, the early edition is inaccurate, incomplete, and marred by seventeenth-century editorial idiosyncracies.[18] Having offered Jeremy Adams a study of the liturgical exploits of Saint-Denis's most famous abbot, it seems fitting in this tribute to Bonnie that I should focus on the benefactions of one of the abbey's leading royal female patrons.

The endowment of 1343 is recorded in an extraordinary pair of acts, each issued jointly by Jeanne, on the one hand, and Abbot Gilles Rigaud and the house of Saint-Denis, on the other. They are not as explicitly anticipative as other acts of Jeanne, but there seems every reason to classify them as such. In the second act Jeanne said explicitly that she had ordained *in her testament* the purchase of the annuities that she specified in one of the acts of 1343 to fund the observances mandated in the other act of 1343—annuities, thus, that she was in fact assigning herself to pay for services whose celebration would commence immediately. It is also interesting that in the first act, commenting at the outset on her choice of burial at Saint-Denis, Jeanne used familiar testamentary language in saying that she had made her decision while healthy in body, by informed decision, and with firm understanding.[19] These phrases evidently refer to her provisions for her burial, presumably contained in a testament,[20] but their presence at the commencement of the act of August 1, 1343, imparts to it a testamentary aura. Prepared with great formality, surely in Jeanne's chancery, the two acts were probably concluded and sealed at Saint-Denis itself,[21] where they were subsequently kept in the abbey's archives. As Damien Berné has observed, the first act is a virtual dialogue between Jeanne and the abbot.[22] Jeanne's is the first name featured in the act, and as benefactor she dominated the exchanges.

The act opens with Jeanne's declaration of her devotion to Saint-Denis and her election of burial there with her late husband. Then follow her announcement and confirmation of a gift she had made to Saint-Denis "during the time," as she put it, of Guy de Châtres (who had served as abbot of Saint-Denis from 1326 until his recent resignation).[23] This gift was "her beautiful reliquary, weighing some fifty-three marks, with all the holy relics it contains." Jeanne enumerated the contents of this *chasse* in detail: a small gold cross containing a portion of the True Cross, a little bejeweled gold plaque containing a bit of the board[24] with Jesus's titles that was behind his head when he hung on the Cross, a small jeweled coronet with a thorn from the Crown of thorns, and finally twelve crystal and gold phials, each with a different relic: some of Christ's blood, his hair, his swaddling clothes, his robe, his clothing at the Last Supper, the sponge thrust at him on the Cross, his sweatband, stone from the Holy Sepulcher and from Calvary, milk of the Virgin, pieces of her kerchiefs, and a portion of the head of Saint John the Baptist. Although Jeanne did not say so,[25] these were bits of the prized relics of the Sainte-Chapelle.[26] Since Jeanne apparently could not bear to part with the reliquary at once, she proposed herself as its guardian during her lifetime, after which it would come to the abbey, which would be bound to keep it forever. Finally Jeanne asked the monks to look with special favor on her husband's soul and on herself.

Next it was the turn of Abbot Gilles Rigaud. He began by declaring that everything set forth in the act had been agreed in chapter during his predecessor's abbacy (although not recorded and sealed), and then rehearsed the many services the abbey would perform for Charles IV and for Jeanne herself in gratitude for her gift. Gilles pledged that "from then on" (*dores en auant*) Charles's anniversary would be solemnly celebrated every year, on the second or third day before Candlemas (February 2, on whose eve Charles had died). Further, the monks would say a special commemoration and prayer for Charles at their monthly services for King Dagobert "and the other kings who were founders of our church," at vespers, vigils, and the Mass. From that very moment (*des maintenant*) Charles's name would be written in the abbey's missal next to the canon, and after her death Jeanne's would be similarly inscribed. All this would be registered in the martyrology of Saint-Denis. Jeanne herself was promised special benefits. During her lifetime all monks who were priests would sing two masses annually, one (of the Holy Spirit) for her, the other (a Requiem mass) for Charles. After her death both masses would be Requiem services for her, Charles, and those friends and relatives she wished to be included. Again this would be registered in the martyrologies and registers of all places where the masses were performed.

Jeanne then resumed the initiative, proffering sums of money that (as she declared in the second act) she had long ago (*pieça*) decreed in her testament the abbey should receive to fund the additional services she instituted. Of the 156 l.t. in annual income she gave the house, 13 l.t. would be distributed to the priories where masses were said for her and Charles. Another 20 l.t. would pay for a sung mass of the Holy Spirit (for her welfare, not Charles's) on or about the second or third day after Saint Mark's feast day (April 25). After her death the abbey would instead commemorate her anniversary by having the office of the dead performed on a day as close as possible to the date of her passing. The largest part of the endowment, 105 l.t. a year, would support two perpetual masses to be sung daily for her, her husband, her children, and her friends, in the Virgin chapel that she had recently refurbished (*nouuellement ordonnee*) in honor of the Virgin and John the Evangelist.[27] Jeanne did not establish new chaplains to sing the masses but rather stipulated that the income would be divided among the officials of the abbey (carefully specified) who said the masses.[28] Finally, 18 l.t. a year would be spent on lighting in the chapel for these and other services.

Jeanne's benefactions did not stop with these annuities. She went on to grant the house three additional precious objects: two immediately, and one prospectively. Like the chasse of the Sainte-Chapelle, Jeanne planned to keep for her lifetime a gold statue of Saint John the Evangelist holding one of his teeth, but the abbey was to receive two other objects at once. The first was a magnificent silver-gilt statue of the Virgin and child (weighing 36 marks 6 ounces) adorned with a fleur-de-lis, holding bits of her milk, hair, and kerchiefs. The second was a majestic jeweled crown, which Jeanne wished hung in the church on solemn feast days with the other crowns the abbey possessed. These objects were never to be alienated, and never to leave the abbey—except, briefly, the crown, which Jeanne decreed should adorn her body after her death until her interment at the abbey. Jeanne thus provided another assurance, if assurance was needed, that her body would lie with her husband's in the royal necropolis.

At the end of the act the abbot thanked Jeanne once more for her gifts, accepted them, and pledged to fulfill all the conditions she prescribed. In a final gesture of gratitude the abbot declared that she, her husband, and all others she designated would thenceforth participate in all good works performed by members of the abbey's community. Further, after her death the abbey would treat her as one of their own, commemorating her as they did each of their dead brothers. The act closed with the announcement of its sealing by queen, abbot, and house.

In the second act Jeanne played the same leading role she did in the first. Here, after alluding to her testament, she set forth the sources from which the annual payments would be drawn, formally assigned them to the abbey, and ensured the abbey full possession of them. Then follows a copy of the authorization and amortization that Philip VI had issued for Jeanne on February 15, 1338/39, which guaranteed that the abbey would receive the gifts free and clear. Only at the end did the abbot intervene, to ratify and accept what Jeanne offered and, with her and the house he governed, to affix their seals to the act.

Why did Jeanne decide to make these spectacular awards?[29] Her eagerness to ensure her burial with her husband at the abbey surely played a part. She may also have been moved by gratitude for the monks' interment of her fifteen-year-old daughter Marie in 1341.[30] But Jeanne's chief reason for making the donations recorded in 1343 was surely the services for herself and her dead husband that she was awarded as countergifts for her generosity, which she must have hoped (and calculated) her pledge to Guy de Châtres would elicit.[31]

Over the years Jeanne's relations with Saint-Denis—and with Guy de Châtres—must have been complicated by the abbey's rejection in January 1329 of one of the two bequests to Saint-Denis that Charles IV had included in his will of October 1324. In his testament Charles bequeathed to the abbey one of four richly endowed chaplaincies he endowed, each worth 50 l.par. a year—on condition that the kings of France appoint to the office.[32] Like Saint-Denis, Notre-Dame of Paris was similarly favored, and like Saint-Denis Notre-Dame refused the bequest because of this condition.[33] Saint-Denis's abbot, the scholar-reformer Guy de Châtres (who had taken office in 1326) must have played a determining rôle in resisting this threat to the abbey's independence. As Damien Berné has stressed, Guy was attentive to the institution of liturgical celebrations at Saint-Denis,[34] and indeed he resigned the abbacy to dedicate himself to the abbey's liturgy.[35] In the case of Charles's bequest, however, it was surely the incursion on Saint-Denis's prerogatives that moved Guy to oppose the bequest.

Since Charles was buried at Saint-Denis, Jeanne must have found the abbey's decision particularly upsetting. Beside the chaplaincies, Charles had left Saint-Denis and Notre-Dame just 200 l. to pay for anniversary celebrations.[36] The limited income from this sum—no more than 20 l.—inevitably meant that Charles's commemoration was slighted and the welfare of his soul (like his tomb) was paid far less attention than he had intended. The agreement between Jeanne and Saint-Denis spectacularly remedied this situation by elevating Charles to a status equal to that of the abbey's most revered royal patrons.

It is far easier to hypothesize Jeanne's motivations in making her gifts than to comprehend the circumstances under which and the process by which—and even precisely when —her agreement with the abbey was reached. The evidence provided by the two acts of August 1, 1343, is difficult to interpret, particularly in light of the fact that they were issued at least two months after Gilles Rigaud became abbot and not immediately upon his assumption of office.[37] Further complications are posed by dates given in two inscriptions, one on Jeanne's Virgin reliquary and the other, recorded by seventeenth- and eighteenth-century historians of the abbey, on the life-size statue of the Virgin that gave its name to the chapel it once adorned, Notre-Dame-la-Blanche.[38]

The two acts demonstrate that although Gilles Rigaud, an ambitious and practical man,[39] was the motive force behind their conclusion, Guy de Châtres, abbot when Charles's chaplaincy was refused, was critically involved in their genesis. In the first act, Gilles Rigaud stated that Jeanne's offer had been made and accepted while Guy de Châtres was still abbot, and that before Guy's resignation the chapter approved all commitments made by the abbey that were enumerated in the documents. According to Gilles, the only formality that had not occurred was the recording and sealing of the agreement. Also important is Gilles's use of the phrase *dores en auant* ("thenceforward," and thus presumably after August 1, 1343) in describing the formal observance of Charles's anniversary at the abbey—

thus implying that no such formal observance had occurred before the date of the acts. This is credible, although Gilles Rigaud's initial statements concerning the transaction are not. That terms as detailed and specific as those set forth in the charters would have been hammered out and agreed to yet never set down and sealed is difficult if not impossible to credit.[40] It seems far more likely that exchanges had been endorsed in principle, and that after Gilles Rigaud became abbot, concrete negotiation of precise terms were carried out until agreement was reached on all details.

The inscriptions on the objects that Jeanne gave to Saint-Denis provide interesting clues to the process of negotiations. A legend on metal bands attached to the base of the Virgin reliquary states that Jeanne gave the magnificent statue on April 28, 1339: "Ceste ymage donna ceans ma dame La Royne Ieh[ann]e Deureux. Royne de france et de Nauarre Compaigne du Roy Challes. le xxviij[e] Iour dauril. lan. M. CCC. xxxix."[41] This inscription must have been added at the abbey after the gift was received. Had Jeanne or her secretaries (or confessor) been responsible for the legend the title *Royne* would surely not have been repeated, and Charles would probably have been referred to as *jadis Roy de france et de nauarre*, or perhaps *son treschier seigneur et espous le .. Roy Charles que diex absoille*.[42] Further, although *Challes* and *Charles* were sometimes used interchangeably, all the acts of Jeanne d'Évreux that I have seen use the form *Charle* or *Charles*.[43] The word *ceans*—"here"—and the failure to mention Saint-Denis also suggest that the inscription was composed at the abbey.[44]

None of this minimizes the significance of the date given in the inscription: April 28, 1339. Its precision suggests that the person who composed the inscription was relying on documentary evidence concerning Jeanne's gift that existed in the archives of Saint-Denis—or that Jeanne made the gift on that date. At this time she was devoting much thought to final things. Only two months before, she had obtained from Philip VI permission to donate amortized annuities worth 500 l.par. a year, and five months afterwards the king approved her plans to execute her testament during her lifetime. But if the gift of the reliquary was promised or made on April 28, 1339, it was not effectively formalized for more than four years. Jeanne's donation to Saint-Denis on August 1, 1343, phrased in the present tense, contains no suggestion that she was confirming a prior gift or that she had already relinquished the Virgin to the abbey.[45]

Placed on the base of a large and imposing statue of the Virgin, the second inscription no longer survives, but Dom Jacques Doublet and Dom Michel Felibien both recorded it. Echoing some words and phrases of the legend on the Virgin reliquary, this inscription declared: "Madame la Royne Iehanne d'Eureux compaigne iadis du Roy Charles: que Diex absoille, a donné ceans cet image & ainsi faict paindre & ordenner ceste Chapelle, où elle a fondé vne Messe perpetuelle qui chacun iour est chantee tantost apres la Messe que l'en dit aux Pelerins, l'an mil trois cens quarante le iour de la My Aoust."[46] Thus, in 1340, on mid-August day, August 15—the feast of the Assumption of the Virgin—Jeanne is said to have given the abbey the imposing stone statue of the Virgin, had the chapel "painted and refurbished [*ordenné*], and endowed a perpetual mass to be said after the mass of the Pilgrims." The references to the chapel's *ordonnement* and the establishment of a mass recall the acts of August 1, 1343, where Jeanne made clear that she had recently had the chapel refurbished and that the chapel had been rededicated to John the Evangelist as well as the Virgin, although there she established *two* masses in the chapel rather than a single one. As in the case of the Virgin reliquary, the specificity of the date August 15, 1340, suggests that Jeanne may have made some sort of pledge to the abbey on that day, just two months prior to October 1340, when she made provision for services at Maubuisson, where Charles IV's entrails were buried and where hers would eventually be interred.[47]

These two inscriptions suggest that Jeanne may have promised or given Guy de Châtres the Virgin reliquary in the spring of 1339 and offered the statue and a single mass (together with refurbishment of the chapel) in August 1340. These dates are worth pondering. As to the spring of 1339, it seems perfectly plausible that Jeanne would have talked to Guy about her plans to execute her will herself, particularly if she was aiming to gain from Saint-Denis appropriate commemoration of her dead husband and trusted that Guy would find her piety and sagacity impressive. Guy was the only ranking ecclesiastic to attend the first auditing session of Jeanne's anticipatory testamentary execution on February 28, 1343,[48] and his presence there suggests that she might well have sought his advice about her project early on. Jeanne might well have made additional commitments in August 1340—including renovation of the Virgin chapel, the offer of a statue of the Virgin, and the institution of a single mass. During this time, Jeanne might have continued trying to persuade Guy to commit the abbey to granting her and her dead husband commemorative services that she judged fitting. For his part, the conservative abbot might have attempted to retain her goodwill while still trying to bring her to moderate the scope of her aspirations—perhaps by making her a material countergift. Such negotiations might explain Jeanne's possession of relics of Saint Peregrinus, given to her by the abbey, which on June 25, 1342, she presented to the Dominicans of Auxerre in a splendid silver chasse.[49] Admittedly, Jeanne might have received the relics at another time. But whenever she obtained them, by making the donation to the Dominicans while she was involved in negotiations with the abbey, Jeanne would have demonstrated clearly to Guy de Châtres and the monks of Saint-Denis that she preferred services to relics as countergifts for her benefactions, both realized and potential.

If the negotiations between Jeanne and Guy lasted from 1339 until Guy's resignation, the chapter of the abbey would surely have become involved and might have accepted in principle the exchange of liturgical commemoration for Jeanne's gifts, especially after learning that she was prepared to part with her spectacular chasse containing portions of the relics of the Sainte-Chapelle. Jeanne might indeed have begun fulfilling some of her pledges to the abbey, since the first act of August 1, 1343, indicates that refurbishment of the chapel of the Virgin and John the Evangelist had already begun[50]—and hence in a sense confirms the inscription on the stone statue of the Virgin. An anticipatory testamentary act that Jeanne issued in February 1343 to benefit the church of Saint-Paul of Saint-Denis, which was adjacent to the abbey church, would have served as a reminder of her readiness to grant cooperative establishments the immediate enjoyment of legacies they would otherwise receive only after her death.[51] By the end of that month, Guy de Châtres had resigned, and Jeanne may have hoped that the endowment of Saint-Paul would inspire his successor to cooperate fully, in hopes of gaining for the abbey even more than she had already pledged. After his installation as abbot, Gilles Rigaud surely continued discussions with Jeanne, perhaps encouraging her to implement fully her planned testamentary bequests and establish two masses rather than a single one in the chapel. And finally, on August 1, 1343, the terms he and Jeanne had agreed upon could be formally announced, with clear acknowledgment of the part Guy de Châtres had played in the negotiations but only vague indication of precisely what his role had been.

Jeanne may in the end have given Saint-Denis more than she intended at the outset, but she received good value for her largesse. Her plans largely succeeded. Charles's memory was spectacularly commemorated at the abbey; she was indeed buried beside him. Her generosity to the abbey inspired her daughter Blanche, whose endowment of the abbey in November 1391 rivaled her mother's.[52] Blanche had already commissioned a tomb for herself and her sister Marie, and after her death in 1393 the two sisters lay together in the chapel her mother had favored.[53] Through its designation as both "la chapelle de la Royne Blanche" and Notre-Dame-la-Blanche, the chapel was linked with Jeanne's name and the statue of the Virgin that may have been one of her earliest outright gifts to the abbey.[54]

Jeanne's endowment of Saint-Denis ensured that she was not forgotten at the abbey. Despite her careful planning, however, she was no more able than her peers to control her property from the grave—particularly the objects she had given to the abbey. Because of the realm's fiscal crisis in 1418, the church relinquished her crown to the king, only, somehow, to recover it.[55] During the abbacy of Charles of Bourbon, cardinal of Vendôme and then Bourbon (r. 1528–57), the reliquary of the Sainte-Chapelle (stripped of its holy remains) was pawned to a Parisian goldsmith, and since it was apparently never recovered, the abbey commissioned a chasse to house its relics in the seventeenth century.[56] In 1590, the reliquary of John the Evangelist was melted to pay a butcher's bill.[57] But the annuities Jeanne had assigned the abbey in 1343 continued to yield considerable profit. In 1514, recalling the revenues from Brie-Comte-Robert that "la feue Royne de France et de Nauarre" had given them (which they were still receiving),[58] the monks successfully petitioned King Louis XII to establish three fairs there to ensure the town's prosperity.[59]

Some two centuries later, through no special fault of their own, the religious of Saint-Denis would forfeit this privilege and income—and indeed all they had—to the cause of liberty, equality, and fraternity. The Revolutionaries sent to the foundry most of the abbey's treasures, including Jeanne's Virgin and the chasse of the Sainte-Chapelle that replaced the reliquary Jeanne had given in 1343. Although the government's commissioners ordered her crown kept (*conserver*), this precious object disappeared with many other regalia. By surprising chance the Virgin escaped destruction.[60] Like the relics in the chasse of the Sainte-Chapelle, those the Virgin once protected in her crystal fleur-de-lis have vanished, but she herself has survived to reign in majesty over the vestiges of Saint-Denis's own treasury, arrayed today in the Galerie d'Apollon at the Louvre.

Appendix
Jeanne's Endowment of Saint-Denis, August 1, 1343

The two acts are edited from the original documents, whose orthography and punctuation I have retained, particularly its system of points and slashes; I have silently expanded abbreviated words and have introduced paragraph breaks.

AN, K 43B, no. 27 is an original act on parchment, ruled in stylus to the end of the act; it measures 515 mm. wide x 495/501 mm. in length; the foldup is 50 mm. deep. The act is copied and decorated in brown ink by the same scribe responsible for no. 27[bis]. Each of these acts was sealed by Jeanne, the abbot, and the monastery. Six seals, thus, were originally attached to the two documents, through three sets of three circular holes cut into both acts; the silk used to attach the seals was threaded through these sets of holes, the middle opening receiving the silk that attached both seals of each party, the left hole receiving the silk that attached the first seal of each party, the right hole that of the second seal. Fragments of four seals survive, sewn into wrappers, three parchment and one cloth; the green silk is today a tangled mass.

In the upper left-hand corner of the face of the act is written in seventeenth- or eighteenth-century script the date "1[er] aoust 1343." On the dorse are the shelfmarks "C x" and "N 5 Liace," the curious fifteenth-century notation "fondacion de la Royne blanche," and various late notations ("deux pieces" twice, "St Denis," "1343," "La Reine," "Lettre de lan 1343"). A description of the act in seventeenth- or eighteenth-century script[61] precedes a reference to "Doublet p. 968 [corrected from *963*]."[62] On the reverse of the foldup is written in strong contemporary script and dark ink "La Royne Iehanne" and in the same hand "ls." On the bottom right edge of the foldup is written in minuscule script "pour ma dame," duplicating the phrase "pour madame" written, similarly, on the bottom right corner of the foldup of no. 27[bis].

AN, K 43B, no. 27[bis] is an original act on parchment, ruled in stylus to the end of the act; it measures 497/495 mm. wide by 492/488 mm. in length; pricking is visible on the right side. On the face of the act is written the date, "1[er] aoust 1343," in the same hand as the date on the face of no. 27; in addition, in a later hand, in heavy black ink, "les deux tiers de la Justice de cheurieres." On the dorse is the Saint-Denis shelfmark and a reference to "Doublet p. 973,"[63] in addition to the contemporary notation "La Royne Iehne [*sic*]" and "ij."

AN, K 43B, no. 27[ter] is a fine late fourteenth- or early fifteenth-century copy of no. 27, ruled in pencil on parchment; the document measures 645 mm. in width x 485 mm. in length. On the dorse are various analyses of the act's contents in different contemporary and later hands, the Saint-Denis shelfmark ("C x"), a reference to the "5[e] Liace," and "Vidimus pour la Royne Iehanne" and "..iiij." in the same contemporary hand, which also wrote "La Royne Iehanne" on the reverse of K 43, nos. 27 and 27[bis].

AN, K 43B, no. 27[quater] is a fine fourteenth-century copy of no. 27[bis], ruled in pencil on parchment; the act measures 500 mm. in width x 390 mm. in length. The initial "I" is decorated with a man's face with jutting lower jaw. On the dorse is the Saint-Denis shelfmark "C x," as well as the notation "N 5[e] Liace"; a brief fourteenth-century description of the act ["Copie des Lettres de la fondacion de la chappelle ma dame la Royne Iehanne d'eureux" with the last word added in later script]; and a lengthy summary in seventeenth-century script, perhaps by Doublet.[64]

1.
AN, K 43B, no. 27

Iehanne par la grace de dieu Royne de france et de Nauarre .. Et Nous Giles par la permission diuine humbles Abbes de Saint Denis en france / Et tout le Conuent de ce meismes lieu .. [65]

Sauoir faisons a tous presens / et auenir / que Nous Iehanne Royne dessus dite aians especial deuocion a leglise monsieur Saint Denis en france / en la quelle nous de certaine science / saine de corps / et ferme dentendement / auons esleue nostre sepulture / auec nostre treschier / et tres ame seigneur et espous Monsieur le Roy charle / dont diex ait lame / Ou temps de Reuerent pere en dieu labbe Guy / eussions nagaires donne et octroie / donnons et octroions desmaintenant a la dite

Eglise / par donnacion faite entre vifz / sanz Iamais Rappeller / nostre bele chace dargent / doree pesant enuiron cincquante trois mars / auecques toutes les saintes Reliques qui dedans sont ..

Cest assauoir vne petite croix dor en la quelle il a de la vraie croix.

Item vn petit tableau dor a petite perrerie / ou il a du tabliau que nostre seigneur[66] ot darriers son chief en la croix / ou son tiltre fu escript.

Item vne petite coronnete dor a menue perrerie / ou il a vn tour de la coronne vne espine de la sainte coronne nostre seigneur.

Item douze petites boiteletes de Cristail garnies dor / ou il a de .xij. Manieres de saintuaires en chascune boitelete son saintuaire. Cest assauoir du saint sanc nostre seigneur. De ses cheueux. Des draps dont il fu enuelopes en senfance /. De sa Robe / Du drap dont il fu Ceint en la Cene / De lesponge dont il fu abiuires en la croix / De son suaire. De la pierre du saint sepulcre. de la pierre du mont descauaire. Du lait nostre dame / De ses queurechiez / et Du chief monsieur Saint Iehan baptiste.

Et desmaintenant tout le droit / seigneurie / et propriete que nous y auons / et pouons auoir du tout transportons en la dite Eglise de Saint Denis / Retenue pardeuers nous La garde et detencion des dites / chace / & saintes Reliques Le cours de nostre vie tant seulement. Et confessons ycelles a tenir et garder ou nom de la dite Eglise / les quelles nous voulons tantost apres nostre deces estre baillees et deliurees enterinement et aplain a la dite Eglise par noz Executeurs / pour y demourer perpetuelment sanz Iamais partir sanz ce que les puissent vendre / despendre / eschangier / translater / engaiger / prester / donner ne allienner / en quelque personne seculiere / ou autre pour quelque cause / ou neccessite que ce soit ou temps auenir / Et Requerons aus diz Religieus que il vueillent auoir par especial Recommandee Lame de nostre dit seigneur / et nous aussi.

Et Nous abbe enfourme par la Relation de nostre predecesseur / et de nostre Couuent / que toutes les choses contenues en ces presentes lettres sont et ont este faites / passees et acordees par bon auis et deliberacion en Chapitre / a lonneur / prouffit et vtilite de nostre Eglise / ou temps de nostre dit predecesseur / combien que lettres nen feussent pas lors grossees et scellees. Encores nous[67] et Couuent dessus diz / sicomme lors fu accorde / en Remuneracion du don et grace fais par nostre dite dame a nostre dite Eglise / accordons / octroions / et promettons / loyaument en bonne foy / pour nous et pour noz Successeurs en la dite Eglise / que nous ferons dores en auant chascun an perpetuelment et sollempnelment lanniuersaire du dit nostre treschier seigneur le Roy Charles le second iour / ou tiers auant la Chandeleur. Et auec ce / nous & noz Successeurs / serons tenuz a tous Iours mais perpetuelment a faire especial memoire / et oroison de nostre dit seigneur chascun mois quant nous faisons / et ferons le seruice du Roy dangoubert / et des autres Roys fondeurs de nostre dite Eglise / tant es vespres / et vegiles comme a la messe / Et sera desmaintenant escript nommeement ou messel empres La canon le nom du .. Roy Charles / et de nostre dite dame apres son deces. Et ainssi est Registre a perpetuel memoire en nostre matrologe. Et en seurquetout auons promis et promettons en la maniere que dit est / que tant comme elle viura / touz les freres prestres de nostre Religion / presens et auenir / ou que il soient demourans / soit a Saint Denis / ou ailleurs ou Royaume sont / et seront tenus tous les anz de Chanter deuz [sic] messes / vne du saint Esperit pour elle / et lautre de Requiem pour lame de son dit Seigneur. Et apres le deces de nostre dite dame / il seront tenuz de chanter perpetuelment chascun an / toutes les dites deux messes de mors / pour les ames de elle / et de son dit seigneur conioinctement[68] / et de ceuls que elle entent. Et en signe de perpetuel memoire sera Registre es matrologes et Registres de tous les lieus / ou les dites messes seront et doiuent estre celebrees / par quoy il ny puisse auoir aucun deffaut / ou oubliance ou temps auenir. Et Proumectons [sic] loyaument / ou nom de nous et de noz Successeurs / sus le veu de nostre Religion / les dites chace & saintes Reliques qui dedans sont garder honorablement en nostre dite Eglise / a touz iours mais perpetuelment sanz iamais partir dycelle a y demourer / sanz ce que nous ne noz Successeurs les puissions vendre / despendre / engaiger / eschangier / transporter / prester /[69] donner / ne alliener en quelque personne que ce soit laye / ou deglise / ne consentir a transporter / ne translater / hors de nostre Eglise / par quelque cause que ce soit / fors tant seulement a noz processions sollempnelz. Et quant a ce obligons enuers les hoirs de nostre dite dame / tout le temporel de nostre dite Eglise. Et voulons / accordons / et octroions / que nostre dite dame ait la garde et detencion de la chace / et saintes Reliques dessus dites / ou nom de nostre dite Eglise / le cours de sa vie tant seulement ..

 ITEM. Nous Royne dessus dite / pour ce que chascun des freres / qui sont demourans es prieures de la dite Eglise sont tenuz comme dit est dessus / a celebrer chascun an perpetuelment deux messes pour nostre dit seigneur / pour nous & noz amis / donnons et octroions treze liures tournois [13 l.t.] de Rente admortie / a distribuer chascun an aus diz Prieurez / aus Comptes qui se font apres la beneicon du lendit / a chascun prieure tel porcion comme il appartendra [sic] par la main du Maistre des Charitez / ou de celluj / qui les dites treze liures Receura / pour faire pittance chascun an aus freres de Chascune Prioure.

 ITEM. Nous Royne dessus dite attendans la bonne voulente & vraie affection que les diz Abbe & Couuent ont a nostre dit treschier seigneur / que diex absoille / et a nous leur donnons encores & octroions desmaintenant a perpetuite / vint liures [20 l.] de Rente admortie / a lusage des Charitez / pour chanter pour nous chascun an tant comme nous viurons / vne messe a note du saint desperit en la dite Eglise[70] le second / ou tiers Iour apres la saint Maarc [sic] ou enuiron. Et apres nostre deces seront tenuz de faire nostre anniuersaire perpetuelment a tel iour comme il escherra / se il est iour que lon puisse / ou doie faire bonnement loffice de mors / ou au iour plus prochain apres que il se pourra faire. Et leur sera faite pittance chascun an de la dite somme / aus iours que il feront les diz seruices ..

ITEM. Pour ce que nous sommes desirrans de nostre Cuer de accroistre le diuin seruice en la dite Eglise / Nous auons donne & donnons a ycelle Cent liures tournois [100 l.t.] de Rente admortie / pour la fondacion de deux messes perpetuels que les diz Abbe / et Couuent doiuent faire chanter dores en auant perpetuelment chascun iour en la dite Eglise / pour le Remede et salut des ames / de nostre dit seigneur / de nous noz enfanz &[71] amis / les quelles deux messes seront chantees chascun iour / en la chapelle de nostre dame que nous y auons nouuellement ordenee / en lonneur de nostre dame / et de monsieur Saint Iehan Euuangeliste .. Cest assauoir La premiere messe / tantost apres celle que lon dit / la messe aus pelerins / la quelle chanteront les / quatre gardes de la dite Eglise / presens et auenir / par sepmaines interpollees lun apres lautre. Et tantost apres sera chantee lautre messe / la quelle chanteront samblablement [sic] trois autres /[72] Cest assauoir le Maistre aus hostes de la dite Eglise / le cheuecier / et souzmaistre aus enfans / et leurs Successeurs. Et pour ce que les dessus diz / qui les dites messes chanteront / soient plus voulentis [sic] de Chanter les dites messes. Nous du consentement des diz Abbe et Couuent / auons ordene / et ordenons / que en accroissement des Rentes que il auoient auant / pour cause de leurs diz Offices qui sont de petite value sicomme nous entendons ceuls qui les dites .ij. messes chanteront / aient et preignent desmaintenant et dores en auant perpetuelment chascun an et par leur main les dites Cent liures de Rente / et soient annexees en leurs diz offices. Cest assauoir les dites quatre gardes Cinquante liures Et les trois autres dessus nommez / pour ce que il sont chargiez dautele / et aussi grans charges / comme les quatre gardes dessus dites / auront les autres Cinquante liures ..

ITEM. Nous donnons a la dite Eglise dixhuit liures tournois [18 l.t.] de Rente admortie / tant pour soustenir les adournemens &[73] vne lampe / qui ardra continuelment nuit et Iour en la dite Chapelle / comme pour le luminaire de Cire / qui sera chascun an alume en la dite Eglise / le Iour que len y Chantera la messe du saint Esperit pour nous a nostre viuant / Et le iour que il [sic] feront nostre anniuersaire apres nostre deces / Et aussi pour querir et soustenir perpetuelment en la dite Chapelle / aus anuels et demi anuelz le luminaire de Cire qui sensuit. Cest assauoir . Pasques / lascention / Penthecouste / la feste dieu / la Toussains / Noel / la Thiphaine / La feste monsieur Saint Denis / son Inuencion / le iour de ses octaues / a la saint Iehan baptiste / Saint Iehan leuuangeliste / a la feste Saint Pierre / et saint Pol / Et a la dedication de leglise / a chascune dycelles / quatre cierges / et a chascune des . Cinq festes nostre dame / Cincq [sic] Cierges / Tous les diz Cierges chascun de deux liures / Les quelz Cierges ardront continuelment en la dite Chapelle aus premieres / et secondes vespres / aus Matines / et a la messe des dites festes. Et aussi pour querir et soustenir deux Cierges chascun de deux liures / qui touz Iours seront allumez en la dite Chapelle / quant len y Chantera les dites deux messes / et deux torches de huit liures / donc [sic] lune sera touz les iours allumee aus dites deux messes / a la eleuation [sic] du corps Ihesucrist / Et la seconde sera tant seulement allumee / aus anuels et demi anuels dessus diz. Et pour les diz luminaires querir et soustenir perpetuelment / Nous voulons et ordenons que le cheuecier de la dite Eglise / present & auenir / ait et prengne [sic] les dites dixhuit liures de Rente admortie par sa main.

ITEM.. Nous donnons a ceuls qui sonneront / et aideront a chanter les dites deux messes Cent souls tournois [100 s.t.] de Rente / a prendre par la main des Chapellains qui les dites messes Chanteront / chascun an a deux termes / moitie a Noel / et moitie a la saint Iehan baptiste

Monte la somme toute des dites Rentes par nous donnees & octroiees pour les causes dessus dites sept vins seze liures [156 l.] de Rente admortie / De la quelle Rente Nous leur auons fait certaines assietes et assignacion sicomme il est plus plainement contenu en noz autres lettres parmi ces presentes annexes ..

ITEM . Pour la grant et especial deuocion / et affection que nous auons a la dite Eglise / y donnons encores vne ymage de nostre dame dargent / dore pesant xxxvj mars. vj. onces / qui tient vne fleur de lix [sic] dor garnie de perrerie / ou il a de son lait / De ses cheueus / et de ses Cueurchiez ..

ITEM. leur donnons vne ymage dor de monsieur saint Iehan euuangeliste / qui tient vne de ses dens ..

ITEM. y donnons vne Coronne dor a viij. florons[74] / dont les Maistres Pierres du corps sont de saphirs / et ya viij tronches[75] de pelles / chascune tronche de ix pelles et vn balay ou Milieu / et sont les florons chascun de quatre balais / et vn saphir ou Milieu et. trois pelles sus les florons / et entre deux florons vn saphir ou Milieu / la quelle nous voulons que soit pendue en leglise / auec les autres aus festes sollempnels. Et la quelle coronne et saintuaires [sic] / Nous auons transporte & transportons desmaintenant en la dite Eglise de monsieur Saint Denis / tout le droit propriete et seigneurie / que nous y auions / et poiions auoir pour y demourer perpetuelment / sanz ce que les diz Religieus les puissent vendre / despendre / eschangier / translater /[76] engaiger / prester / donner / ne autrement alliener / en quelque personne deglise ou seculiere / par quelque tiltre / ou pour quelque cause ou neccessite que ce soit ores / ou au temps auenir / Retenue pardeuers nous le cours de nostre vie tant seulement la garde du dit saintuaire de monsieur Saint Iehan leuangeliste / Reserue aussi a nous / que quant nous serons trespassee de cest siecle / les diz Religieus seront tenuz de enuoier par deux des freres de la dite Eglise la dite coronne / au lieu / ou nous trespasserons / pour estre mise en nostre chief / aus lieus / et Eglises / ou nostre corps sera portez /

Mais des lors que nostre corps sera enterrez en la dite Eglise de monsieur Saint Denis ycelle Coronne sera Remise en la dite Eglise / pour y demourer perpetuelment en la maniere que dit est dessus ..

Et Nous Abbe & Couuent dessus diz / Considerans La deuocion que nostre dite dame a a nostre dite Eglise / et a Nous / et les grans bienfais / dons / et graces / que fais a si liberaument a nostre dite Eglise Desirans de tout nostre Cuer acomplir sa bonne voulente / et saint desir / sicomme accorde a este ou temps de nostre predecesseur comme dit est dessus / Toutes les choses dessus dites et chascune dycelles / en la maniere que elles sont plus plainement ci dessus specifiees / et diuisees. Auons gres / Ratiffiees & accordees en nostre Chapitre. Et ycelles greons Ratiffions / et accordons par nous et noz successeurs en la dite Eglise. Et les dites Cent liures [100 l.] de Rente / octroiees par nostre dite dame / pour chanter les dites deux messes / transportons / et annexons perpetuelment es offices des personnes / qui les dites deux messes chanteront .. Les quelles personnes / et leurs successeurs es diz offices prendront par leur main / et leueront la dite Rente / auecques les Cent souls [100 s.] de Rente que il sont tenus[77] a paier a ceuls qui sonneront / et aideront a chanter Les dites deux messes. Et samblablement accordons et promettons a garder les diz saintuaires & coronne / faire les diz seruices & anniuersaires / et faire faire les luminaires dessus diz tout en la fourme et maniere que ci dessus est escript et diuisie.

Et en Regraciant et merciant nostre dite dame / des biens et des honneurs que elle a fais si deuotement / et si charitablement a nostre dite Eglise et a nous / Nous auons acompaigne et acompaignons desmaintenant nostre dite dame a mort & a vie / nostre dit treschier seigneur le Roy Charles /[78] et ceuls que elle y entent a acompaignier / en toutes les messes / Matines / vigiles / heures & oroisons / penitences & autres bienfais qui par nous et par noz Successeurs seront fais ou temps auenir en nostre dite Eglise / et par toute nostre Religion / Et ferons autant pour elle apres son deces / comme nous faisons pour vn des propres freres de nostre dite Eglise .. Proumettons loyaument / en bonne foy / pour nous / et pour noz Successeurs en nostre dite Eglise / tenir et acomplir Les choses dessus dites / et chascune dycelles. Et en obligons / nous / noz Successeurs / et tout le temporel de nostre dite Eglise ..

Et pour ce que ce soit ferme chose et estable perpetuelement a tous Iours .. Nous Royne .. Abbe et Couuent dessus diz / auons scelle ces presentes lectres de noz seauls .. Donne le premier Iour Daoust .. lan de grace Mil trois Cenz Quarante et trois ...

2.
AN, K 43B, no. 27[bis]

Iehanne par la grace de dieu. Royne de france et de Nauarre . . Et Nous Giles par La permission diuine Humbles Abbes [sic] de Saint Denis en France Et tout le Couuent de ce meismes lieu Salut.

Sauoir faisons a touz presenz & auenir. Que comme Nous Iehanne Royne dessus dite / pour certaines et iustes causes contenues en noz autres lettres ouuertes es queles ces presentes sont annexees / aions donne & octroie a leglise Monsieur Saint denys en france / certaines Rentes / les queles Nous[79] auions pieca ordene par nostre testament estre achetees pour la dite Eglise / Pour les causes plus aplain esclarcies en noz dites autres lettres / Dont la Somme des dites Rentes monte. Sept vinz Seze Liures tournois [156 l.t.] de Rente par an. Et nostre treschier seigneur & Cousin le .. Roy de france / Nous ait octroie par ses lettres ouuertes scellees en soie & en Cire vert ci dessouz encorporees / que des conquez / et achaz / que nous auons faiz et ferons en ses fiez /[80] arrerefiez & censiues / Iusques a la Somme de Cincq Cenz liures parisis [500 l.par.] de Rente Nous en puissons donner & aumosner a Eglises & personnes deglise Religieux [*sic*] / et autres / et distribuer & diuiser en autres piteables vsages. Excepte forteresces / Chastiaux / fiez de Chief de baronnie et haute Iustice.

Et nous aions acquis par tiltre dachat de Monsieur Iehan de Compiengne Cheualier & de Madame Beatrix du Mes sa fame / Certaines Rentes et Reuenues toutes Mouuens en fie du Roy sanz Moien / Des queles Rentes Nous auons partie donne & aumosne aus Religieuses de nostre dame de Maubuisson delez pontoise. Et partie en auons donne pour la fondation de certaines Messes / & Chapellenies que nous auons fonde en la dite Eglise de nostre dame. Et pour ce que Nous auons Regarde / que Le seurplus de la dite Rente est et sera prouffitable / et bien seant a leglise de Monsieur Saint denys. Nous ycelle Rente leur auons baille / & assis / baillons et asseons aus Lieux et en La Maniere qui sensieut.

Cest assauoir a fresnay en biauuoisins[81] Certaines auenes que nous y auons achetees des diz / cheualier et dame / et les deniers qui sont deuz auec les dites auenes / qui croissent & appetissent / et les doiuent les habitanz de la dite ville chascun an paier depuis la feste Saint Remy[82] / qui sont extimees a soixante Muis a la Mesure du dit lieu / qui font a la Mesure de Paris. quinse [*sic*, i.e., 15] Muis / Prisiez / Rabatuz les fraiz de le leuer et cuillir / Trente deux liures parisis [32 l.par.] de Rente par an.

Item a Cheurieres[83] Onze[84] vins et nuef [229] chapons de Cens que nous y auons aussi achetez des diz Cheualier et dame / deuz chascun an le Iour de Noel / le Chapon prisie .xij. deniers parisis valent Onze liures nuef soulz [11 l. 9 s.par.] parisis de Rente par an ..

Item vn fie que tient Iehan de Gauchi escuier / qui vault enuiron Cincquante liures parisis [50 l.par.] de terre / prisie la liure. douze deniers / qui valent Cincquante soulz parisis [50 s.par.] de Rente par an.

Item vn fie que Raoul destrees tient qui vault enuiron dix liures parisis de terre / vault au pris dessus dit .x. soulz parisis [10 s.par.] de Rente.

Item les deux pars de la Haute Iustice de Cheurieres prisiee ou fuer de enuiron. soixante soulz parisis [60 s.par.] de Rente par an / que le Roy a nostre Requeste a octroie que les diz Religieux puissent tenir si comme il appert par certaines lectres ouuertes seellees en soye & en cire vert / Reserue aus dites Religieuses de leglise de Maubuisson et aus Chapellains que nous auons fondez en ycelle eglise / que ou cas que il auroient aucun empeechement que Ia nauiengne en leurs dites Rentes / que donnees et aumosnees leur auons comme dit est. ycelles Religieuses et Chapellains presens / et auenir auront / et pourront auoir Recours pardeuers les Genz du Roy pour contraindre et Iusticier les Rebelles de paier / sanz appeller a ce les diz Religieux de Monsieur Saint denys. Et sanz ce aussi que ce tourne en aucune Maniere / ou en autre cas en preiudice de la dite Haute Iustice que nous auons donne comme dit est aus diz Religieux /

Monte la Somme a eulx assise par les dites parties. Quarante nuef liures nuef soulz parisis [49 l. 9 s.par.] / qui valent a tournois soixante vne liures Seze souls [*sic*] trois deniers tournois [61 l. 16 s. 3 d.t.] de Rente par an / Dont nous leur auons fait baillier la possession et saisine

Et ainsi demeurent encore [*sic*] a asseoir aus diz Religieux pour la perfection de la Rente que donnee leur auons comme dit est dessus.. Quatre vinz quatorze liures iij. s. ix. d.[85] tournois [94 l. 3 s. 9 d. t.] de Rente annuele et perpetuele lequel demourant non assis / Nous auons voulu / ordone / & accorde / voulons / ordenons / et accordons / de certaine science / que yceuls Religieux presens & auenir / aient et prengnent [*sic*] franchement / enterinement et aplain / dores en auant chascun an sus la Recepte de nostre Chastellenie de Braye Conte Robert / iusques a tant que la dite Rente leur soit autre part baillee et assise toute admortie.

Et quant a ce obligons enuers les diz Religieux nostre dite Chastellenie / et touz les proffiz / Reuenues / & emolumenz dycelle. Mandons et commandons par la teneur de ces presentes lectres a touz noz Receueurs Gruiers et autres officiers presenz & auenir qui les proffiz et emolumenz de nostre dite Chastellenie Receuront / que eulx sanz autre Mandement attendre de Nous / ne de noz successeurs paient et deliurent sanz nul contredit / et sanz nul delay aus diz Religieux . ou a leur[86] certain commandement la dite Rente a deux termes / Cest assauoir la Moitie a la tous Sains[87] / et lautre a lascenion ensiuant / et ainsi dan en an / et de terme en terme. Iusques atant que la dite Rente leur soit autre part bailliee et assise toute admortie comme dit est. Et commenceront A la[88] Receuoir a la toussains prochain / Et les Sommes qui paiees auront este aus diz Religieux pour la dite cause par noz Dites[89] Genz. Nous voulons quelles soient Rabatues de leur Recepte.

Et ou cas que noz diz Receueurs / Gruiers / ou autres Officiers / ou noz hoirs / & successeurs serions Refusanz / ou deffaillanz que Ia nauiengne de paier aus diz Religieux la dite Rente aus termes dessus diz. Nous voulons et expressement consentons que les diz Religieux / ou leurs dites[90] Genz puissent faire plaine execution par les Genz du Roy de ce qui leur seroit deu de la dite Rente sus les proffiz / yssues et emolumenz de nostre dite Chastellenie.

Et quant aus choses dessus dites tenir et fermement acomplir / Nous obligons / Nous / Noz hoirs / & successeurs / et ceuls qui de nous auront cause / nostre dite Chastellenie / Les Rentes / proffiz et Reuenues dycelle.

Et sil auenoit que Ia diex ne vueille que nous trespassissiens [sic] de cest Siecle auant que nous leur eussiens fait assiete et deliure a plain / la dite Rente admortie / ou que aucun empeechement leur y seroit mis par noz hoirs ou sucesseurs / ou par le seigneur de qui la dite Chastellenie est / et sera tenue en fie / par quoy les diz Religieux / nen peussent paisiblement Ioir / Comme dit est dessus. Nous voulons et consentons desmaintenant que les diz Religieux puissent faire vendre perpetuelment a touz iours par les Genz du Roy tant des biens / Rentes / proffiz / et Reuenues de nostre dite Chastellenie / que yceuls Religieux puissent du pris qui en sera euz auoir / et acquerer les dites . Quatre vinz quatorze[91] liures . iij . s. ix deniers tournois [94 l. 3 s. 9 d.t.] de Rente admortie a noz propres cous et despens. Aus queles [sic] Genz du Roy / Nous donnons quant a ce plain pouoir et auctorite par la teneur de ces presentes lettres. de faire la dite vente / de obliger / les biens / emolumens / proffiz et Reuenues de nostre dite Chastellenie pour garantir ycelle vente / et de faire tout ce que en tel cas puet appartenir / Et que nous mesmes pourriens [sic] faire se nous faisions la dite vente en nostre propre personne ..

La teneur de la lettre du Roy est tele ..

Philippe .. par la grace de dieu Rois de france .. Sauoir faisons a touz presenz et auenir . Que Nous[92] consideranz lamour & affection que Nous et nostre treschiere / et amee dame. la .. Royne Iehanne Royne de france et de Nauarre / Compaigne Iadis de nostre treschier seigneur & Cousin le .. Roy Charle que diex absoille / auons eu touz iours ensemble / Li auons octroie a sa Requeste / et octroions de grace especial / et de certaine science par ces lectres / que pour ce que elle a entente / & en propos / de donner ou aumosner a Eglises / ou personnes deglise Iusques a la Montance de Cincq Cenz liures parisis de Rente annuele & perpetuele / et que ycelle Rente elle puisse donner / aumosner / translater et deuiser ensemble / ou par parties pour le proufit et salut de same / et de ceuls que elle y voudra acompaignier / en quelconques eglises / ou personnes[93] deglises[94] / Religieus[95] [sic] & autres / et distribuer et diuiser en autres piteables vsages. en tant de lieux comme il lui plaira / Mais il nest pas nostre entente que de ce que elle acquerra ainsi elle donne aumosne ou baille a eglises / personnes deglises / ou Religieux comme dit est forteresces / ne chastiaux ne fie de chief de baronnie / ne de Chastellenie / ne Haute Iustice. Et est nostre entente que se elle a Ia fait aucuns tels acquez en noz fiez / Arrierefiez [sic] / ou Censiues quil soient compris en nostre presente grace. Et se par aduenture aduenoit que elle naqueriert enterinement a son viuant toute la dite Rente / ou se ainsi estoit ores que elle leust ia acquise et non distribuee du tout auant son decez .. Si voulons nous et li octroions de grace especial / que ses executeurs puissent acquerre des biens de sa execution la dite Rente / ou ce qui en defaudroit / et ycelle aumosner / translater / et distribuer en la Maniere dessus dite pour le salut de same / selonc lordenance que elle en fera / et le pouoir que elle en a donne / ou donrra [*sic*] a ses Executeurs sur ce par son testament / Codicille / darraine voulente / ou autrement. Voulans que les eglises personnes & lieux / es queles la dite Rente sera bailliee / assignee / translatee / et deuisee comme dit est / la puissent tenir / possider et posseser paisiblement a touz iours mais perpetuelment sanz ce que euls / ou aucuns de euls soient / ou puissent estre contrains de la vendre / ou mettre hors de leurs mains / & sanz Iamais paier pour ce aucune finance a nous / ou a noz successeurs Roys de france. Et lui octroions desmaintenant / et quittons tout le droit qui a nous / ou a noz successeurs puet et pourroit appartenir / soit pour quint denier ou pour autre cause / des achaz que elle faiz / et fera / ou ses executeurs feront des dites Rentes. Et voulons et octroions de certaine science / que en la Maniere / et selonc ce que nostre dite dame a son viuant / ou ses Executeurs apres son decez acquerront ycelles Rentes il les puissent par leurs lettres donner aumosner et distribuer en la Maniere dessus dite .. les queles lettres nous voulons de certaine science et de grace especial apres estre Ratiffiees et confermees du seel Royal en soie et en Cire vert par nostre Chancellier qui ores est et qui pour le temps sera sanz difficulte aucune / ou autre Mandement attendre de nous ou de noz successeurs Rois [*sic*] de france. Et pour ce que ce soit ferme chose et estable perpetuelment a touz iours. Nous auons fait mettre nostre seel a ces presentes lettres. Sauf en autres choses nostre droit / et en toutes lautrui. Donne a Paris lan de grace Mil trois Cenz trente & Huit le Quinzieme Iour du mois de feurier.

 Et Nous Abbe / & Conuent dessus diz / Consideranz la dite assiete et autres choses dessus dites / estre faites au proffit / et vtilite de nostre dite Eglise. ycelle assiete loons / Ratiffions / & acceptons / Et la dite assignacion a nous faite de partie de la dite Rente sus la dite Chastellenie de Braye Iusques atant que nostre dite dame la nous ait autrement assise comme dit est aggreons et approuuons.

 Et pour ce que ce soit ferme chose et estable a touz Iours / Nous .. Royne .. Abbe & Couuent dessus diz auons fait mettre noz seauls en ces presentes lettres / qui furent faites le premier Iour Daoust .. lan de grace Mil Trois Cenz . Quarante & trois.

NOTES

1. I intend to provide full bibliography in a forthcoming study of Jeanne's anticipatory testamentary execution and her last will, part of a collaborative project to edit the corpus of medieval French royal testamentary acts on which I am working with Xavier Hélary, Élisabeth Lalou, and Romain Telliez. For the moment, see as well my article, "Les testaments de Jeanne d'Évreux et leur exécution," which will soon be published in *Le Moyen Âge*. The date of Jeanne's birth is unknown. The fundamental works on Jeanne are: Barbara Drake Boehm, "Jeanne d'Évreux, Queen of France," in Boehm, Abigail Quandt, and William D. Wixom, *The Hours of Jeanne d'Evreux. Acc. No. 54.I.2. The Metropolitan Museum of Art, The Cloisters Collection, New York: Commentary* (Lucerne: Faksimile Verlag Luzern; New York: The Metropolitan Museum of Art, 2000), pp. 35–87, at p. 67n14 (hereafter *Hours*); Barbara Drake Boehm, "Le mécénat de Jeanne d'Évreux," in *1300 . . . L'art au temps de Philippe le Bel. Actes du Colloque international, Galeries nationales du Grand Palais, 24 et 25 juin 1998*, ed. Danielle Gaborit-Chopin and François Avril, with Marie-Cécile Bardos, XVIe Rencontres de l'École du Louvre, septembre 2001 (Paris: École du Louvre, 2001), pp. 15–31; and Carla Lord, "Jeanne d'Évreux as a Founder of Chapels: Patronage and Public Piety," in *Women and Art in Early Modern Europe: Patrons, Collectors, and Connoisseurs*, ed. Cynthia Lawrence (University Park: Pennsylvania State University Press, 1997), pp. 21–36. Indispensable for Jeanne and her family are vols. 2 and 3 of Patrick Van Kerrebrouck's series, Nouvelle histoire généalogique de l'auguste Maison de France: *Les Capétiens, 987–1328* (Villeneuve d'Ascq: Patrick Van Kerrebrouck, 2000) and *Les Valois* (Villeneuve d'Ascq: Patrick Van Kerrebrouck, 1990). Brie-Comte-Robert lies some thirty km. southeast of Paris. My deep thanks to Ghislain Brunel, Olivier Canteaut, and Richard C. Famiglietti for their generous counsel.

2. In his second and third wills, and in the codicil he drew up on November 28, 1314, Philip the Fair, for example, provided for the completion of the house of Poissy should it not be finished before his death: Paris, Archives nationales (hereafter AN), J 403, no. 13 (will of March 1298), nos. 17–17[bis] (testament of May 17, 1311), and no. 18, attached to no. 17[bis] (codicil). See my article, "Royal Salvation and Needs of State in Early-Fourteenth-Century France," in *The Monarchy of Capetian France and Royal Ceremonial*, Collected Studies 345 (Aldershot: Variorum, 1991), no. 4 (pp. 11, 14, 16–18). Similarly, in his will of October 1324, Charles IV ordered that if he had not fully executed his father's and brothers' wills before his own death, his executors were to carry out their provisions with dispatch (AN, J 404A, no. 29 [AE II 333]).

3. AN, J 405, no. 1, an exemplification made in Paris in the Chambre des comptes on December 5, 1336, by Pierre Tuepain de Gressio, clerk of the diocese of Sens, who with Hugues Boilleau (also rendered Boisleau and Boileau), Jeanne's councillor, collated the act with the original; in the notary's attestation Hugues is designated "Magistro hugone boisleau," and their work described as "diligentem collacionem." The king's act was said to be "infixis per quasdam alias litteras & clausas / sub sigillo paruo / illustrissime domine / domine Iohanne," evidently Jeanne's will.

4. See the preceding note for its presence in the Chambre des comptes in 1336. Presumably it was destroyed or discarded after Jeanne made other wills. Jeanne's final will and codicils were in the Chambre des comptes when Menant copied them in the seventeenth century; see n. 8 below.

5. AN, J 405, no. 2, formerly sealed in red wax on a parchment strip ("par Monsieur le Regent. Ia. de Vertus"). The abbreviation l.t. stands for *livre tournois*, which was worth 4/5 of the *livre parisis* (l.par.); thus, 4 l.par. = 5 l.t. Other abbreviations: d. = denier, s. = sou. It

is impossible to give modern equivalents for the sums dispensed by Jeanne, but they were clearly impressive and substantial.

6. AN, J 405, no. 3 ("Autre fois signee Ainssi par Monsieur le Regent. Ia. de vertus. Renouuelee par vous du commandement le Roy. Feauz").

7. Marie-Laure Lemonnier-Surget, *Les "ennemis du roi": parenté et politique chez les Evreux-Navarre (1298-1425)* (Lille: Atelier national de reproduction des thèses, [2004]), Annexes, pp. 98–101; Anatole de Montaiglon, "Joyaux et pierreries donnés au couvent des Grands Carmes de la Place Maubert à Paris par la reine Jeanne d'Évreux en 1349 et 1361," *Archives de l'art français. Recueil de documents inédits relatifs à l'histoire des arts en France* 11 (2nd ser., 1) (1861): 448–53, at pp. 448–52 (from the original acts, in AN, L 1527); cf. Boehm, "Jeanne d'Évreux," in *Hours*, pp. 52–53.

8. Rouen, Bibliothèque municipale, MS 3403, Leber 5870, Menant VI (hereafter Rouen, Menant VI), fols. 72–122 (the execution of Jeanne's testament, from September 28, 1372, through January 1372/73); fols. *122–33 (testament dated at Crécy-en-Brie in March 1366/67; Easter fell on April 5 in 1366 and on April 18 in 1367); fols. *133–39 (codicil dated at Brie-Comte-Robert in October 1370, attached to the testament); fol. 139v (another codicil, dated the same day, unattached to the will); fol. 140v (commission of Charles V for the execution of the will, dated at Bois de Vincennes on July 5, 1372). Gaspard-Moïse-Augustin de Fontanieu (1694–1767) had Menant's transcriptions copied for inclusion in his collection of documents relating to the history of France: Paris, Bibliothèque nationale de France (hereafter BnF), n. acq. fr. 7614 (Portefeuilles de Fontanieu 90–91), fols. 205–236v. An independent and far fuller copy of the execution is found in BnF, fr.7855, pp. 341–415; unfortunately this copy does not include the end of the execution (including expenses) nor Jeanne's testament and codicils; it terminates with the list of "autres biens et joyaux de ladite execution lesquels nont pas este trouuez en escript ou dit inuentoire . . . Item vne petite fourure de gris prisiee ii. frans et demi. Somme viii^{xx}. frans." Whether this copy was made from the original or from another copy is unclear. Jean-Michel-Constant Leber published a portion of Menant's transcription, in *Collection des meilleurs dissertations, notices et traités particuliers relatifs à l'histoire de France, composée, en grande partie, de pièces rare, ou qui n'ont jamais été publiés séparément pour servir à compléter toutes les collections de mémoires sur cette matière*, 20 vols. (Paris: G.-A. Dentu, 1838) 19:120–69 (from Rouen, Menant VI, fols. 72–97); this partial edition is unreliable and must be verified against Menant's transcriptions. Cf. Lemonnier-Surget, *Les "ennemis du roi,"* pp. 296–317, esp. pp. 296–97.

9. AN, J 405, no. 8.

10. The text of this letter is included in the second act of August 1, 1343, edited below (AN, K 43B, no. 27bis).

11. AN, J 405, no. 9.

12. In "Les testaments de Jeanne d'Évreux et leur exécution" (see n. 1 above), I offer editions of AN, K 43B, no. 21bis (May 31, 1342, for Longchamp), and L 845, no. 41 (February 1342/43, for the church of Saint-Paul located near the abbey of Saint-Denis). For Jeanne's endowment of the church of Saint-Étienne at Brie-Comte-Robert, see Edmond Michel, "La reine Jeanne d'Evreux à Brie-Comte-Robert (1326–70)," *Bulletin et Compte-Rendu de la Société d'histoire et d'archéologie de Brie-Comte-Robert, Mormant, Tournan et la vallée de l'Yères* 1 (1898–1901): 9–15, 22–25, at pp. 13–15 (giving extracts and a summary); cf. Boehm, "Jeanne d'Évreux," in *Hours*, p. 44.

13. In her testament Jeanne declared: "Et pour ce ayans fait autres fois certains Testamens & Codiciles, Et d'Iceux a nostre viuant fait faire certains payemenz & satisfactions

tant en deniers comme en rentes que nous auons donnees et assizes a certaines Eglises, Religions & autres lieux piteables, & aussy a nos Seruiteurs en remuneracion & guerredon de leur Seruices que fait nous auoient." See Rouen, Menant VI, fol. 122v.

14. These were held on February 28, 1342/43, February 12, 1343/44, May 1349, and August 26, 1354; see Jeanne's testament of March 1366/67, in Rouen, Menant VI, fol. 123.

15. Jeanne was to collect this sum from half the proceeds of royal moneying rights at Tournai and Saint-Quentin.

16. Eva Leistenschneider has discussed Jeanne's foundation in "Die Grabkapellen des 14. Jahrhunderts im Querhaus von Saint-Denis," in *Hofkultur in Frankreich und Europa im Spätmittelalter. La culture de cour en France et en Europe à la fin du Moyen Âge*, ed. Christian Freigang and Jean-Claude Schmitt et al., Passagen/Passage; Deutsches Forum für Kunstgeschichte/Centre allemand d'histoire de l'art 11 (Berlin: Akademie Verlag, 2005), pp. 328–37; and in *Die französische Königsgrablege Saint-Denis. Strategien monarchischer Repräsentation 1223-1461* (Weimar: VDG, Verlag und Datenbank für Geisteswissenschaften, 2008), pp. 142–55.

17. After preparing the acts for edition, I had the pleasure of meeting Damien Berné, who graciously permitted me to read his thesis, "Architecture et liturgie. Étude d'une interaction spatiale et mémorielle à Saint-Denis à l'époque gothique," 2 vols. (Thèse pour le diplôme d'archiviste paléographe, École nationale des chartes, 2008), in which he reedited Jeanne's acts (with modernized capitalization, accents, and punctuarion); like Jacques Doublet (see n. 18 below), he omitted from the second act the exemplification of Philip VI's letter of August 7, 1339 (2:79–86). In his thesis (2:504–5) Berné also edited the charter of February 1343 that I mention in n. 12 above. A summary of Berné's thesis can be found on http://theses.enc.sorbonne.fr/document 1128.html, 8. See also his article, "L'action mémorielle des princesses capétiennes à Saint-Denis au XIVe siècle," *Histoire de l'art* 63 (Oct. 2008): 1–10.

18. AN, K 43B, nos. 27–27bis. Jacques Doublet's "modernized" edition contains many errors and omits the royal letter of February 15, 1339, exemplified in the second act (*Histoire de l'Abbaye de S. Denys en France. . .* [Paris: Iean de Heuqueville, 1625], pp. 968–75). Doublet discussed this endowment again in chapters on both the abbey's treasury (pp. 336–37, where his descriptions echo those of the abbey's inventories) and Jeanne's tomb (pp. 1298–99). Although Michel Felibien often reedited acts Doublet had published, he simply summarized these long documents in *Histoire de l'Abbaye Royale de Saint-Denys en France . . .* (Paris: Frederic Leonard, 1706), pp. 275–76. In their edition of the abbey's inventories, Blaise de Montesquiou-Fezensac and Danielle Gaborit-Chopin included extracts from Doublet's edition relating to the objects Jeanne gave the abbey: *Le trésor de Saint-Denis*, 3 vols. (Paris: A. et J. Picard, 1973–77) 1:110–12, no. 5 (the chasse with relics from the Sainte-Chapelle); 1:113–14, no. 7 (the statue of Saint John); 1:114–15, no. 8 (the reliquary of the Virgin); 1:176, no. 104 (Jeanne's crown); see also 2:30–34 (the chasse of the Sainte-Chapelle), 2: 39–41; 2:216–21 (Jeanne's crown); and 3:27–28 and pl. 10A (the reliquary of John the Evangelist); 3:28–32 and accompanying pls. 9–13 (the Virgin reliquary); 3:75–76 and pl. 64A (Jeanne's crown); see also the long extract 1:10–11. In in his book, *Histoire de la ville de Brie-Comte-Robert (des origines au XVe siècle)* (Paris: Dujarric, 1902), pp. 214–15, 217, n. 3, Edmond Michel gave long extracts from the summary of the two acts contained in a cartulary of Saint-Denis, AN, LL 1191, pp. 397–400.

19. "de certaine science / saine de corps / et ferme dentendement"; cf. Jeanne's will of March 1366/67, where she declared herself "ferme & Seure d'Entendement & Saine de Corps," and used the phrase "de certaine Science" four times in announcing different

provisions (Rouen, Menant VI, fols. 122, 123v, 126v, 128v, 129). See also her codicil of October 1370, in which she stated that she was "En bonne Sante de Corps Saine de pensee Et de bon Entendement" (fol. 139v).

20. The surviving copy of Jeanne's will of March 1366/67 is incomplete; it includes no clause stipulating where her body, heart, and entrails were to be interred, although it contains clauses concerning her funeral (and the crown she had given to Saint-Denis, which was to adorn her body) and also the tombs for her body and heart (which had already been made and "mises ez lieux ou Il doiuent estre mis"), as well as the entrail tomb that her executors were to have made if she had not seen to this before she died (which was to be placed "au lieu ou [nos Entrailles] Seront Enterrees telle comme bon Semblera a nos Executeurs") (Rouen, Menant VI, fols. 127v–128). In the event, her body was buried at Saint-Denis, her heart at the church of the Dominicans in Paris, and her entrails at Maubuisson (Van Kerrebrouck, *Les Capétiens*, p. 171).

21. Ghislain Brunel (to whom I extend deep gratitude) recognized in the animal-head decoration found on the first letter of both acts of 1343 (*I* for *Iehanne*) a motif favored by a scribe who worked in the royal chancery during the reigns of Charles IV and Philip VI. For another example see the letter dated April 19, 1326, reproduced in Ghislain Brunel, *Images du pouvoir royal. Les chartes décorées des Archives nationales, XIIIe–XVe siècle* (Paris: Somogy; Centre historique des Archives nationales, 2005), p. 40, fig. 6 (AN, J 567, no. 1). As Olivier Canteaut kindly pointed out to me, the secretary responsible for this act, Jean du Temple, died in 1330 or 1332, but the act itself may well have been penned by another hand. Whether the scribe responsible for the act of 1326 actually prepared the acts of 1343 or whether his motif was imitated by a scribe he had trained (or who had worked with him) is difficult to say. Both current and former clerks of the royal chancery were surely employed in Jeanne's writing office, whose professionalism is attested by the elegantly executed (and decorated) accounts for 1328–36 preserved in AN, KK 3B; those for 1364 (AN, KK 4) are less fine. Olivier Canteaut has shown that the notary Henri de Dompierre worked for decades both as Jeanne's secretary and as a scribe in the royal chancery and the Chambre des comptes. Dompierre signed chancery acts between 1322 and 1338 and worked in the Chambre des comptes until 1349. See Canteaut's article, "Du notaire au clerc du secret : le personnel de la chancellerie des derniers Capétiens directs dans les rouages du pouvoir," which he kindly permitted me to read before its publication and which has now appeared in *"De part et d'autre des Alpes" (II). Chancelleries et chanceliers des princes à la fin du Moyen Âge. Actes de la table ronde de Chambéry, 5 et 6 octobre 2006*, ed. Guido Castelnuovo and Olivier Mattéoni, Collection Sociétés, religions, politiques 19 (Chambéry: Université de Savoie, Laboratoire Langages, littératures, sociétés, 2011), pp. 231–85, at 243, n. 50, and 276.

Ghislain Brunel has observed that the green silk used in sealing the acts of August 1, 1343, was foreign to the royal writing office, and that the royal office did not employ the protective covering found on the seals attached to these acts. Similar green silk was used to attach seals (now missing) to other royal donations to Saint-Denis. See, e.g., an act of Blanche of France (1253–1320), daughter of Louis IX and Marguerite of Provence, dated March 21, 1313/14, AN, K 38, no. 11^2 (with the shelfmark of the abbey); and an act of Marguerite of France (1309–82), countess of Flanders, daughter of Philip V and Jeanne of Artois and Burgundy, dated May 1363 and sealed (as Jeanne d'Évreux's acts had been) by the abbot and monastery as well, AN, K 48, no. 30 (again with the shelfmark of the abbey). Like the acts of August 1, 1343, the acts of Blanche and Marguerite do not designate the place of issuance. An act of Charles V issued at Saint-Denis in May 1372 (AN, K 49 no. 62) is sealed on green and red silk, with the seal enclosed in a parchment sheath; an act of John II for Saint-Denis dated September 1362 at the manor of Tournoye near Provins (AN, K 49, no. 71) and a confirmation that Charles VI issued at Saint-Denis in October 1404 (AN, K 49, no. 63) are also sealed on green and red silk.

22. Berné discussed the rhetoric of the first act in "Architecture et liturgie," 1:144–47.

23. In her testament of March 1366/67, listing those who had attended the first auditing session of the accounts of her anticipatory execution on February 28, 1343, Jeanne described Guy as "lors desmis" (Rouen, Menant VI, fol. 123). Precisely when the resignation occurred is unknown. Felibien stated that Guy ruled the abbey until 1343 and commented of his resignation, "il se démit de sa charge par l'effet d'une humilité du moins aussi rare dans ce siécle-là, [*sic*] que dans le nostre" (*Histoire*, p. 274). The inscription on Guy's grave lauded him as an abbot "qui viuat in astris," who "contempsit honores, Despexit namque mundum, armen, Sathanamque, Mira quidem fecit Christi detentus amore, Se sic subiecit quod sic priuauit honore" (Doublet, *Histoire*, p. 1374; Felibien, *Histoire*, pp. 374–75). (Guy was buried beneath a metal plaque near the similar plaque of Gilles de Pontoise, near the tomb of Francis I.) Not until June 12, 1343, did Pope Clement VI write to Philip VI and his son Jean to commend to them Guy's successor, Gilles Rigaud: Clement VI, *Lettres closes, patentes et curiales publiées ou analysées d'après les registres du Vatican*, ed. Eugène Déprez, Jean Glénisson, and Guillaume Mollat, 4 vols., Bibliothèque des Écoles françaises d'Athènes et de Rome, 3d ser., 3 (Paris: E. de Boccard, 1901–61) 1:71–74, nos. 222–23.

24. In the charter the word is *tableau*; cf. Matthew 27:37 ("super caput eius causam ipsius"), Mark 15:26 ("titulus cause eius"), Luke 23:38 ("superscriptio scripta super eum").

25. Nor did Jeanne describe the reliquary, which inventories of the sixteenth century and later show was supported on four silver-gilt lions and was decorated with enamels depicting the Nativity, the Crucifixion, and the Resurrection. At some point the reliquary received a small leather case containing a cross engraved with a crucifix on one side and Saint Louis on the other, inscribed "Here a piece of the True Cross that Saint Louis, king of France, carried on his person" ("Icy a de la vraye Croix que St Louis, Roy de France, souloit porter sur luy"); this was missing by 1634, but in that year there was found in the reliquary a piece of white satin containing a bone of Louis of Toulouse or Marseille. The arms of the abbey were added to the reliquary. See *Trésor*, ed. Montesquiou-Fezensac and Gaborit-Chopin, 1:110–12; 2:29–30 (source dated 1505, referring to Saint Louis and the piece of the Cross).

26. In his will, Charles left Jeanne a jeweled brooch he wore and also "la chasse nouuele que Ie ay fete faire / a la semblance de la chace de paris de nostre chapele," which evidently had some connection with the Sainte-Chapelle—and perhaps with the reliquary Jeanne pledged to Guy de Châtres (AN, J 404B, no. 29 [AE II 333]). In July 1267 Louis IX bestowed on the abbey of Vézelay parts of six relics he had bought from the emperor of Constantinople: wood from the Cross, two thorns, Christ's swaddling clothes, his sweatband, the purple garment in which he was tormented, and part of the *lintheum* that he wore when washing the feet of the disciples at the Last Supper (AN, J 462, no. 25). Louis had the relics placed in the hand of a reliquary holding the arm of Mary Magdalene which he also sent to the abbey, in gratitude for the relics of the Magdalene the house had given him when her body was translated at Vézelay the year before.

27. Jeanne's phraseology indicates that the rededication of the chapel was linked to her redecoration of the space: "que nous y auons nouuellement ordenee / en lonneur de nostre dame / et de monsieur Saint Iehan Euuangeliste." Both masses were to be sung after the

so-called Mass of the Pilgrims. A treatise "De la Deuotion des Treschrestiens Roys de france et de tous les autres Chrestiens auparauant eux, enuers le glorieux Martyr S. Denys Areopagite," written after 1636, probably by Dom Germain Millet (BnF, lat. 13817, fols. 93–111, at 96v) suggests that only one mass instituted by Jeanne was being sung after the pilgrims' mass, whereas another one, said at prime in the chapel, had just been inaugurated. This report may simply reflect the inscription on the statue of the Virgin in the chapel, for which see below at n. 44.

28. Jeanne specifically designated the different officials who were to say the masses; later, in granting 100 s.t. (or 5 l.t.) to those who rang bells and assisted at the masses, she referred to those who said the masses (and who would disburse this sum) as *Chapellains*, as in fact they were.

29. In 1636, Dom Germain Millet declared that Jeanne gave Saint-Denis the chasse containing portions of the relics of the Sainte-Chapelle "en contreschange" for the head of Saint Louis, which was transferred from Saint-Denis to the Sainte-Chapelle in 1306: *Tresor sacré*, pp. 73, 87 (where Millet stated that Jeanne herself "fit mettre [le Chef] à la Saincte Chappelle de Paris, où il se voit"); the first passage was quoted from the 4th ed. of 1645, in *Trésor*, ed. Montesquiou-Fezensac and Gaborit-Chopin, 2:318, no. XXIV. Once launched, the notion of an exchange between Jeanne and the Sainte-Chapelle proved popular: 2:31–32, no. XIII (source dated 1714) and 2:32, no. XIV (source dated 1726).

30. Precisely where Marie was originally buried is unclear, but her body eventually rested beside that of her sister Blanche (who died in 1393) in the chapel Jeanne had begun refurbishing. See below at n. 51.

31. Michel (*Histoire de la ville*, p. 349) believed that Jeanne made her gifts in exchange for "services funèbres pour l'âme de son mari," but the transaction was more complex than this suggests.

32. For Charles's will, see AN, J 404A, no. 29 (AE II 333): "Et Retieng a Moy / et a mes successeurs Roys de france la collaction [*sic*] / & linstitucion des diz chapelains." The other two chaplaincies were established at Saint-Louis of Poissy and at Becoiseau (Becoisel-en-Brie, near the forest of Crécy), which presumably gratefully accepted them. Charles left both Notre-Dame and Saint-Denis 20 l. to support his anniversary celebration, 100 l. to Poissy, and nothing further to Becoiseau.

33. Jules Viard, ed., *Documents parisiens du règne de Philippe VI de Valois (1328–1350). Extraits des registres de la chancellerie de France*, 2 vols., Société de l'histoire de Paris et de l'Île-de-France, Documents 11–12 (Paris: Henri Champion, 1899–1900), 1:35–38, no. XXXII, at p. 36; see Berné, "Architecture et liturgie," 1:136–38, who did not mention Notre-Dame.

34. Berné, "Architecture et liturgie," 1:136–39. Unlike Berné, I consider critical Charles IV's novel requirement that the chaplains be named by the kings of France, which I believe caused both Notre-Dame and Saint-Denis to reject the chaplaincy. Despite the fact that he was one of the executors of Louis X's widow Clementia of Hungary, Guy de Châtres was surely instrumental in modifying the uses to which the endowment she left was put— which I believe less objectionable than did Berné (ibid., 138–39); see my "Chapels and Cult of Saint Louis at Saint-Denis," *Mediaevalia: A Journal of Medieval Studies* 10 (1984; pub. 1988): 279–331, at pp. 289–92. In her testament of October 5, 1328, Clementia left 30 l.par. a year (not a large sum) to support performance of a daily mass for the dead "en une determinee chapelle," for the souls of her husband, herself, and their friends. The bequest was rejected because the abbey was said to be overburdened with masses for kings, queens,

and other benefactors. Eventually, however, the abbey agreed to accept a chaplaincy in the "new chapel of Saint Louis," whose incumbent (paid 20 l.par. a year) would say three masses for the dead every week; the other 10 l.par. of Clementia's bequest would fund a pittance to be distributed on or about October 3, the anniversary of Clementia's death. See AN, K 42, no. 8b, an act of March 7, 1331, issued by three of Clementia's executors; on May 25, 1331, the same three executors guaranteed the abbey that celebration of the masses would be contingent on their receiving the promised revenue (AN, K 42, no. 9). Berné discussed these acts in "Architecture et liturgie," 2:281–84. For the wall painting honoring Clementia, Louis, and their son Jean that was installed in the chapel, see Brown, "Chapels," cited above.

35. Before his death in 1350, Guy completed his *Sanctilogium*, a collection of lives of saints who were venerated at the abbey, and was surely involved in the liturgical reform that took place at the abbey during those years. See Brown, "Les testaments de Jeanne d'Évreux et leur exécution" (see n. 1 above); Henri Omont, "Le *Sanctilogium* de Gui de Châtres, abbé de Saint-Denys," *Bibliothèque de l'École des chartes* 86 (1925): 407–10, and "Gui de Châtres, abbé de Saint-Denys, auteur d'un Sanctilogium," *Histoire littéraire de la France*, vol. 36, *Suite du quatorzième siècle* (Paris: Imprimerie nationale, 1927), pp. 627–30; Kyunghee Choi, "Illuminating Liturgy and Legend: The Missal of St.-Denis (London, Victoria and Albert Museum Ms. L. 1346–1891) and the Royal Abbey in the Fourteenth Century" (Ph.D. dissertation, Institute of Fine Arts, New York University, 2004); (as Kyunghee Pyun), "Foundation Legends in the Illuminated Missal of Saint-Denis: Interplay of Liturgy, Hagiography, and Chronicle," *Viator* 39, 2 (2008): 143–91.

36. I have found no evidence that Jeanne was similarly perturbed about the situation at Notre-Dame, perhaps because the assignment of the two rejected chaplaincies to the Sainte-Chapelle meant that Charles's memory was richly honored in the heart of Paris.

37. See n. 23 above.

38. On this statue, which the church of Saint-Germain-des-Prés acquired after the Revolution, see Charles Saunier, "Les réclamations d'objets d'art par la fabrique de Saint-Germain-des-Prés, à l'époque du Concordat," *Bulletin de la Société historique du VIe arrondissement de Paris* 2 (1899): 62–76, at p. 75, esp. n. 1; cf. Georges Huard, communication delivered on February 16, 1938, *Bulletin de la Société nationale des antiquaires* (1938): 95–104. I am grateful to Charles T. Little for bringing Saunier's article to my attention.

39. Gilles Rigaud left Saint-Denis after having been made cardinal priest of S. Prassede on December 17, 1350; he died in 1351 and was buried at the abbey. See Felibien, *Histoire*, pp. 274–75; *Gallia Christiana*, 7:399–400.

40. The person who in the eighteenth century summarized the act for the abbey's inventory of charters was evidently puzzled by this aspect of the agreement and wrote that the actual letters had been "passées et accordées par bon auis et deliberation en Chapitre, par ledit abbé Guy et Le Conuent" but had not been "par Eux Grossoyées et scellées [engrossed and sealed]" (AN, LL 1191, p. 398). Had this actually occurred, the earlier acts could simply have been exemplified, a relatively simple operation that could have taken place as soon as Gilles Rigaud entered office.

41. *Trésor*, ed. Montesquiou-Fezensac and Gaborit-Chopin, vol. 3, pl. 11; in their notice, the editors stated (p. 28) that the statue "fut offerte à l'abbaye de Saint-Denis, en 1339, par Jeanne d'Évreux," and "fut confirmée par un acte de 1343"; they made the same statement concerning the reliquary of John the Evangelist (3:27). According to Françoise Baron, in Baron et al., *Les Fastes du Gothique. Le siècle de Charles V*, exhibition catalogue, Galeries nationales du Grand Palais, 9 October 1981–1 February 1982 (Paris: Ministère

de la Culture; Éditions de la Réunion des musées nationaux, 1981), pp. 232–33, no. 186, "l'inscription [atteste] la donation . . . confirmée en 1343." Boehm ("Le mécénat," p. 19) stated that the act of 1343 "fait mention du don d'une figure, en argent doré éclatant" and that the statue itself "mentionne notamment la date du don, 1339."

42. In an act of May 31, 1342, the abbess and nuns of Longchamp referred to Charles as "nostre treschier seigneur .. le Roy Charle que dieux absoille / Iadiz son seigneur & espouz" and as "le .. Roy charle son seigneur que dieux absoille" (AN, K 43B, no. 21bis). In an act of February 1343 for the church of Saint-Paul of Saint-Denis, Jeanne termed him "nostre treschier seigneur et epous le .. Roy Charles que diex absoille" (AN, L 845, no. 41); see also Jeanne's will of March 1366 (Rouen, Menant VI, fols. 124, 129v). See n. 12 above.

43. For both forms, *Charles* and *Challe*, see the will of Charles of Valois of December 22, 1320 (AN, J 404A, no. 24).

44. Cf. Doublet's transcription of the epitaph for Charles IV and Jeanne at Saint-Denis, which described Jeanne's gifts (*Histoire*, p. 1298): "laquelle Royne donna ceans ceste Chace . . . Item donna cette image de Nostre Dame."

45. Louis Duval-Arnould usefully distinguished between a juridical act (such as the handing over ["remise"] of a charitable donation) and the written document recording the act, in "Les aumônes d'Aliénor, dernière comtesse de Vermandois et dame de Valois (+ 1213)," *Revue Mabillon* 60 (1984): 395–463, at pp. 406–7n37.

46. Doublet, *Histoire*, p. 1299 (reading *peoiedre & orduer*); Felibien, *Histoire*, p. 533, with minor differences, including the phrase, surely correct, *paindre & ordenner*. The chapel was at some point decorated with statues of Jeanne, Charles, and their two daughters: Boehm, "Jeanne d'Évreux," in *Hours*, p. 47, citing Doublet, *Histoire*, p. 329 ("Aux quatre coins . . . sur quatre colonnes de pierre, sont esleuees quatre statuës de pierre de liais.").

47. Adolphe Dutilleux and Joseph Depoin, eds., *Cartulaire de l'abbaye de Maubuisson (Notre-Dame-la-Royale)*, 2 vols., Documents édités par la Société historique du Vexin (Pontoise: Lucien Paris, Société historique du Vexin, 1890–1913), 1:78–80, no. LXXX; see also ibid., pp. 81–82, nos. LXXXI–LXXXIII (supplementary acts of October 1340, February 2, 1341, and February 27, 1345); on the foundation, see also Dutilleux and Depoin, eds., *L'abbaye de Maubuisson (Notre-Dame-la-Royale). Histoire et cartulaire publiés d'après des documents entièrement inédits*, 4 vols., Documents édités par la Société historique du Vexin (Pontoise: Amédée Paris, 1882–85), 1:24–25.

48. Rouen, Menant VI, fol. 123; see also above, n. 23. In this act (Jeanne's testament of March 1366), Jeanne did not say where the session was held, but it seems likely to have been at Brie-Comte-Robert. In addition to Jeanne herself, her brother Philip, king of Navarre, and her daughter Blanche, duchess of Orléans, attended this session.

49. Paul Guérin, ed., *Les petits Bollandistes: Vies des saints de l'Ancien et du Nouveau Testament, des Martyrs, des Pères, des Auteurs sacrés et ecclésiastiques . . . d'après le Père Giry . . .* , 7th ed., vol. 5 (Paris: Bloud et Barral, 1885), p. 564; and Boehm, "Jeanne d'Évreux," in *Hours*, p. 51. For the relics of Saint Pelerin (Peregrinus), see Millet, *Tresor sacré*, pp. 51–53.

50. "la chapelle de nostre dame que nous y auons nouuellement ordenee . . ." See appendix, section 1.

51. For this act, see nn. 12 and 41 above. The endowment was small, just 50 s.t. a year to be distributed to those who attended an annual mass of the Virgin sung in Jeanne's honor (with a prayer for Charles IV's soul), to be replaced after she died by an anniversary commemoration of the day of her death, to be performed jointly for her and Charles.

52. AN, S 2311, no. 4; BnF. lat. 17111 (a copy of an original charter kept at the abbey,

made for Roger de Gaignières), pp. 143–50; edited in Berné, "Architecture et liturgie," 2:97–108, at pp. 99–102.

53. Alain Erlande-Brandenburg, in Erlande-Brandenburg, Jean-Pierre Babelon, Françoise Jenn, and Jean-Marie Jenn, *Le roi, la sculpture et la mort. Gisants et tombeaux de la Basilique de Saint-Denis*, 3rd ed. (Saint-Denis: Conseil général de la Seine-Saint-Denis, Archives départementales, 1996), p. 23, no. 45.

54. See Brown, "Les testaments de Jeanne d'Évreux et leur exécution" (see n. 1 above).

55. *Trésor*, ed. Montesquiou-Fezensac and Gaborit-Chopin, 2:216–21, 314–15, esp. p. 315n1; 3:75–76, pl. 4 (T), pl. 64.

56. Ibid., 2:30–33, no. XIV, esp. p. 32; and 3:3.

57. Ibid., 2:39–41.

58. The second act of August 1, 1343, specified that 94 l. 3 s. 9 d.t. of the total sum of 156 l.t. would be assigned on Brie-Comte-Robert until another source was provided, but evidently the original assignment was never modified.

59. Doublet, *Histoire*, pp. 1155–56; the royal act was issued in Paris in November 1514, shortly before the king's death on January 1, 1515, and just a few months after he endowed the abbey with an annuity of 250 l. to be drawn from his daughters Claude's and Renée's *comté* of Montfort-l'Amaury, in memory of their mother, his recently deceased wife, Anne de Bretagne: AN, K 81, no. 5, for which see Doublet, *Histoire*, pp. 1150–53, and *Anne de Bretagne, une histoire, un mythe*, exhibition catalogue (Paris: Somogy Éditions d'art; Nantes: Musée du Château des ducs de Bretagne, 2007), p. 103.

60. The guidebook to the abbey's treasury annotated by the officials responsible for the triage is preserved in the Cabinet des médailles of the BnF, shelfmark Theta 1005 H: *Le Trésor de l'abbaye royale de S.-Denys en France; qui comprend les Corps Saints & autres Reliques précieuses qui se voient, tant dans l'Eglise, que dans la Salle du Trésor* (Paris: Philippe-Denis Pierres, 1783), pp. 7–8, 15; another copy (unannotated) is in the BnF, 8-Lj9 569 (F). The Virgin and the chasse of the Sainte-Chapelle, as well as the reliquary made to replace Jeanne's image of John the Evangelist, were marked *id.* (*idem*), following the notation *fondre*; the other notation used by the commissioners was *laisser*. Most crowns (including Saint Louis's crown with a thorn from the Crown of Thorns) were ordered to be melted, although the coronation crown (and other regalia, including Charlemagne's sword) was ordered kept; ibid., pp. 5, 7, 8, 9, 11, 13, 14–15. See *Trésor*, ed. Montesquiou-Fezensac and Gaborit-Chopin, 2:44–45, 3:28, 29, for the final fate of the Virgin, and 3:76, for Jeanne's crown.

61. "Cheurieres & fresnoy & Bray Comte Robert. Fondation de Lanniuersaire de Ieanne Reyne de france & de Nauarre & donation de fiefs & Justice Cheurieres, & fresnoy & de 94 l. 3 s. 9 d. de Rente sur bray Comte robert du 1[er] aoust 1343." This notation is written in the same hand as the lengthy analysis on the dorse of no. 27[quater] and may be Doublet's.

62. Doublet's edition of K43B, no. 27 appears in *Histoire*, pp. 968–73.

63. Doublet's edition of K 43B, no. 27[bis] is found in *Histoire*, pp. 973–75.

64. "Brie conte Robert. [Coppie de la, *inserted*] Chartre de Lan [*two dates linked by* et *and heavily crossed out, with* 1343 *written above the second date*] par laquelle Jeanne Roine de france et de Nauarre. Donne a LEglize et abbaye St Denis 156 l. tournois de rente en plusieurs parties Scauoir 32 l. parisis de rente deubz par Les habitans de fresnay en beauuoisins a Cheurieres 11 l. 9 s. de cens pour Lestimation de 229 chappons Cinquante Solds parisis de rente sur Jean de Gauchy esc., 10 s. par. aussj de rente sur La Haulte Justice de cheurieres, Plus 94 l. 3 s. 9 d. tournois de rente a prendre sur La Chastellenie de brie conte Robert en Suitte de Laquelle chartre est La coppie d'vne Lettre du Roy philippe comme Il permet A

Lad. Dame et Reine [Iusques *crossed out*] de donner aux eglizes Jusques a 500 l. de rente A Les tenir par ceux ausquels elle en aura fait Le don comme Amortis, Auec vne autre chartre Dicelle Reine datté de Lan 1343 Comme elle fait pareillement donation a Lad. abbaye de Sa belle Chasse dargent doréé pesant 53 marcs Auec Les reliques estant dedans, 33 l. de rente aux Charittez, 100 l. de rente pour La fondation de La Chapelle nre. dame, 18 l. aussj de rente pour fournir aux ornementz et Lentretien d'vne Lampe, & cent sols pour Les sonneurs Le tout montant par an 156 l. quj est pareille somme que celle mentionnéé en la chartre precedente, Le tout amorty, Plus vne Image d'argent doré pesant 36 marcz vne Image dor de st. Jean Leuangeliste & vne couronne dor enrichie de pierres precieuzes, Le tout a La Charge par Les Religieux de dire plusieurs obitz et messes." After this is written in ink in the eighteenth- (or nineteenth-) century hand that corrected the preceding summary: "Doublet p 973 vers le millieu de la page."

65. Curiously, the act omits the traditional *Salut*, found in the accompanying act.
66. MS *nres'*. I have expanded this abbreviation as *nostre seigneur* throughout the act, and have expanded *nre'* as *nostre*.
67. *Abbe/Abbes* omitted.
68. MS *conio'inctement*.
69. I supply the bar; in the act, the line ends with *prester* and the next line begins with *donner*.
70. *Eglise* is written over an erasure.
71. *nos enfanz &*, squeezed in over an erasure.
72. I have inserted the bar; one line ends with *autres* and the next begins *Cest*.
73. *soustenir les adournemens &*, written over an erasure.
74. Jeanne's postmortem inventory listed one other *couronne*: "vne couronne dor dEmeraudes ou il y a 10 florons et sur chacun floron vne perle, et y a 10 troches de perles chacune de vj perles et en chacune troche vn petit rubiet dalexandrie," valued at 359 or 360 *francs d'or*: Leber, *Collection*, 19:122–23, here corrected from Rouen, Menant VI, fol. 74; BnF, fr. 7855, p. 343. The inventory also included two *coronnettes dor* (one valued at 120 and the other at 48 fr. d'or) and thirteen *chapels* and *chapelets*, of which one *bon chapel* with various large stones was valued at 4000 *francs d'or* and another *chapel* at a fifth of this sum. Menant omitted the texts of four entries (describing six of the thirteen *chapels* or *chapelets*), which are found in BnF, fr. 7855, p. 344.
75. I.e., *troches* (bouquets); see Leber, *Collection* 19:123.
76. I have added this bar.
77. MS *ten'*, *tenuz* in Doublet. But note *tenus* above.
78. The bar is written over an erasure.
79. Corrected from *Nos*.
80. I have added this bar; one line ends *fiez* and the next begins *arrerefiez*.
81. Probably Fresnoy-en-Thelle (Oise, ar. Senlis, c. Neuilly-en-Thelle), some thirty km. southeast of Beauvais.
82. January 13.
83. Chevrières (Oise, ar. Compiègne, c. Estrées-Saint-Denis) is located due west of the forest of Compiègne, approximately fifteen km. southwest of Compiègne.
84. *Onze* is corrected over an erasure.
85. From *Quatre* through *d.*, several letters are written over erasures.
86. *aus ... leur* written over an erasure.
87. *s Sains /* written over an erasure, with letters widely spaced.

88. *admortie . . . A la* written over an erasure and squeezed into the space.
89. MS *dces'*.
90. MS *dces'*.
91. *quatorze* is written over an erasure, squeezed in.
92. *Nous* is written over an erasure.
93. *ou personnes* written over an erasure.
94. MS *deglis'*; below, *personnes deglises.*
95. Generally the scribe who wrote this act spelled this word *Religieux* and hence I have silently expanded all abbreviated *Relig'* (when the plural noun is required) to *Religieux*; in no. 27, the plural noun is regularly rendered *Religieus.*

Contributors

Dorsey Armstrong is Associate Professor of Medieval Literature in the English Department at Purdue University, where she teaches courses on late medieval literature, Anglo-Saxon language and literature, gender and Women's Studies, and the medieval world. Her main research interest is Arthurian literature; her book *Gender and the Chivalric Community in Sir Thomas Malory's Morte d'Arthur* was published by University Press of Florida in 2003. She has recently become the editor-in-chief of *Arthuriana*, the premier academic quarterly on Arthurian subjects.

Geoffrey Ashe is the author of more than twenty-five books, mainly on historical and legendary topics, especially the Arthurian legend. They have been translated into French, German, Spanish, Japanese, and Korean. He has contributed to *Speculum* and other journals and held visiting professorships at universities in the US and Canada. He was co-founder and secretary of the Camelot Research Committee, which excavated Cadbury Castle in Somerset and established the importance of this reputedly Arthurian site in post-Roman Britain. He received an MBE, "Historian: For Services to Heritage," from Queen Elizabeth II in 2012. He is married with four sons and a daughter. (See further the biography in *Contemporary Authors*, vol. 192 [Gale Group, 2002], pp. 14–34).

Ann W. Astell (PhD, 1987) was Professor of English and chair of Medieval Studies at Purdue University prior to her appointment as Professor at the University of Notre Dame in 2007 in the Department of Theology. The recipient of an NEH Fellowship and of a John Simon Guggenheim Memorial Fellowship, she is the author of six books: *The Song of Songs in the Middle Ages*

(1990); *Job, Boethius, and Epic Truth* (1994); *Chaucer and the Universe of Learning* (1996); *Political Allegory in Late Medieval England* (1999); *Joan of Arc and Sacrificial Authorship* (2003); and *Eating Beauty: The Eucharist and the Spiritual Arts of the Middle Ages* (2006). She is the editor of five essay collections: *Divine Representations: Postmodernism and Spirituality* (1994); *Lay Sanctity, Medieval and Modern: A Search for Models* (2000); (with Bonnie Wheeler) *Joan of Arc and Spirituality* (2003); (with Justin Jackson) *Levinas and Medieval Literature* (2009); and (with Sandor Goodhart) *Sacrifice, Scripture, and Substitution: Readings in Ancient Judaism and Christianity* (2011).

Elizabeth A. R. Brown attended Swarthmore College and received her AM and PhD from Radcliffe Graduate School and Harvard. She has taught at Harvard, the Ecole pratique des Hautes Etudes, NYU, and Yale, and is Professor of History Emeritus from Brooklyn College and the Graduate School, The City University of New York. Her publications include *The Monarchy of Capetian France and Royal Ceremonial* (1991), *Politics and Institutions in Capetian France* (1991), *Customary Aids and Royal Finances in Capetian France: The Marriage Aid of Philip the Fair* (1992), and *Saint-Denis, la basilique* (2001). She is a Fellow, former President of the Fellows of the Academy, and President of the Medieval Academy of America in 2010–11, and also a corresponding member of the Société nationale des antiquaires and the Société de l'histoire de France.

Annemarie Weyl Carr has published *Byzantine Illumination 1150–1250: The Study of a Provincial Tradition* (University of Chicago Press, 1987), *A Byzantine Masterpiece Recovered: The Thirteenth-Century Murals of Lysi, Cyprus* (University of Texas Press, 1991), *Cyprus and the Devotional Arts of Byzantium in the Era of the Crusades* (Ashgate, 2005), and many articles on Byzantine and Levantine art during the Crusades. She edited and contributed extensively to a volume on the church of Asinou, Cyprus (forthcoming, Dumbarton Oaks), edited the journal *Gesta*, served as the president of the International Center of Medieval Art, and taught for years at Southern Methodist University, where she is University Distinguished Professor of Art History Emerita.

Howell Chickering is the G. Armour Craig Professor of Language and Literature in the English Department at Amherst College. He is the author of *Beowulf: A Dual-Language Edition* (1977; 3rd ed., 2006) and numerous articles on Old English poetry, Middle English poetry, and Chaucer. He co-edited (with Thomas H. Seiler) the TEAMS volume *The Study of Chivalry: Resources and Approaches* (1988) and has edited four other books on medieval music, literature, and interdisciplinary pedagogy. He has been a co-leader, staff member, or evaluator on eight NEH medieval projects. He is currently co-editing (with Allen Frantzen and R. F. Yeager) *Teaching "Beowulf" in the Twenty-first Century*, to be published by the Arizona Center for Medieval and Renaissance Studies in the MRTS series in 2013, and is writing a book to be entitled *Chaucer and the Sound of Poetry*.

WILLIAM W. CLARK is Professor of Art History at Queens College of the City University of New York. He is a specialist in twelfth-century architecture and sculpture, as well as nineteenth-century French architectural photography, who has published on a number of Gothic churches in northern France, including the cathedrals of Paris, Laon, Lisieux, and Reims, as well as the abbeys of Saint-Denis and Saint-Germain-des-Prés and other Parisian monuments. His most recent book is *Medieval Cathedrals*, published by Greenwood in 2006.

JEFFREY JEROME COHEN is Professor of English and Director of the Medieval and Early Modern Studies Institute at the George Washington University. His books include *Hybridity, Identity and Monstrosity in Medieval Britain: Of Difficult Middles*; *Medieval Identity Machines*; and *Of Giants: Sex, Monsters, and the Middle Ages*. He is the editor of the collections *Cultural Diversity in Medieval Britain: Archipelago, Island, England*; *Thinking the Limits of the Body*; *The Postcolonial Middle Ages*; *Becoming Male in the Middle Ages*; and *Monster Theory: Reading Culture*. His articles have appeared in *Exemplaria*, *Speculum*, and the *Journal of Medieval and Early Modern Studies*.

GILES CONSTABLE is Professor Emeritus at the Institute for Advanced Study in Princeton. Previously he taught at the University of Iowa and Harvard University, and was Director of Dumbarton Oaks in Washington, DC. He is a Fellow and past President of the Medieval Academy of America. He has written and edited some twenty volumes and over a hundred articles. His main interests are in the religious life of the eleventh and twelfth centuries, especially monasticism and the Crusades.

KELLY R. DEVRIES is Professor of History at Loyola University Maryland and the author of more than sixty articles on medieval military history and technology. His books include (among others) *Joan of Arc: A Military Leader*; *The Artillery of the Dukes of Burgundy, 1363–1477* (with Robert D. Smith); and *Medieval Military Technology*. His *Cumulative Bibliography of Medieval Military History and Technology* (and updates) received the 2007 J. F. Verbruggen Prize for achievement in medieval military history. He was recently appointed Honorary Historical Consultant at the Royal Armouries, UK.

D. THOMAS HANKS, JR., has been writing and teaching about Malory, with excursions into Chaucer, since 1987. His chief works on Malory's style have appeared in *Arthurian Literature* (2006); *Re-Viewing Le Morte Darthur*, ed. D. S. Whetter and Raluca L. Radulescu (2005); *Arthuriana* (2003); *The Malory Debate* (2000), ed. Bonnie Wheeler et al.; and seminally, with Jennifer Fish, in "Beside the Point: Medieval Meanings vs. Modern Impositions in Editing Malory's Morte Darthur," *Neuphilologische Mitteilungen* 98 (1997): 273–89. A professor of English at Baylor University since 1976, Hanks has won every teaching award the university offers.

KEVIN HARTY is Professor and Chair of English at La Salle University in Philadelphia. He is the author or editor of a dozen books and has published more than sixty refereed scholarly essays. His recent scholarship focuses on literature and film about Robin Hood, King Arthur, and Joan of Arc.

DONALD L. HOFFMAN is Emeritus Professor at Northeastern Illinois University. He has published widely on Arthurian topics in Medieval and Modern literature and culture. His co-edited book (with Elizabeth Sklar), *King Arthur in Popular Culture*, appeared in 2002. His most recent publication is "Chahine's *Destiny*: Prophetic Nostalgia and the Other Middle Ages," in *Race, Class, and Gender in "Medieval" Film*, ed. Lynn T. Ramey and Tison Pugh (Palgrave, 2007).

WILLIAM CHESTER JORDAN is Dayton-Stockton Professor of History and Chair of the Department of History at Princeton University. He is the author of several books dealing with French political history in the thirteenth century, serfdom and manumission, Jewish-Christian relations, women and credit, the Great Famine of the early fourteenth century, and church-state relations in the same period. His most recent book (2009) is a comparative study of two great English and French abbeys, *A Tale of Two Monasteries: Westminster and Saint-Denis in the Thirteenth Century*.

MAURICE KEEN was educated at Winchester College and at Balliol College, Oxford, graduating with Honours in History in 1957, and going on afterwards to doctoral research. In 1961 he was elected a Fellow of Balliol as Tutor in Medieval History, which post he held till his retirement in 2000. In 1990 he was elected a Fellow of the British Academy. He wrote half a dozen books on medieval topics, including his *Chivalry* (1984), which won the Wolfson Prize for history. He died in 2012.

EDWARD DONALD KENNEDY is Professor Emeritus of English and Comparative Literature at the University of North Carolina at Chapel Hill. His publications include *Chronicles and Other Historical Writing* (vol. 8 of *A Manual of the Writings in Middle English*, ed. A. E. Hartung [New Haven: Connecticut Academy of Arts and Sciences, 1989]), and *King Arthur: A Casebook* (Garland, 1996; Routledge, 2002) and close to one hundred articles and reviews, primarily on Arthurian subjects and chronicles. He was editor of *Studies in Philology* for twelve years and served as subject editor for English and Scottish chronicles for the forthcoming *Encyclopedia of the Medieval Chronicle* (Brill, 2010).

ALAN LUPACK, Director of the Rossell Hope Robbins Library and an Adjunct Professor of English at the University of Rochester, is the author of *The Oxford Guide to Arthurian Literature and Legend*. Former President of the North American Branch of the International Arthurian Society, he is co-author of *King Arthur in America* and editor or co-editor of four collections of post-medieval Arthurian texts. He serves as the Associate editor of the TEAMS Middle English Texts Series, for which he has edited two volumes; and he is the creator of the electronic database The Camelot Project.

NADIA MARGOLIS specializes in the later French Middle Ages, having mainly published on Christine de Pizan and Joan of Arc. Currently Visiting Professor of French and Medieval Studies at Mount Holyoke College, she has lectured and taught at universities in Europe and the UK as well as in the United States. Her latest book, *An Introduction to Christine de Pizan*, was published by the University Press of Florida in 2011.

ELIZABETH S. SKLAR is Professor of English at Wayne State University, where she teaches Old and Middle English language and literature. Her area of scholarly specialization is Arthurian Studies. She has published extensively on the Matter of Arthur, both medieval and modern. Her co-edited book (with Donald L. Hoffman), *King Arthur in Popular Culture*, appeared in 2002. She has served two terms on the Executive Advisory Council of the International Arthurian Society/North American Branch, and recently completed a ten-year term as Area Chair for the Arthurian Legend section of the Popular Culture Association. She is currently a member of the editorial board of *Arthuriana*.

STEPHEN STALLCUP (1970–2009) studied Medieval Studies and English at Southern Methodist University, where he was awarded an NEH Young Scholar Fellowship. He received his PhD from Princeton University. He had been an Assistant Professor of English at the University of North Carolina at Greensboro, where he taught courses in medieval and early modern literature. His scholarship focused on Arthurian topics and Ricardian literature, and he was revising a book manuscript on *Representing the King in Ricardian England*. He died unexpectedly of meningitis during the preparation of this volume, shortly after this article was completed.

Lorraine Kochanske Stock teaches Chaucer, Middle English, and continental medieval literature and films that adapt medieval texts at the University of Houston. She has published many articles on various aspects of Medieval Studies and medievalism including medieval drama, Chaucer, *Piers Plowman*, the Gawain-Poet, Froissart's illustrators and translators, Dante, the *Roman de Silence*, the *Roman de la Rose*, the Wild Man and Woman, the Green Man, and Robin Hood. In 2005 she published *The Medieval Wild Man* (Palgrave). She currently is completing a monograph about medieval primitivism and the Wild Man figure.

Toshiyuki Takamiya was born in Tokyo in 1944. Professor Takamiya took a BEc, BA, MA at Keio University, Tokyo, and then went to Cambridge, UK, for three years of research. His academic interests lie in Malory and Caxton, the reception of the Middle Ages, and digital bibliography, about which subjects he has given a number of papers at international conferences and has published many books and articles in English and in Japanese. He has served as Director of the Humanities Media Interface Project at Keio University, digitizing more than a dozen sets of the Gutenberg Bible. He has an Honorary LittD from the University of Sheffield and an Honorary DLitt from the University of Glasgow. He has been a Director of the Early Book Society. In 2012 he edited, jointly with R. F. Yeager, *The Medieval Python: A Festschrift in Honour of Terry Jones*.

Anne Bagnall Yardley is Associate Professor of Music and Associate Academic Dean at Drew Theological School. She is the author of *Performing Piety: Musical Culture in Medieval English Nunneries* published by Palgrave/Macmillan in 2006, as well as numerous articles on music in medieval nunneries. She has also published on a variety of other topics including nineteenth-century Methodist music and the pedagogy of music in the seminary. Yardley received her undergraduate education at Whitman College and her musicological training at Columbia University where she received a PhD in 1975.

Index

Note: Page numbers in italics indicate figures and tables.

Abbey, Edwin Austin, 103
Abdullah (king of Saudi Arabia), 117
Abelard, Peter, 10–11
Acta Pilati, 189
Adams, Jeremy DuQuesnay, 3, 9, 219
"Adam Scriveyn" (Chaucer), 34
Adelaide de Maurienne: children of, 12, 201 (*see also* Constance de France); nunneries founded by, 13, 216n53; seal of, 204, 214n27; second marriage of, 216n53
Admont Abbey (Austria), 11, 155
advertisements and marketing: "Holy Grail" in, 112, 113, 115–18, 119nn6–7; of *Joan the Woman*, 139; of Michelin tires, 101, *102*; of Moreau's WWI memoir, 133; of music, 106
Agincourt, English victory at, 125
Alanus de Insulis, 76
Aldgate Priory chants, 171, 178, 181n14
Alençon, duke of, 126, 127, 128
Alexander III (pope), 202, 210
Alexander of Lincoln, 72, 76
Alfred of Beverley, 62
Allen, Rosamund, 81, 82
alliteration: in *The Knight's Tale*, 55; in *Le Morte Darthur*, 83, 84–85, 88n17
L'Alouette (The Lark, play), 10, 146, 147–48, 150n21
Ambrosius (Merlin), 73. *See also* Merlin

Anderson, George, 4–5
Andrew of Wyntoun, 92
Andronikos II Palaiologos, 188
Angelic Pope, 77–78
Anglicization, 25–26
Anouilh, Jean: Hellman's adaptation of play by, 10, 147–48, 150n21; Joan of Arc play of, 146, 147–48; as "penseur artisanal" (artistic thinker), 145; WORKS: *L'Alouette* (The Lark), 146, 147–48, 150n21; *Antigone* (adaptation), 145; *Pauvre Bitos*, 145
Anselme de Sainte Marie, Augustin Déchaussé, 201
Antigone (play), 145, 146
De antiquitate Glastoniensis ecclesie (William of Malmesbury), 65
Antoine (duke of Brabant), 125
ANZAC (Australian and New Zealand Army Corps), 135, 140n10
Apokaukos, John, 187
Apollo (deity), 192–93
Arcite: fall of, 47–53; fury that spooked horse of, 6, 44–47, 56–57n12; line 2689 concerning, 48, 53, 54–56; questions about, 43–44
Argus (periodical), 135
Armes Prydein ("The Omen of Britain," poem), 72
Arrabit, John, 202

Arthour and Merlin (Auchinleck Manuscript), 52
Arthur (king): English kings' appropriation of story, 62–68; failure of kingdom, 89, 91; Geoffrey's history of, 7, 30, 61–65, 67; Joan of Arc compared with, 9; in *Lancelot of the Laik* and *Lancelot do Lac*, 89–94; "Poisoned Apple" episode of, 93–94; pseudo-prophecies about, 75, 76; seal of, 68; as symbol of Welsh glory, 30, 64, 71; tomb supposedly discovered, 7, 61–62, 64–65, 67; wise man's lecture to, 91–92, 94. See also *Le Morte Darthur*
Arthuriana: approach to studying, 6–9; French claims to authority juxtaposed to, 62–63; Geoffrey's history as framework for, 71 (see also *History of the Kings of Britain*); popularity among WWI youth, 8; "strength of ten" idea in, 8, 97, 99, 101, 103–4, 106–8. See also Arthur; Arthurian youth groups; Galahad; Geoffrey of Monmouth; Googled Grail; Guenevere; Holy Grail; Lancelot; Malory, Thomas; Merlin; Tennyson, Alfred Lord; *The Wife of Bath's Tale*
Arthuriana (journal), 2–3, 81, 82
Arthurian Society (Oxford University), 6
Arthurian Studies in Honour of P. J. C. Field (Wheeler), 6
Arthurian youth groups: Burne-Jones's plan for, 98; Galahad as model for, 101, 103–4, *105*, 106–7; manual of, 103, *105*. See also chivalry
Arts and Entertainment (A&E) Network, 3
Arviragus (British king), 67
Ashe, Geoffrey: essay by, 71–79; references to, 7
Assertion (John Leland), 68
Astell, Ann W.: introduction by, 1–14; references to, 148
Auchinleck Manuscript (*Arthour and Merlin*), 52
audience: oral/aural prose for, 81–87; reading vs. listening of, 80–81
Augustine (saint), 73–74
aural/oral culture: *Le Morte Darthur* in context of, 81–87
Australia: Joan of Arc referenced in WWI films of, 133–35, 140–41n11
Australian and New Zealand Army Corps (ANZAC), 135, 140n10
Australian Variety (periodical), 133
Auxerre: Dominicans of, 224; treaty signed at, 124
Avalon: Glastonbury's connection to, 61–62, 65–66
Aveline de Beaussault, 160
awenyddion (Welsh seers), 74

Bacon, Roger, 77
Bacqué, Patrick, 214n29
Baltimore *Sun*, 108
Baltoyianne, Chrysanthe, 191
Barbour, John, 92
Barking Abbey (London): chants listed, *174*; *Dominus Ihesus* chant at, 180n5; *Mandatum pauperum* at, 11–12, 169, 172–74, 177; ordinal of, 171, 172–73, 178, 181n14
Baron, Françoise, 243–44n41
Barthélemy de Fontaines, 160
Bartholomew (saint), 192
Bartlett, Robert, 25
battles: Agincourt, 125; in Armagnac-Burgundian civil war, 124–25; Joan of Arc's attack on Paris, 9–10, 123, 125–29; Loos, 133–34, 140n9. See also World War I
Baudouin (Constance's son), 202, 212n11
Bautier, Robert-Henri, 205
BBC, 3
Becoisel-en-Brie Abbey, 242n32
Bede (saint), 63
Bedos-Rezak, Brigitte, 204, 205
Beidler, Peter G., 37–38, 42n26
Benedictines. See Barking Abbey
Benedict XVI (pope), 117
Beowulf: Japanese studies of, 19–21, 23n8; *Ukiyoe* block prints juxtaposed to scenes of, 17, 22n1; women's role in, 20–22. See also "Grendel's Mother"

Berger, Thomas, 107
Berné, Damien, 219, 222, 239n17, 242–43n34
Bernstein, Leonard, 147
Bertram, William, 135
Besson, Benno, 143
Bethduras citadel (plain of Ascalon), 202, 209
Betrayal (Bouts), 184, 187, 191
Betrayal (Dürer), 184
Bibb, Eloise Alberta, 103, 109n21
biblical references: Genesis, 189, 191; Judges, 52; Psalms, 51; Lamentations, 50–51; Matthew, 177; Mark, 170; Luke, 12, 170, 172; John, 169, 170, 172; Revelation, 1–2
Biddick, Kathleen, 32n8
Bival Abbey (France): charters recording grants to, 11, 160, 166; debts of, 162–63, 166; decline of conditions at, 165–67; disobedient (*diffamati*) nuns of, 160–62, 164; forged charter of, 159; stability at, 163–64
Black Sheep Brewery, 117
Blaetz, Robin, 138
Blair, Tony, 117
Blake, N. F., 88n17
Blanche of France (Jeanne d'Évreux's daughter), 217, 225, 242n30, 244n46, 244n48
Blanche of France (Louis IX's daughter), 240–41n21
Blessed Bastard (Lehmann), 97
Blome, John, 65–66
Board, Marilynn Lincoln, 97–98
Boardman, Steve, 96n13
Boar of Cornwall, 75, 76
Boccaccio, Giovanni: *chiose* (glosses) of, 47; Christine de Pizan's response to, 1; on fury that spooked Arcite's horse, 6, 43, 44–45, 46–47, 56–57n12; works: *The Book of Theseus*, 46, 57n15; *De mulieribus claris*, 1. See also *Teseida*
Body of Polycye (Christine de Pizan), 91
Boethius, 1
Bonaventure (saint), 188
Bond, George, 13

Bondeville Abbey (France), 159
Boniface VIII (pope), 64
The Book of the City of Ladies (*Le Livre de la Cité des Dames*, Christine de Pizan), 1
The Book of Theseus (Boccaccio), 46, 57n15
Boss, Eleanor, 101
Boston Public Library murals, 103
Bourgeois of Paris, 128–29
Bouts, Dirk, 184, 187, 191
Bouvier, Jacques, 127
Bower, Walter, 92
"boy problem," 103, 106
Bragadin, Marcantonio (Venetian general), 12, 192–93
Braithwaite, Richard, 36
Brasillach, Robert, 10, 145
Brecht, Bertolt: "epic theater" idea of, 143; on HUAC, 145; influences on, 143–44; Joan of Arc plays of, 10, 143–45; WORKS: *Dreigroschenoper* (Threepenny Opera), 143; *Galileo*, 144–45; *Die Gesichte der Simone Machard* (The Visions of Simone Machard), 143; *Die Heilige Johanna der Schlachthöfe* (Saint Joan of the Stockyards), 10, 143–44; *Der Prozess der Jeanne d'Arc zu Rouen* (The Trial of Joan of Arc at Rouen, adaptation), 143
Brennius (legendary king), 68
Brie-Comte-Robert: Jeanne d'Évreux's last days at, 217, 238n8, 244n48; location of, 237n1; revenues from, 226, 245n58
Brobdingnagian Bards (band), 118
Brown, Dan, 112, 119n4, 169
Brown, Elizabeth A. R.: essay by, 217–47; references to, 12, 13
Browne, Peter Emerson, 136
Brown University, Wheeler as student at, 4–5, 14n5
The Bruce (Barbour), 92
Brunel, Ghislain, 240–41n21
Brutus (legendary founder), 75
Budrys, Algis, 107
Bukofzer, Manfred F., 180n2, 181n8
Burne-Jones, Edward, 97–98, 99

258   Index

Burns, James, 99, *100*, 101
Burri, Emil, 143
Bury St. Edmunds chants, 179, 181n14
business development: "Holy Grail" of, 112, 113–15, 119n6. *See also* advertisements and marketing
Byron, Robert, 184
Byzantine tradition: *Christ Drawn to the Cross* icon of, *186*, 187–88; iconography of Passion of, 12, 184, 187–89, 194–95n6, 195n7; metaphors of Christ's body in, 189, 191, 193; single Christ Helkomenos icons and, 189, *190*, 191–92. See also *Espolio* (El Greco)

Cagny, Perceval de, 125, 126–27
Canteaut, Olivier, 240n21
The Canterbury Tales (Chaucer): authorial anxiety about critics of, 34–35; Riverside edition noted, 44, 47; vernacular and context of writing, 26; SPECIFIC: *The Franklin's Tale*, 30; *The Man of Law's Tale*, 5, 30; *The Merchant's Tale*, 29; *The Miller's Tale*, 37; *The Nun's Priest's Tale*, 29; *Sir Thopas*, 5–6, 29; *The Squire's Tale*, 29, 99; *The Summoner's Tale*, 28; *Troilus and Criseyde* (Chaucer), 5, 30, 34, 35, 45. See also *The Knight's Tale*; *The Wife of Bath's Tale*
Capetians, 62–63. See also Constance de France; Jeanne d'Évreux
Caradoc, 62
Carley, John, 66
Carmarthen, 72, 73
Carr, Annemarie Weyl: essay by, 183–98; references to, 12
Carter, Jimmy, 108
cartoons, 108
Cather, Katherine Dunlap, 106
Catholic Church: Henry VIII's Arthurian-based claims in rejecting, 68; letter from abbot to abbess in, 11, 155–57; penance process in, 171. *See also* chants; Jesus Christ; Joan of Arc; monasteries and abbeys; Virgin Mary; *and specific institutions, popes, and saints*

Cavell, Edith: films about, 135, 140–41n11, 141n12; as WWI martyr and heroine, 10, 134–35
Caxton, William, 68, 89, 93
Celestine V (pope), 77
Celts: Arthuriana linked to, 31, 62; Chaucer on, 29–30; druidism and, 72; as "fringe," 25; hopes for resurgence, 75. *See also* Wales
Chailly, Hugh de, 209
Chakrabarty, Dipesh, 25
chants: as aural incense, 174–75; instructions for, 169–70; list of, 181n8; Mary Magdalene–related, 172, 177, 178–79, 182n21; BY LOCATION: Aldgate Priory, 171, 178, 181n14; Barking Abbey, *174*, 180n5; Bury St. Edmunds, 179, 181n14; Fécamp Abbey, 177, 179; Origny Ste-Benoîte, 177; St. Mary's Abbey, 179, 181n14; BY NAME: *In diebus illis mulier*, 172, 181–82n15; *Dominus Ihesus*, 170, 180n5; *Mandatum fratrum*, 170; *Mandatum novum*, 170, 171, 173, *174*, 180n2; *Maria ergo unxit*, 172, 173, *174*, 182n15; *O mirum et magnum*, *174*, 175–76; *Visitatio sepulchri*, 176. See also *Mandatum pauperum*
Chapuys, Eustace, 68
Charlemagne (Charles the Great), 62–63, 78
Charlemagne, Second. *See* Second Charlemagne
Charles (count of Claremont), 127
Charles IV (king of France): burial of and masses for, 219–20, 221, 222–23, 224, 225; chaplaincies endowed but two refused, 222, 242n32, 242–243n34; death of, 217; inscription references to, 223–24, 244n42; statue for chapel at Saint-Denis, 244n46; third wife and widow of (*see* Jeanne d'Évreux); will of, 237n2, 241n26
Charles V (king of France), 68, 218, 241n21
Charles VI (king of France), 124, 125
Charles VII (king of France): crowning of,

125; Joan of Arc's trial and, 146; role in failure of Joan's attack on Paris, 9, 123, 126, 127–28
Charles VIII (king of France), 78
Charles of Bourbon (abbot), 225–26
Charles of Navarre (Charles the Bad), 217
charters: Bival Abbey, 11, 159, 160, 166; Montmartre nunnery, 209, 210; Saint-Denis Abbey, 204, 209; Saint-Victor Abbey, 202, *203*, 204, 208–9, 215n40. *See also* Constance de France
Chartier, Jean, 125
Chatzedakes, Manoles, 184, 197n37
Chaucer, Geoffrey: alliteration used by, 55; authorial anxiety of, 34–35; background of, 26; Dame Natura as *magistra* and, 1; definitional looseness of, 54; England/Britain as described by, 28–32; Lady Murasaki compared with, 5; *Lancelot of the Laik* compared with works of, 90; rhyme structure of, 58n44; sources used by, 6, 45, 47–48, 95n4; status and legacy of, 31–32; WORKS: "Adam Scriveyn," 34; *Legend of Good Women*, 90. See also *The Canterbury Tales*
Cherewatuk, Karen, 81
Chester Processional, 171, 178, 181n14
Chesterton, G. K., 31
Le Chevalier de la Charrette (Chrétien de Troyes), 93, 94, 95n4, 95n7
Chicago Daily Tribune, 108
Chickering, Howell: introduction by, 1–14
children: Joan of Arc referenced in films for, 135–36, *137*, 138. *See also* youth
chivalry: Americanization of, 104, 106–7; Edward III's order for, 65; Galahad as model for, 103–4, *105*; moral view of, 99, 101, 106–7, 108. *See also* Arthuriana; Arthurian youth groups
Chrétien de Troyes, 93, 94, 95n4, 95n7
Christ. *See* Jesus Christ
Christ Drawn to the Cross (icon), *186*, 187–88. *See also Helkomenos epi Stavrou* (*Christ Drawn to the Cross*, icon)
Christ Helkomenos (icon), 189, *190*, 191–92

Christian Church: Glastonbury excavation interests of councils of, 66–67; Last Supper chalice and, 112–13; prophetic tradition of, 73–74, 77–78. *See also* Catholic Church; Jesus Christ; Orthodox Church; Virgin Mary
Christian Science Monitor, 108
Christine de Pizan: Joan of Arc and, 9, 142–43, 148; women celebrated by, 1; WORKS: *Body of Polycye*, 91; *The Book of the City of Ladies* (*Le Livre de la Cité des Dames*), 1; *Ditié de Jehanne d'Arc*, 142–43; *Mutacion de Fortune*, 149n3
Chronique (Saint-Rémy), 127
Church of the Holy Cross (Pelendri, Cyprus), *186*, 187–88
Cistericans. *See* Bival Abbey
Clairvaux, P. (abbot), 155–57
Clark, William W.: essay by, 201–16; references to, 12–13
class struggle: of Brecht's Joan of Arc, 143–44. *See also* Marxism; social class
Clement VI (pope), 241n23
Clementia of Hungary, 242–43n34
Clin, Marie Véronique, 9
Cohen, Jeffrey Jerome: essay by, 25–33; references to, 5, 8
Coleman, Joyce, 81, 82
Coleman, William, 57n15
Committee on Teaching Medieval Studies (Medieval Academy of America), 2
Confessio Amantis (Gower), 90, 91
Congress of Arras (1435)
Constable, Giles: essay by, 155–58; references to, 11
Constance de France (Countess of Saint-Gilles, sister of Louis VII): approach to studying, 11–12; biographical information on, 201–2, 211n3, 212n6, 213n12; charters of, listed, 208–10; Holy Land pilgrimage of, 202, 216n43; participation in charters of husband, 211–12n4; political identity of, 202, 204–5, 208; Saint-Denis charter of, 204, 209; Saint-Victor charter of, 202, *203*, 204, 208–9, 215n40; seal of, 202, *203*, 204–5, *206*, 208, 212n9;

Vincennes property of, 209, 215nn39–40. *See also* seals
Constantine the Great (emperor), 64, 67, 68
Conventual Maundy (weekly), 169–70, 172, 177, 178–79. *See also* Maundy Thursday ritual
Correale, Robert M., 56n5
Council of Constance, 66
Council of Editors of Learned Journals, 3
Council of Pisa, 66–67
Council of Siena, 66
Counter-Reformation, 184
Craft of Dying (text), 91
Crete: El Greco's departure from, 183, 191; El Greco's *Espolio* linked to icons of, 184, 187
Cronica de rebus Glastoniensibus (John of Glastonbury), 65
Crosby, Ruth, 82
Cutting, Mary S., 107
Cyprus: Christ in loincloth on icon of, 195n7; *Helkomenos epi Stavrou* (*Christ Drawn to the Cross*) icon of, *186,* 187–89; Venetian general flayed in, 12, 192–93

Dadaism, 18
Dagobert (king), 205, 220
Damascene, John, 191–92
The Damned (band), 116
Dante: Beatrice as *magistra* and, 1; on Celestine V and Joachim of Fiore, 77; Chaucer's reading of, 45; Furies of, 56–57n12, 56n5; Lancelot versions and, 90–91, 94; WORK: *Paradiso*, 77
Davidov, Aleksandra, 191
Davies, R. D., 25, 26
The Da Vinci Code (Brown), 169
Davis, Norman, 43
Dawes, Christopher, 116–17
Dean, Priscilla, 136
De Grasse, Joseph, 136, 138
della Porta, Guglielmo, 192
DeMille, Cecil B., 10, 138–39
Deruvian (missionary), 66
DeVries, Kelly R.: essay by, 123–31; references to, 9–10

Diana (deity), 43
Dick, Philip K., 132
The Disrobing of Christ (El Greco). See *Espolio*
Ditié de Jehanne d'Arc (Christine de Pizan), 142–43
Doe, Denisot, 131n23
Dominus Ihesus (chant), 170, 180n5
Dompierre, Henri de, 240n21
Donaldson, E. Talbot: on Arcite's injury, 6, 43, 44; Festschrift for, 13; on "pighte" and "pomel," 48–49, 50, 52, 54, 55; Wheeler as student of, 6, 14n7
Doncoeur, Paul, 146, 150n15
Doublet, Jacques, 223, 227, 239nn17–18
Douglass, Frederick, 103, 109n21
drama: Anouilh's Joan of Arc play, 146; Brecht's Joan of Arc plays, 143–45; female ogre tradition in, 22; Hellman's Joan of Arc play, 147–48; Joan of Arc deployed in, 10, 138, 142–43, 148–49
dreams: of Holy Grail, 116; *Lancelot of the Laik* framed as, 90, 91
Dreigroschenoper (Threepenny Opera, play), 143
Dreyer, Carl, 150n15
Dryden, John, 31, 46, 54
Dürer, Albrecht, 184
Duval-Arnould, Louis, 244n45

eBay, 116–17
Ecce Homo (icon), 189, 197n37
Edward I (king of England), 64–65, 68
Edward II (king of England), 65
Edward III (king of England), 65–66
Eglinton Tournament, 108
Eleanor of Aquitaine, 1, 12, 61, 63, 205, 208
Eleanor of Aquitaine (Parsons and Wheeler), 12
Eleanor of Castile, 64
El Greco (Domenikos Theotokopoulos): background and style of, 183–84, 194n4; icons of Christ Helkomenos in time of, 191–92. See also *Espolio*
Eliot, George, 78
Eliot, T. S., 107
Elliott, Robert, 136

England: Anglicization and its consequences in, 25–26; Arthur's story appropriated by monarchy, 62–68; Chaucer's version of, 5, 28–32; cult of Saint George appropriated in, 65, 67; iconography of Christ's Passion in, 188; romantic poem as colonial project of, 27–29; WWI battles of, 132–33. *See also* Arthuriana; Barking Abbey; Glastonbury Abbey; Westminster Abbey; *and specific kings*
Epiphanios of Salamis (saint), 189, 191
Ernis of Saint-Victor (abbot), 201, 202, 215n40
Espolio (El Greco): approach to studying, 12; illustration of, *185*; red robe symbol in, 12, 187–88, 189, 191; sources of, *186*, 187–88, *190*, 191–94; style of, 183–84, 194n4
Esztergom Staurathek (enamel), 187
Eudes Rigaud (abbot and archbishop), 11, 160–67, 201
Europe: call to provincialize, 25; Charlemagne's European unity of, 78; prophecies popular in, 75–76, 77–78. *See also specific countries*
Eustace (heir to English throne), 201, 202, 208, 211n3

fairy and fairie: definition of, 33n15; in *Sir Orfeo*, 27–29. *See also* Arthuriana
Farnese, Ottavio, 192, 193
Farnham, Clive, 133
Fauquembergue, Clément de, 126
Faust (Goethe), 143–44
Fécamp Abbey (Normandy), 177, 179
Felibien, Michel, 223, 239n18, 241n23
Feminea Medievalia I (journal), 5
Ferrar, Geraldine, 10, 138
Feuchtwanger, Lion, 143
Field, P. J. C.: on clause phenomenon, 88n14; edited collection in honor of, 6, 13; on Malory, 80, 81, 88n17
film: of Cavell as martyr and heroine, 134–35, 140–41n11; Joan of Arc, listed (pre-WWI era), 140n3; Joan of Arc referenced in and subject of (WWI era), 10, 132–39, *137*; of Moreau's WWI memoir, 133–34
flaying, 12, 191–93, 198n43
Flaying of Marsyas (Titian), 192–93
Fleming, Richard, 66
Fleming, Victor, 150n15
Floris and Blancheflour (text), 52
Floyd, Malcolm, 171
Fontanieu, Gaspard-Moïse-Augustin de, 238n8
Fontevrault, M. (abbess), 155–57
food and drinking: "Holy Grail" of, 117–18, 119nn6–7
footwashing. *See* Maundy Thursday ritual
Forbrush, William Byron, 103, *105*, 106
Foskolou, Vassilike, 188
France: Armagnac-Burgundian civil war in, 124–25; Capetian authority in, 62–63; Glastonbury tombs and England's precedence over, 66–67; Joan of Arc figure deployed in politics of, 10, 142–46, 148–49; post-WWII purge of rightists in, 145; rationale for Edward I's war with, 64; WWI battles of, 132–33. *See also* Paris; Toulouse; *and specific institutions*
France, Marie de, 27–28
The Franklin's Tale (Chaucer), 30
Freedberg, Sidney, 193
Freeman, Luba, 192
French Revolution, 143, 226, 245n60
Fresh Verdicts on Joan of Arc (Wheeler and Wood), 9
Fries, Maureen, 7, 13
Frome, Nicholas, 66
Fry, Christopher, 147, 148
Fury and furies: readings and misreadings of, 6, 44–47

Gaborit-Chopin, Danielle, 239n18, 243n41
Galahad: as model for American boys, 99, *100*, 101, 103–4, *105*, 106–7. See also *Sir Galahad*; "Sir Galahad"
Galehot (or Galiot), 90, 91, 92
Galen Representation And Integration Language (GRAIL), 117

Galileo (play), 144–45
Gaulle, Charles de, 145
Gavin, John C., 135
Gawain: in *Lancelot of the Laik*, 90, 92; tales of, 34, 37, 38, 42n23
Gene Recognition and Assembly Internet Link (GRAIL), 119n5
Geoffrey of Monmouth: Arthur depicted by, 7, 30, 61–65, 67; Chaucer's protagonists' names from, 30; Henry VIII's belief in, 68; Joan of Arc and, 142; Merlin depicted by, 7, 71, 72–77; on Welsh warrior, 28; WORKS: *The Prophecies of Merlin*, 72–76, 142. See also *History of the Kings of Britain*
George (saint), 65, 67
Gerald of Wales, 27, 61–62, 63, 74
Gérard de Caigni, 160
Germany: folk terms in, 39; icon of Christ's Passion in, 188. See also Brecht, Bertolt; World War I
Gerson, Jean, 9
Die Gesichte der Simone Machard (The Visions of Simone Machard, play), 143
Gilles Rigaud (abbot): departure from Saint-Denis, 243n39; endowments for abbey of, 219, 220, 222–23, 241n23, 243n40; installation as abbot, 225. See also Saint-Denis Abbey
Glastonbury Abbey (England), 7, 61–62, 64–66, 67
Goddess worship, 39
Godefroi de Leigni, 95n7
Goethe, Johann Wolfgang von, 143–44
Golden Legend (text), 170–71
Googled Grail: approach to studying, 8–9, 111–12, 118–19n2; defining, 112–13; parsing, 113–15; selling, 115–18
Gospel in Florence frieze, 194–95n6
Gospel Paris frieze, 194–95n6
Gower, John, 34, 37–38, 90, 91
grace: Catholic writing on, 155–57
Grail. See Googled Grail; Holy Grail
GRAIL (Galen Representation And Integration Language), 117
GRAIL (Gene Recognition and Assembly Internet Link), 119n5

Gray, Phoebe, 104
Great Britain. See England; Ireland; Scotland; Wales
Greco. See El Greco
Greece: iconography of Christ's Passion in, 184, 188. See also Crete; Cyprus
Gregory the Great (pope), 170–71
"Grendel's Mother" (Nagase): approach to studying, 5; composition of, 19–20; Nagase's remarks on, 20–21; text of, 20
Gressio, Pierre Tuepain de, 237n3
Gripiotis, John, 191
Guenevere (queen): in *Lancelot of the Laik* and *Lancelot do Lac*, 89–90, 92, 93–94; as *magistra*, 1; "Poisoned Apple" episode of, 93–94; tomb supposedly discovered, 7, 61–62, 64–65; in Vulgate *Lancelot*, 93; in *The Wedding of Sir Gawain and Dame Ragnell*, 38
Guy de Châtres (abbot): endowments for abbey of, 219, 221–22, 224–25, 241n23, 241n26, 242–43n34; liturgical lessons of, 243n35. See also Saint-Denis Abbey

Hadjinicolaou, Nicos, 184, 187
"hag": as category of female otherness, 35–36; etymology of, 36–39; use of term, 5–6
Hall, Winfield Scott, 106
Hallum, Robert, 66
Hamby, William H., 107
Hamel, Mary, 56n5
Hanks, D. Thomas, Jr.: essay by, 80–88; references to, 7
Hardyng, J., 67
Harper, Frances Ellen Watkins, 103
Harris, Julie, 147
Harty, Kevin: essay by, 132–41; references to, 10
Haruta, Setsuko, 21–22
Hary (Henry the Minstrel), 92
Haskins, Susan, 171
Hauptmann, Elisabeth, 143
Hayes, Gilbert, 91
Hearn, Lafcadio, 19
Die Heilige Johanna der Schlachthöfe (Saint

Joan of the Stockyards, play), 10, 143–44
Helena (saint), 67
Helkomenos epi Stavrou (*Christ Drawn to the Cross*, icon): examples of, *186*, *190*; iconography and context of, 187–89, 191–94
Hellman, Lillian, 10, 146, 147–48, 150n21
Heloise (abbess of the Paraclete), 1, 10–11
Heloise and the Paraclete (McLaughlin), 11
Hengist (leader), 73
Henry I (king of England), 75
Henry II (king of England): Arthurian interests of, 7, 61–64; Bival charter and, 159; daughter's marriage and, 208
Henry III (king of England), 163
Henry V (Holy Roman Emperor), 204
Henry V (king of England), 66, 67
Henry VI (king of England), 131n23
Henry VII (king of England), 67
Henry VIII (king of England), 7, 68
Hersey, Iain Ashley, 118
Hildegard of Bingen, 1, 77
Hill, Lucienne, 147
Hinton, Jane, 147
History Channel, 3
History of the Kings of Britain (*Historia regum Britanniae*, Geoffrey of Monmouth): Arthur's story in, 61–65, 67; Chaucer's characters' names drawn from, 30; English use of, 92; goal in writing of, 71; Merlin as character in, 72–77
Hoffman, Donald L.: essay by, 111–19; references to, 8–9
Hokusai, Katsushika, 17
Hollis, Stephanie, 37
Holmes, Lillian, 104
Holy Grail: Avalon/Glastonbury connection in romances about, 65–66; Burns's revision of story, 99, *100*, 101; clichéd nature of, 108, 118; current alternative beliefs about, 119n4; current common understandings of, 112–13; definitions of, 8; didactic Galahad tales of, 106; Googled grails compared with, 114–15; healing and drinking associations of, 117; Lancelot's failed quest for, 89. *See also* Googled Grail
"Holy Grail" (songs), 112, 118
"The Holy Grail" (Tennyson), 108
"The Holy Grail of Infosecurity" (essay), 119n5
Holy Land: Constance's pilgrimage to, 202, 216n43. *See also* Knights Templar
Hospitalers of Saint John (Jerusalem), 202, 209
Hrothgar (king of Danes), 22
HUAC (House Un-American Activities Committee), 145, 147, 148
Hugh of Saint-Germani-des-Prés (abbot), 201
Hugues Boilleau (Boisleau or Boiseau), 237n3
Hugues d'Oiry, 160
Hundred Years War (1337–1453), 124–25, 128
Hunters and Collectors (band), 112, 118

"Ibaraki" (Kabuki play), 22
icons and iconography: as influence on painting (see *Espolio*); of Passion of Christ, 12, 184, *186*, 187–94, *190*, 194–95n6, 195n7; seals linked to, 214n33
Idylls of the King (Tennyson), 104
The Impostor (film), 132
In diebus illis mulier (chant), 172, 181–82n15
Ine (Anglo-Saxon king), 63–64
Ingham, Patricia Clare, 33n14, 33n19
De instructione principum (Gerald of Wales), 61
International Arthurian Society—North American Branch. See *Arthuriana* (journal)
International Joan of Arc Society (Société Internationale de l'étude de Jeanne d'Arc), 9
Iola Leroy (Harper), 103
Ireland: English kings' authority in, 62–63, 67; English romantic writers on fairy world of, 27–29; marginalization of, 25, 26, 33n19

Ireland, John, 91
Isaac II Angelos (Byzantine emperor), 187, 196n15
Isabelle of Tarines (nun), 161
Italy: iconography of Christ's Passion in, 188
Iviron 5 (illuminated book), 188

James III (king of Scotland), 92–93, 96n16
Jansen, Katherine L., 171
Japan: *Beowulf* studies in, 19–21, 23n8; earthquake in Tokyo (1923), 18; female ogre tradition of, 22, 24n20; *Ukiyoe* block prints of, 17, 22n1. *See also* "Grendel's Mother"; Nagase, Kiyoko
Jeanne d'Arc. *See* Joan of Arc
Jeanne d'Évreux (queen of France): approach to studying, 13; burial of and masses for, 219–20, 221, 240n20; postmortem inventory for, 246n74; reliquary and relics of, 219–24, 241nn25–26, 242n29; statue for chapel at Saint-Denis, 244n46; testamentary activities of, summarized, 217–18; TESTAMENTARY ENDOWMENT OF SAINT-DENIS: description, 219–26; explanation of French text, 226–27; French text, 227–36
Jeffery, Peter, 171, 172, 180n2
Jehannine theater. *See* drama
Jerome (saint), 51
Jesmok, Janet, 81, 88n15
Jesus Christ: body symbolized by purple robe, 189, 191, 193; chants for resurrection of, 176; iconography of Passion of, 12, 184, *186*, 187–94, *190*, 194–95n6, 195n7; relics of, 189, 219–21, 241nn25–26; on treatment of others, 177. *See also Espolio* (El Greco); Last Supper; Maundy Thursday ritual
Joachim of Fiore, 77–78
Joanna (queen of Sicily), *207*, 208, 215n36
Joan of Arc: approaches to studying, 9–10; canonization of, 139n2, 143; Christine de Pizan and, 1, 142–43, 148; film treatments of (WWI era), 10, 132–39, *137*; Paris attacked by, 9–10, 123, 125–29; politicized in theatrical dramas, 10, 142–49; trial and death of, 9, 139n2, 146
Joan of Arc (Clin and Pernoud), 9
Joan of Arc (film), 150n15
Joan of Arc (trans. Adam; Wheeler), 9
Joan of Arc (Trask), 148
Joan of Arc and Spirituality (Astell and Wheeler), 9
The Joan of Arc of Loos (film), 133–34, 136, 140n7
Joan of Plattsburg (originally called *Joan of Flatbush*, film), 10, 136, *137*, 142n14
Joan the Woman (film), 10, 138–39
Johanek, P., 63
John of Damascus, 189
John of Fordun, 92
John of Gaunt, 26
John of Glastonbury, 65–66, 67
Johns, Susan M., 213n24
Johnston, Annie Fellows, 8, 104, 106
John the Baptist (saint), 220
John the Evangelist (saint): Saint-Denis chapel and relics of, 220–21, 224, 225, 226, 241–42n27; status of, 13
John the Fearless: Joan of Arc compared with, 9; lessons of, 128–29; Paris captured by, 123, 124–25
Jordan, William Chester: essay by, 159–68; references to, 11
Joseph of Arimithea, 7, 65–67
Journal du siège d'Orléans, 123, 128
Die Jungfrau von Orleans (The Maid of Orleans, play), 138, 143–44, 149n9

Kagan, Richard, 193
Keen, Maurice: essay by, 61–70; references to, 7
Kelemen, Pál, 194n4
Kennedy, Edward Donald: essay by, 89–96; references to, 7–8
Kerrebrouck, Patrick Van, 212n6
Kilkenny, Statutes of, 26
Kindrick, Robert L., 6
King, Jane, 133
Kirk, Elizabeth D., 4–5, 13

Knepler, Henry, 148
Knights of King Arthur (club), 103, 106
The Knight's Tale (Chaucer): alliteration in, 55; approach to studying, 6; definitions and contexts of words in, 47–53; *occupatio* device in, 90; readings and misreadings of fury in, 44–47; verbal problems in, 43. *See also* Arcite
Knights Templar, 209. *See also* Hospitalers of Saint John
Kolve, V. A., 46, 47
Kosmas the Melode, 187, 195n14
Ku Klux Klan, 139
Kuniyoshi, Utagawa, 17
Kuriyagawa, Fumio, 19

Lambert, Mark, 80
Lancelot: in Chaucer's tales, 29; in *Lancelot of the Laik* and *Lancelot do Lac*, 89–94; Malory's alliteration and, 84–85; Malory's and Scots-English versions compared, 89, 91–94; in *The Marriage of Sir Gawain*, 38; "Poisoned Apple" episode of, 93–94; "strength of ten" phrase linked to, 107; in Vulgate *Lancelot*, 93
Lancelot do Lac (noncyclic French prose): Lancelot's knighting in, 93–94; Malory's plotline and, 8; optimistic ending of, 89, 90–91; Vulgate *Lancelot* based on, 93; wise man's lecture to Arthur in, 91–92, 94
Lancelot of the Laik (Scots-English text): approach to studying, 7–8; date of, 92–93; description of, 89–92; *Le Morte Darthur* compared with, 91–94
Langland, William, 37
Langtoft, Peter, 64
language: *magister/magistra* in medieval Latin, 2; periodization of English, 30–31; style distinguished from, 80; Wheeler's study of Old Norse, 14n5. *See also* Middle English
Lansing, Frank, 135
The Lark (*L'Alouette*, play), 10, 146, 147–48, 150n21
Last Judgment (Michelangelo), 192, 193

Last Supper: Christ's chalice at, 112–13; Mary Magdalene's presence felt at, 11–12, 169–71, 172; relics of, 220, 241n26. *See also* Holy Grail; *Mandatum pauperum*; Maundy Thursday ritual
Last Supper (Leonardo da Vinci), 169
Lateran Council, Fourth, 171
Layamon (priest), 57n17, 63
Leber, Jean-Michel-Constant, 238n8
lectio difficilior principle, 56
Leder, Gary, 132
Lefévre de Saint-Rémy, Jean, 127
Lefévre-Pontalis, Germain, 131n23
Legend of Good Women (Chaucer), 90
Leges Eadwardi Confessoris (text), 63
Lehmann, Ruth P. M., 97
Leland, John, 68
Léonard, Emile G., 211–12n4, 214n30
Leonardo da Vinci, 169
Le Pen, Jean-Marie, 142
The Letters of Heloise and Abelard (McLaughlin, completed by Wheeler), 11
Lewis, Andrew W., 212n6
Life of St. Gildas (Caradoc), 62
Lille, Alan de, 1
Lincoln, W. J., 135, 141n12
Linguistics for Students of Literature (Traugott and Pratt), 80
Lionel of Antwerp, 26
Listening to Heloise (Wheeler), 11
The Little Patriot (film), 135–36
Little Sir Galahad (Gray), 104
Little Sir Galahad (Holmes), 104
Le Livre de la Cité des Dames (*The Book of the City of Ladies*, Christine de Pizan), 1
Lloyd's Weekly News, 133, 140nn5–6
Loewen, Jan van, 146
Loomis, R. S., 31
Loos, battle of (1915), 133–34, 140n9
Louis VI (king of France), 12, 201, 216n53
Louis VII (king of France): death of, 204; Montmartre nunnery size and, 210; seal of, 205, *206*, 208; sister of (*see* Constance de France)

Louis VIII (king of France), 63
Louis IX (saint; king of France), 241nn25–26, 242n29
Louis X (king of France), 242–43n34
Louis XII (king of France), 226, 245n59
Louis of Orléans (duke), 124
Lucas, Angela M., 42n25
Luchaire, Achille, 212n6
Lupack, Alan: essay by, 97–110; references to, 8
Lupack, Barbara Tepa, 109n21
Lyall, R. J., 91
Lynch, Kathryn L., 33n15
Lyon, Bryce, 14n5

Macé, Laurent, 205, 214n29, 214n33
magistra doctissima title, 1–2
Major Barbara (play), 143
Malory (Lambert), 80
Malory, Thomas: approach to studying, 7; manuscript culture as context of, 80–82; poetic diction of, 83–85; prose style of, summarized, 86–87; rhetorical balance of, 85–86; sources of, 8, 93–94. See also *Le Morte Darthur*
The Malory Debate (Kindrick, Salda, and Wheeler), 6
mandatum: etymology of, 180n2; Jesus and Mary Magdalene both reflected in, 177
Mandatum fratrum (chant), 170
Mandatum novum (chant), 170, 171, *172*, 173, *174*, 180n2
Mandatum pauperum (chant): at Barking Abbey, 172–77, *174*, *175*–76; Mary Magdalene as key to, 11–12, 169, 177; ritual described, 169–70; sources on, 171–72, *172*, 178–79, 181n14. See also Last Supper; Mary Magdalene; Maundy Thursday ritual
Manly, John M., 58n36
Mannyng, Robert, 64
The Man of Law's Tale (Chaucer), 5, 30
manuscript culture, 81–82
Map, William, 27
Mapstone, Sally, 90, 94, 96n16
Marcellus II, 77

Margolis, Nadia: essay by, 142–51; references to, 7, 10
Marguerite of Aunay (abbess), 160–64
Marguerite of Cristot (abbess), 164–66
Marguerite of France (Philip V's daughter), 240–41n21
Maria ergo unxit (chant), 172, 173, *174*, 182n15
Marie of France (Jeanne d'Évreux's daughter), 217, 221, 225, 242n30, 244n46
The Marriage of Sir Gawain (tale), 34, 38
Mars (deity), 43
Marsh, Jeannette (earlier, Jeannette Marshall Denton), 83
Marsyas myth, 192–93
Martyrdom of Nurse Cavell (film), 135
Martyrium Chapel (Montmartre), 209
Marxism: Brecht's dramas and, 143–45; Hellman's version of, 147–48; Joan of Arc and variations of, 10. See also class struggle; social class
Mary Magdalene (saint): added to Last Supper image, 169; chants listed, 178–79; cult of and liturgy for, 11–12, 172, 177, 182n21; medieval understanding of, 170–71; relics of, 241n26; ritual reenactment of footwashing, 173–77. See also *Mandatum pauperum*; Maundy Thursday ritual
Mary of Champagne (abbess), 155
Mason, C. Post, 135
Mathilda (empress), 204
Mathilda I of Anjou (abbess), 155
Mathilda II (abbess), 155
Mathilda III (abbess), 155
Mathilda of Boulogne (queen of England), 201, 204
Maubuisson: endowments and burials at, 224, 240n20
maundy: etymology of, 180n2
Maundy, conventual (weekly), 169–70, 172, 177, 178–79
Maundy Thursday ritual: description of, 169–70; icon associated with, 197n37; instructions for, 173–74; Mary Magdalene as key to, 11–12, 169, 177; music

during, 171–72, *172, 175–76*; penitential understanding of, 171; sources on, 171–72, *172*, 178–79, 181n14. See also *Mandatum pauperum*
McCarthy, Terence, 88n17
McCarthy era (and HUAC), 145, 147, 148
McCoy, Bernadette Marie, 57n15
McLaughlin, Mary Martin, 11, 13
Meadows Museum of Spanish Art (Southern Methodist University), 183
Measure of Wysdome (Ireland), 91
Medici, Lorenzo de, 192, 198n43
Medieval Academy of America, Committee on Teaching Medieval Studies, 3
Medieval Institute Publications, 2
Medieval Mothering (Parsons and Wheeler), 5, 18
medieval studies: attitudes toward emendation of text, 55; multidisciplinary approach to, 4. See also Middle Ages; Wheeler, Bonnie
Medieval Studies in North America (journal), 3
Melkin (soothsayer), 65
Menant, Jacques, 218, 238n8
The Merchant's Tale (Chaucer), 29
Merlin, 7, 71, 72–77
Merlin (text), 53
Meroure of Wysdome (Ireland), 91
Metrical Chronicle (Robert of Gloucester), 49–50
Meyer, Robert J., 42n23
Micha, Alexandre, 93
Michel, Edmond, 239n18, 242n31
Michelangelo, 12, 192, 193
Michelet, Jules, 142, 149n2
Michelin tire advertisement, 101, *102*
Middle Ages: epistemological dismantling in, 25; influential books of, 71 (see also *History of the Kings of Britain*); letter to abbess in, 155–57; mothering in, 5, 18–22; otherness of, 30–31; romantic genre of, 27–30; saddles in, 53, 54–55. See also medieval studies
Middle English: *magister/magistra*, 2; *wyf* and *hag*, 35–36. See also Old and Middle English literature

Middle English Dictionary (*MED*), 48–49, 52, 57–58n28
Middle English Texts Series, 2
The Miller's Tale (Chaucer), 37
Millet, Germain, 242n29
Minamoto-no-Raiko, 22
Monaco, Lorenzo, 188
monasteries and abbeys: episcopal visitations to nunnery, 160–67; founding of Montmartre nunnery, 13; letter from abbot to abbess of, 155–57; relations among, 159–60. See also Byzantine tradition; Catholic Church; chants; charters; icons and iconography; Maundy Thursday ritual; relics; *and specific institutions*
Monemvasia (Greece): church and icon in, 187, 196n15; possible gift to, 188
Monreale mosaic, 187
Monstrelet, Enguerrand de, 125
Montesquiou-Fezensac, Blaise de, 239n18, 243n41
Montmartre nunnery (France), 13, 209–10
Montmorency, Adele (or Adelaide) de, 216n53
Montmorency, count of, 127, 128
Montmorency, Matthew de, 216n53
Monty Python and the Holy Grail (film), 117, 119n5, 119n7
Moreau, Émilienne, 10, 133–34, 136, 140nn5–6
Le Morte Darthur (Malory): approaches to studying, 7–8; English monarchial claims and, 68; *Lancelot of the Laik* compared with, 89, 91–94; manuscript culture as context of writing, 80–82; poetic diction of, 83–85; "Poisoned Apple" episode of, 93–94; prose style of, summarized, 86–87; rhetorical balance of, 85–86; "Tale of Lancelot" in, 94, 96n17
mothering. See "Grendel's Mother"
Moving Picture World (periodical), 136
De mulieribus claris (Boccaccio), 1
murals, 103
Murasaki Shikibu, 5

268   Index

music: advertisements for, 106; "Holy Grail" in, 116, 117–18; hymns noted, 187, 189, 196–97n30; processionals, 171, 176, 177–79, 181n14. *See also* chants
Mutacion de Fortune (Christine de Pizan), 149n3
Myrddin, 72. *See also* Merlin

Nagase, Kiyoko: approach to studying, 5; background of, 18–19, 22; WORK: "Grendel's Mother," 19–21
National Front Party (France), 142
nativism, 138–39
Natsume, Soseki, 19, 23n8
Nelson, William, 82
Nennius (monk), 73
Newman, John Henry, Cardinal, 117
The New Middle Ages series, 3
New Yorker (magazine), 108
Nishiwaki, Junzaburo, 19
Normand, Mabel, 136, *137*, 142n14
Norris, Chuck, 113
Nostradamus, 75–76
Notre-Dame Abbey (Paris), 222, 242n32, 242–243n34
Notre-Dame-la-Blanche chapel, 222, 225
nuns and spirituality: approach to studying, 10–12; letter from abbot to abbess, 155–57; penance process for, 171. *See also* Barking Abbey; Bival Abbey; Byzantine tradition; *Mandatum pauperum*; Mary Magdalene; Montmartre nunnery
The Nun's Priest's Tale (Chaucer), 29
Nurse Cavell (film), 135, 141n12

Ogura, Michiko, 24n20
Old and Middle English literature: "hag" as category of female otherness in, 35–36; Japanese teaching of, 19–20, 23n8; "Loathly Lady" or "Irish Sovereignty" type tales in, 34–39; Wheeler's study of, 4–5. *See also* Arcite; Chaucer, Geoffrey; "Grendel's Mother"; Nagase, Kiyoko
Old Norse language, 14n5

"The Omen of Britain" (*Armes Prydein*, poem), 72
O mirum et magnum (chant), *174*, *175–76*
On Arthurian Women (Tolhurst and Wheeler), 6–7
The Once and Future King (White), 107
oral/aural culture: *Le Morte Darthur* in context of, 81–87
Order of Sir Galahad, 103
O'Reilly's Holy Grail Tavern (San Francisco), 118
Origny Ste-Benoîte chants, 177
Orsi, Lelio, 192
Orthodox Church: Christ's robe and Passion considered in, 189
Osborn, Marijane, 17, 22n1
Osborne, Baby Marie, 135
Oxford English Dictionary (*OED*), 48–49, 50, 52
Oxford University, Arthurian Society, 6

Pan and His Pipes and Other Tales for Children (Cather), 106
Paradiso (Dante), 77
Paris (France): Cabochien revolt in, 125; Constance de France living in, 201, 204; fortifications in fifteenth century, 123–24; Joan of Arc's attack on, 9–10, 123, 125–29; John the Fearless's capture of, 123, 124–25
Parkes, Matthew B., 87n8
Parsons, John Carmi, 5, 12
La Passion de Jeanne d'Arc (film), 150n15
Patmos monastery, 189, *190*, 197n37
Pauvre Bitos (play), 145, 146
Pearsall, Derek, 31, 33n23
Peiresc, Nicolas-Claude Fabri de, 205, 214n30
Peregrinus (saint), 224
Perlesvaus (French romance), 93
Pernoud, Régine, 9, 13
Perruchei, Symon de, 209
Peter Monoculus (abbot), 155
Petit, Jean, 124
Le Petit Parisien (periodical), 133, 140n5
Phagan (missionary), 66
Pharos Chapel relics, 189

Phelps, Elizabeth Stuart, 103
Phi Beta Kappa Society, 3
Philip (Louis VII's son), 201, 202, 210
Philip II Augustus, 63, 123
Philip IV (Philip the Fair, king of France), 64, 237n2
Philip VI (Philip of Valois), 218, 221, 223, 241n23
Philippe of Navarre, 244n48
Philip the Good (duke of Burgundy), 128
Philological Quarterly, 5
Piers Plowman (Langland), 37, 51–52
pitch, *pighte*, and *picchen*, 48–52, 54, 57n22
pitchfork, 58n29
Plato, 3
Plautus, 51–52
Pluto (deity), 27, 29, 44, 46
Poetica (journal), 5
Polton, Thomas, 66–67
pomel, 48, 52–53, 54, 55–56, 58n32
Pontius of Polignac (abbot), 155
Pottier, Abbé, 208, 215n36
Poulson, Christine, 101
Powell, F. York, 19, 22
Pratt, Mary Louise, 80
print culture, 81–82, 87n8
prophecies: Christian tradition of, 73–74, 77–78; Geoffrey's exploration of Merlin's, 72–76, 142; of Nostradamus, 75–76
The Prophecies of Merlin (Geoffrey of Monmouth), 72–76, 142
prose style: aurality and poetic diction in, 83–85; claims of unattainability of Grail and, 113–14; literary cultural context of, 80–82; *occupatio* device in, 90; rhetorical balance in, 85–86; semantic deterioration in, 115; summary, 86–87
Der Prozess der Jeanne d'Arc zu Rouen (The Trial of Joan of Arc at Rouen, play), 143
punctuation, 81–82, 87n8
Python (programming language), 119n5

queens. *See* royal women; *and specific queens*

Radbertus, Paschasius, 51
Raphael, 192
Ratis Ravyng (text), 91
Rat Scabies (punk rocker), 116–17
Raymond V (count of Toulouse): charters of, 211–12n4; divorce of, 201; illegitimate children of, 213n12; royal symbolism adopted by, 205, 208; seals of, 205, *207*, 212n9, 214nn29–30
Raymond VI: brother of, 212n11; charters of, 211–12n4; political identity of, 208; seal of, 205; wives of, 215n37
Raymond VII, 205
Redbook (periodical), 107
Register (Eudes Rigaud), 11, 160, 163, 164, 165, 166
Regnault of Chartres, 127
Regularis concordia (text), 169–70
Reid, Wallace, 138
Reinhart in Love (Berger), 107
relics: lost in French Revolution, 226, 245n60; in Pharos Chapel, 189. *See also under* Saint-Denis Abbey
René of Anjou (duke of Bar), 127
Representations of the Feminine in the Middle Ages (Wheeler), 5
La Revanche (film), 135, 141n12
Rhys ap Gruffydd (Lord Rhys), 62
Rice, David Talbot, 184
Richard II (king of England), 26
Rigaud, Eudes. *See* Eudes Rigaud
Rimbaud, Arthur, 151n31
Rishanger, William, 64
Robert of Bruges (abbot), 155
Robert of Gloucester, 49–50, 61, 64
Robertson, Jean, 133
Robinson, Fred C., 17
Roger of Moulins, 202, 209
Romance and Chronicle (Field), 80
Roman de Brut (Wace), 61–62, 63, 64
Roman d'Eneas (text), 52–53
Roman du Graal (text), 96n17
Romano, Giulio, 192
Romanos the Melode, 189, 196–97n30
Romola (Eliot), 78
Rossetti, Dante Gabriel, 97, *98*
Routt, William D., 135

royal women: approach to studying, 12–13; patronage of, 208–10; typical shapes of seals of, 204, 213n24. *See also* Constance de France; Eleanor of Aquitaine; Jeanne d'Évreux
Ryder, Jeff, 27

Saint-Denis Abbey (Paris): acts sealed on silk at, 240–41n21; chapel refurbished and rededicated at, 220–21, 223–25, 241–42n27, 244n46; Charles V's endowment rejected by, 222, 242n32, 242–243n34; Constance's charter donation for, 204, 209; Jeanne d'Évreux's endowment of, 219–27; Jeanne d'Évreux's endowment of (French text), 227–36; liturgical reform of, 243n35; relics of, 219–24, 241nn25–26, 242n29
Sainte-Chapelle: chaplaincies endowed for, 243n36; relics of, 220, 221, 225–26, 241n26, 242n29
Saint-Étienne church (Brie-Comte-Robert), 238n12
Saint Joan (play), 143, 147–48
Saint-Louis de Poissy monastery (France), 242n32
Saint Mary Abbey (York), 170
Saint-Paul church of Saint-Denis, 225, 244n42
Saintsbury, George, 80, 88n18
Saint-Victor Abbey (Paris), 202, *203*, 204, 208–9, 215n40
Salda, Michael N., 6
Sarum rite, 178, 180n5, 181n14
Sato, Sonosuke, 19
Saturn (deity), 44, 46
Savigny, Congregation of, 159. *See also* Bival Abbey
Savonarola, 78
Schäfer, Thomas, 180n2
Schiller, Johann Christoph Friedrich von, 138, 143–44, 149n9
science. *See* technology developments
Scotland: in Chaucer's tales, 30; English kings' authority in, 62–63, 64, 65, 67; Forest of Celidon in, 72; marginalization of, 25, 26, 33n19

Scott, Walter, 80
Scoundrel Time (Hellman), 148
seals: of Constance de France, 202, *203*, 204–5, *206*, 208; as field of study, 213n19; iconographic connections between, 214n33; of Raymond V, 205, *207*, 212n9, 214nn29–30; of royal women in general, 12–13, 213n24; silk used to attach, *203*, 226, 240–41n21
Second Charlemagne, 78
Secreta secretorum (trans. Hayes), 91
Segheres, Anna, 143
"Selling in Wartime" (exhibition), 109n14
Sery, Luc, 204, 211n3
SGGK. *See Sir Gawain and the Green Knight*
Shaw, George Bernard, 143, 146, 147–48
sigilography. *See* seals
Silverstein, Theodore, 37
Sir Degaré (text), 29
Sir Ferumbras (text), 50
Sir Galahad (Burns), 99, *100*, 101
"Sir Galahad" (Tennyson): approach to studying, 8; artists inspired by, 97–99; illustrations of, *98*, *100*; Michelin tire advertisement using, 101, *102*; modern literary allusions to, 107–8
Sir Galahad (Watts): artist's rejection of Tennysonian links, 98–99; didactic Galahad tales published with, 106; as model for American boys, 101, 103–4; stained-glass works based on, 101; Tennyson's "Sir Galahad" linked to, 8
Sir Gawain and the Green Knight (tale), 37, 42n23
Sir Orfeo (text), 27–29
Sir Thopas (Chaucer), 5–6, 29
Sistine Chapel *Last Judgment* (Michelangelo), 192, *193*
Sklar, Elizabeth S.: essay by, 111–19; references to, 8–9
Smith, Jeremy, 88nn17–18
Snowdonia (Wales): legends of, 71, 73
social class: Christine de Pizan and, 142, 149n3; Joan of Arc and, 142–43. *See also* class struggle; Marxism

Société Internationale de l'étude de Jeanne d'Arc (International Joan of Arc Society), 9
Socrates, 3
Sorel, Agnès, 146
Southern Methodist University, Meadows Museum of Spanish Art, 183
Spain: iconography of Christ's Passion in, 183–84, 191
Speculum (periodical), 159
speculum regis literature, 91, 92–93
Speght, Thomas, 46
The Sphere (periodical), 101, *102*
spirituality. See Christian Church; nuns and spirituality
The Squire's Tale (Chaucer), 29, 99
Stallcup, Stephen: death of, 14n7, 58n39; essay by, 43–58; references to, 5–6
Standing, Herbert, 135
Stanza della Segnatura (Raphael), 192
Statius, 45, 57n13
Statutes of Kilkenny, 26
stede, 55–56
Steinbeck, John, 8, 107
Stephen (king of England), 201, 208, 211n3
St. Mary's Abbey chants (York), 179, 181n14
Stock, Lorraine Kochanske: essay by, 34–42; references to, 5–6
Stone of Scone, 65
Stowe, Madeline, 132
"Straight Dope" (website), 112
Strayer, Joseph R., 11, 159, 166, 167n3
"strength of ten": American use of, 101, *102*, 103–4, 106–7; Burns's use of, 99, 101; in Tennyson's "Sir Galahad," 8, 97, 101, 108
The Strength of Ten (Hall), 106
Studies in Arthurian and Courtly Cultures Series, 6
style definitions, 80. See also prose style
Sully, Maurice de, 201
The Summoner's Tale (Chaucer), 28
Sweet, Henry, 30
Swift, Jonathan, 80

Taillefer, William, 209
Taisho Democracy Movement, 19
Takamiya, Toshiyuki: essay by, 17–24; references to, 5
Tale of Florent (Gower), 34, 37–38
The Tale of Genji (Lady Murasaki), 5
The Tale of Heike (epic), 19
teacher/mentor: midwife metaphor for, 3
The Teaching Company, 3
Teaching Medieval Studies (TEAMS), 2
technology developments: "Holy Grail" of, 112, 113–14, 117, 119n3, 119n5. See also Googled Grail
Temple, Jean du, 240n21
Tennyson, Alfred Lord, 8, 97, *98*, 104–8. See also "Sir Galahad"
Teseida (Boccaccio): on Arcite's fall and injury, 47–48, 53; on fury that spooked Arcite's horse, 6, 43, 44–45, 46–47, 56–57n12
testamentary activities, anticipatory execution. See Jeanne d'Évreux
Theatetus (Plato), 3
Theatre Magazine (Australia), 133
Theophanes Stretlitzas Bathas, 184, 187, 195n11
Theotokopoulos, Domenikos. See El Greco
Theseus, 43, 46, 57n15
Tholl, Susan E. von Daum, 172, 180n7
Thomas, Susanne Sara, 42n29
Thorpe, Lewis, 73
Thrupp, Sylvia, 167n3
Titian, 12, 192–93
Toledo cathedral. See *Espolio* (El Greco)
Tolhurst, Fiona, 7
Toulouse (France): as dowry, 208. See also Constance de France
Toulouse-Lautrec family, 212n11
Trask, William, 148
Traugott, Elizabeth Closs, 80
Trémoïlle, Georges de la, 127
Trivet, Thomas, 53
Troilus and Criseyde (Chaucer), 5, 30, 34, 35, 45
Trojans and Troy, 71, 74
Tucker, George Loane, 136, *137*

Two Little Knights of Kentucky (Johnston), 8, 104
Twomey, Michael, 81

Ueda, Bin, 18
Uncyclopedia (website), 113
Unholy Grail (band), 118
United States: Joan of Arc figure deployed in politics of, 147–48; "strength of ten" phrase deployed in, 101, *102*, 103–4, 106–7. *See also* Arthurian youth groups
"Urban Dictionary" (website), 113
Uther (Arthur's father), 67

Venus (deity), 44, 47, 56–57n12, 90
Versailles, Treaty of (1919), 143
Vézelay Abbey (France), 241n26
Victor Talking Machine Company, 106
Vinaver, Eugène, 6, 80, 81
Virgil, 45, 56–57n12
Virgin Mary: in iconography of Christ's Passion, 188, 189; as *magistra*, 1; Saint-Denis chapel and relics of, 220–21, 222, 223–25, 241–42n27; status of, with Christ, 13
The Vision of Sir Launfal (Lowell), 104
Visitatio sepulchri (chant), 176
Vital Parts (Berger), 107
Voragine, Jacob, 171
Vortigern (king), 73
Vulgate (Lancelot-Grail) Cycle: Lancelot depicted in, 90–91, 93–94; Malory influenced by, 8, 89

Wace: Merlin's prophecies excluded by, 76; WORK: *Roman de Brut*, 61–62, 63, 64
Wade, James, 33n15
Wagner, Richard, 106
Wala (Cadwallader princess), 63–64, 67
Wales: Arthur as symbol in, 30, 64, 71; bardic poetry and prophetic tradition of, 72, 73–75, 76–77; English kings' authority in, 62–63, 64–65, 67; English romantic writers on fairy world of, 27–29; hopes for resurgence of, 72, 75; marginalization of, 25–26, 30; Merlin's depiction and political aspirations in,

7; Trojan descent claimed by, 71, 74. *See also* Celts; Geoffrey of Monmouth
Walker, Barbara, 39
Wallace, David, 32n7
The Wallace (Hary), 92
Warner, Marian, 135
wars: Hundred Years, 124–25, 128. *See also* battles; World War I
The Waste Land (Eliot), 107
Watanabe-no-Tsuna, 19, 22
Watts, George Frederic. See *Sir Galahad* (Watts)
WBT. See *The Wife of Bath's Tale*
The Wedding of Sir Gawain and Dame Ragnell (tale), 34, 37, 38
Welsh seers (*awenyddion*), 74
Westminster Abbey (London), 64, 68
Wethey, Harold E., 184, 193, 194n4, 195n9
Wheeler, Bonnie: academic contributions, 2–4, 183; Arthuriana interests of, 6–8; editorial work of, 2–3, 6–7; honored as *magistra doctissima*, 1–2, 13, 219; Joan of Arc interests of, 9; on Malory's paratactic style, 80; on midwife metaphor for teacher/mentor, 3; nuns and spirituality as interests of, 10–11; Old and Middle English literature interests of, 4–5; royal women as interests of, 12; Stallcup as student of, 6; WORKS: *Arthurian Studies in Honour of P. J. C. Field*, 6; *On Arthurian Women* (with Tolhurst), 6–7; "Dante, Chaucer and the Ending of *Troilus and Criseyde*," 5; *Eleanor of Aquitaine* (with Parsons), 12; *Fresh Verdicts on Joan of Arc* (with Wood), 9; "Grammar, Genre, and Gender in Chaucer and Murasaki Shikibu," 5; *Heloise and the Paraclete* (McLaughlin, completed by Wheeler), 11; *Joan of Arc* (trans. Adam), 9; *Joan of Arc and Spirituality* (with Astell), 9; "Joan of Arc's Sword in the Stone," 9; *The Letters of Heloise and Abelard* (McLaughlin, completed by Wheeler), 11; *Listening to Heloise*, 11; list of edited volumes, 3; *The Malory Debate*

(with Kindrick and Salda), 6; *Medieval Mothering* (with Parsons), 5, 18; "The Project of Arthurian Studies," 6; *Representations of the Feminine in the Middle Ages*, 5; ""Trouthe without Consequences, 5

White, T. H., 107

The Wife of Bath's Tale (Chaucer): approaches to studying, 5–6; danger of fairy allure in, 29–30; "hag" in, 35–39; as pastoral history, 33n14; romantic version of Welsh hero in, 28; Wife as *magistra* in, 1

The Wild Cat of Paris (film), 136, 138

William (earl of Ulster), 26

William II (king of Sicily), 208

William de Brailes, 188

William of Malmesbury, 65

William of Newburgh, 27

William the Breton, 63

William the Lion (king of Scotland), 62

Willoughby, George, 133–34, 140n7

Wilton Processional, 171, 176, 177, 179, 181n14

Winchester Manuscript, 6, 82, 83–85

Winter of Our Discontent (Steinbeck), 8

women: celebrations of, 1–4; gender issues in Joan of Arc film, 138–39; as "hags," 5–6, 34–39; Taisho Democracy Movement and, 19. *See also* Joan of Arc; royal women

Wood, Charles T., 9, 13

Wooden, John, 108

Worcester, William, 67

World War I: Cavell as martyr in, 134–35, 140–41n11; end of, 143; Gallipoli disaster in, 135, 140n10; Joan of Arc referenced in films during, 10, 132–39, *137*; Michelin tire advertisement in, 101, *102*; recruitment in, 99, *100*, 101; siege of Loos in, 133–34, 140n9; *Sir Galahad* and soldiers of, 8

"wyf": etymology of, 35–39; use of term, 5–6; as witch, 37, 42n20

Yardley, Anne Bagnall: essay by, 169–82; references to, 11–12

Yarnell, Mark, 116

Ye Grete Lawis of Scotland (text), 91

Yoshitoshi, Tsukioka (or Taiso), 17

"Your Dictionary" (website), 112

youth: Joan of Arc referenced in films for, 135–36, *137*, 138; Sir Galahad as model for, 99, *100*, 101, 103–4, *105*, 106–7. *See also* Arthurian youth groups

Typeset in 10/13 Adobe Caslon Pro
Composed by Tom Krol
Manufactured by Cushing-Malloy, Inc.

Medieval Institute Publications
College of Arts and Sciences
Western Michigan University
1903 W. Michigan Avenue
Kalamazoo, MI 49008-5432
http://www.wmich.edu/medieval/mip

WESTERN MICHIGAN UNIVERSITY